Shojo Beat

The Magic Touch

Oyayubi kara Romance

Vol. 1

Story & Art by Izumi Tsubaki

CONTENTS

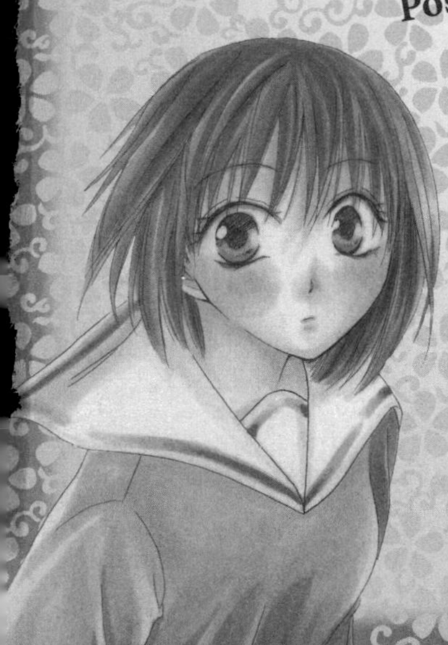

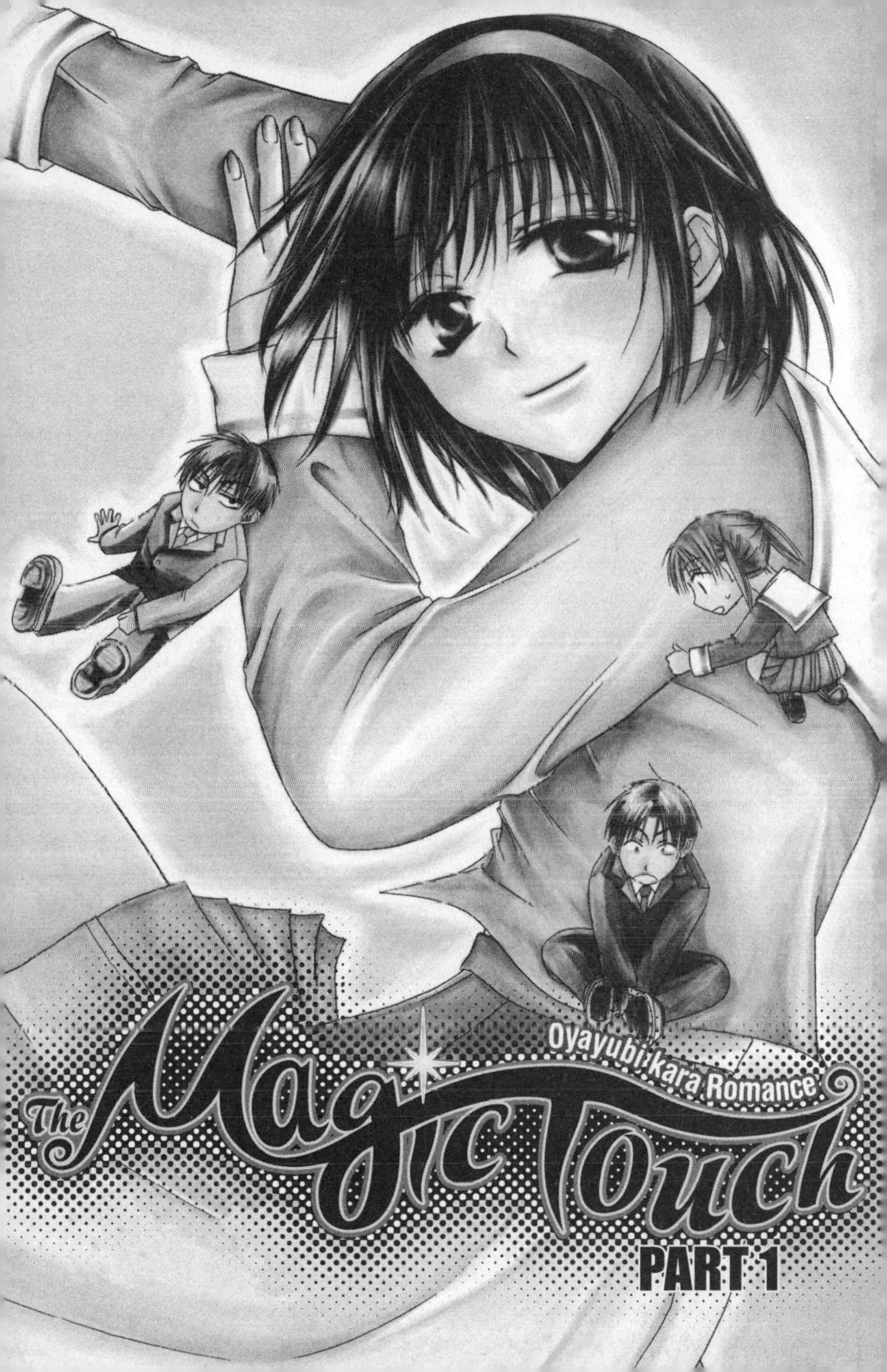
The Magic Touch
Oyayubi kara Romance
PART 1

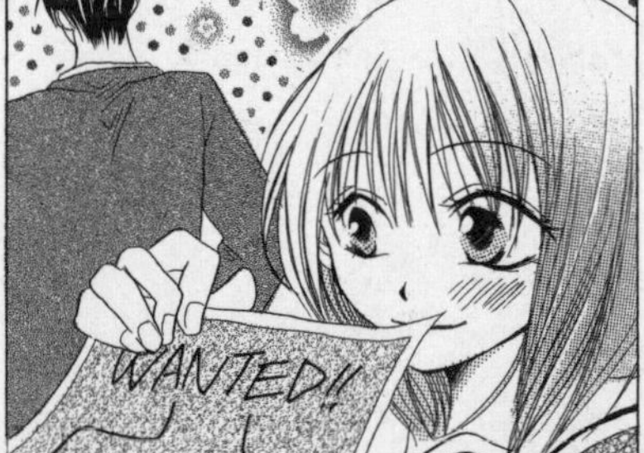
WANTED!!

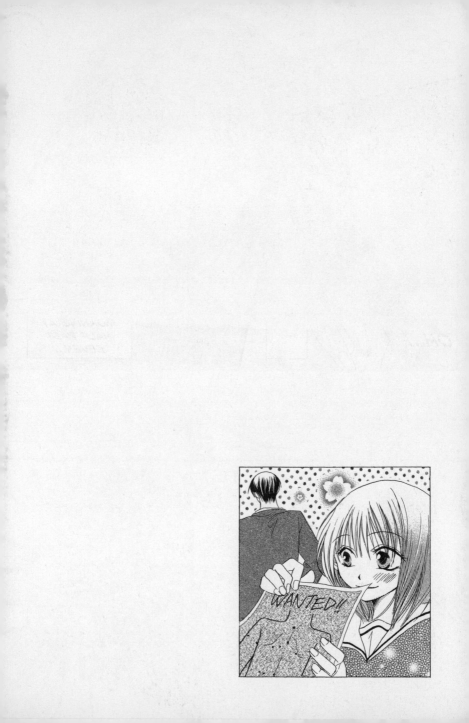

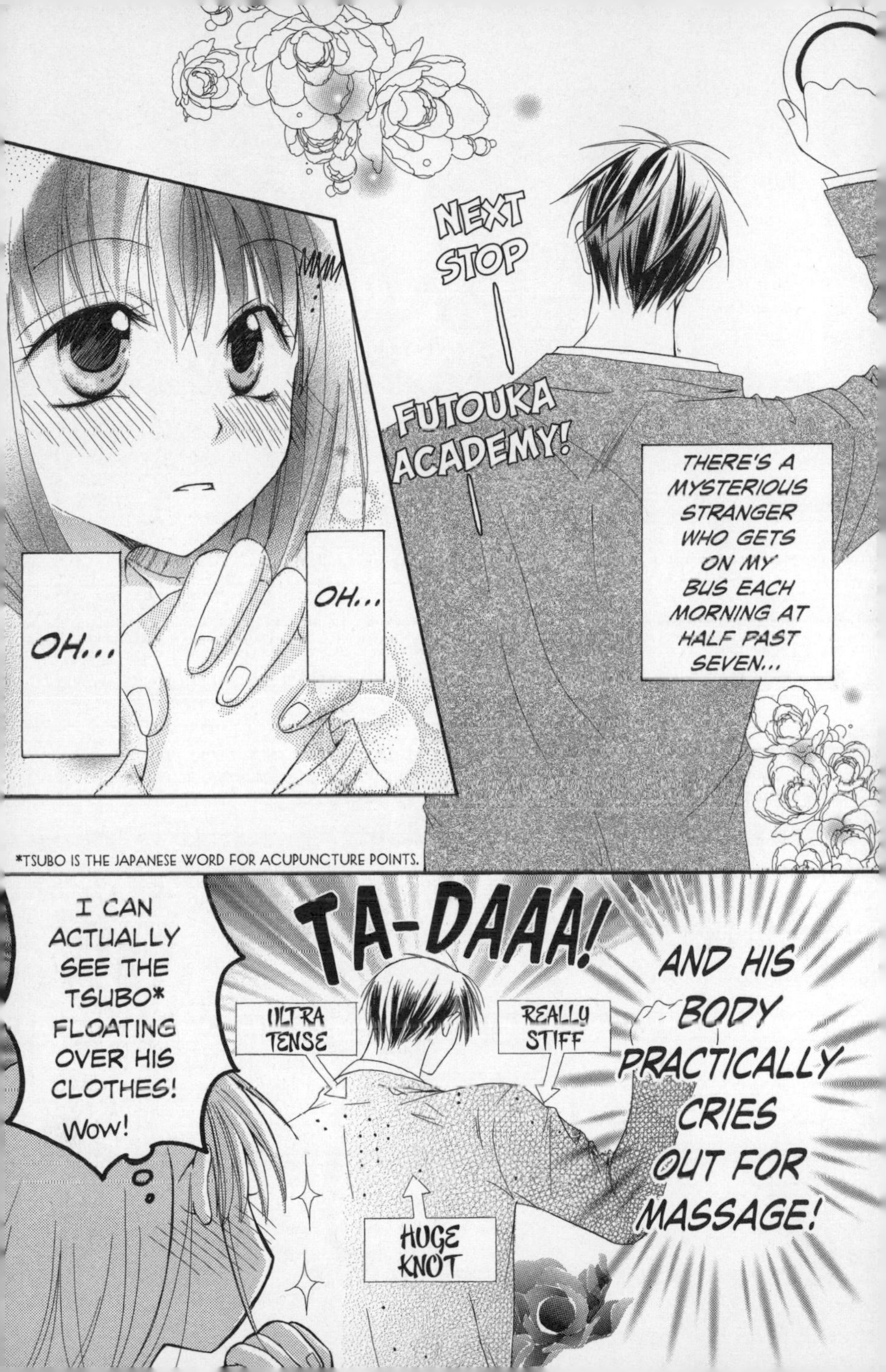
NEXT STOP
FUTOUKA ACADEMY!
THERE'S A MYSTERIOUS STRANGER WHO GETS ON MY BUS EACH MORNING AT HALF PAST SEVEN...
OH...
OH...
AND HIS BODY PRACTICALLY CRIES OUT FOR MASSAGE!
TA-DAAA!
REALLY STIFF
ULTRA TENSE
HUGE KNOT
I CAN ACTUALLY SEE THE TSUBO* FLOATING OVER HIS CLOTHES!
Wow!

*TSUBO IS THE JAPANESE WORD FOR ACUPUNCTURE POINTS.

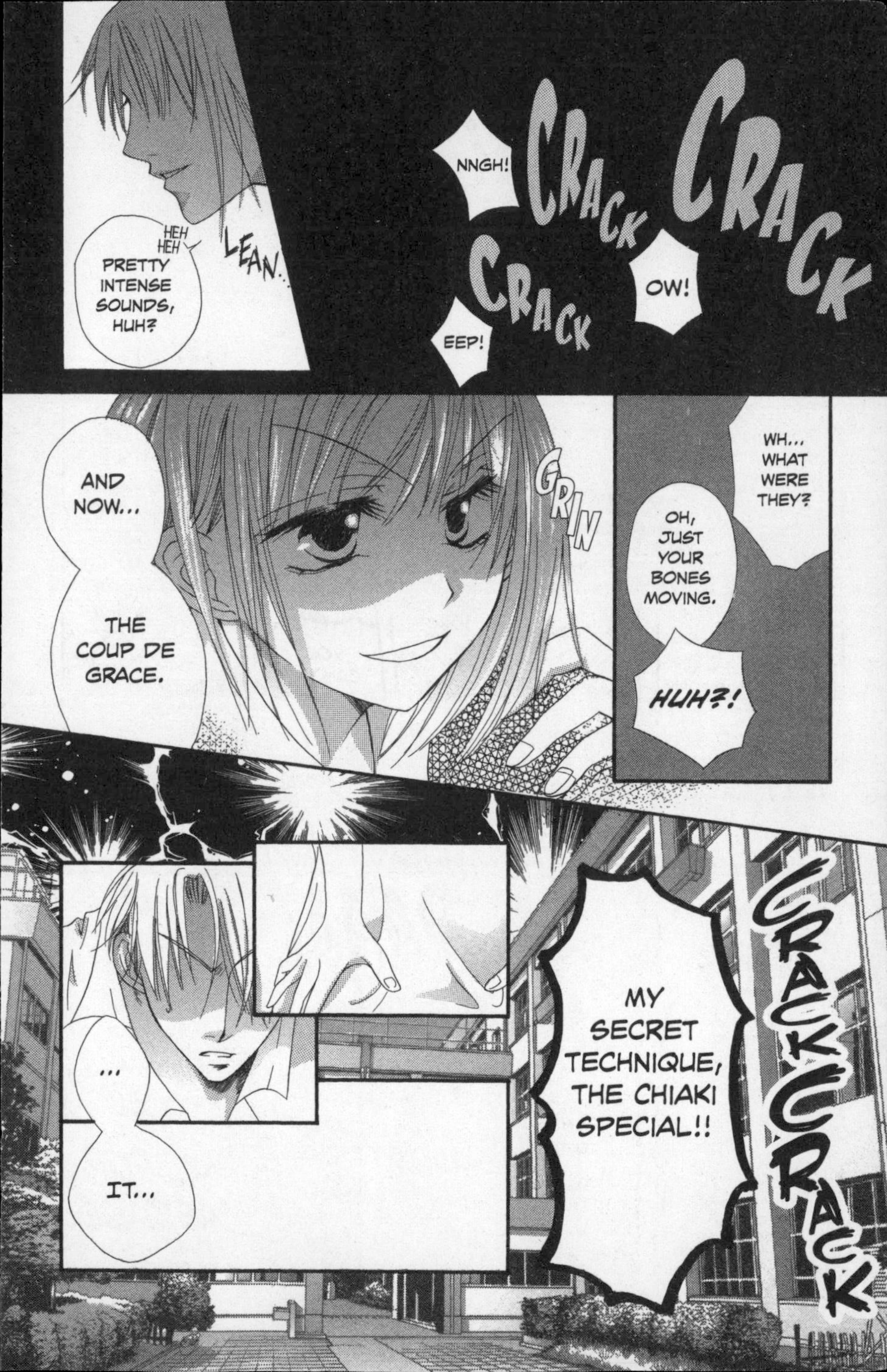
CRACK
CRACK
NNGH!
CRACK
OW!
CRACK
EEP!
HEH HEH
LEAN...
PRETTY INTENSE SOUNDS, HUH?
WH... WHAT WERE THEY?
OH, JUST YOUR BONES MOVING.
HUH?!
GRIN
AND NOW...
THE COUP DE GRACE.
CRACK CRACK CRACK
MY SECRET TECHNIQUE, THE CHIAKI SPECIAL!!
...
IT...

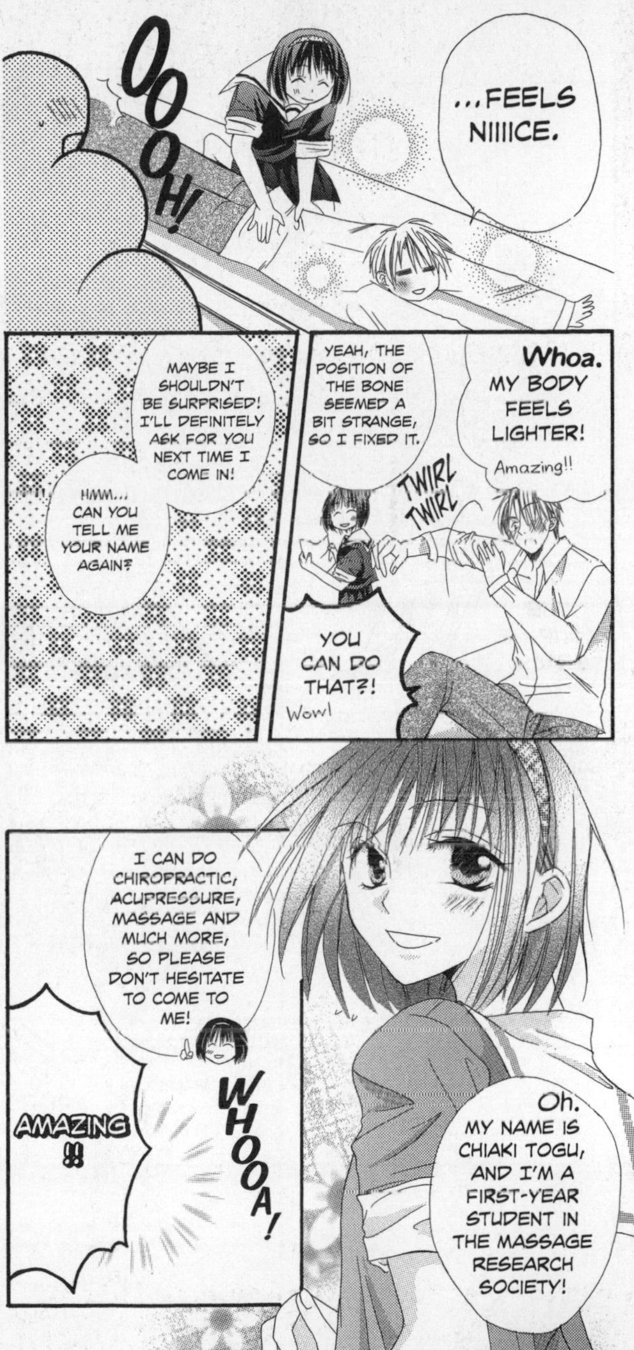
...FEELS NIIIICE.
OOOH!
Whoa. MY BODY FEELS LIGHTER!
Amazing!!
YEAH, THE POSITION OF THE BONE SEEMED A BIT STRANGE, SO I FIXED IT.
TWIRL TWIRL
YOU CAN DO THAT?!
Wow!
MAYBE I SHOULDN'T BE SURPRISED! I'LL DEFINITELY ASK FOR YOU NEXT TIME I COME IN!
HMM... CAN YOU TELL ME YOUR NAME AGAIN?
Oh. MY NAME IS CHIAKI TOGU, AND I'M A FIRST-YEAR STUDENT IN THE MASSAGE RESEARCH SOCIETY!
I CAN DO CHIROPRACTIC, ACUPRESSURE, MASSAGE AND MUCH MORE, SO PLEASE DON'T HESITATE TO COME TO ME!
WHOOA!
AMAZING!!

Nice To Meet You!

Thank you for reading this book! Let's see, this is my first manga...I guess that's why I feel really nervous. This isn't a dream, is it?! Wow! Since I have this space, I'll introduce myself... even though there isn't that much to talk about.

<Profile>

Name: Izumi Tsubaki
Birthday: December 11
Blood type: A
Hobby: Collecting ermine stuff (since the sixth grade!)

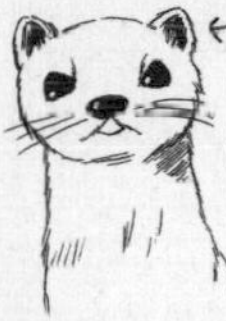
← Ermines look like this. I love how you can't tell if their eyes look nice or mean!

Special Talents:
Ability to sleep anywhere; ability to stay up all night.

...And that's about it!

Please keep reading my books!!

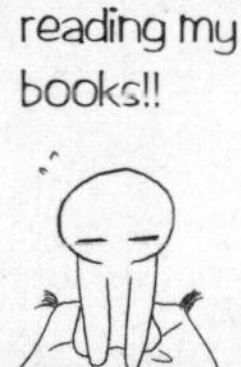

椿いづみ
Izumi Tsubaki

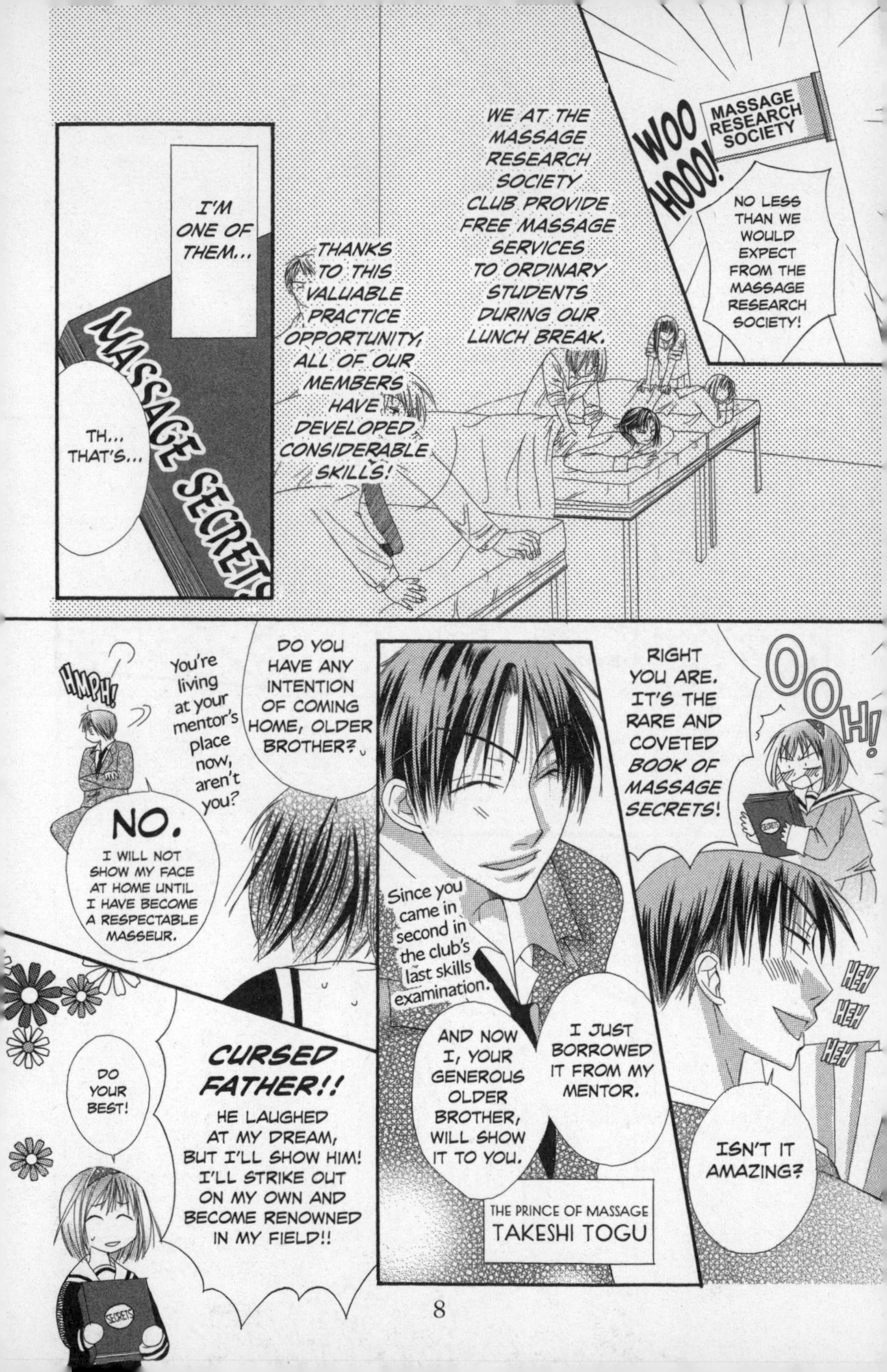
WOO HOOO!
MASSAGE RESEARCH SOCIETY
NO LESS THAN WE WOULD EXPECT FROM THE MASSAGE RESEARCH SOCIETY!
WE AT THE MASSAGE RESEARCH SOCIETY CLUB PROVIDE FREE MASSAGE SERVICES TO ORDINARY STUDENTS DURING OUR LUNCH BREAK.
THANKS TO THIS VALUABLE PRACTICE OPPORTUNITY, ALL OF OUR MEMBERS HAVE DEVELOPED CONSIDERABLE SKILLS!
I'M ONE OF THEM...
MASSAGE SECRETS
TH... THAT'S...
OOH!
RIGHT YOU ARE. IT'S THE RARE AND COVETED BOOK OF MASSAGE SECRETS!
SECRETS
HEH HEH HEH
ISN'T IT AMAZING?
I JUST BORROWED IT FROM MY MENTOR.
Since you came in second in the club's last skills examination.
AND NOW I, YOUR GENEROUS OLDER BROTHER, WILL SHOW IT TO YOU.
THE PRINCE OF MASSAGE TAKESHI TOGU
DO YOU HAVE ANY INTENTION OF COMING HOME, OLDER BROTHER?
HMPH!
You're living at your mentor's place now, aren't you?
NO.
I WILL NOT SHOW MY FACE AT HOME UNTIL I HAVE BECOME A RESPECTABLE MASSEUR.
CURSED FATHER!!
HE LAUGHED AT MY DREAM, BUT I'LL SHOW HIM! I'LL STRIKE OUT ON MY OWN AND BECOME RENOWNED IN MY FIELD!!
DO YOUR BEST!
SECRETS

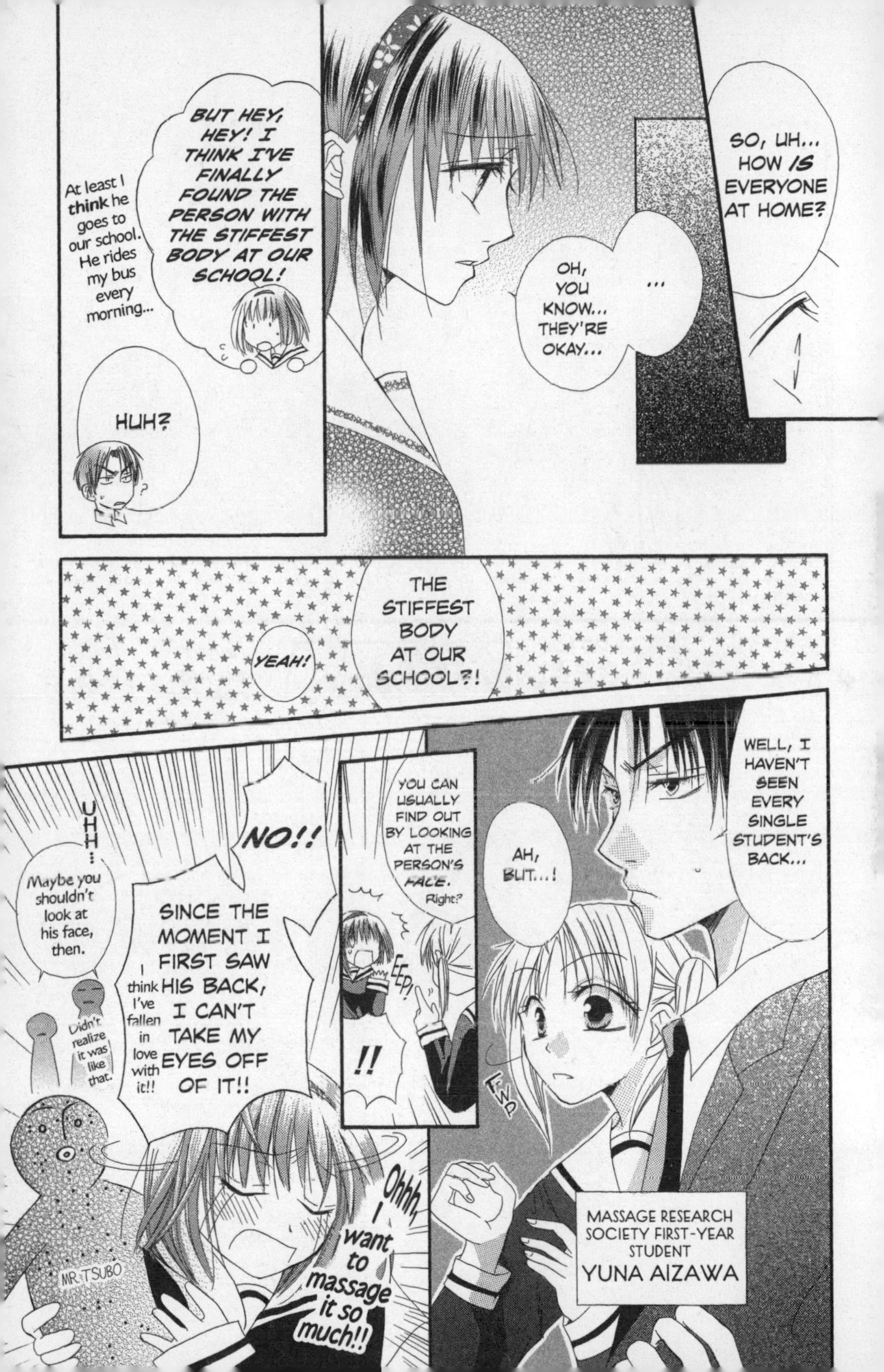
SO, UH... HOW *IS* EVERYONE AT HOME?
...
OH, YOU KNOW... THEY'RE OKAY...
BUT HEY, HEY! I THINK I'VE FINALLY FOUND THE PERSON WITH THE STIFFEST BODY AT OUR SCHOOL!
At least I **think** he goes to our school. He rides my bus every morning...
HUH?
THE STIFFEST BODY AT OUR SCHOOL?!
YEAH!
WELL, I HAVEN'T SEEN EVERY SINGLE STUDENT'S BACK...
AH, BUT...!
FWP
MASSAGE RESEARCH SOCIETY FIRST-YEAR STUDENT YUNA AIZAWA
YOU CAN USUALLY FIND OUT BY LOOKING AT THE PERSON'S *FACE*. Right?
EEP!
!!
NO!!
SINCE THE MOMENT I FIRST SAW HIS BACK, I CAN'T TAKE MY EYES OFF OF IT!!
I think I've fallen in love with it!!
UHH...
Maybe you shouldn't look at his face, then.
Didn't realize it was like that.
Ohhh, I want to massage it so much!!
MR. TSUBO

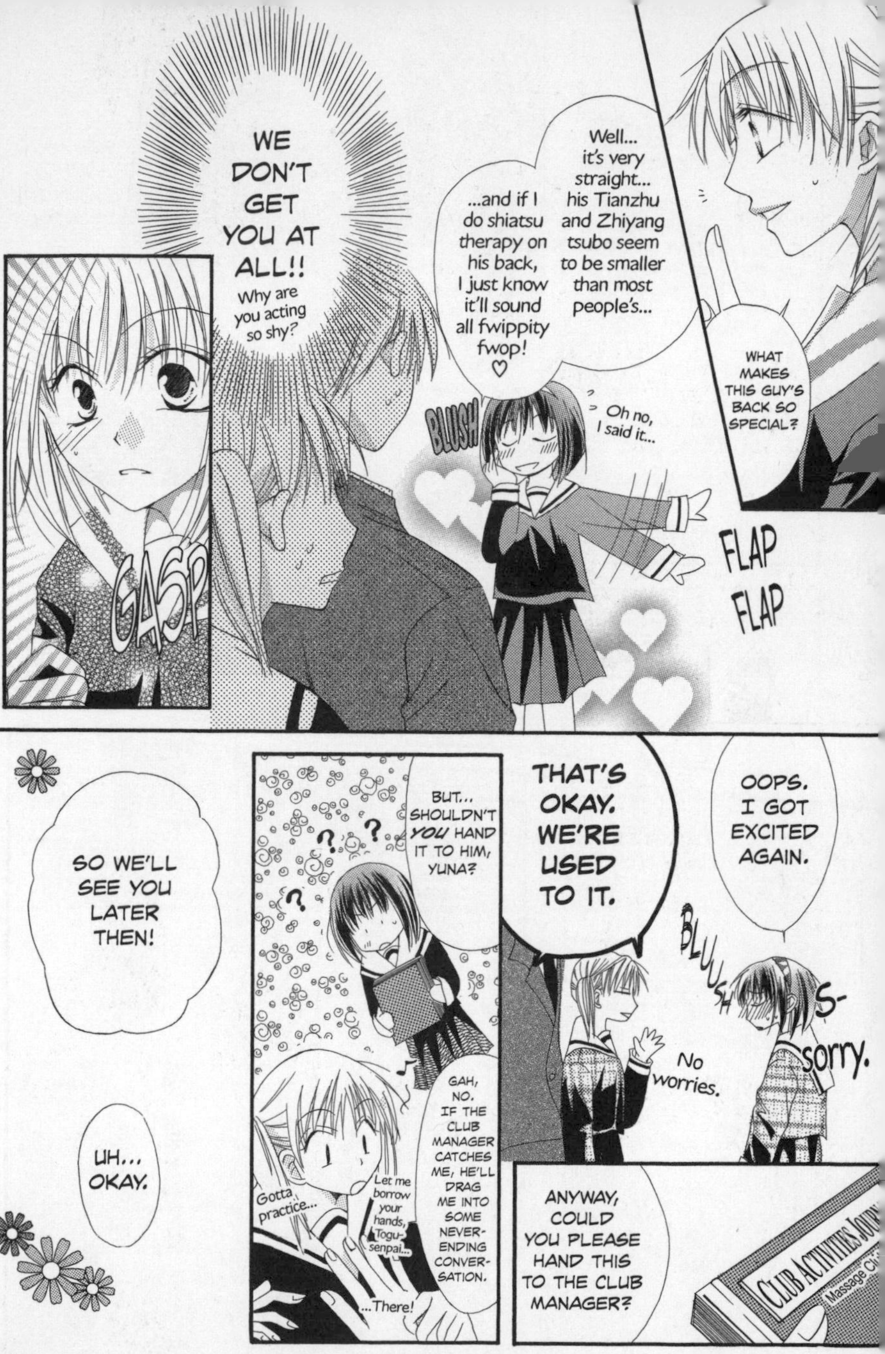
WHAT MAKES THIS GUY'S BACK SO SPECIAL?
Well... it's very straight... his Tianzhu and Zhiyang tsubo seem to be smaller than most people's...
...and if I do shiatsu therapy on his back, I just know it'll sound all fwippity fwop! ♡
BLUSH
Oh no, I said it...
FLAP FLAP
WE DON'T GET YOU AT ALL!!
Why are you acting so shy?
GASP
OOPS. I GOT EXCITED AGAIN.
BLUUSH
S-sorry.
THAT'S OKAY. WE'RE USED TO IT.
No worries.
ANYWAY, COULD YOU PLEASE HAND THIS TO THE CLUB MANAGER?
BUT... SHOULDN'T *YOU* HAND IT TO HIM, YUNA?
GAH, NO. IF THE CLUB MANAGER CATCHES ME, HE'LL DRAG ME INTO SOME NEVER-ENDING CONVERSATION.
Let me borrow your hands, Togu-senpai...
Gotta practice...
...There!
SO WE'LL SEE YOU LATER THEN!
UH... OKAY.

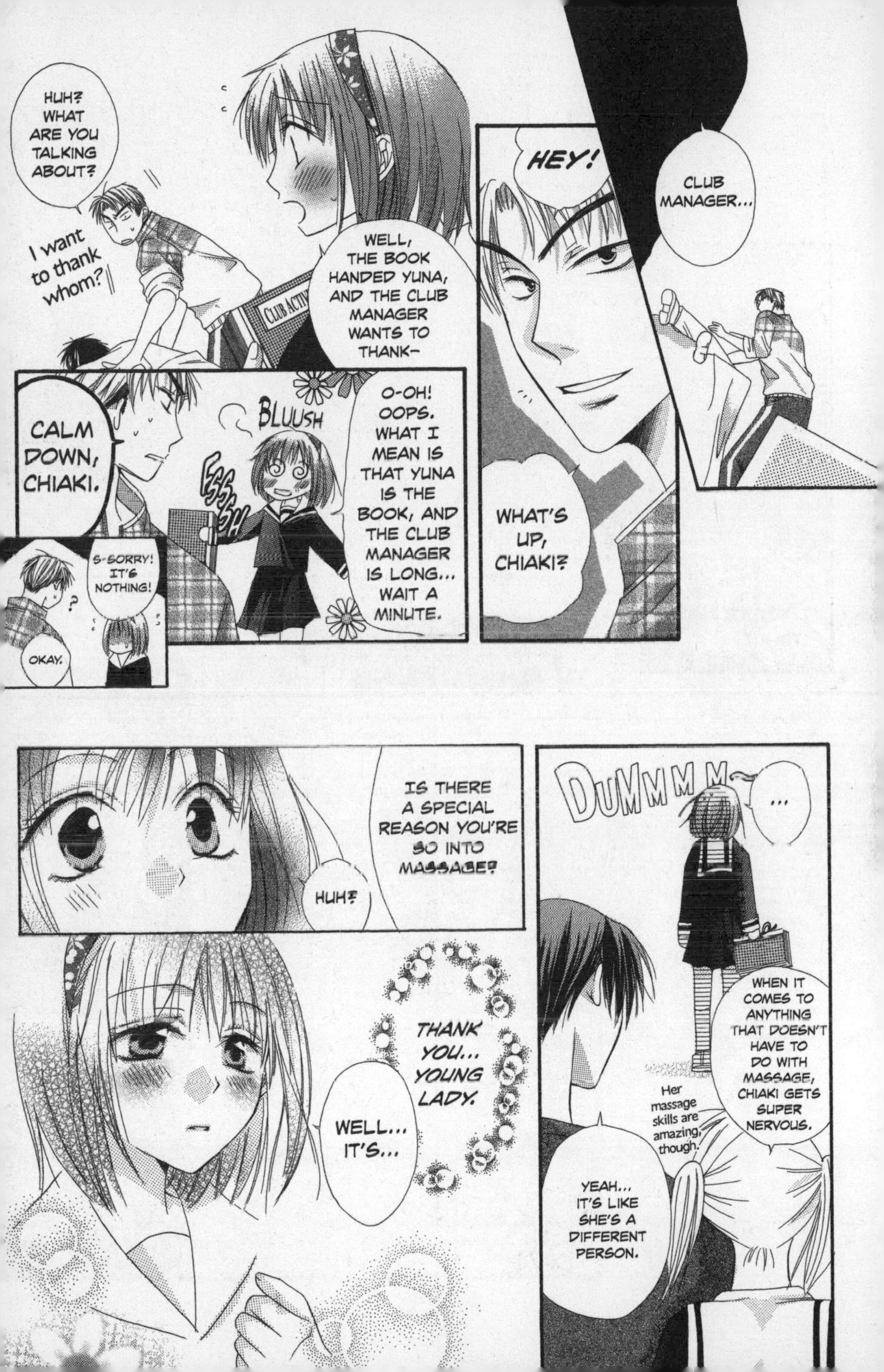
CLUB MANAGER...
HEY!
WHAT'S UP, CHIAKI?
WELL, THE BOOK HANDED YUNA, AND THE CLUB MANAGER WANTS TO THANK–
HUH? WHAT ARE YOU TALKING ABOUT?
I want to thank whom?
O-OH! OOPS. WHAT I MEAN IS THAT YUNA IS THE BOOK, AND THE CLUB MANAGER IS LONG... WAIT A MINUTE.
BLUUSH
CALM DOWN, CHIAKI.
S-SORRY! IT'S NOTHING!
?
OKAY.
DUMMMM
...
WHEN IT COMES TO ANYTHING THAT DOESN'T HAVE TO DO WITH MASSAGE, CHIAKI GETS SUPER NERVOUS.
Her massage skills are amazing, though.
YEAH... IT'S LIKE SHE'S A DIFFERENT PERSON.
IS THERE A SPECIAL REASON YOU'RE SO INTO MASSAGE?
HUH?
THANK YOU... YOUNG LADY.
WELL... IT'S...

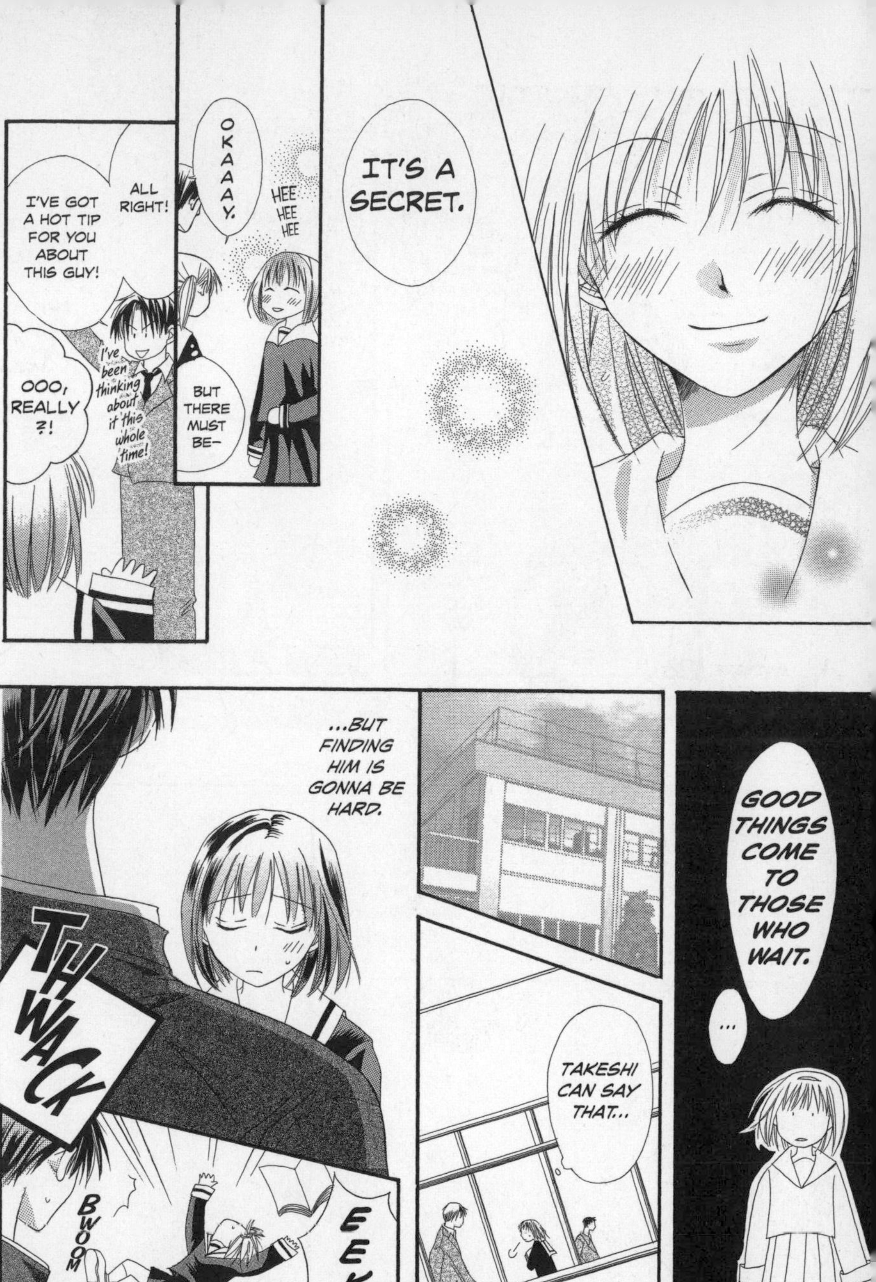
IT'S A SECRET.
HEE HEE HEE
OKAAAY.
BUT THERE MUST BE-
ALL RIGHT!
I'VE GOT A HOT TIP FOR YOU ABOUT THIS GUY!
I've been thinking about it this whole time!
OOO, REALLY?!
GOOD THINGS COME TO THOSE WHO WAIT.
...
TAKESHI CAN SAY THAT...
...BUT FINDING HIM IS GONNA BE HARD.
EEK!!
THWACK
BWOOM

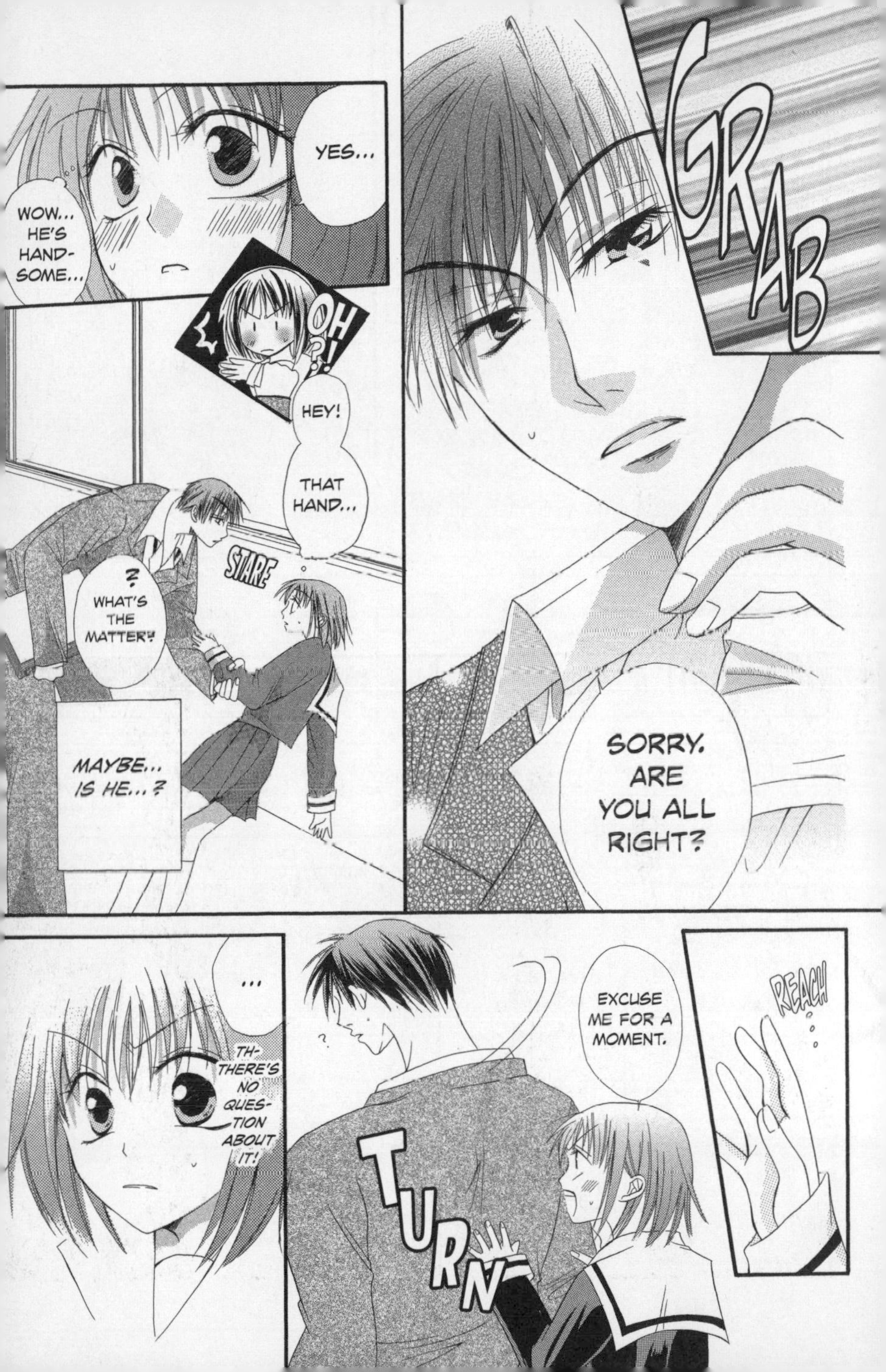
GRAB
SORRY. ARE YOU ALL RIGHT?
YES...
WOW... HE'S HANDSOME...
OH!?
HEY! THAT HAND...
STARE
? WHAT'S THE MATTER?!
MAYBE... IS HE...?
REACH
EXCUSE ME FOR A MOMENT.
TURN
...
TH-THERE'S NO QUESTION ABOUT IT!

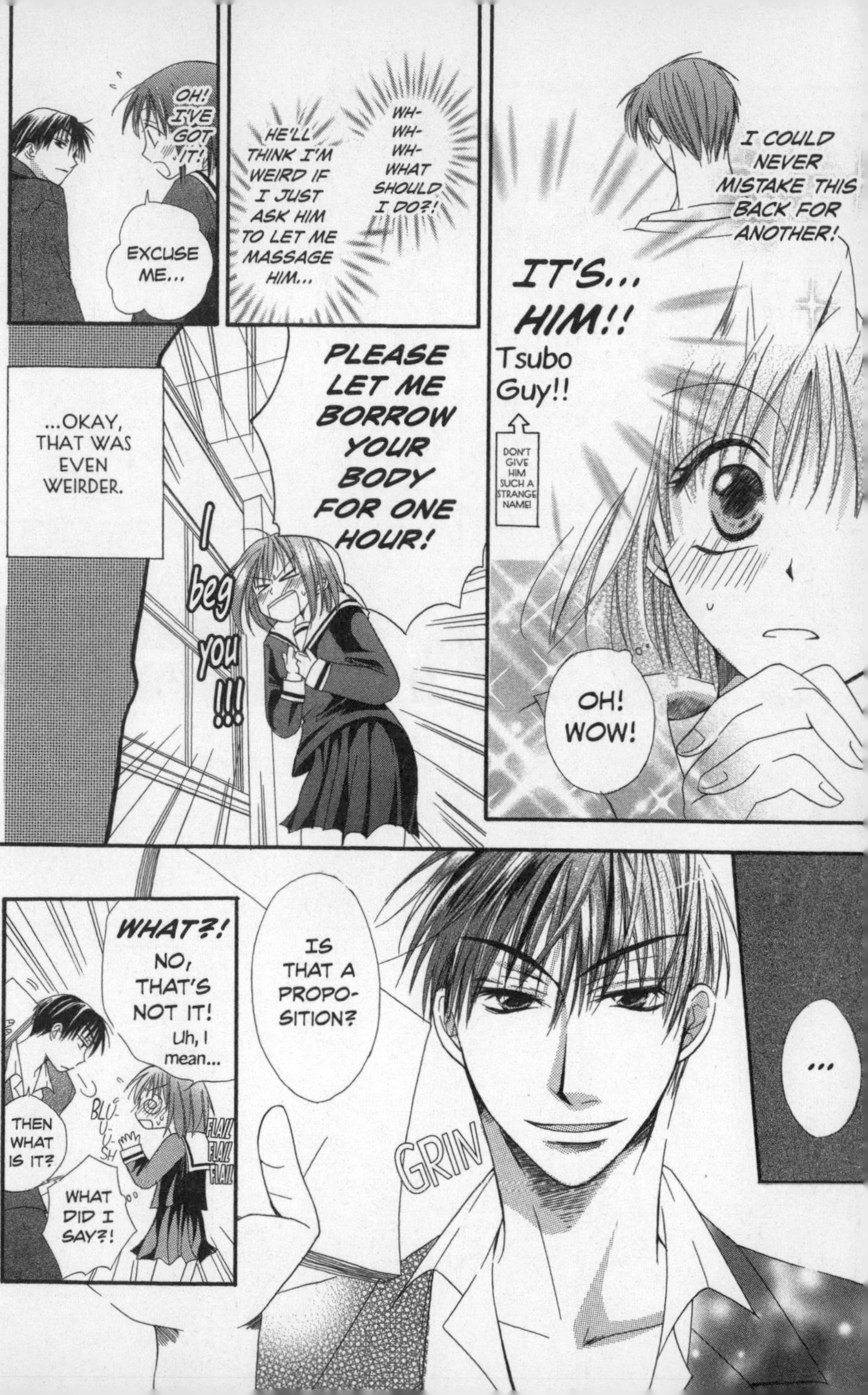

I COULD NEVER MISTAKE THIS BACK FOR ANOTHER!
IT'S... HIM!!
Tsubo Guy!!
DON'T GIVE HIM SUCH A STRANGE NAME!
OH! WOW!
WH-WH-WH-WHAT SHOULD I DO?!
HE'LL THINK I'M WEIRD IF I JUST ASK HIM TO LET ME MASSAGE HIM...
OH! I'VE GOT IT!
EXCUSE ME...
PLEASE LET ME BORROW YOUR BODY FOR ONE HOUR!
I beg you!!!
...OKAY, THAT WAS EVEN WEIRDER.
...
IS THAT A PROPO-SITION?
GRIN
WHAT?!
NO, THAT'S NOT IT!
Uh, I mean...
THEN WHAT IS IT?
BLU-U-U-SH
FLAIL FLAIL FLAIL
WHAT DID I SAY?!

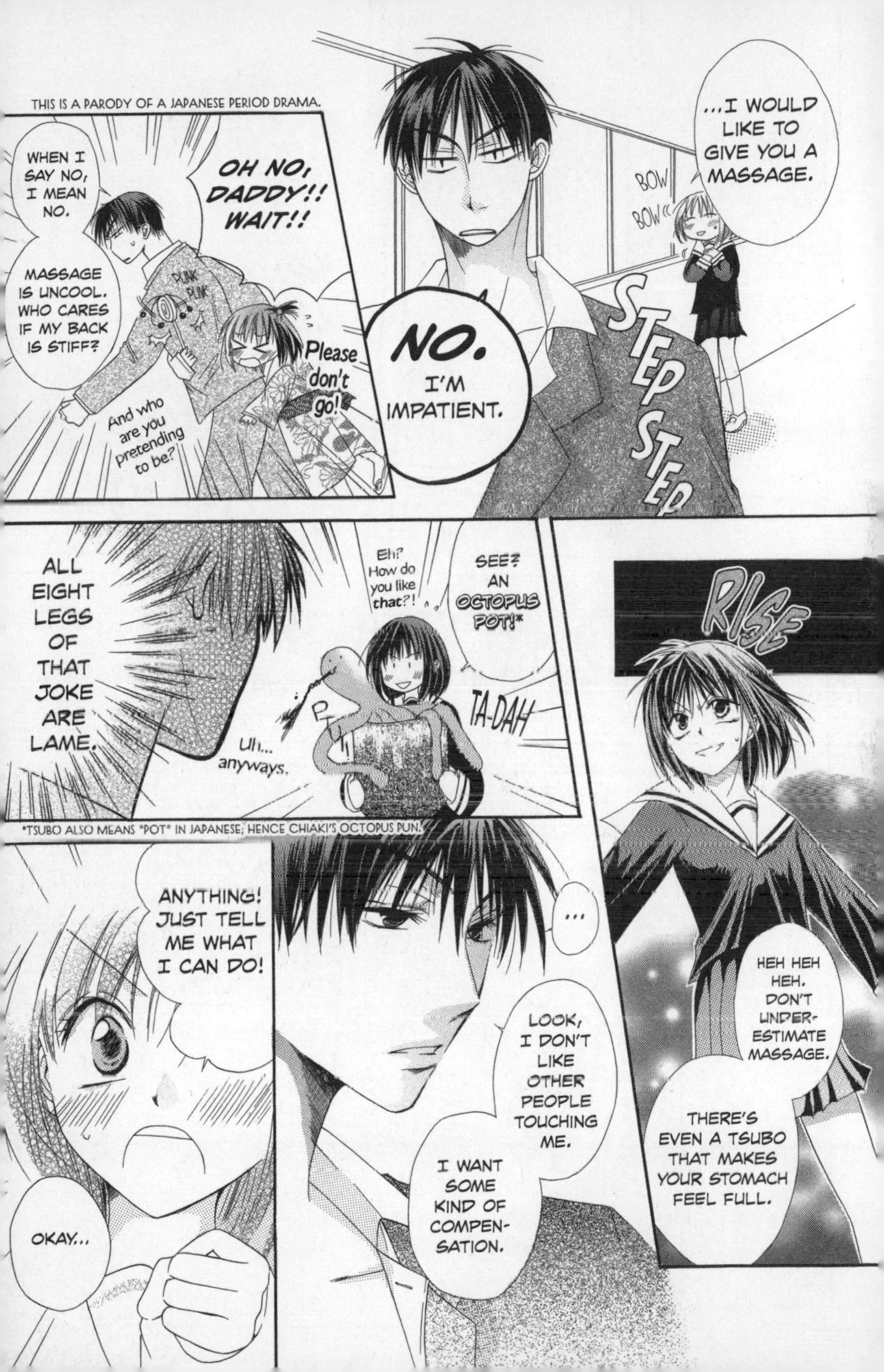
...I WOULD LIKE TO GIVE YOU A MASSAGE.
BOW BOW
STEP STEP
NO. I'M IMPATIENT.
THIS IS A PARODY OF A JAPANESE PERIOD DRAMA.
OH NO, DADDY!! WAIT!!
WHEN I SAY NO, I MEAN NO.
MASSAGE IS UNCOOL. WHO CARES IF MY BACK IS STIFF?
Please don't go!
And who are you pretending to be?
RISE
HEH HEH HEH. DON'T UNDER-ESTIMATE MASSAGE.
THERE'S EVEN A TSUBO THAT MAKES YOUR STOMACH FEEL FULL.
SEE? AN OCTOPUS POT!*
Eh? How do you like that?!
TA-DAH
Uh... anyways.
ALL EIGHT LEGS OF THAT JOKE ARE LAME.
*TSUBO ALSO MEANS "POT" IN JAPANESE; HENCE CHIAKI'S OCTOPUS PUN.
...
LOOK, I DON'T LIKE OTHER PEOPLE TOUCHING ME.
I WANT SOME KIND OF COMPEN-SATION.
ANYTHING! JUST TELL ME WHAT I CAN DO!
OKAY...

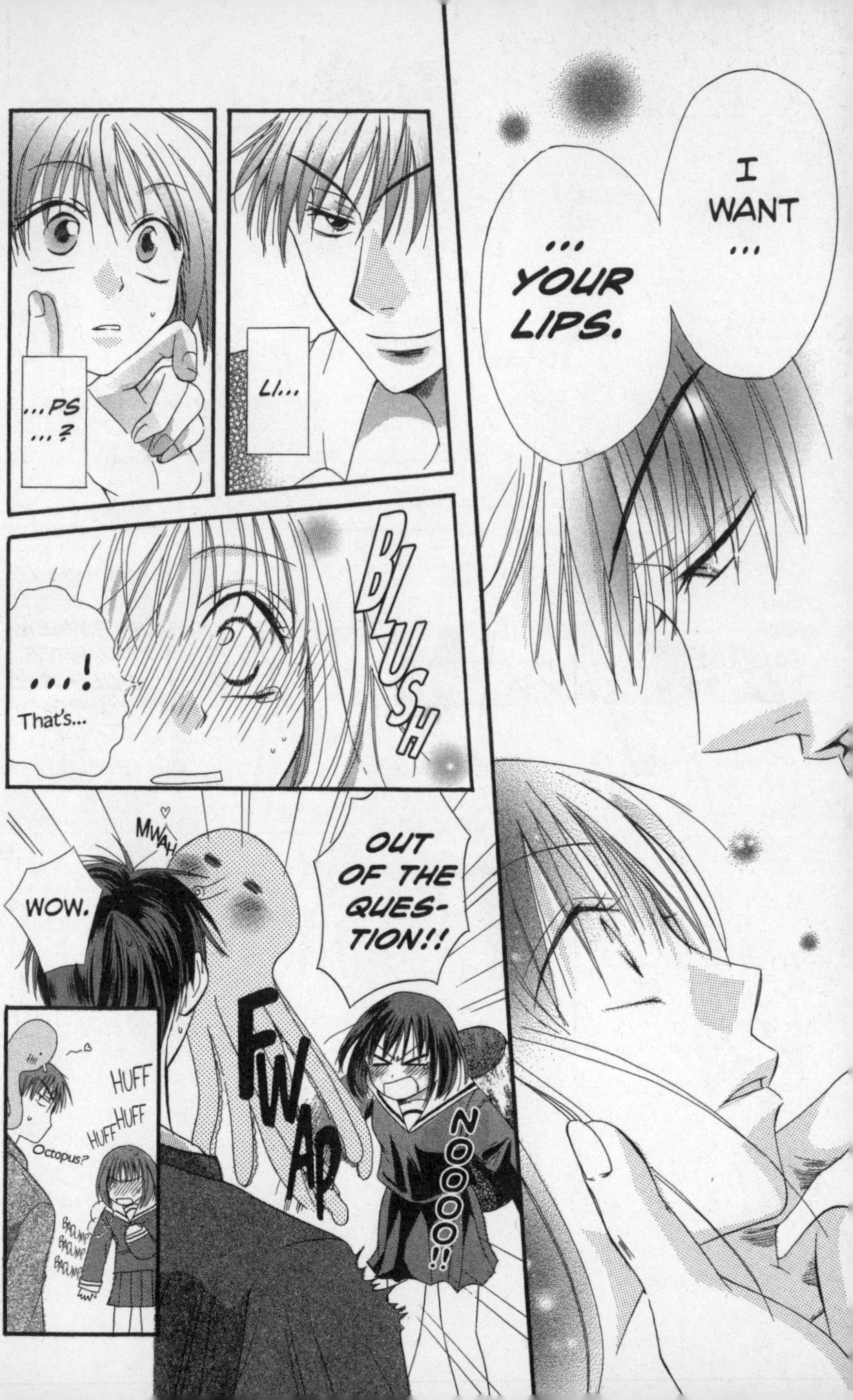
I WANT ...
... YOUR LIPS.
LI...
...PS ...?
BLUSH
...! That's...
OUT OF THE QUES-TION!!
MWAH
WOW.
FWAP
NOOOOO!!
HUFF HUFF HUFF
Octopus?
BADUMP BADUMP BADUMP

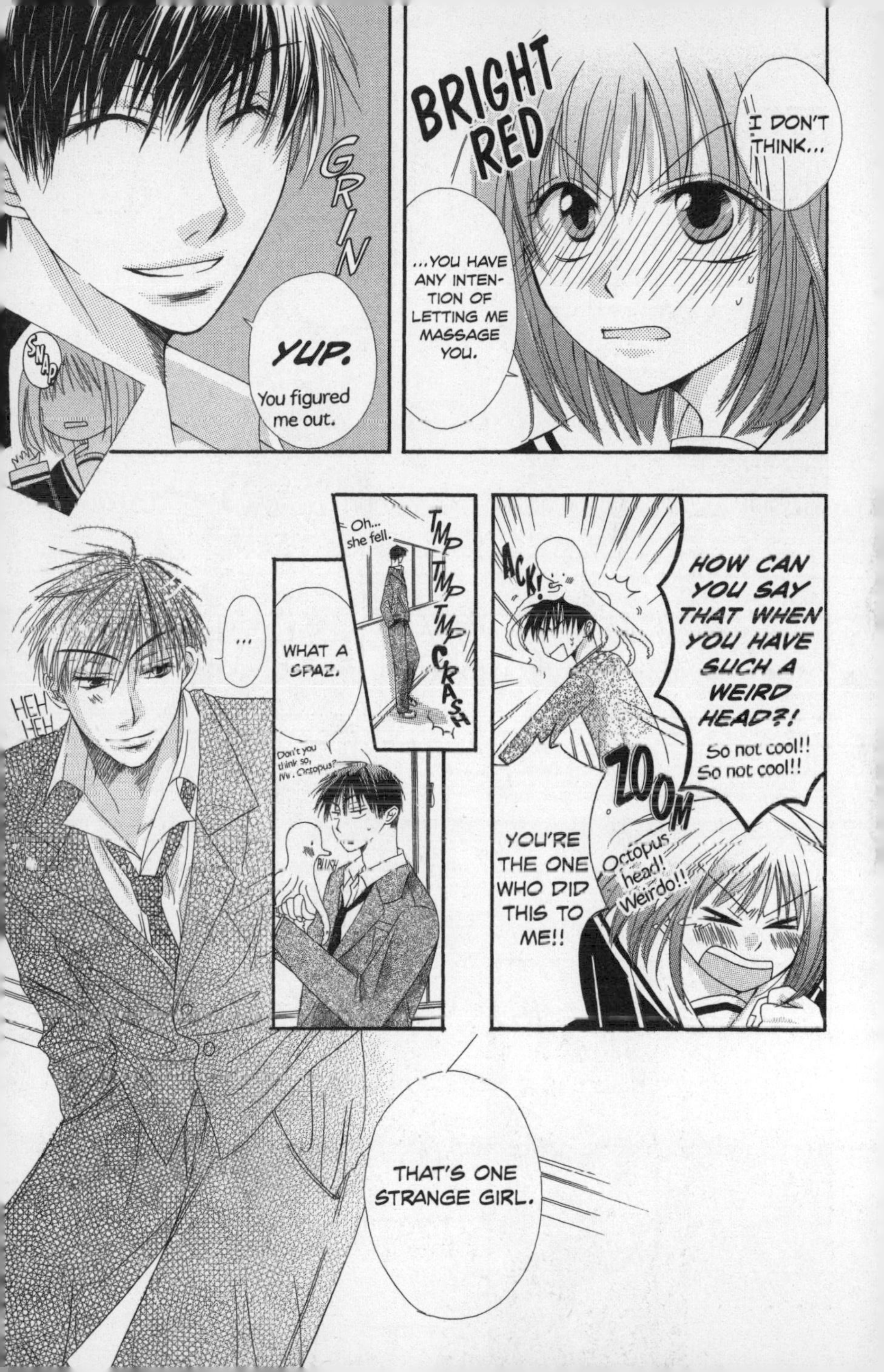
I DON'T THINK...
BRIGHT RED
...YOU HAVE ANY INTENTION OF LETTING ME MASSAGE YOU.
GRIN
YUP.
You figured me out.
SNAP
HOW CAN YOU SAY THAT WHEN YOU HAVE SUCH A WEIRD HEAD?!
ACK!
So not cool!! So not cool!!
ZOOM
YOU'RE THE ONE WHO DID THIS TO ME!!
Octopus head! Weirdo!!
Oh... she fell.
TMP TMP TMP CRASH
WHAT A SPAZ.
Don't you think so, Mr. Octopus?
...
HEH HEH
THAT'S ONE STRANGE GIRL.

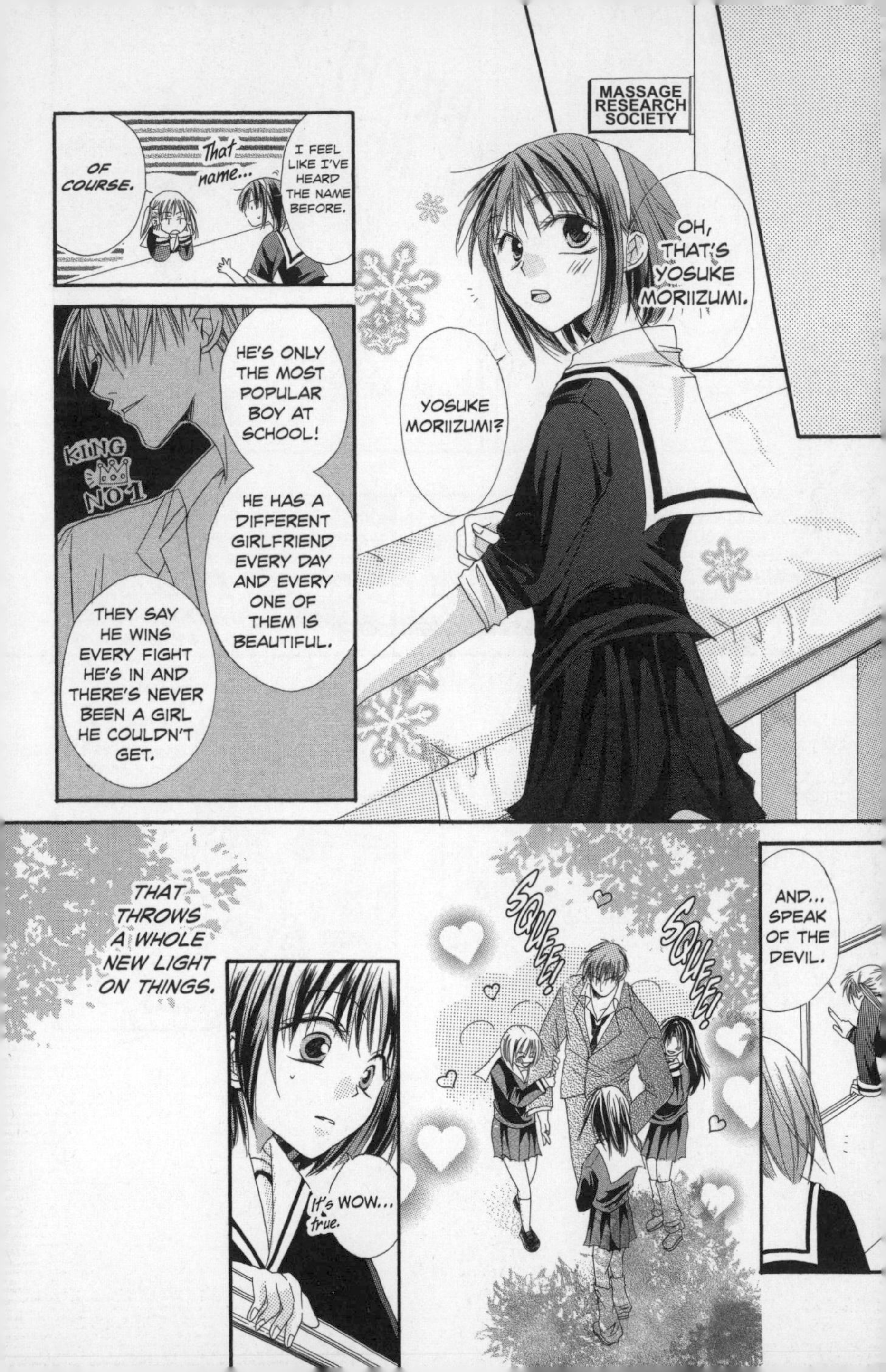
MASSAGE RESEARCH SOCIETY
OH, THAT'S YOSUKE MORIIZUMI.
YOSUKE MORIIZUMI?
I FEEL LIKE I'VE HEARD THE NAME BEFORE.
That name...
OF COURSE.
HE'S ONLY THE MOST POPULAR BOY AT SCHOOL!
KING NO.1
HE HAS A DIFFERENT GIRLFRIEND EVERY DAY AND EVERY ONE OF THEM IS BEAUTIFUL.
THEY SAY HE WINS EVERY FIGHT HE'S IN AND THERE'S NEVER BEEN A GIRL HE COULDN'T GET.
AND... SPEAK OF THE DEVIL.
SQUEE!
SQUEE!
THAT THROWS A WHOLE NEW LIGHT ON THINGS.
WOW...
It's true.

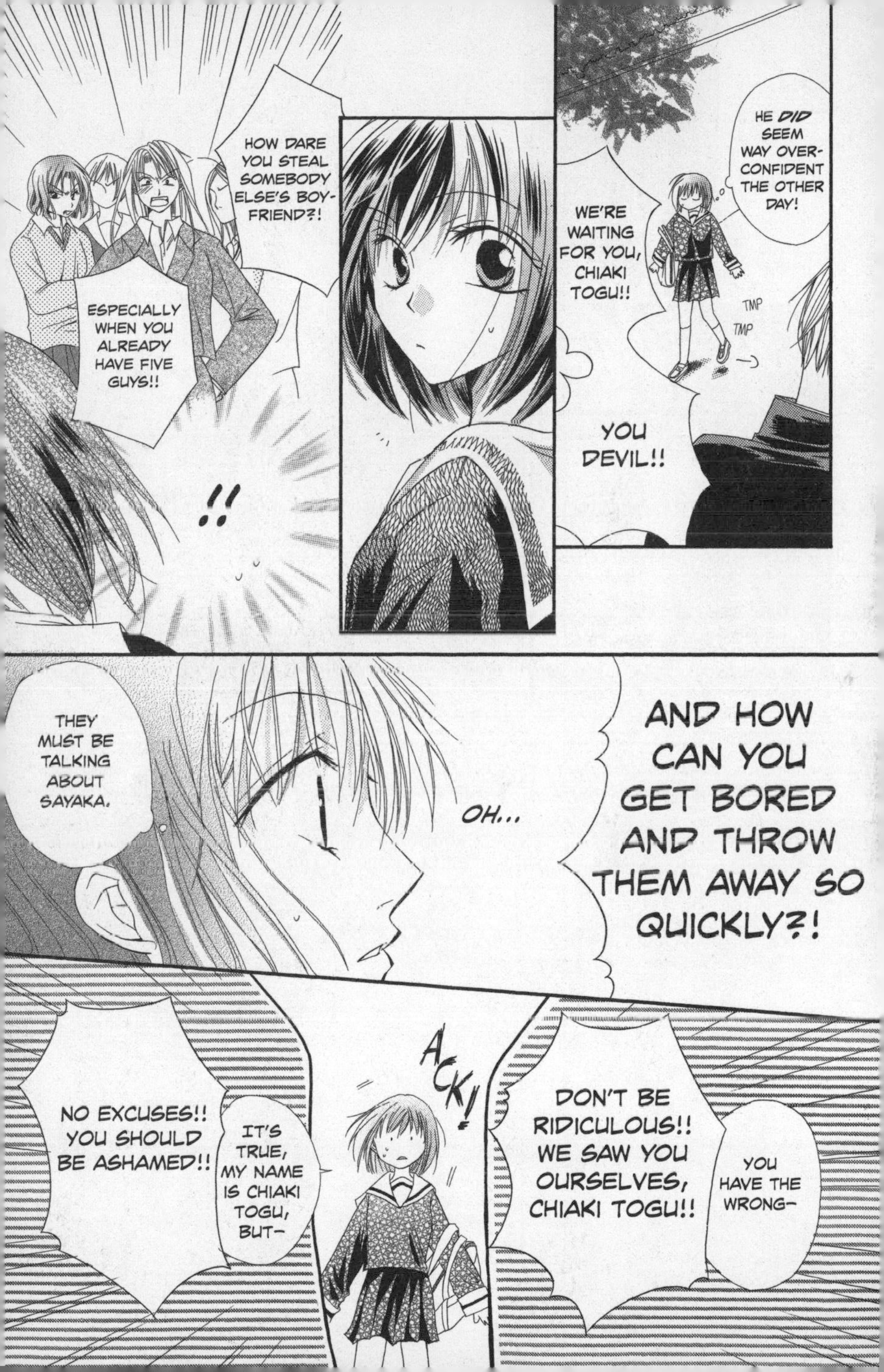
HE DID SEEM WAY OVER-CONFIDENT THE OTHER DAY!
TMP
TMP
WE'RE WAITING FOR YOU, CHIAKI TOGU!!
YOU DEVIL!!
HOW DARE YOU STEAL SOMEBODY ELSE'S BOY-FRIEND?!
ESPECIALLY WHEN YOU ALREADY HAVE FIVE GUYS!!
!!
AND HOW CAN YOU GET BORED AND THROW THEM AWAY SO QUICKLY?!
OH...
THEY MUST BE TALKING ABOUT SAYAKA.
YOU HAVE THE WRONG-
DON'T BE RIDICULOUS!! WE SAW YOU OURSELVES, CHIAKI TOGU!!
ACK!
IT'S TRUE, MY NAME IS CHIAKI TOGU, BUT-
NO EXCUSES!! YOU SHOULD BE ASHAMED!!

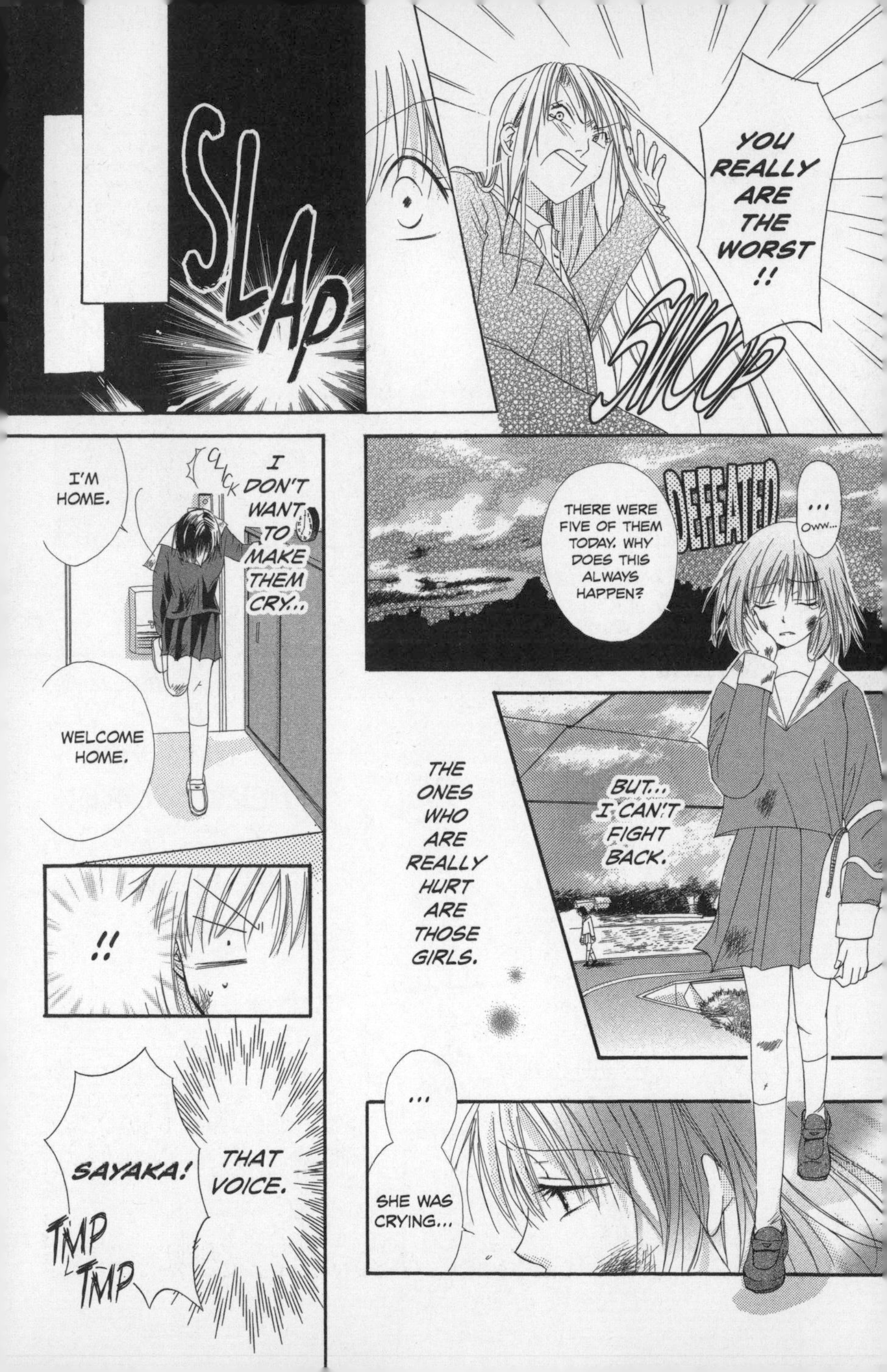
YOU REALLY ARE THE WORST!!
SWOOP
SLAP
... OWW...
DEFEATED
THERE WERE FIVE OF THEM TODAY. WHY DOES THIS ALWAYS HAPPEN?
BUT... I CAN'T FIGHT BACK.
THE ONES WHO ARE REALLY HURT ARE THOSE GIRLS.
...
SHE WAS CRYING...
I DON'T WANT TO MAKE THEM CRY...
CLICK
I'M HOME.
WELCOME HOME.
!!
THAT VOICE.
SAYAKA!
TMP TMP

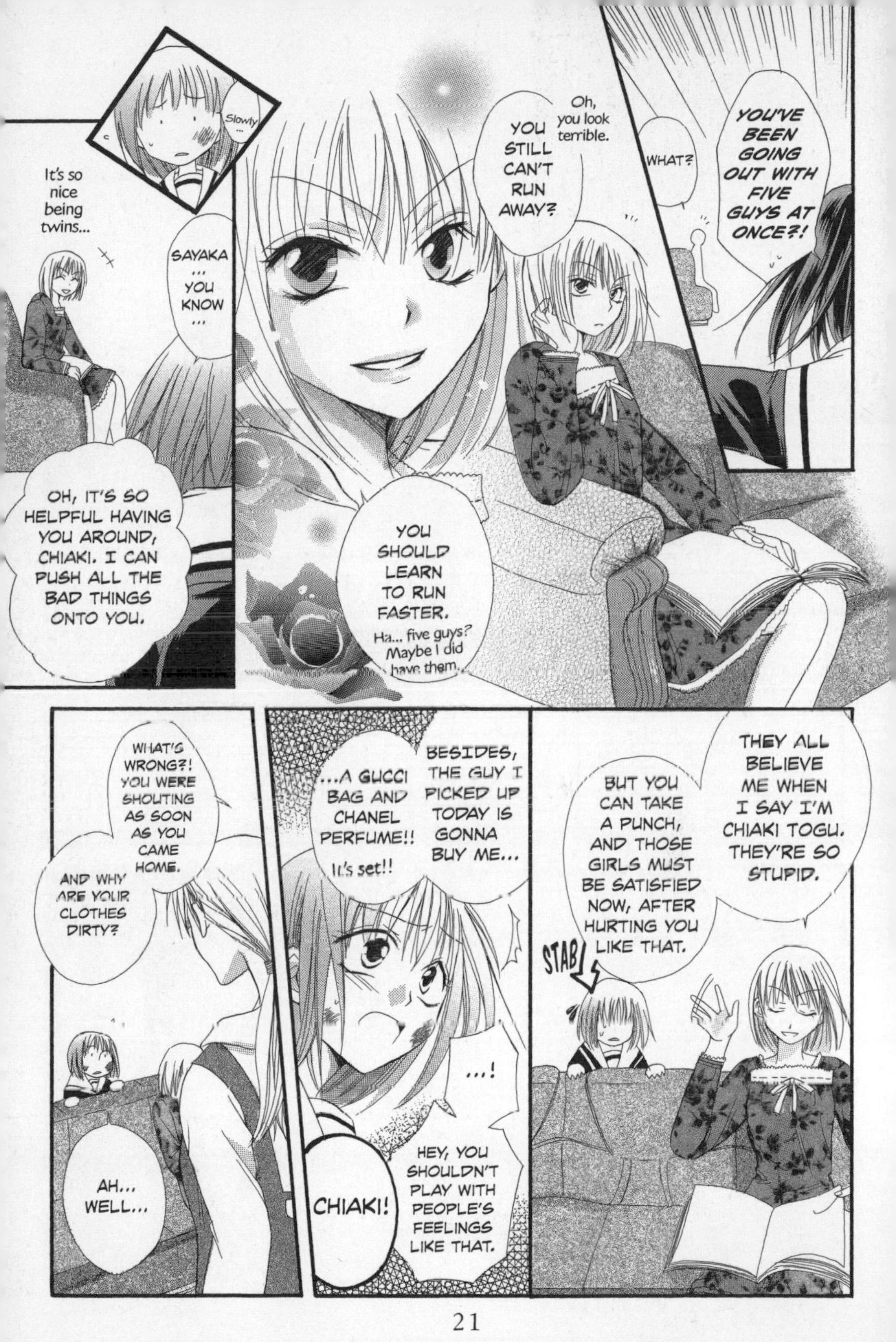
YOU'VE BEEN GOING OUT WITH FIVE GUYS AT ONCE?!
WHAT?
Oh, you look terrible.
YOU STILL CAN'T RUN AWAY?
YOU SHOULD LEARN TO RUN FASTER.
Ha... five guys? Maybe I did have them.
Slowly...
SAYAKA... YOU KNOW...
It's so nice being twins...
OH, IT'S SO HELPFUL HAVING YOU AROUND, CHIAKI. I CAN PUSH ALL THE BAD THINGS ONTO YOU.
THEY ALL BELIEVE ME WHEN I SAY I'M CHIAKI TOGU. THEY'RE SO STUPID.
BUT YOU CAN TAKE A PUNCH, AND THOSE GIRLS MUST BE SATISFIED NOW, AFTER HURTING YOU LIKE THAT.
STAB
BESIDES, THE GUY I PICKED UP TODAY IS GONNA BUY ME...
...A GUCCI BAG AND CHANEL PERFUME!!
It's set!!
...!
HEY, YOU SHOULDN'T PLAY WITH PEOPLE'S FEELINGS LIKE THAT.
CHIAKI!
WHAT'S WRONG?! YOU WERE SHOUTING AS SOON AS YOU CAME HOME.
AND WHY ARE YOUR CLOTHES DIRTY?
AH... WELL...

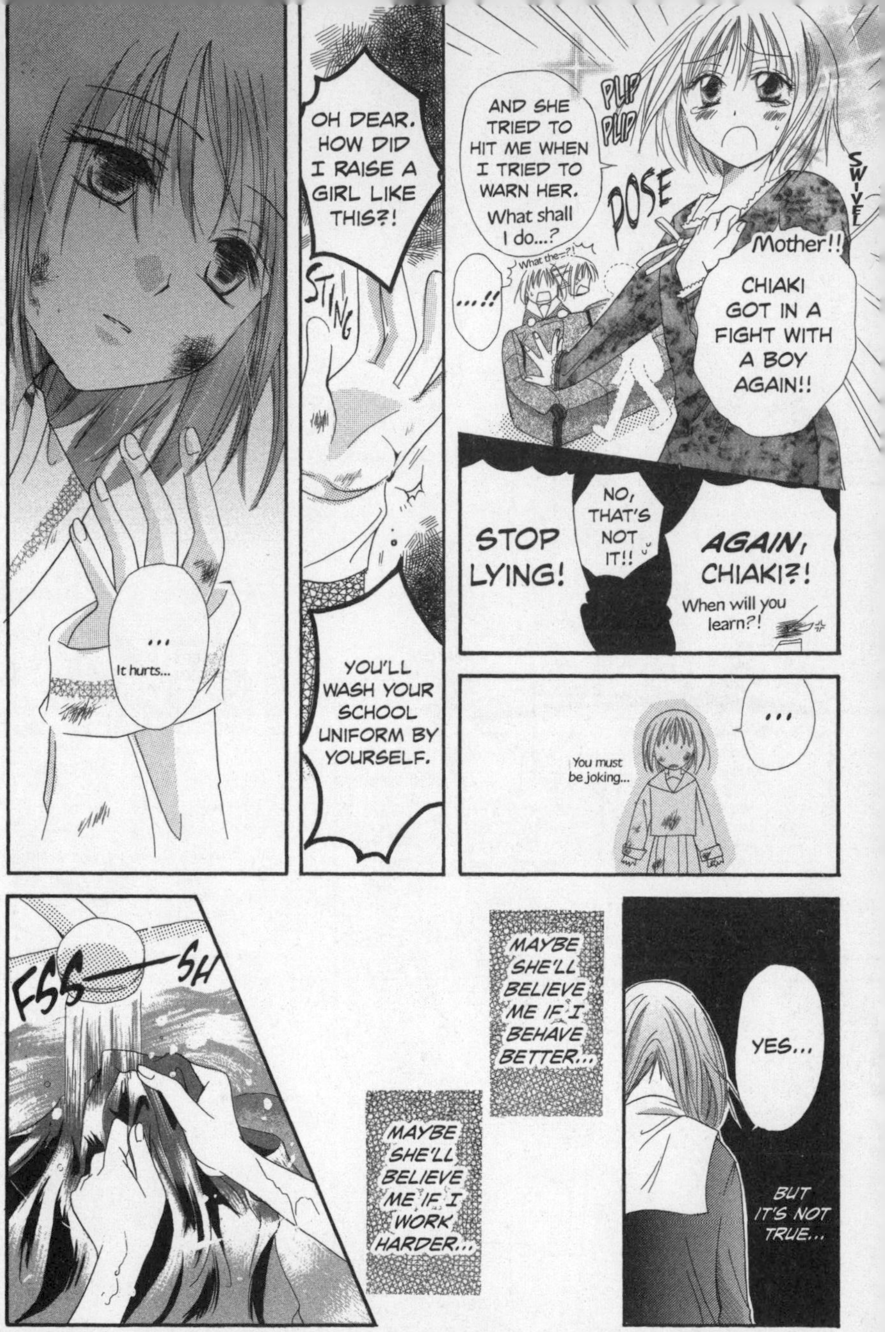
SWIVEL
Mother!!
CHIAKI GOT IN A FIGHT WITH A BOY AGAIN!!
PLIP PLIP
POSE
AND SHE TRIED TO HIT ME WHEN I TRIED TO WARN HER.
What shall I do...?
...!!
What the-?!
AGAIN, CHIAKI?!
When will you learn?!
NO, THAT'S NOT IT!!
STOP LYING!
...
You must be joking...
OH DEAR. HOW DID I RAISE A GIRL LIKE THIS?!
STING
YOU'LL WASH YOUR SCHOOL UNIFORM BY YOURSELF.
...
It hurts...
YES...
BUT IT'S NOT TRUE...
MAYBE SHE'LL BELIEVE ME IF I BEHAVE BETTER...
MAYBE SHE'LL BELIEVE ME IF I WORK HARDER...
FSS SH

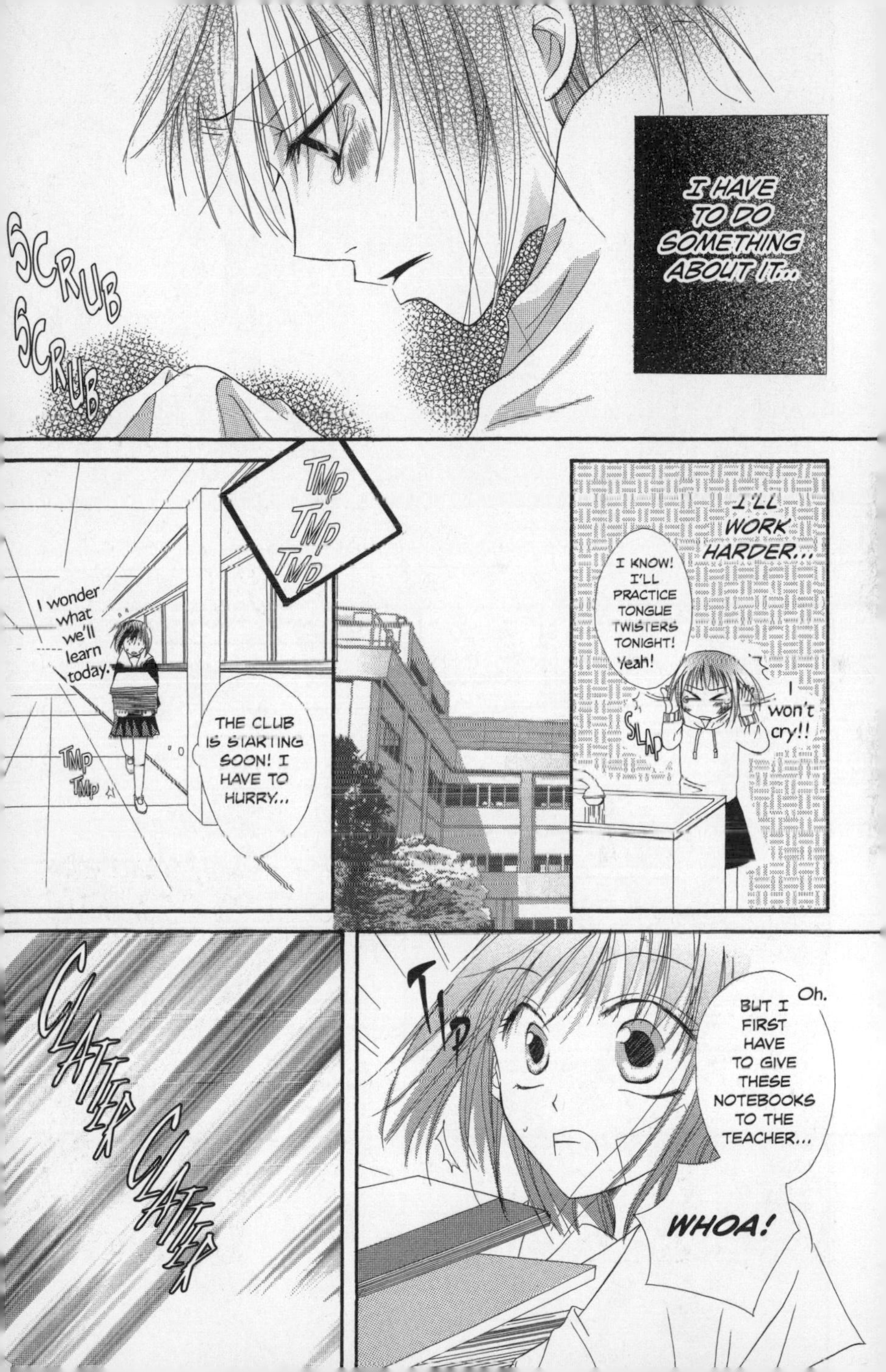
I HAVE TO DO SOMETHING ABOUT IT...
SCRUB SCRUB
I'LL WORK HARDER...
I KNOW! I'LL PRACTICE TONGUE TWISTERS TONIGHT! Yeah!
SLAP
I won't cry!!
TMP TMP TMP
THE CLUB IS STARTING SOON! I HAVE TO HURRY...
I wonder what we'll learn today.
TMP TMP
Oh.
BUT I FIRST HAVE TO GIVE THESE NOTEBOOKS TO THE TEACHER...
WHOA!
CLATTER CLATTER

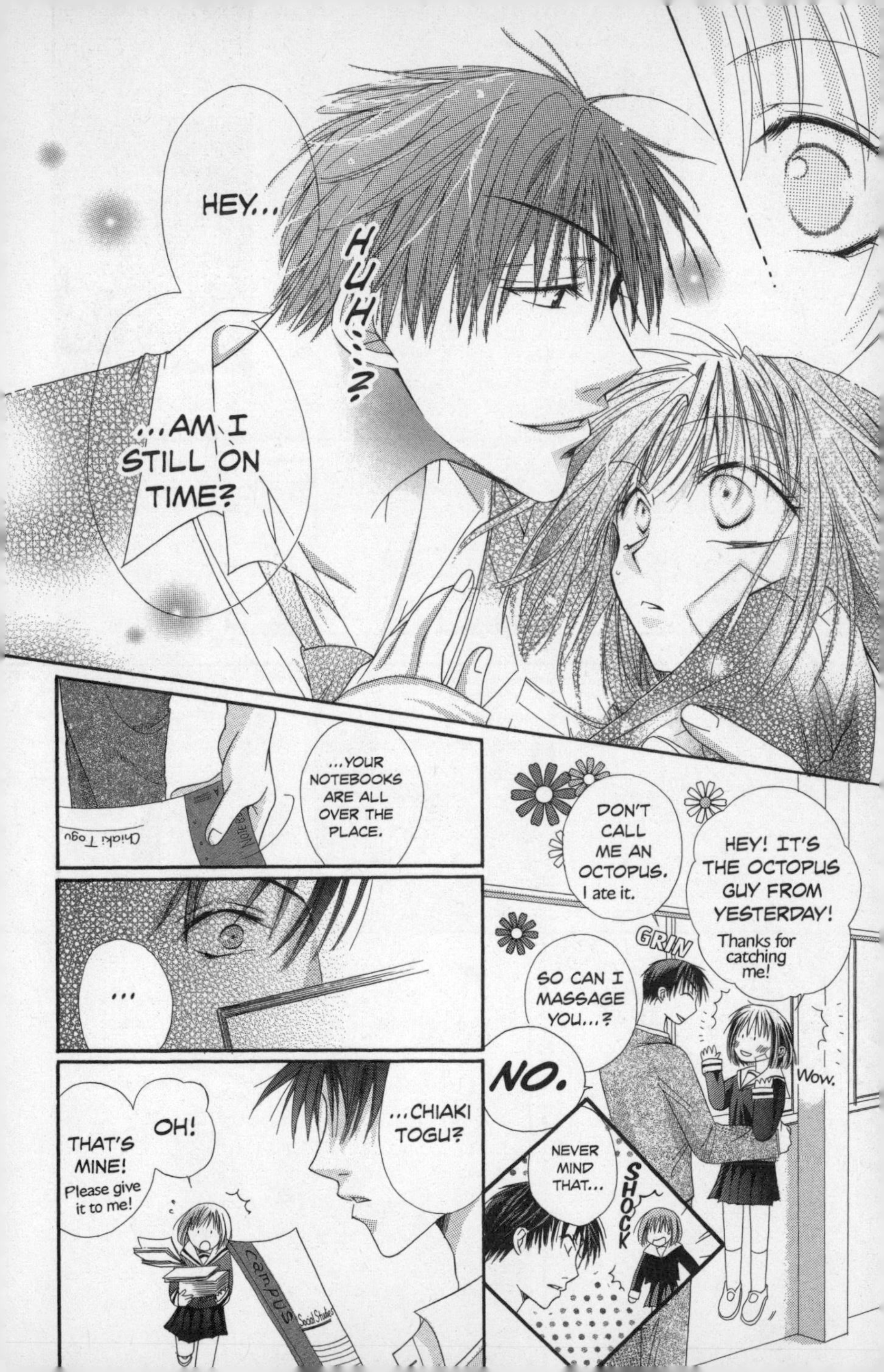
HUH...?
HEY...
...AM I STILL ON TIME?
HEY! IT'S THE OCTOPUS GUY FROM YESTERDAY!
Thanks for catching me!
Wow.
DON'T CALL ME AN OCTOPUS.
I ate it.
GRIN
SO CAN I MASSAGE YOU...?
NO.
NEVER MIND THAT...
SHOCK
...YOUR NOTEBOOKS ARE ALL OVER THE PLACE.
Chiaki Togu
...
...CHIAKI TOGU?
OH!
THAT'S MINE!
Please give it to me!
Campus
Social Studies

YAMADA IS A VERY COMMON LAST NAME, WHEREAS TOGU SOUNDS ARISTOCRATIC.

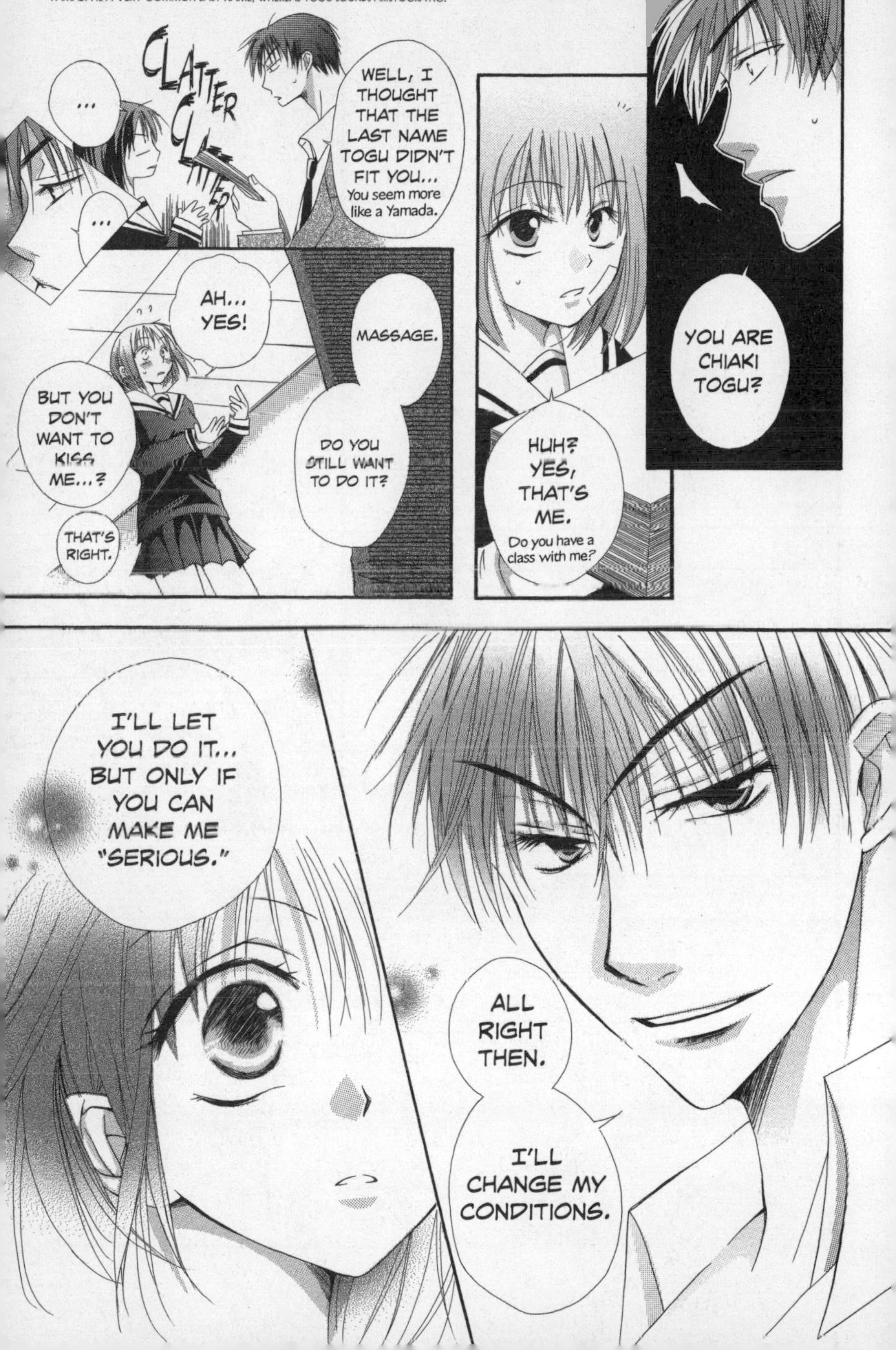
YOU ARE CHIAKI TOGU?
HUH? YES, THAT'S ME. Do you have a class with me?
WELL, I THOUGHT THAT THE LAST NAME TOGU DIDN'T FIT YOU... You seem more like a Yamada.
CLATTER CLATTER
...
...
MASSAGE.
DO YOU STILL WANT TO DO IT?
AH... YES!
BUT YOU DON'T WANT TO KISS ME...?
THAT'S RIGHT.
ALL RIGHT THEN.
I'LL CHANGE MY CONDITIONS.
I'LL LET YOU DO IT... BUT ONLY IF YOU CAN MAKE ME "SERIOUS."

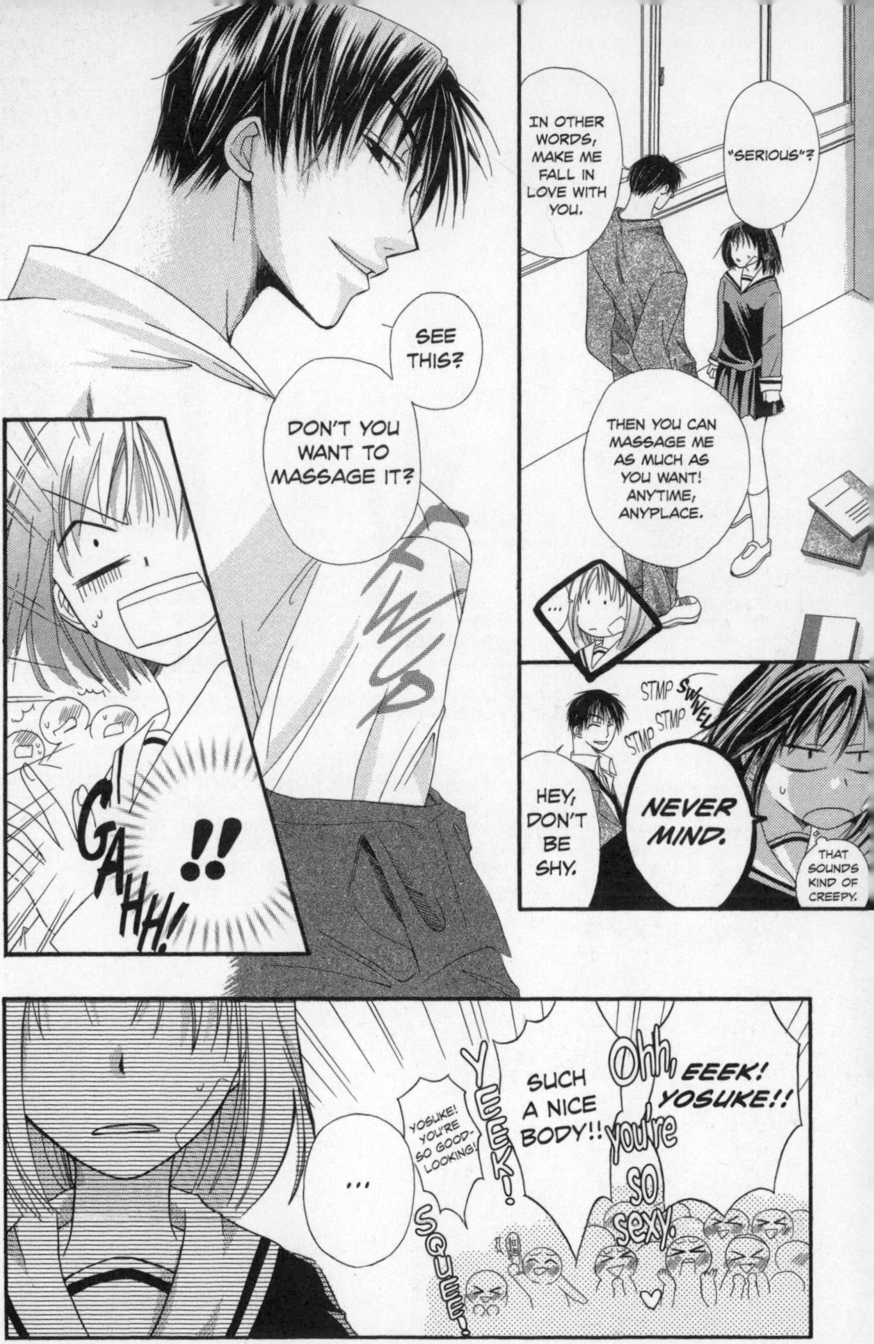
"SERIOUS"?
IN OTHER WORDS, MAKE ME FALL IN LOVE WITH YOU.
THEN YOU CAN MASSAGE ME AS MUCH AS YOU WANT! ANYTIME, ANYPLACE.
...
STMP STMP STMP
THAT SOUNDS KIND OF CREEPY.
NEVER MIND.
HEY, DON'T BE SHY.
SEE THIS?
DON'T YOU WANT TO MASSAGE IT?
GAHH!!
EEEK! YOSUKE!!
Ohh, you're so sexy.
SUCH A NICE BODY!!
YEEEK!
YOSUKE! YOU'RE SO GOOD-LOOKING!
SQUEEE!
...

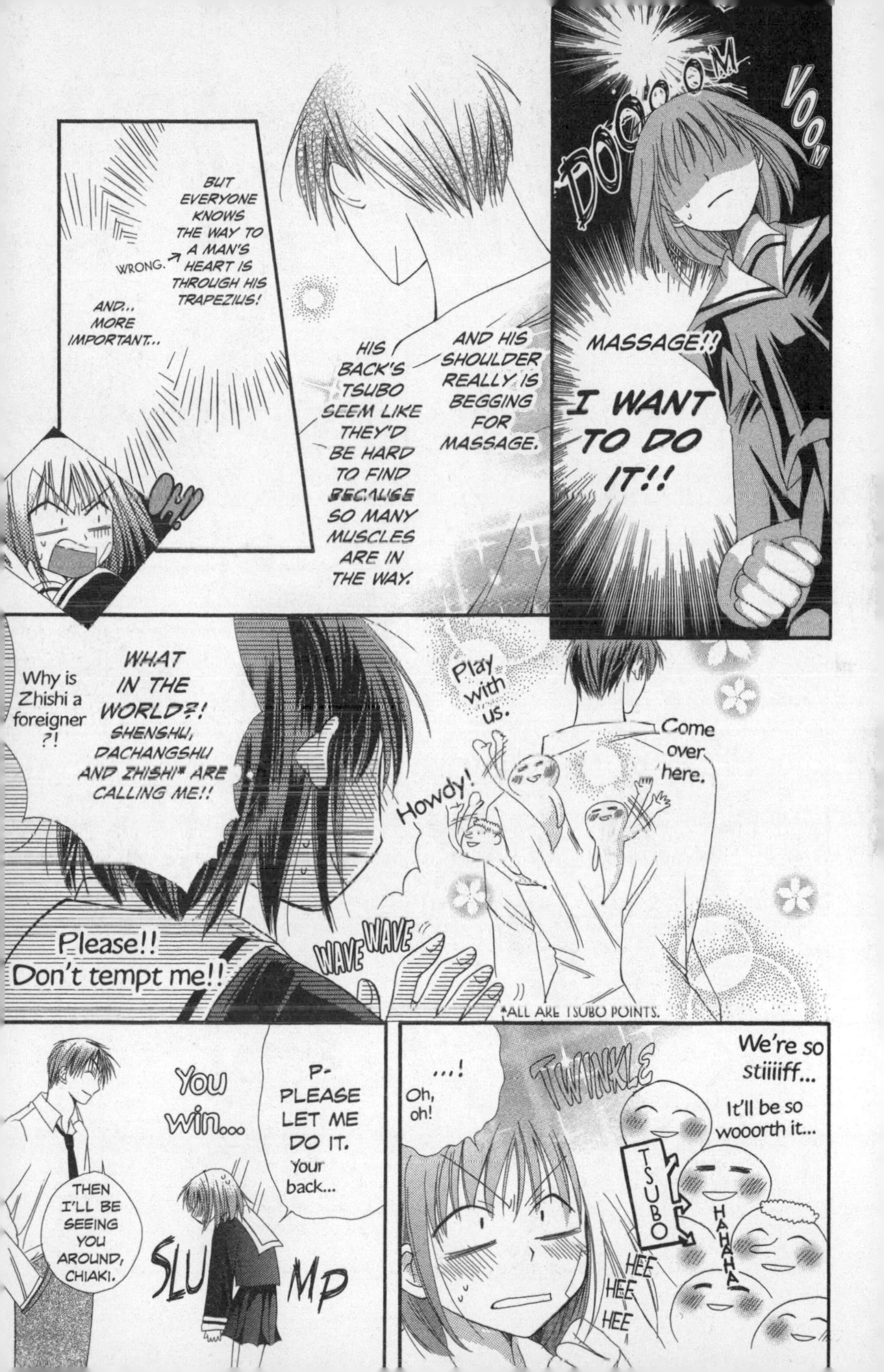
DOOOOOM
VOOM
MASSAGE!!
I WANT TO DO IT!!
BUT EVERYONE KNOWS THE WAY TO A MAN'S HEART IS THROUGH HIS TRAPEZIUS!
WRONG.
AND... MORE IMPORTANT...
AND HIS SHOULDER REALLY IS BEGGING FOR MASSAGE.
HIS BACK'S TSUBO SEEM LIKE THEY'D BE HARD TO FIND BECAUSE SO MANY MUSCLES ARE IN THE WAY.
Come over here.
Play with us.
Howdy!
WAVE WAVE
WHAT IN THE WORLD?! SHENSHU, DACHANGSHU AND ZHISHI* ARE CALLING ME!!
Why is Zhishi a foreigner?!
Please!! Don't tempt me!!
*ALL ARE TSUBO POINTS.
We're so stiiiiff...
It'll be so wooorth it...
TWINKLE
...!
Oh, oh!
TSUBO
HAHAHA
HEE HEE HEE
P-PLEASE LET ME DO IT.
Your back...
You win...
THEN I'LL BE SEEING YOU AROUND, CHIAKI.
SLUMP

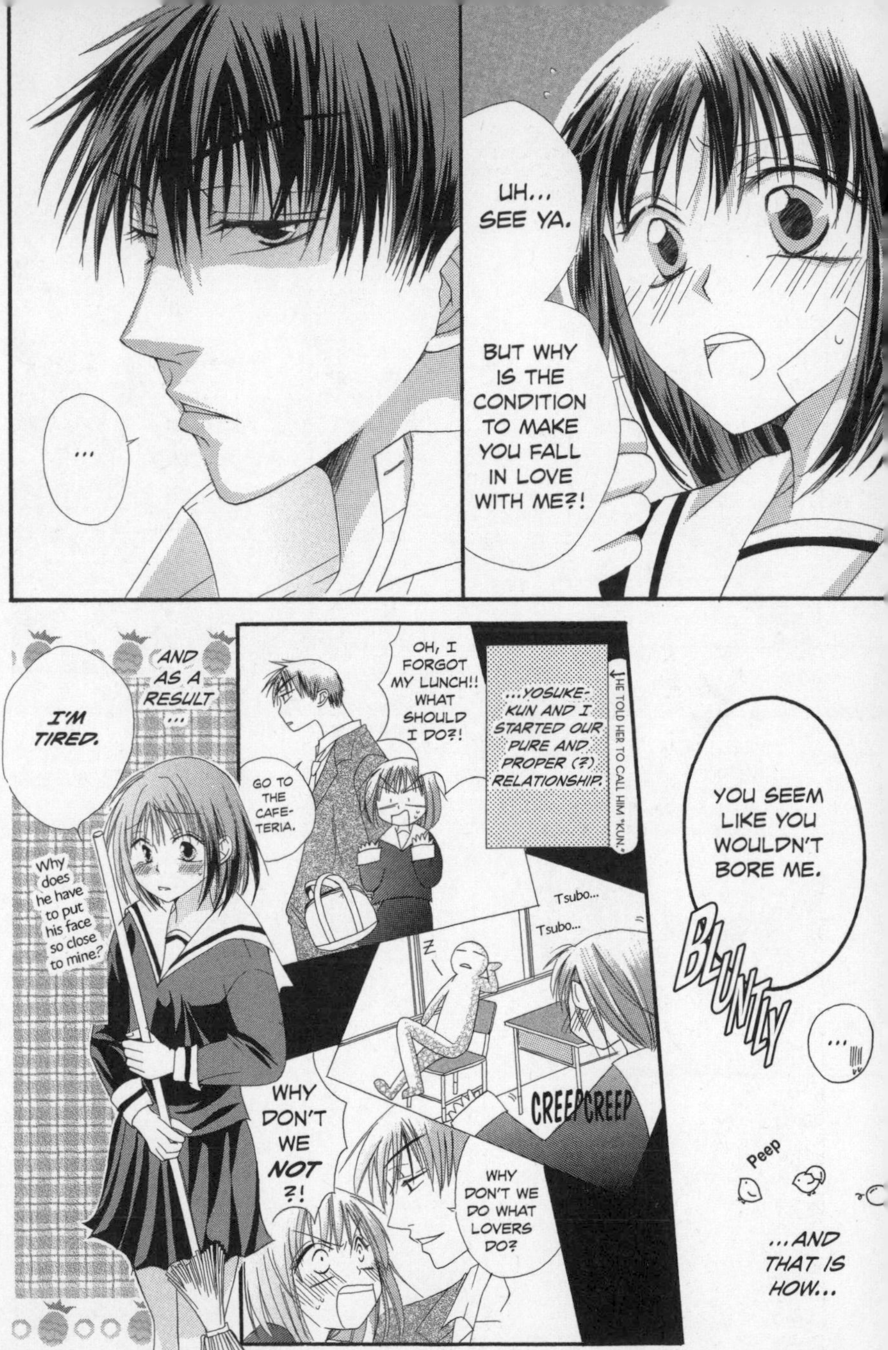
UH... SEE YA.
BUT WHY IS THE CONDITION TO MAKE YOU FALL IN LOVE WITH ME?!
...
YOU SEEM LIKE YOU WOULDN'T BORE ME.
BLUNTLY
...
Peep
...AND THAT IS HOW...
...YOSUKE-KUN AND I STARTED OUR PURE AND PROPER (?) RELATIONSHIP.
HE TOLD HER TO CALL HIM "KUN."
OH, I FORGOT MY LUNCH!! WHAT SHOULD I DO?!
GO TO THE CAFETERIA.
Tsubo...
Tsubo...
CREEPCREEP
WHY DON'T WE DO WHAT LOVERS DO?
WHY DON'T WE NOT?!
AND AS A RESULT...
I'M TIRED.
Why does he have to put his face so close to mine?

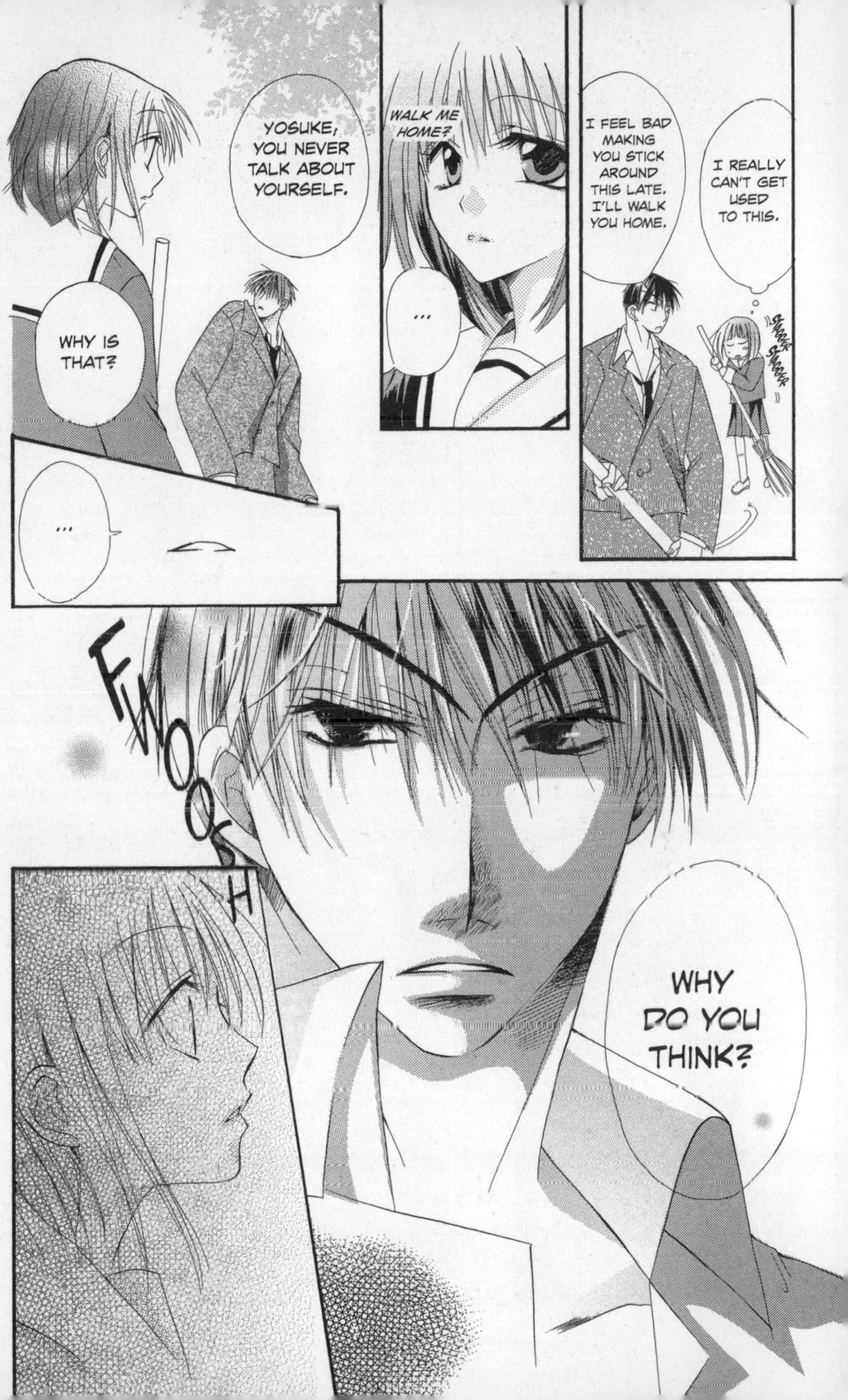
I REALLY CAN'T GET USED TO THIS.
I FEEL BAD MAKING YOU STICK AROUND THIS LATE. I'LL WALK YOU HOME.
WALK ME HOME?
...
YOSUKE, YOU NEVER TALK ABOUT YOURSELF.
WHY IS THAT?
...
WHY DO YOU THINK?
FWOOSH

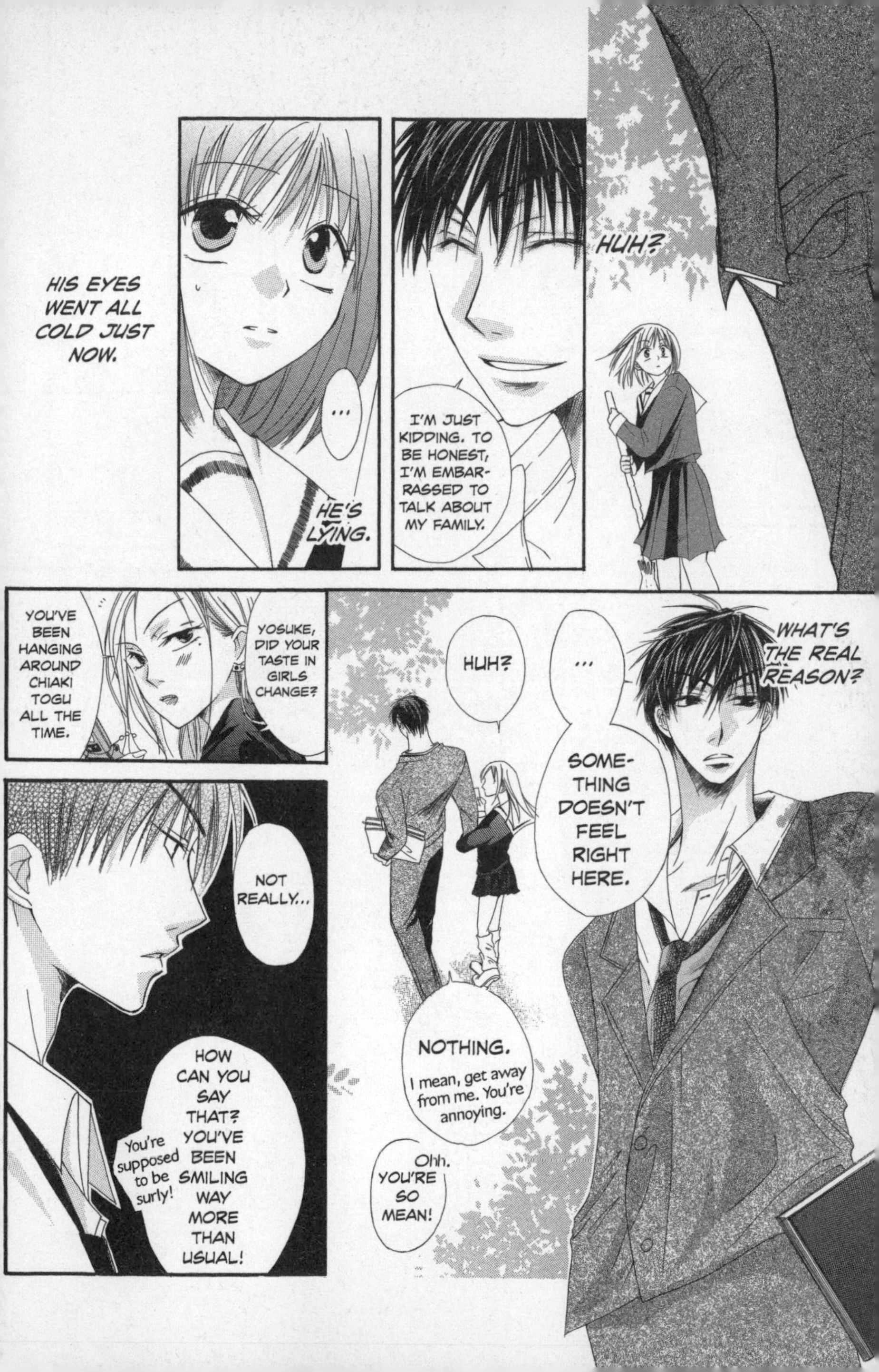
HUH?
I'M JUST KIDDING. TO BE HONEST, I'M EMBARRASSED TO TALK ABOUT MY FAMILY.
...
HE'S LYING.
HIS EYES WENT ALL COLD JUST NOW.
WHAT'S THE REAL REASON?
...
SOMETHING DOESN'T FEEL RIGHT HERE.
HUH?
NOTHING.
I mean, get away from me. You're annoying.
Ohh. YOU'RE SO MEAN!
YOSUKE, DID YOUR TASTE IN GIRLS CHANGE?
YOU'VE BEEN HANGING AROUND CHIAKI TOGU ALL THE TIME.
NOT REALLY...
HOW CAN YOU SAY THAT? YOU'VE BEEN SMILING WAY MORE THAN USUAL!
You're supposed to be surly!

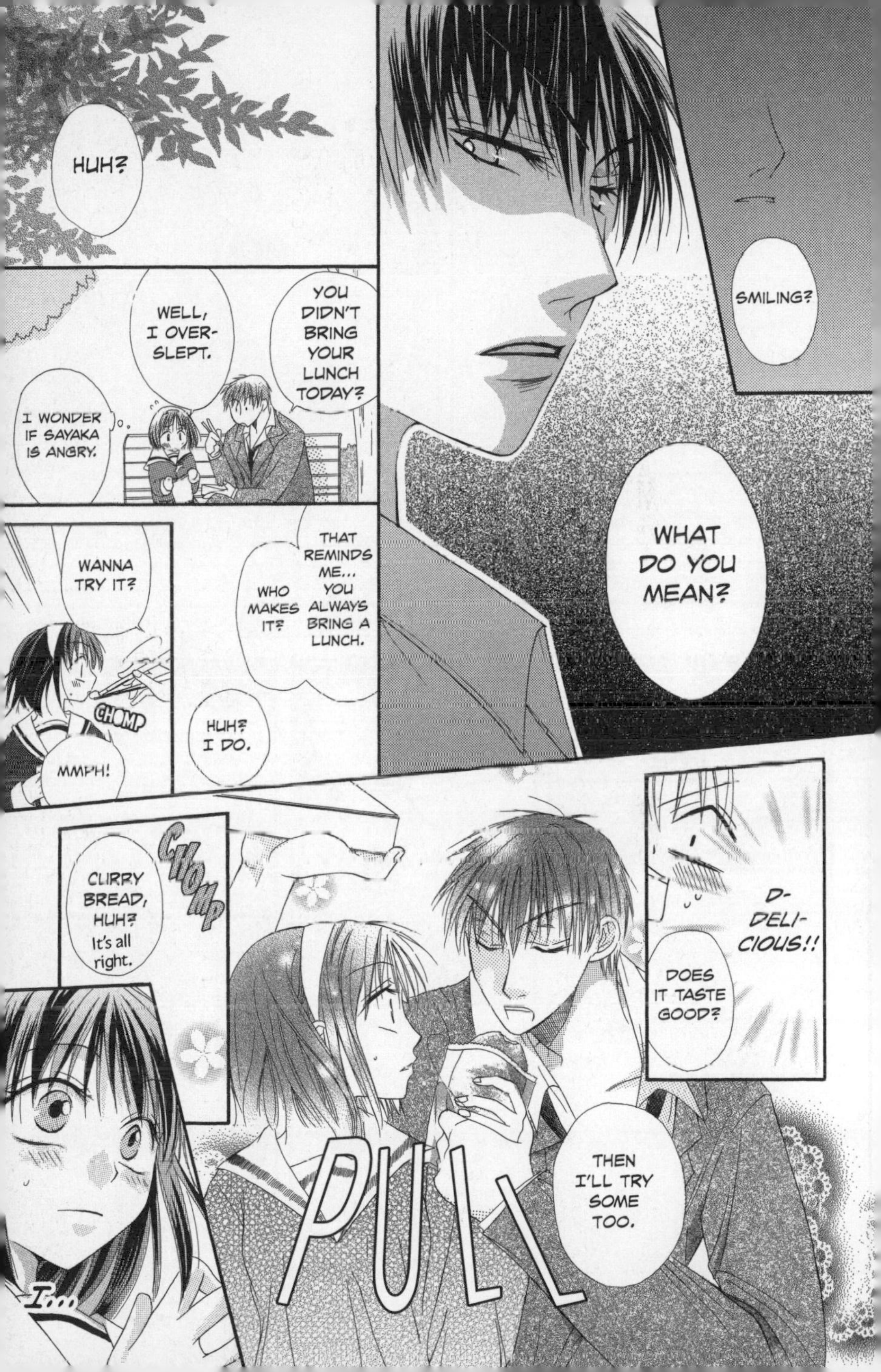
SMILING?
WHAT DO YOU MEAN?
HUH?
YOU DIDN'T BRING YOUR LUNCH TODAY?
WELL, I OVER-SLEPT.
I WONDER IF SAYAKA IS ANGRY.
THAT REMINDS ME... YOU ALWAYS BRING A LUNCH.
WHO MAKES IT?
HUH? I DO.
WANNA TRY IT?
CHOMP
MMPH!
D-DELI-CIOUS!!
DOES IT TASTE GOOD?
THEN I'LL TRY SOME TOO.
PULL
CHOMP
CURRY BREAD, HUH? It's all right.

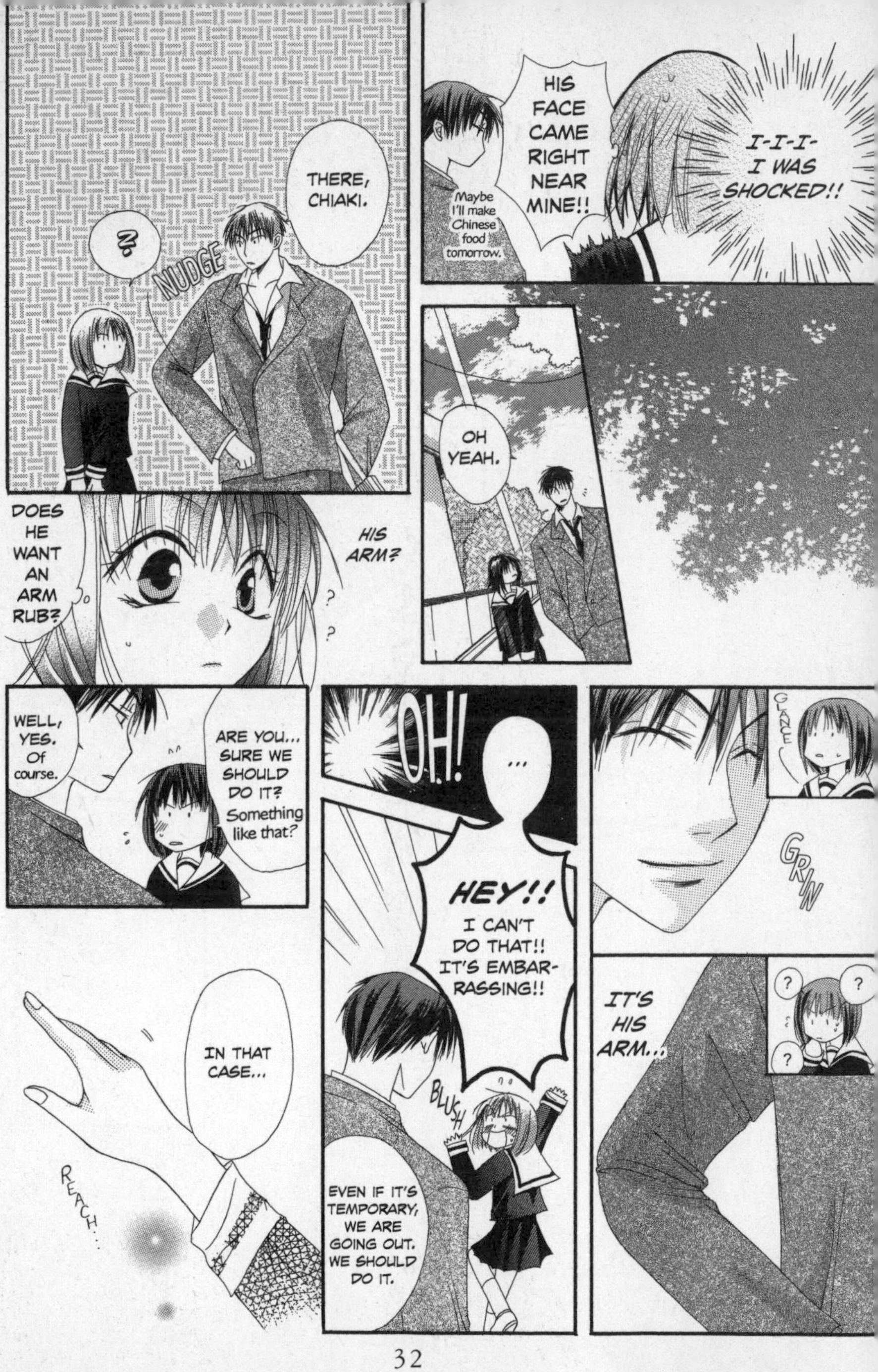
HIS FACE CAME RIGHT NEAR MINE!!
Maybe I'll make Chinese food tomorrow.
I-I-I-I WAS SHOCKED!!
THERE, CHIAKI.
?
NUDGE
OH YEAH.
HIS ARM?
DOES HE WANT AN ARM RUB?
GLANCE
GRIN
IT'S HIS ARM...
OH!
...
HEY!! I CAN'T DO THAT!! IT'S EMBARRASSING!!
BLUSH
EVEN IF IT'S TEMPORARY, WE ARE GOING OUT. WE SHOULD DO IT.
ARE YOU... SURE WE SHOULD DO IT? Something like that?
WELL, YES. Of course.
IN THAT CASE...
REACH...

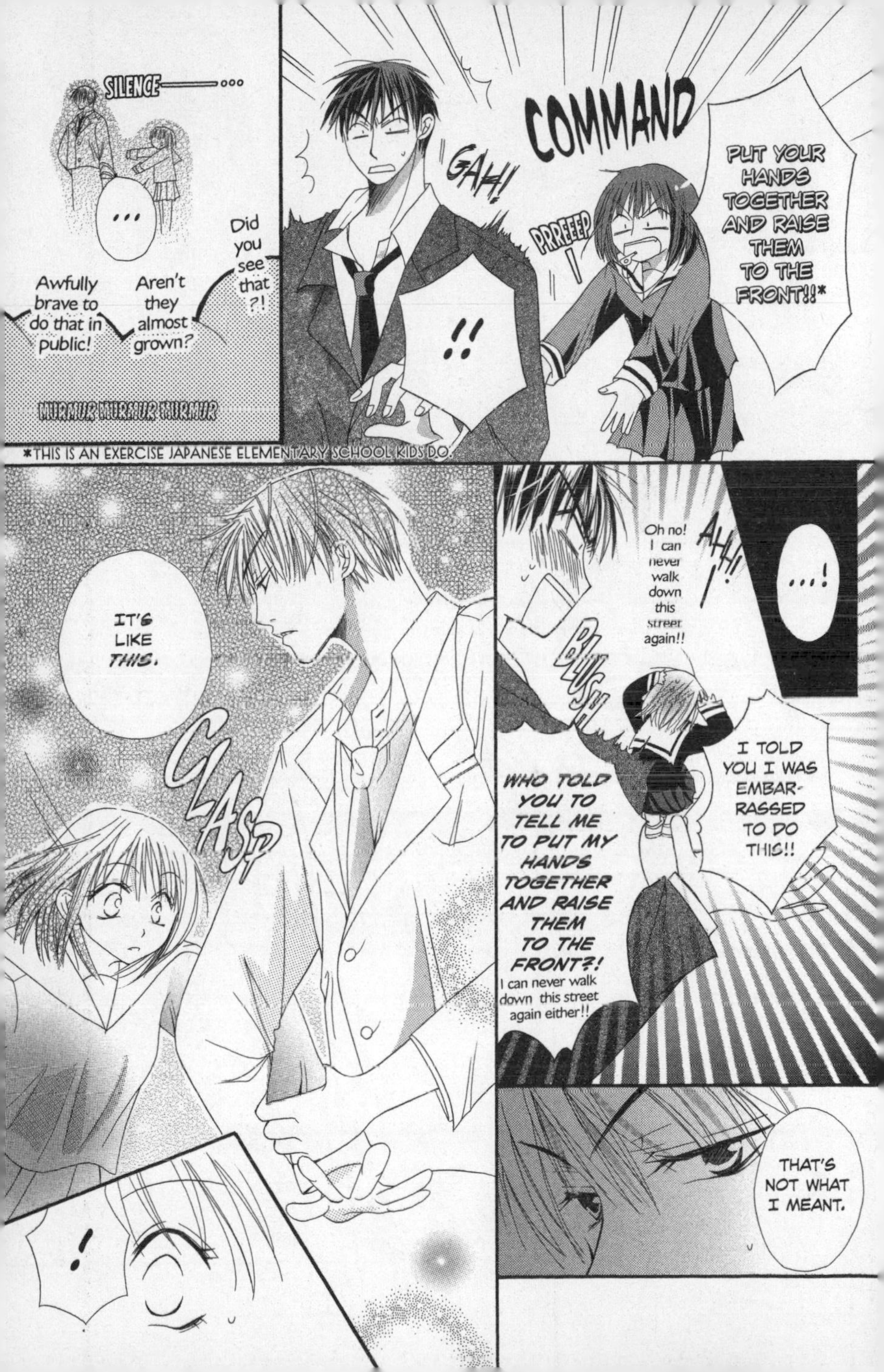
COMMAND
PUT YOUR HANDS TOGETHER AND RAISE THEM TO THE FRONT!!*
PRREEEP!
GAH!
!!
SILENCE———...
...
Did you see that?!
Aren't they almost grown?
Awfully brave to do that in public!
MURMUR MURMUR MURMUR
*THIS IS AN EXERCISE JAPANESE ELEMENTARY SCHOOL KIDS DO.
...!
AHH!
Oh no! I can never walk down this street again!!
BLUSH
I TOLD YOU I WAS EMBARRASSED TO DO THIS!!
WHO TOLD YOU TO TELL ME TO PUT MY HANDS TOGETHER AND RAISE THEM TO THE FRONT?!
I can never walk down this street again either!!
THAT'S NOT WHAT I MEANT.
IT'S LIKE THIS.
CLASP
!

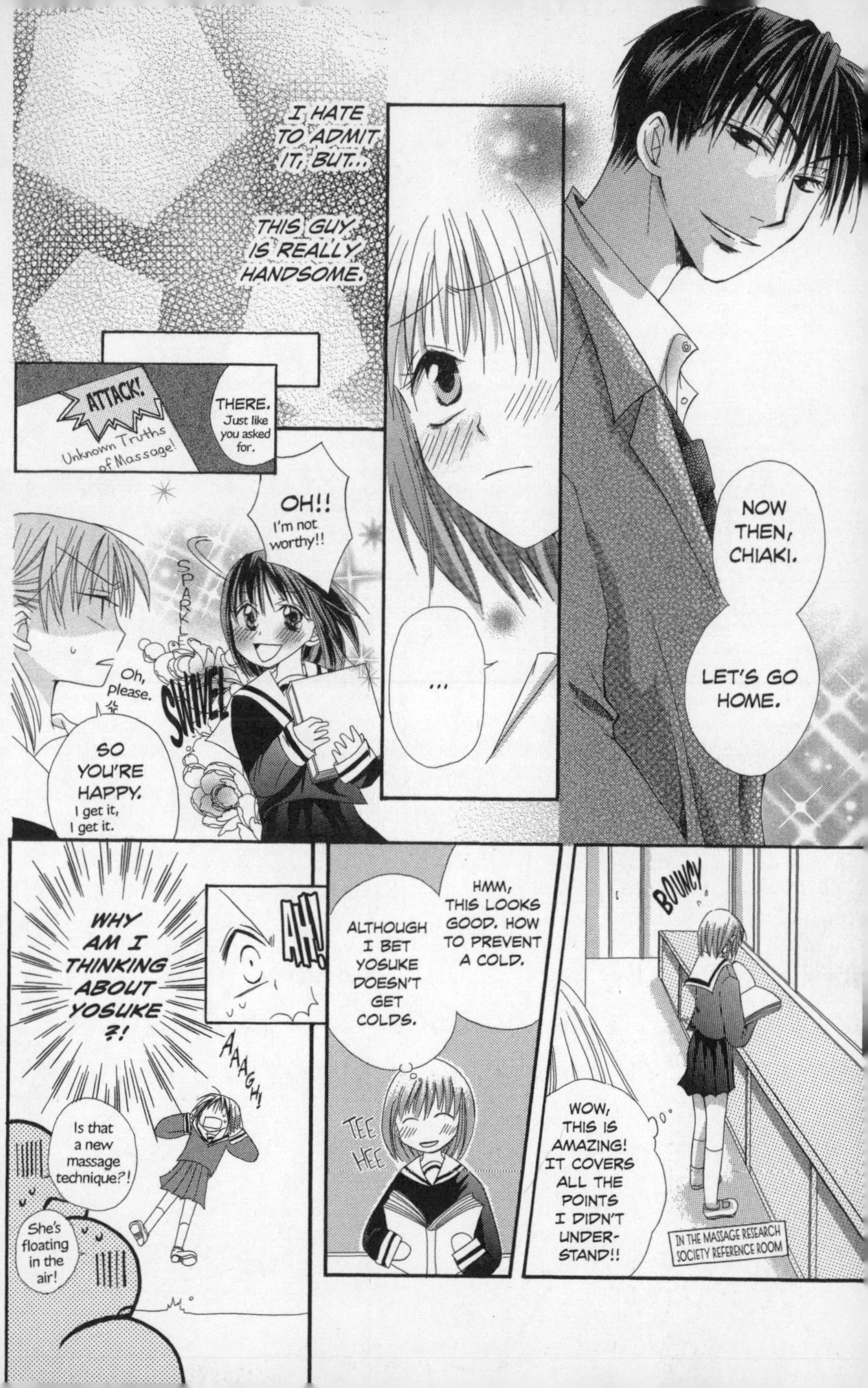
NOW THEN, CHIAKI.
LET'S GO HOME.
...
I HATE TO ADMIT IT, BUT...
THIS GUY IS REALLY HANDSOME.
ATTACK!
Unknown Truths of Massage!
THERE. Just like you asked for.
OH!! I'm not worthy!!
SPARKLE
SWIVEL
Oh, please.
SO YOU'RE HAPPY. I get it, I get it.
BOUNCY
IN THE MASSAGE RESEARCH SOCIETY REFERENCE ROOM
WOW, THIS IS AMAZING! IT COVERS ALL THE POINTS I DIDN'T UNDER-STAND!!
HMM, THIS LOOKS GOOD. HOW TO PREVENT A COLD.
ALTHOUGH I BET YOSUKE DOESN'T GET COLDS.
TEE HEE
AH!
WHY AM I THINKING ABOUT YOSUKE?!
AAAGH!
Is that a new massage technique?!
She's floating in the air!

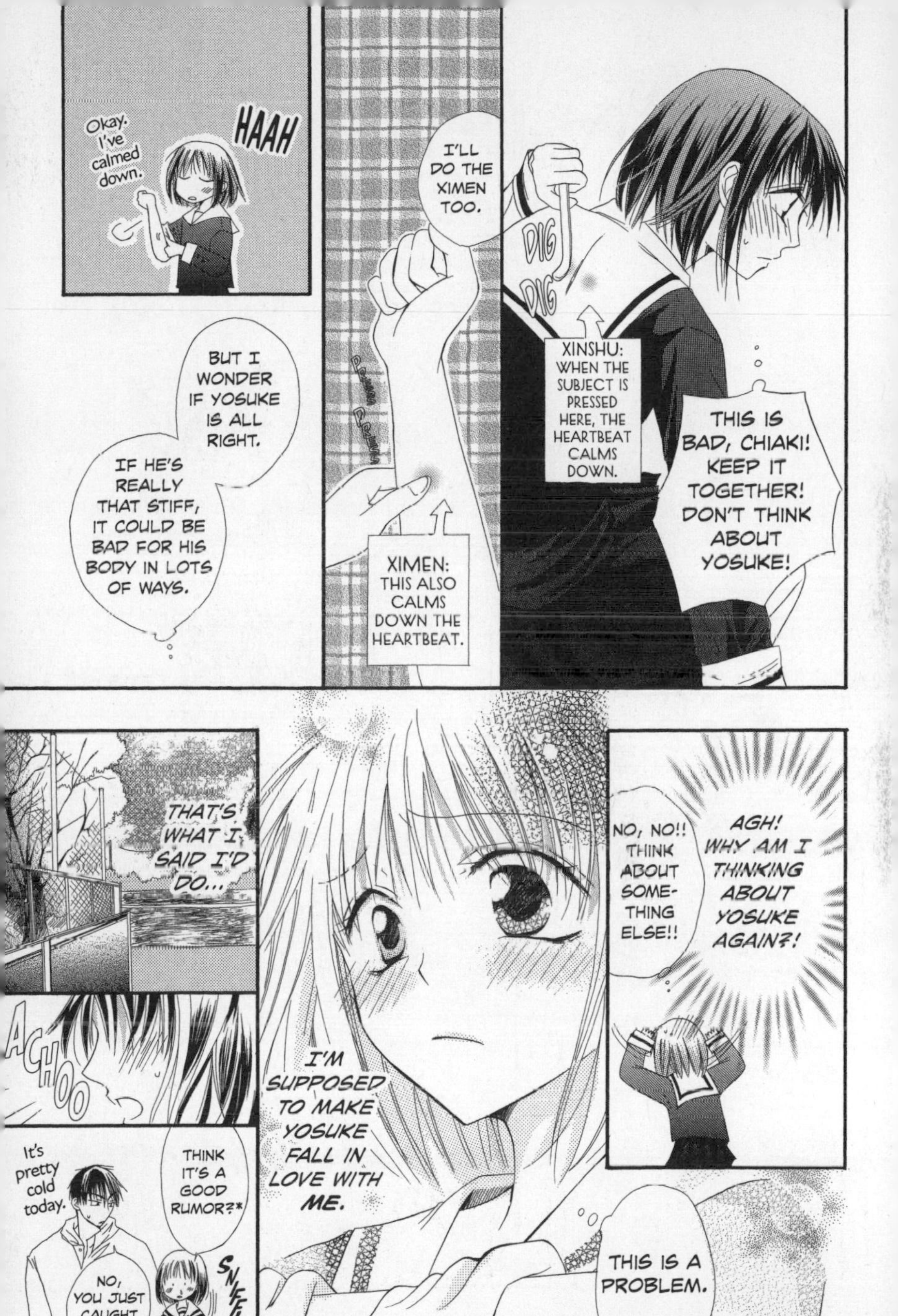
DIG
DIG
XINSHU: WHEN THE SUBJECT IS PRESSED HERE, THE HEARTBEAT CALMS DOWN.
THIS IS BAD, CHIAKI! KEEP IT TOGETHER! DON'T THINK ABOUT YOSUKE!
I'LL DO THE XIMEN TOO.
XIMEN: THIS ALSO CALMS DOWN THE HEARTBEAT.
HAAH
Okay. I've calmed down.
BUT I WONDER IF YOSUKE IS ALL RIGHT.
IF HE'S REALLY THAT STIFF, IT COULD BE BAD FOR HIS BODY IN LOTS OF WAYS.
AGH! WHY AM I THINKING ABOUT YOSUKE AGAIN?!
NO, NO!! THINK ABOUT SOME-THING ELSE!!
I'M SUPPOSED TO MAKE YOSUKE FALL IN LOVE WITH ME.
THIS IS A PROBLEM.
THAT'S WHAT I SAID I'D DO...
ACHOO
THINK IT'S A GOOD RUMOR?*
It's pretty cold today.
NO, YOU JUST CAUGHT A COLD.
SNIFFLE

*JAPANESE SUPERSTITION HAS IT THAT PEOPLE SNEEZE WHEN OTHER PEOPLE ARE TALKING ABOUT THEM.

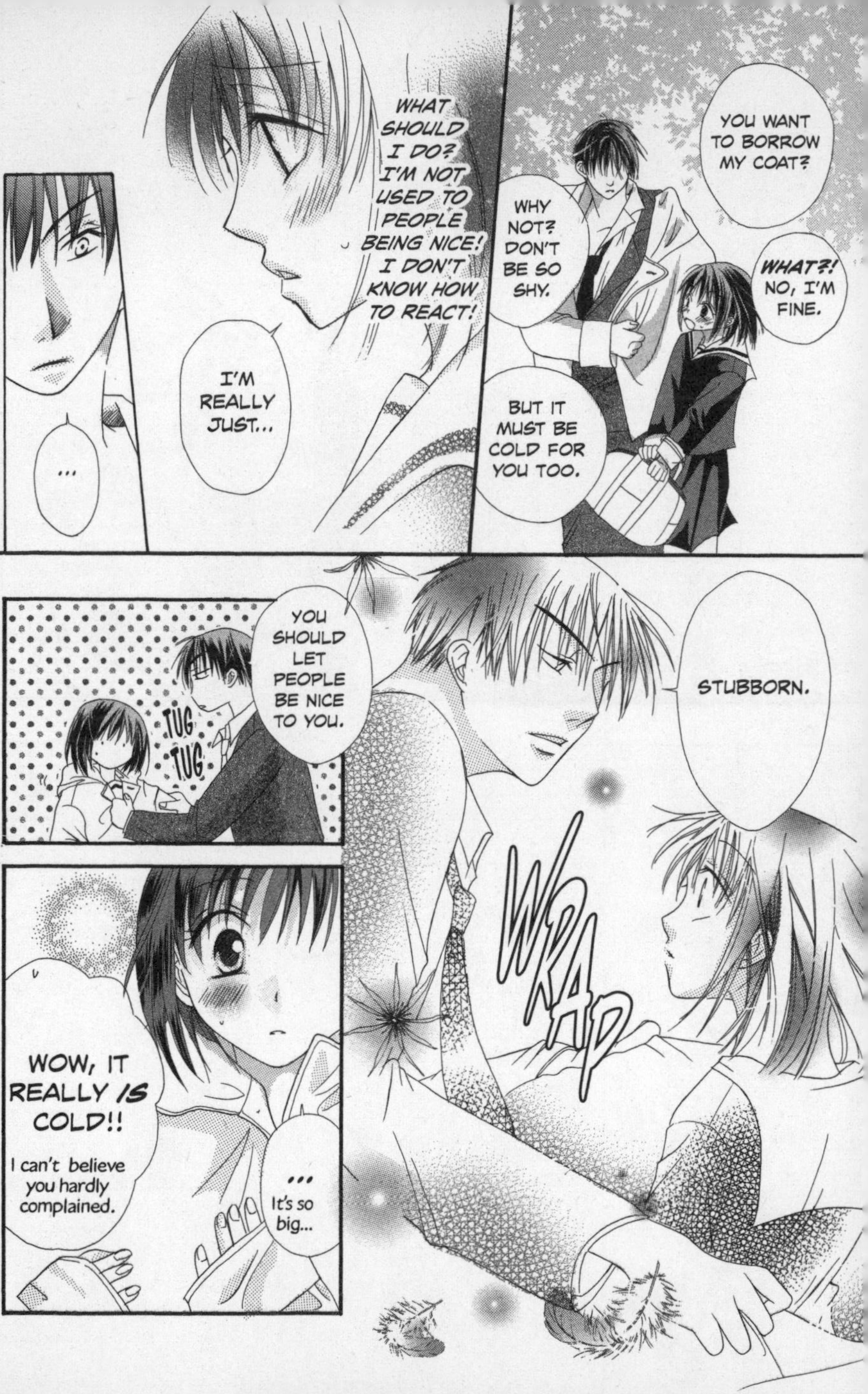
YOU WANT TO BORROW MY COAT?
WHAT?! NO, I'M FINE.
WHY NOT? DON'T BE SO SHY.
BUT IT MUST BE COLD FOR YOU TOO.
WHAT SHOULD I DO? I'M NOT USED TO PEOPLE BEING NICE! I DON'T KNOW HOW TO REACT!
I'M REALLY JUST...
...
STUBBORN.
WRAP
YOU SHOULD LET PEOPLE BE NICE TO YOU.
TUG TUG
... It's so big...
WOW, IT REALLY *IS* COLD!!
I can't believe you hardly complained.

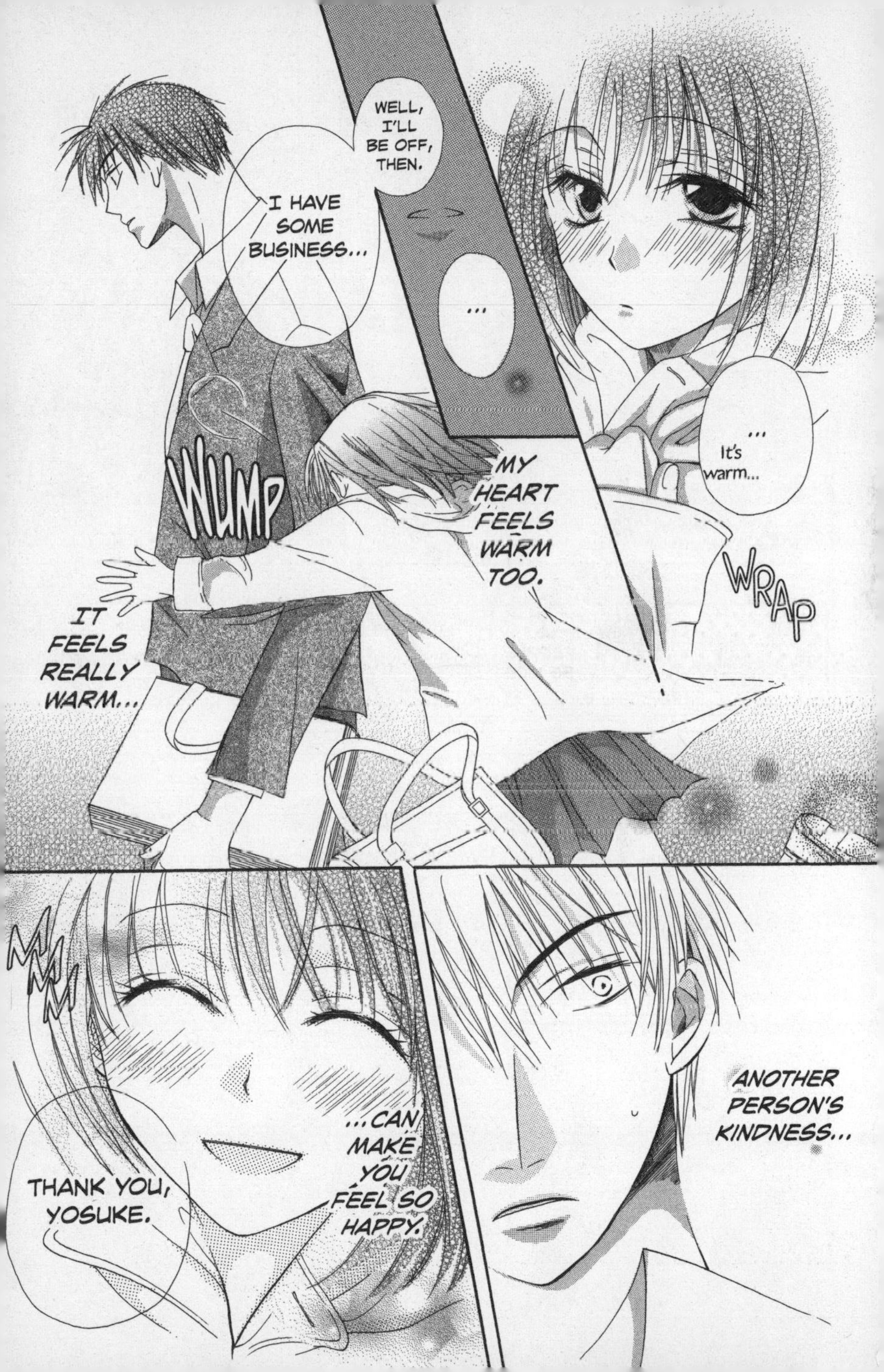
... It's warm...
WELL, I'LL BE OFF, THEN.
...
I HAVE SOME BUSINESS...
WRAP
MY HEART FEELS WARM TOO.
WUMP
IT FEELS REALLY WARM...
ANOTHER PERSON'S KINDNESS...
MMM
...CAN MAKE YOU FEEL SO HAPPY.
THANK YOU, YOSUKE.

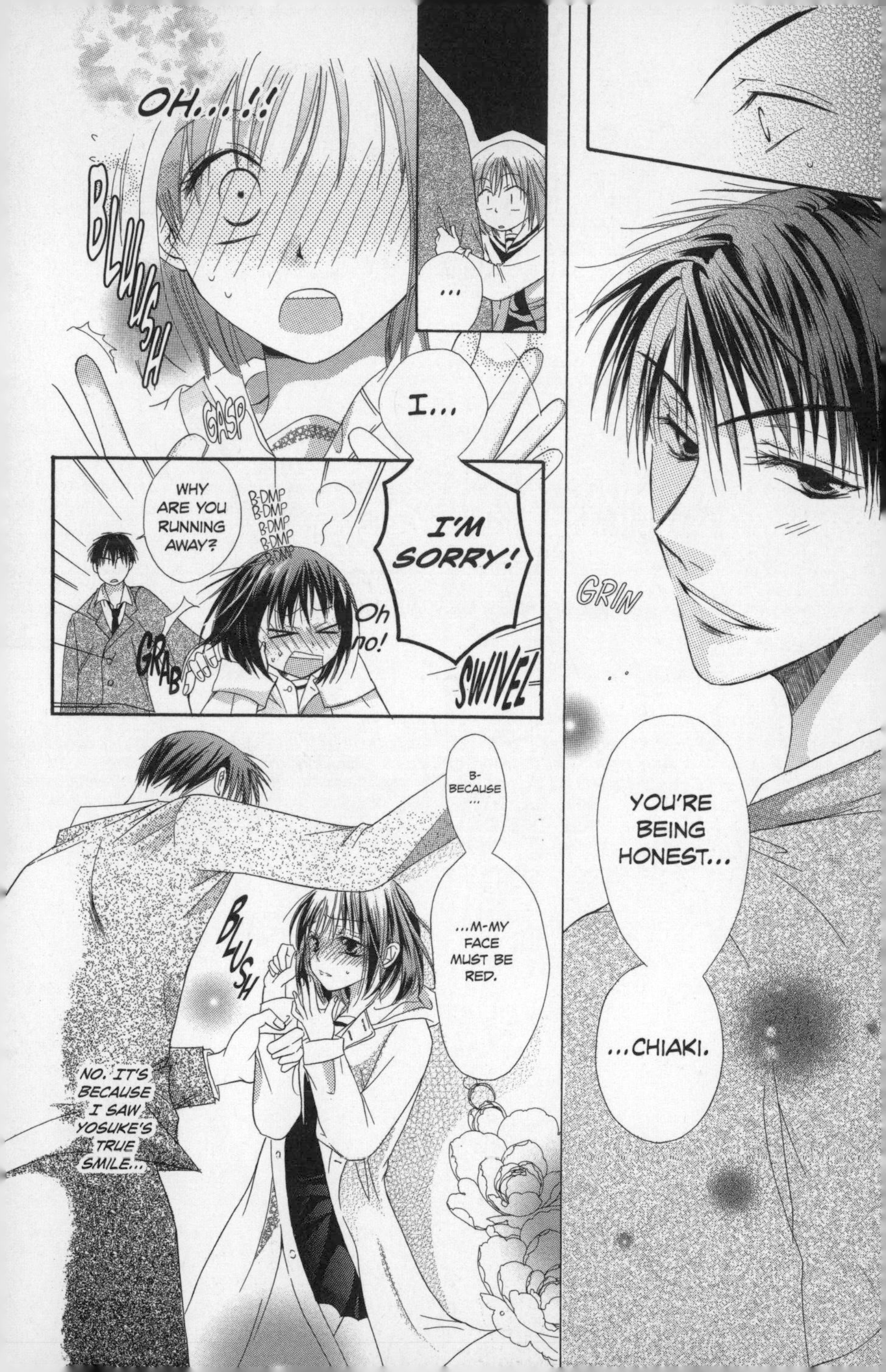
GRIN
YOU'RE BEING HONEST...
...CHIAKI.
...
OH...!!
BLUSH
GASP
I...
I'M SORRY!
SWIVEL
Oh no!
WHY ARE YOU RUNNING AWAY?
B-DMP B-DMP B-DMP B-DMP
GRAB
B-BECAUSE ...
...M-MY FACE MUST BE RED.
BLUSH
NO. IT'S BECAUSE I SAW YOSUKE'S TRUE SMILE...

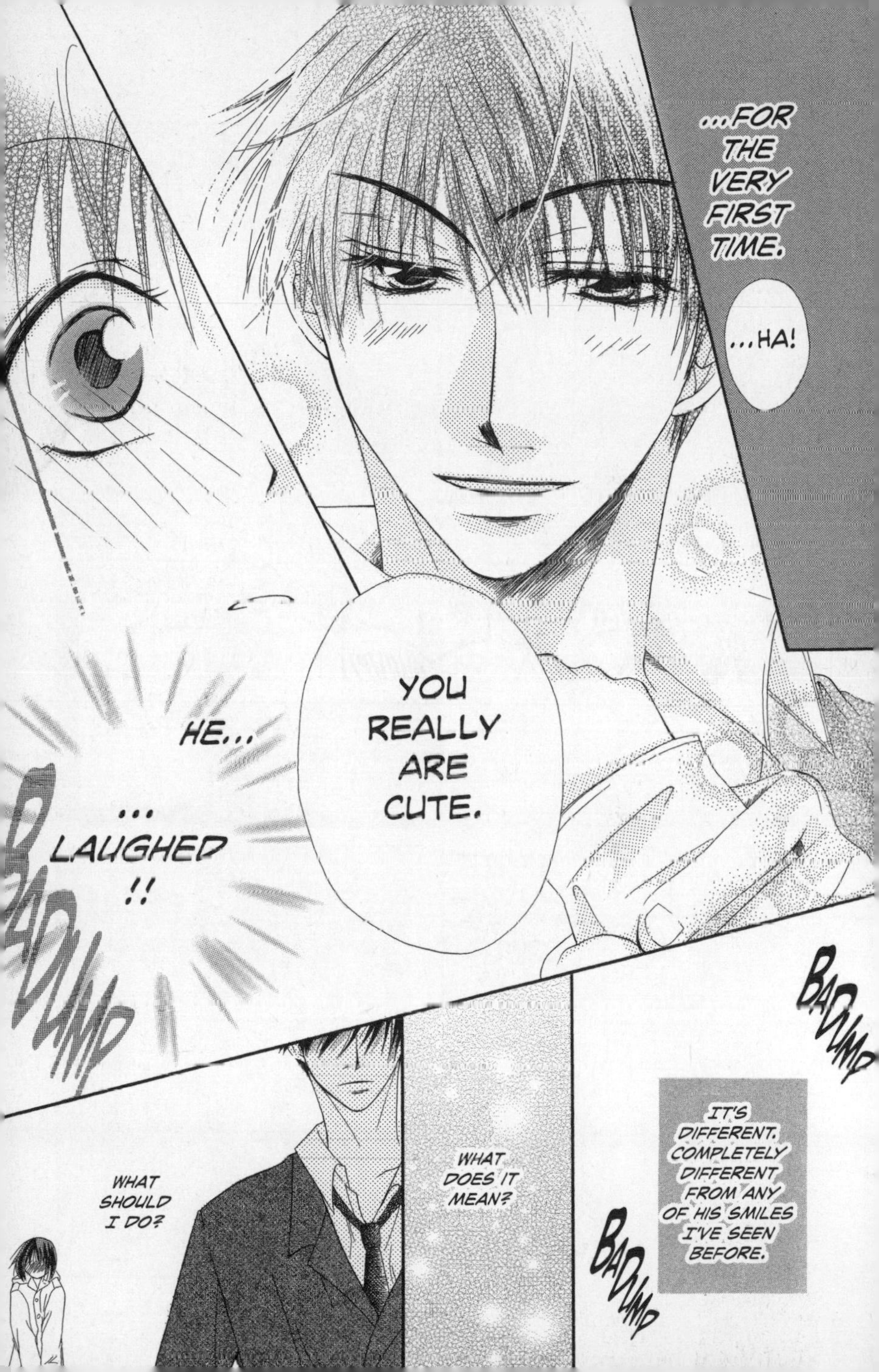
...FOR THE VERY FIRST TIME.
...HA!
YOU REALLY ARE CUTE.
HE...
...LAUGHED!!
BADUMP
BADUMP
IT'S DIFFERENT. COMPLETELY DIFFERENT FROM ANY OF HIS SMILES I'VE SEEN BEFORE.
BADUMP
WHAT DOES IT MEAN?
WHAT SHOULD I DO?

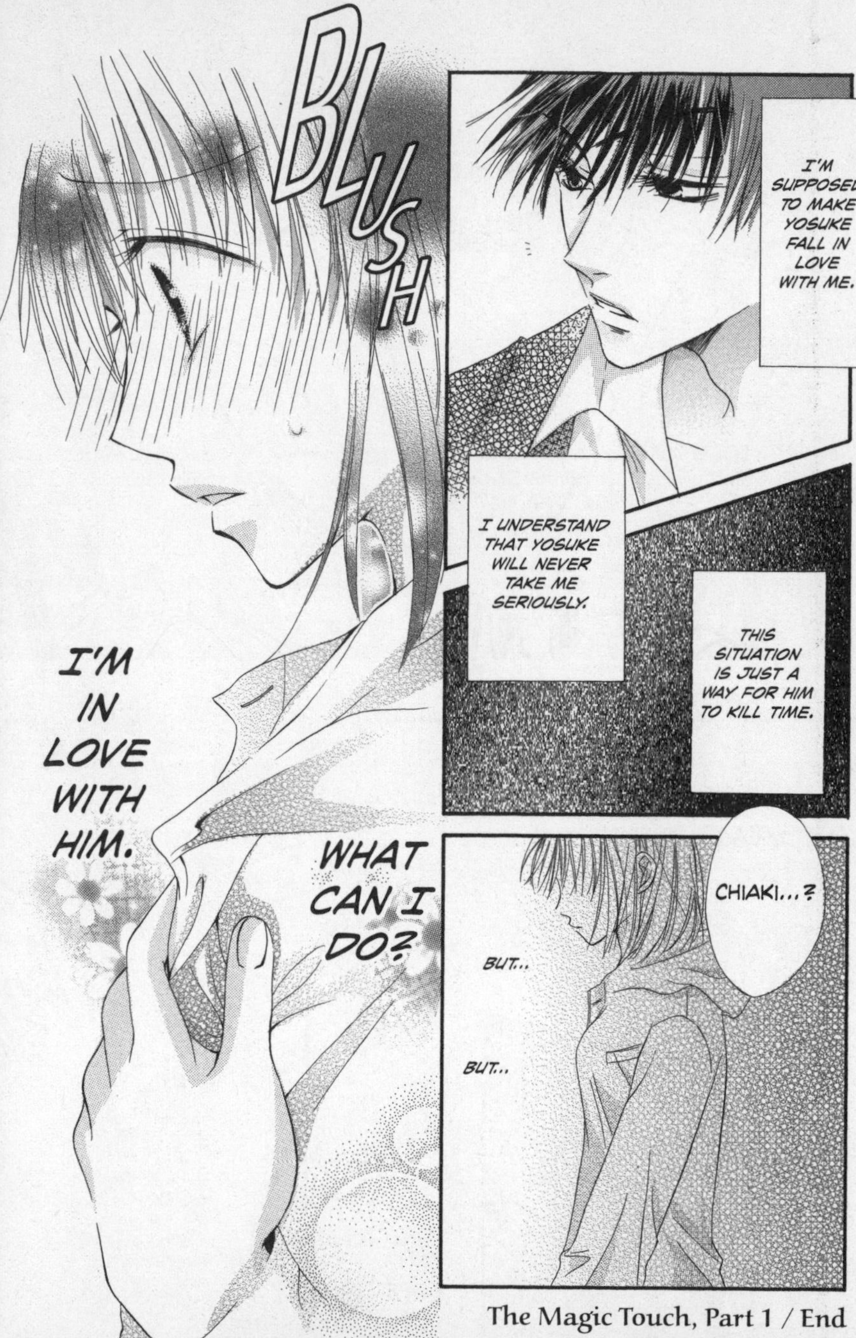
I'M SUPPOSED TO MAKE YOSUKE FALL IN LOVE WITH ME.
I UNDERSTAND THAT YOSUKE WILL NEVER TAKE ME SERIOUSLY.
THIS SITUATION IS JUST A WAY FOR HIM TO KILL TIME.
CHIAKI...?
BUT...
BUT...
BLUSH
I'M IN LOVE WITH HIM.
WHAT CAN I DO?

The Magic Touch, Part 1 / End

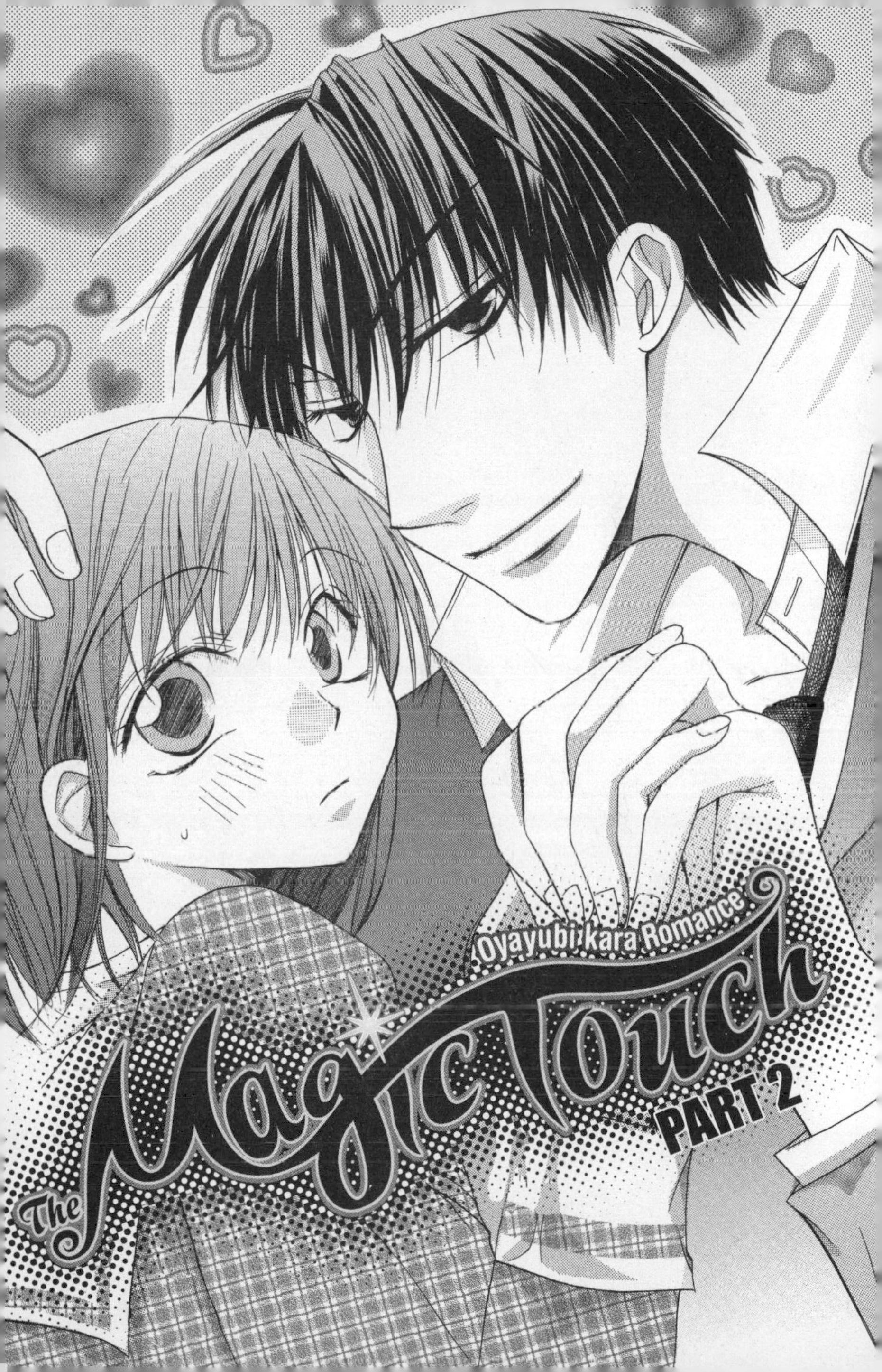
Oyayubi kara Romance
The Magic Touch
PART 2

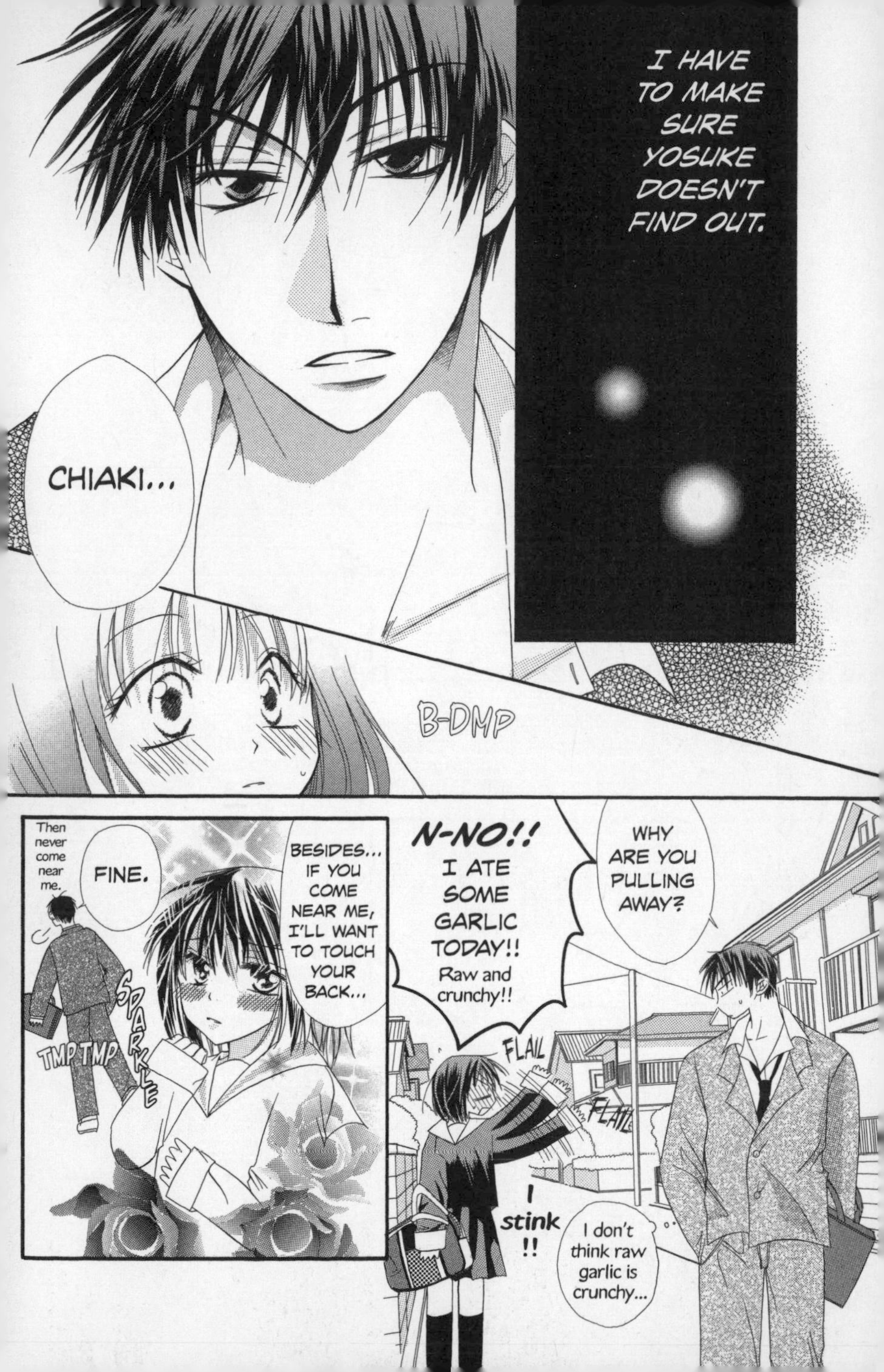
I HAVE TO MAKE SURE YOSUKE DOESN'T FIND OUT.
CHIAKI...
B-DMP
WHY ARE YOU PULLING AWAY?
N-NO!! I ATE SOME GARLIC TODAY!! Raw and crunchy!!
FLAIL
FLAIL
I stink!!
I don't think raw garlic is crunchy...
BESIDES... IF YOU COME NEAR ME, I'LL WANT TO TOUCH YOUR BACK...
SPARKLE
FINE.
Then never come near me.
TMP TMP

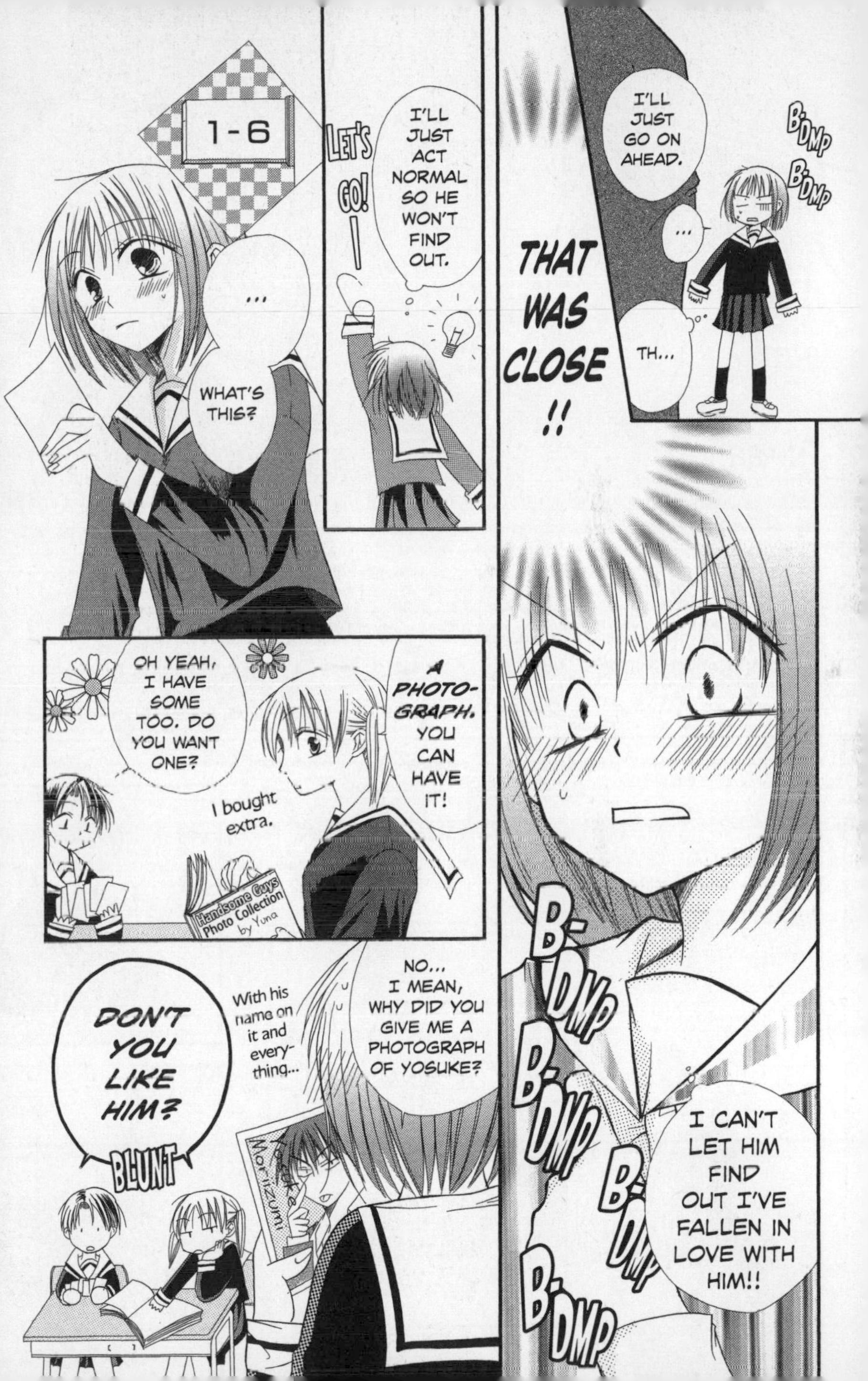
I'LL JUST GO ON AHEAD.
...
TH...
B-DMP B-DMP
THAT WAS CLOSE!!
B-DMP B-DMP B-DMP B-DMP
I CAN'T LET HIM FIND OUT I'VE FALLEN IN LOVE WITH HIM!!
I'LL JUST ACT NORMAL SO HE WON'T FIND OUT.
LET'S GO!
1-6
...
WHAT'S THIS?
A PHOTOGRAPH. YOU CAN HAVE IT!
OH YEAH, I HAVE SOME TOO. DO YOU WANT ONE?
I bought extra.
Handsome Guys Photo Collection by Yuna
NO... I MEAN, WHY DID YOU GIVE ME A PHOTOGRAPH OF YOSUKE?
With his name on it and every-thing...
DON'T YOU LIKE HIM?
BLUNT
Yosuke Morizumi

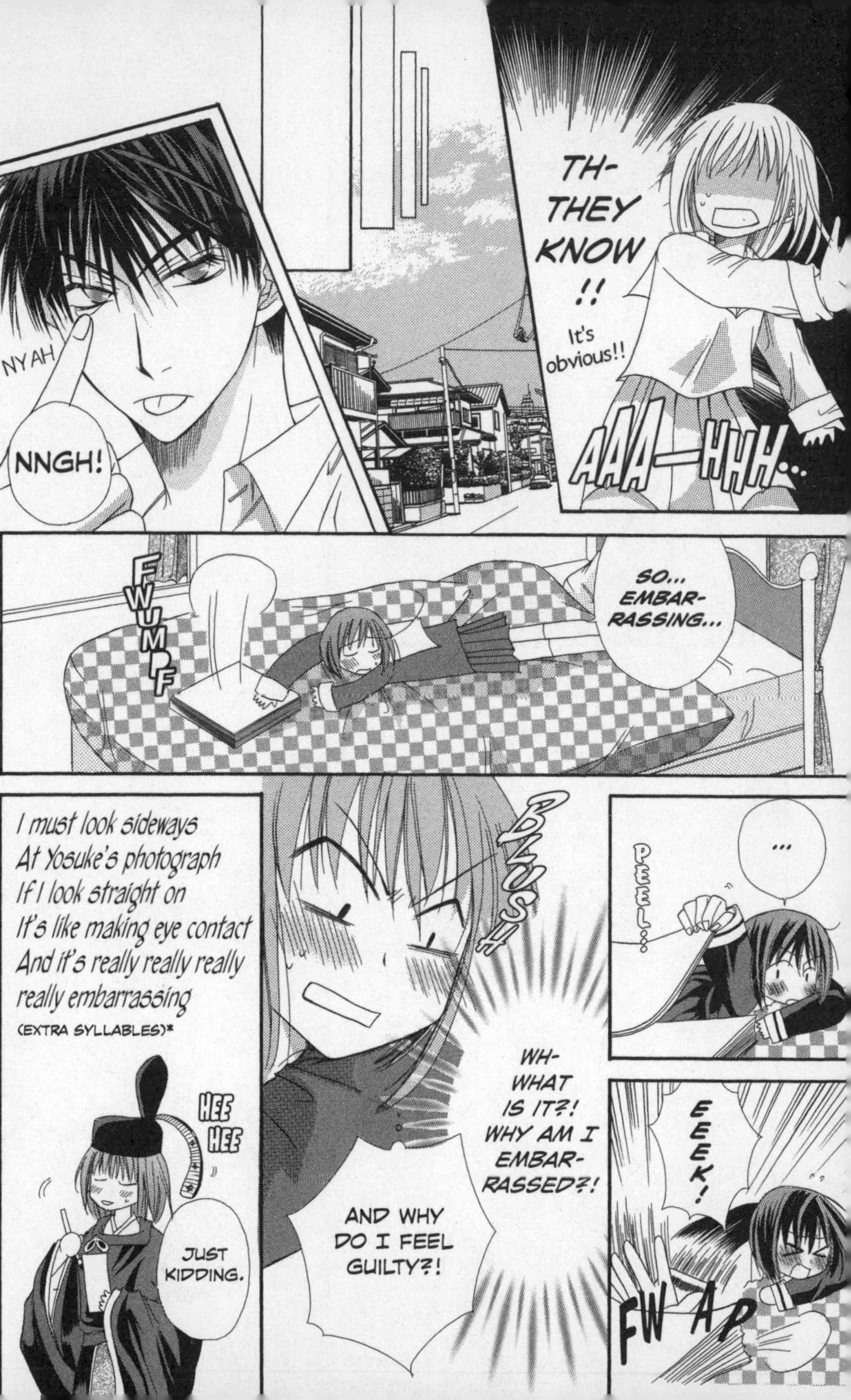
TH-THEY KNOW!!
It's obvious!!
AAA—HHH...
NYAH
NNGH!
SO... EMBARRASSING...
FWUMPF
...
PEEL...
EEEK!
FWAP
BLUSH
WH-WHAT IS IT?! WHY AM I EMBARRASSED?!
AND WHY DO I FEEL GUILTY?!
I must look sideways
At Yosuke's photograph
If I look straight on
It's like making eye contact
And it's really really really
really embarrassing
(EXTRA SYLLABLES)*
HEE HEE
JUST KIDDING.

*THIS IS TANKA, A TYPE OF JAPANESE POETRY THAT TRADITIONALLY USES A 5-7-5-7-7 SYLLABLE PATTERN.

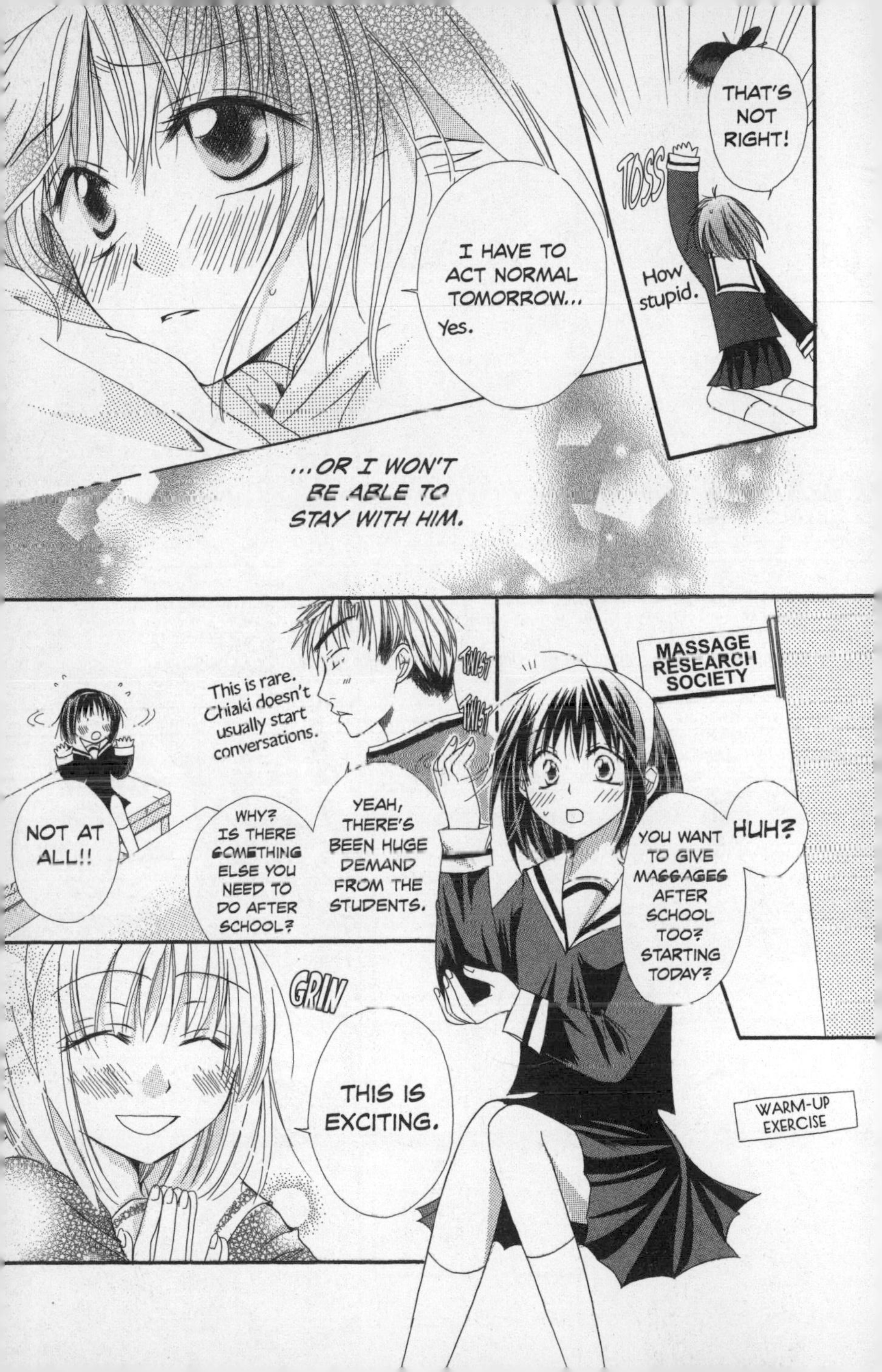
THAT'S NOT RIGHT!
TOSS
How stupid.
I HAVE TO ACT NORMAL TOMORROW...
Yes.
...OR I WON'T BE ABLE TO STAY WITH HIM.
MASSAGE RESEARCH SOCIETY
HUH?
YOU WANT TO GIVE MASSAGES AFTER SCHOOL TOO? STARTING TODAY?
TWIST
TWIST
YEAH, THERE'S BEEN HUGE DEMAND FROM THE STUDENTS.
WHY? IS THERE SOMETHING ELSE YOU NEED TO DO AFTER SCHOOL?
This is rare. Chiaki doesn't usually start conversations.
NOT AT ALL!!
WARM-UP EXERCISE
GRIN
THIS IS EXCITING.

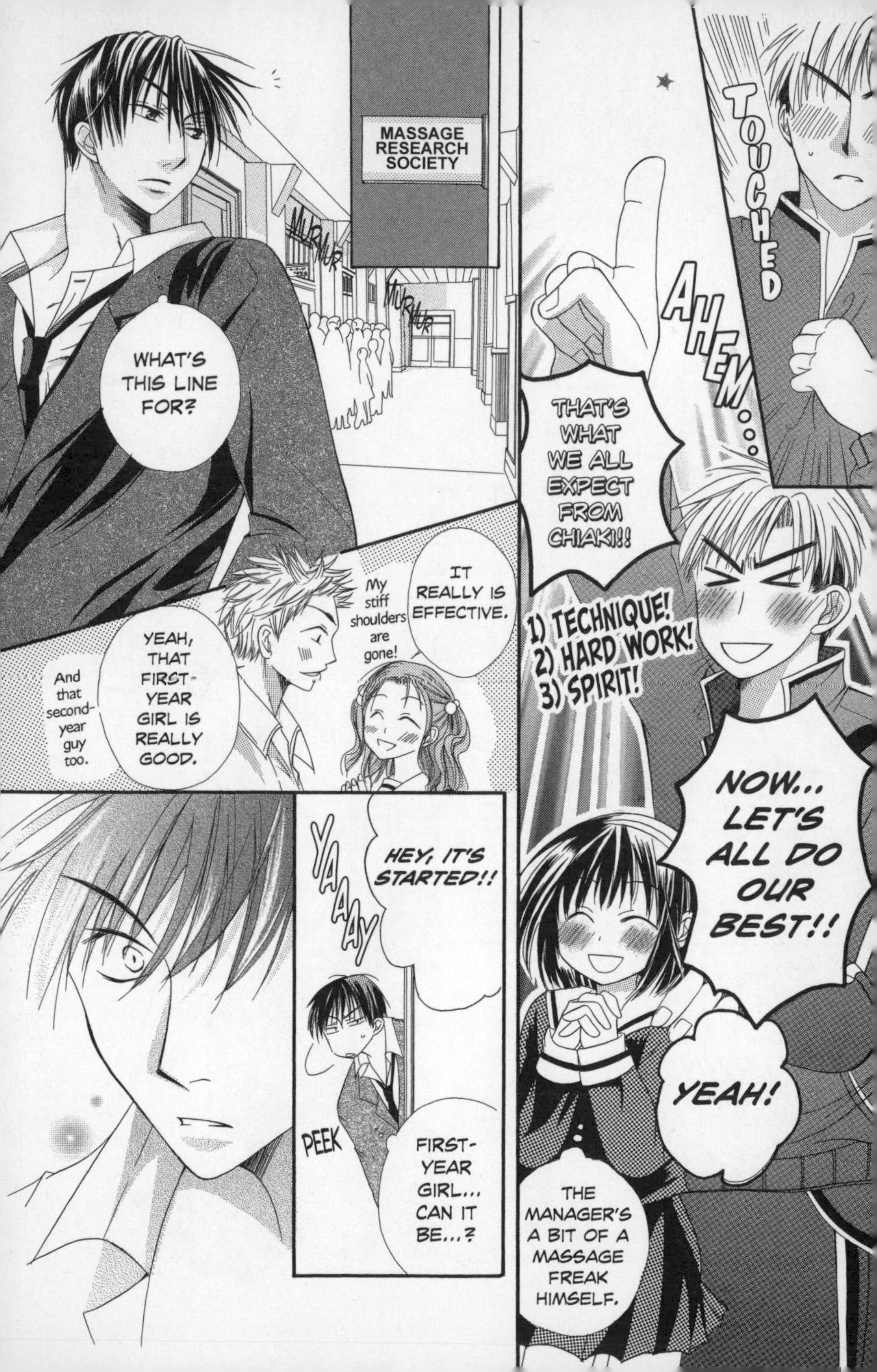
TOUCHED
AHEM...
THAT'S WHAT WE ALL EXPECT FROM CHIAKI!!
1) TECHNIQUE! 2) HARD WORK! 3) SPIRIT!
NOW... LET'S ALL DO OUR BEST!!
YEAH!
THE MANAGER'S A BIT OF A MASSAGE FREAK HIMSELF.
MASSAGE RESEARCH SOCIETY
MURMUR
MURMUR
WHAT'S THIS LINE FOR?
IT REALLY IS EFFECTIVE.
My stiff shoulders are gone!
YEAH, THAT FIRST-YEAR GIRL IS REALLY GOOD.
And that second-year guy too.
YAAAAY
HEY, IT'S STARTED!!
PEEK
FIRST-YEAR GIRL... CAN IT BE...?

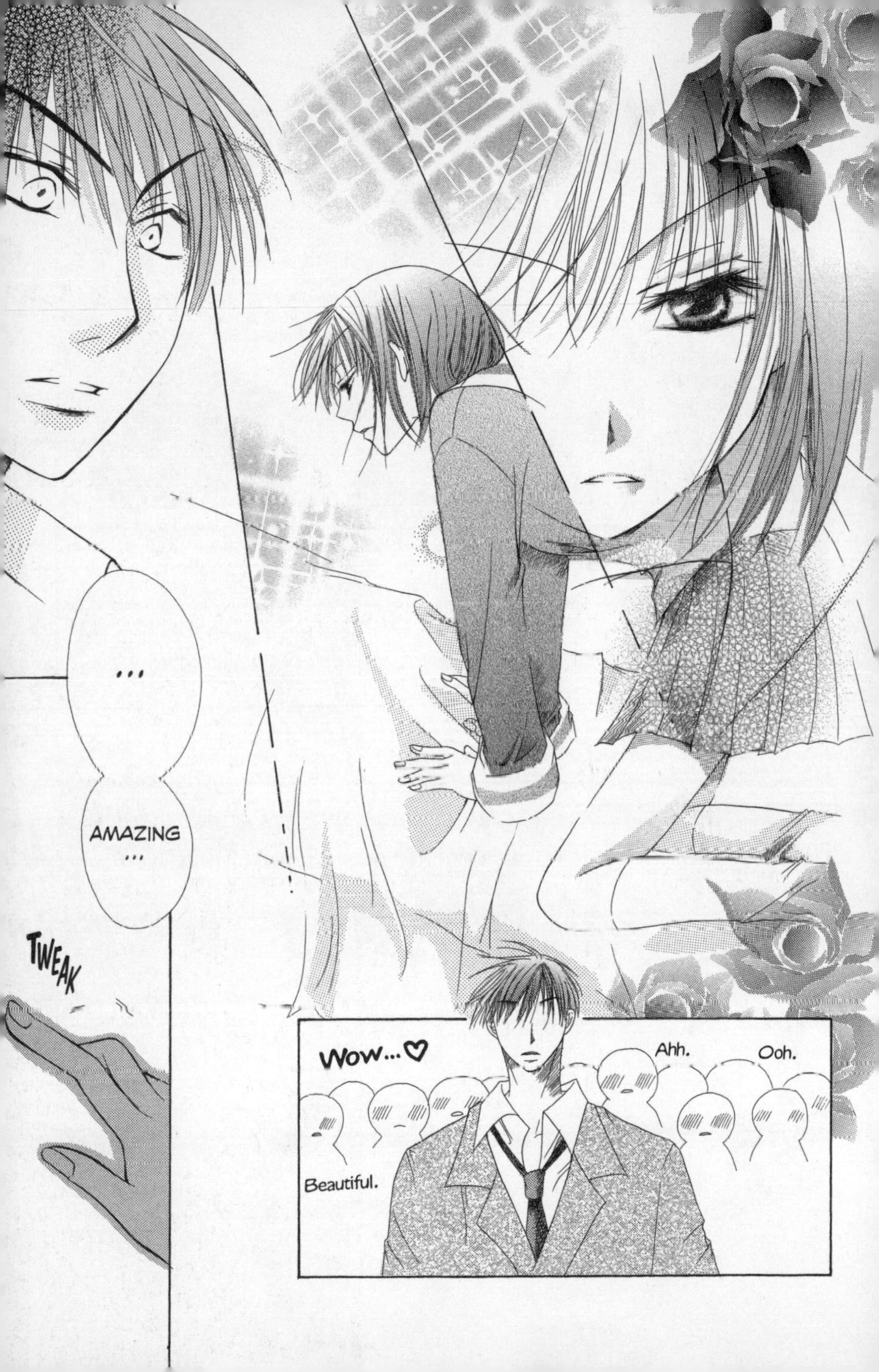
Ooh.
Ahh.
Wow...♡
Beautiful.
...
AMAZING...
TWEAK

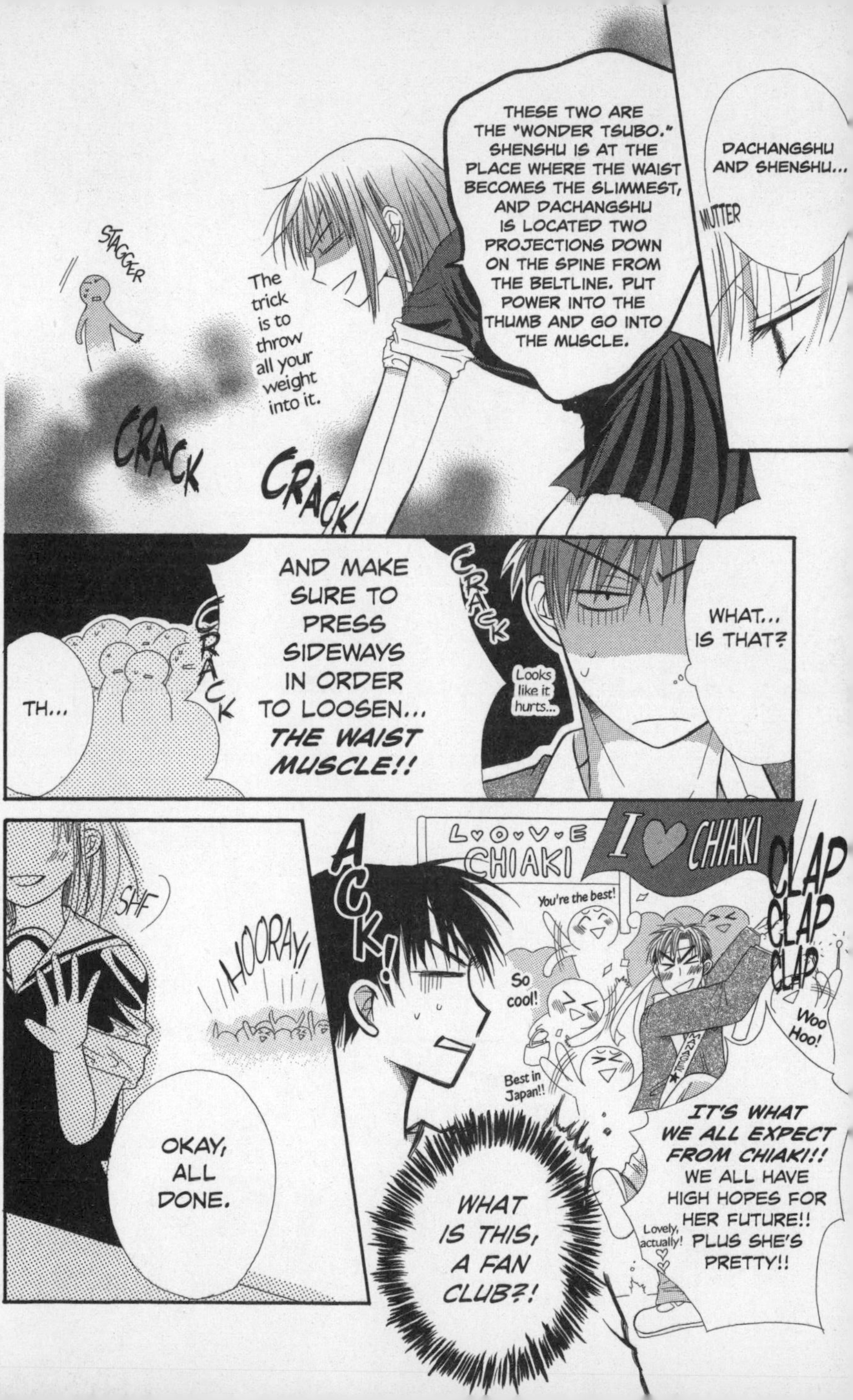
DACHANGSHU AND SHENSHU...
MUTTER
THESE TWO ARE THE "WONDER TSUBO." SHENSHU IS AT THE PLACE WHERE THE WAIST BECOMES THE SLIMMEST, AND DACHANGSHU IS LOCATED TWO PROJECTIONS DOWN ON THE SPINE FROM THE BELTLINE. PUT POWER INTO THE THUMB AND GO INTO THE MUSCLE.
The trick is to throw all your weight into it.
STAGGER
CRACK
CRACK
WHAT... IS THAT?
Looks like it hurts...
CRACK
AND MAKE SURE TO PRESS SIDEWAYS IN ORDER TO LOOSEN... *THE WAIST MUSCLE!!*
CRACK
TH...
CLAP CLAP CLAP
I ♥ CHIAKI
L-O-V-E CHIAKI
You're the best!
So cool!
Woo Hoo!
Best in Japan!!
IT'S WHAT WE ALL EXPECT FROM CHIAKI!! WE ALL HAVE HIGH HOPES FOR HER FUTURE!! PLUS SHE'S PRETTY!!
Lovely, actually!
WHAT IS THIS, A FAN CLUB?!
ACK!
HOORAY!
SHF
OKAY, ALL DONE.

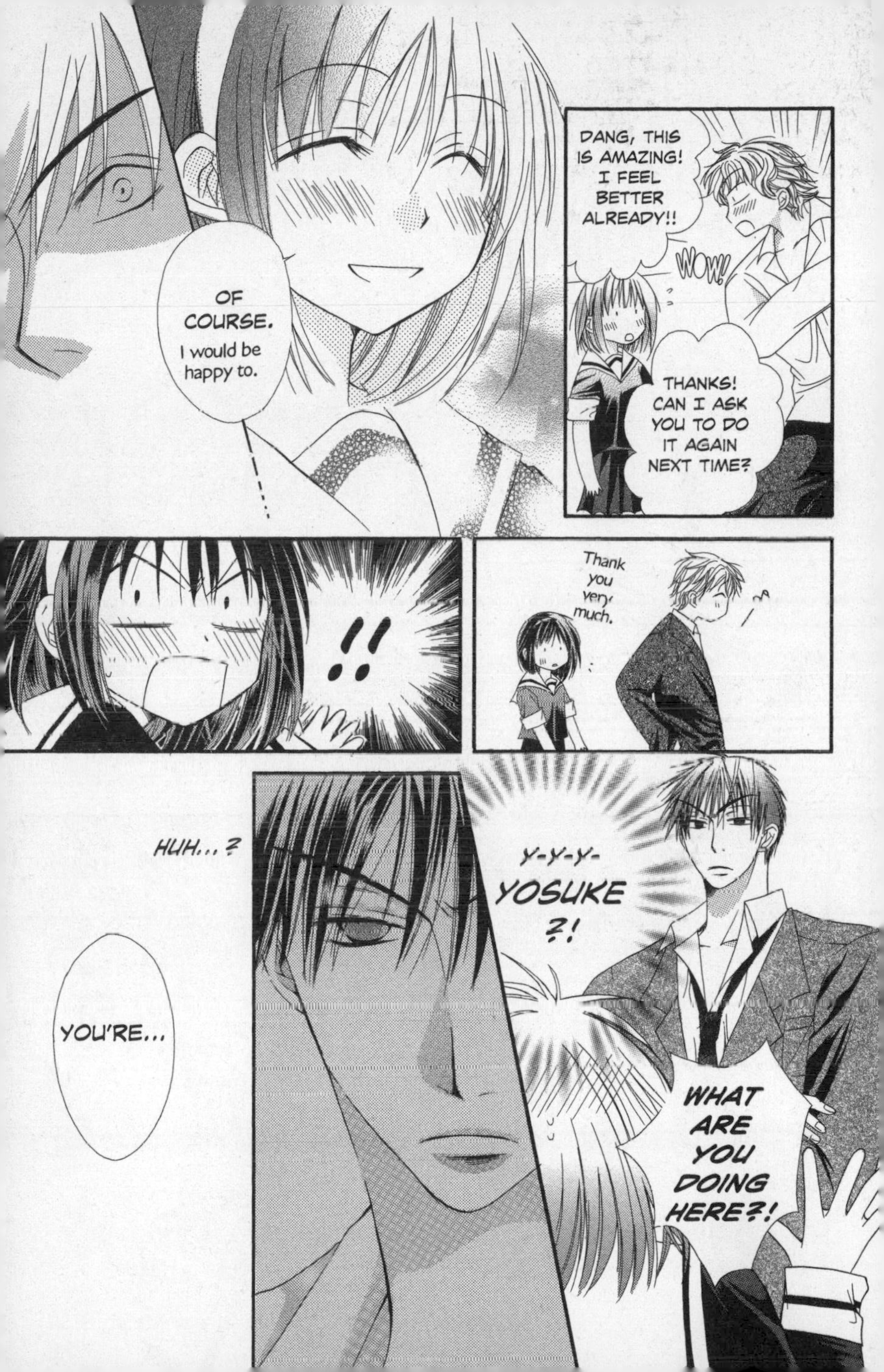
DANG, THIS IS AMAZING! I FEEL BETTER ALREADY!!
WOW!
THANKS! CAN I ASK YOU TO DO IT AGAIN NEXT TIME?
OF COURSE. I would be happy to.
Thank you very much.
!!
Y-Y-Y- YOSUKE?!
WHAT ARE YOU DOING HERE?!
HUH...?
YOU'RE...

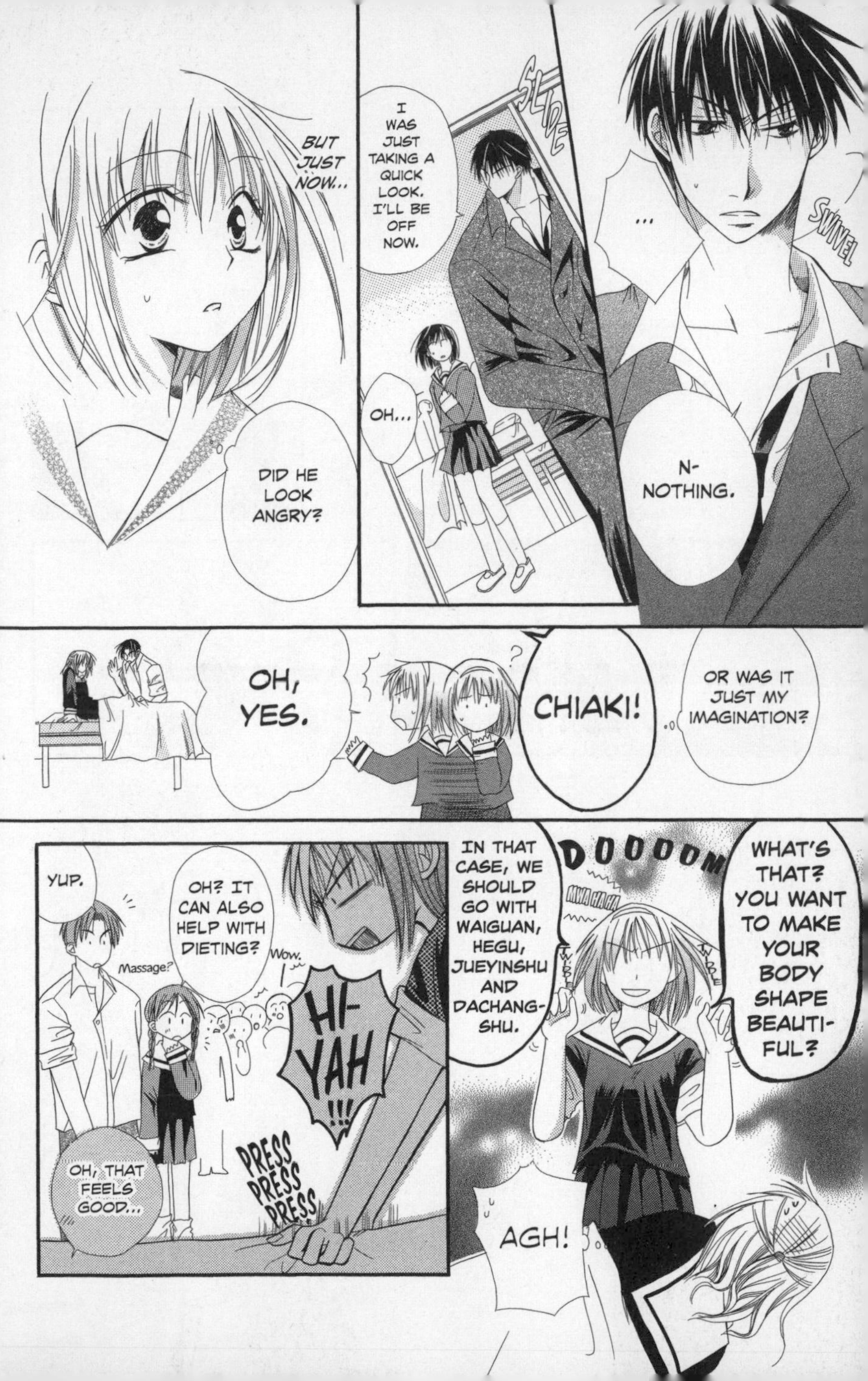
...
SWIVEL
N-NOTHING.
SLIDE
I WAS JUST TAKING A QUICK LOOK. I'LL BE OFF NOW.
OH...
BUT JUST NOW...
DID HE LOOK ANGRY?
OR WAS IT JUST MY IMAGINATION?
CHIAKI!
OH, YES.
WHAT'S THAT? YOU WANT TO MAKE YOUR BODY SHAPE BEAUTIFUL?
DOOOOM
MWA HA HA
IN THAT CASE, WE SHOULD GO WITH WAIGUAN, HEGU, JUEYINSHU AND DACHANGSHU.
AGH!
HI-YAH!!!
PRESS PRESS PRESS
OH? IT CAN ALSO HELP WITH DIETING?
Wow.
YUP.
Massage?
OH, THAT FEELS GOOD...

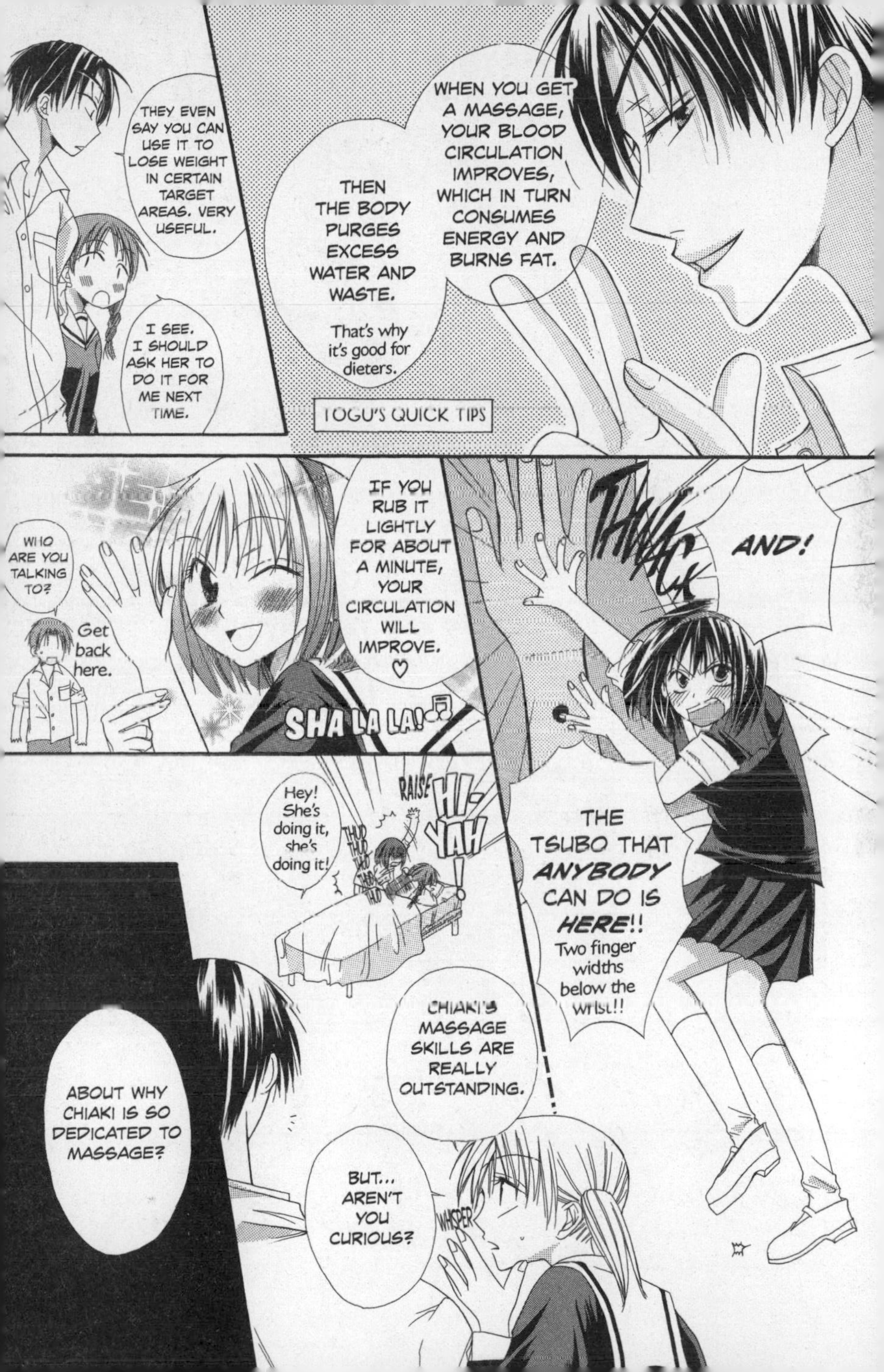
WHEN YOU GET A MASSAGE, YOUR BLOOD CIRCULATION IMPROVES, WHICH IN TURN CONSUMES ENERGY AND BURNS FAT.
THEN THE BODY PURGES EXCESS WATER AND WASTE.
That's why it's good for dieters.
TOGU'S QUICK TIPS
THEY EVEN SAY YOU CAN USE IT TO LOSE WEIGHT IN CERTAIN TARGET AREAS. VERY USEFUL.
I SEE. I SHOULD ASK HER TO DO IT FOR ME NEXT TIME.
AND!
THWACK
THE TSUBO THAT *ANYBODY* CAN DO IS *HERE*!! Two finger widths below the wrist!!
IF YOU RUB IT LIGHTLY FOR ABOUT A MINUTE, YOUR CIRCULATION WILL IMPROVE. ♡
SHA LA LA!
WHO ARE YOU TALKING TO?
Get back here.
RAISE
HI-YAH!
Hey! She's doing it, she's doing it!
THUD THUD THUD THUD THUD
CHIAKI'S MASSAGE SKILLS ARE REALLY OUTSTANDING.
BUT... AREN'T YOU CURIOUS?
WHISPER
ABOUT WHY CHIAKI IS SO DEDICATED TO MASSAGE?

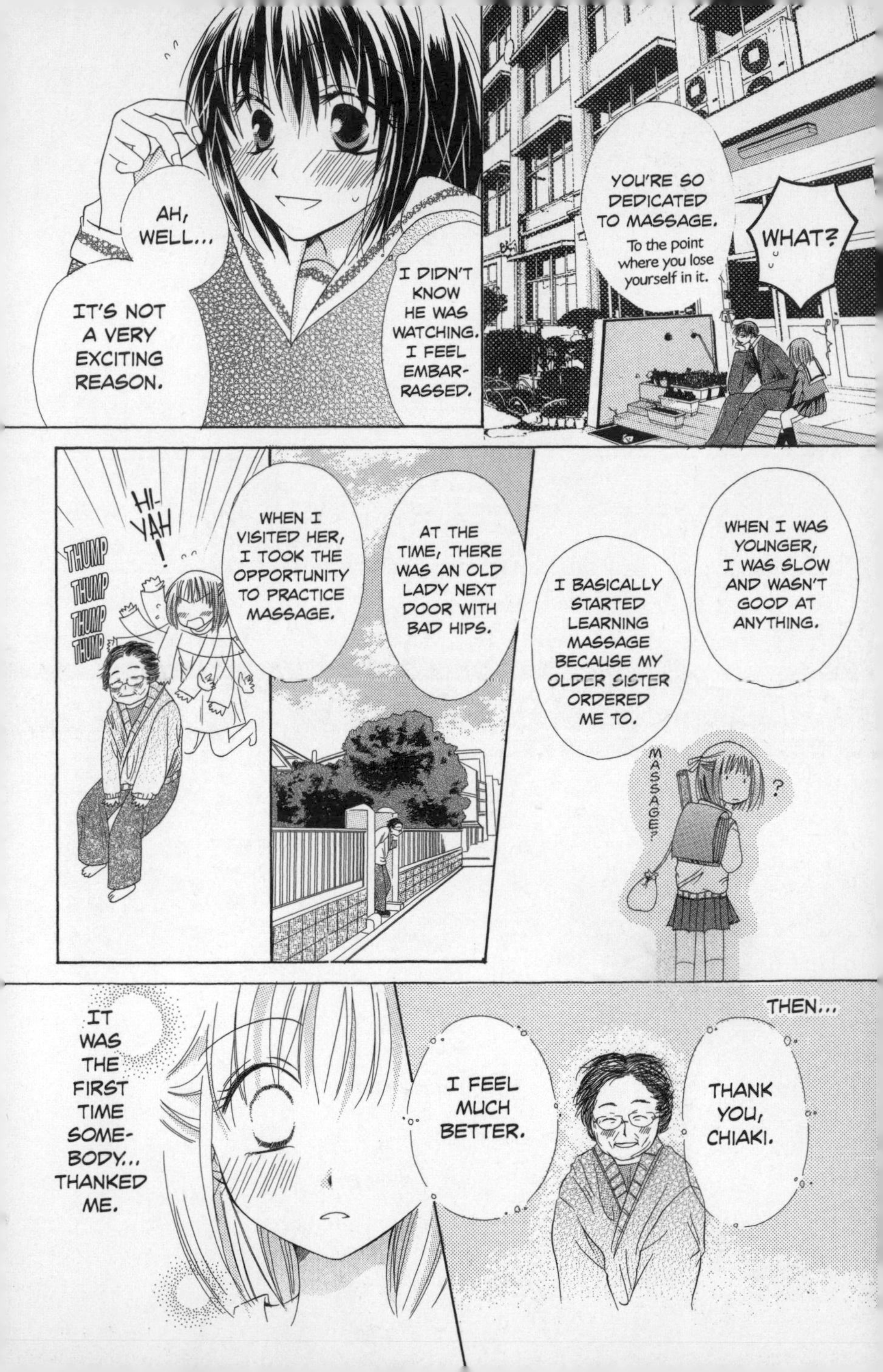
YOU'RE SO DEDICATED TO MASSAGE.
To the point where you lose yourself in it.
WHAT?
AH, WELL...
I DIDN'T KNOW HE WAS WATCHING. I FEEL EMBARRASSED.
IT'S NOT A VERY EXCITING REASON.
WHEN I WAS YOUNGER, I WAS SLOW AND WASN'T GOOD AT ANYTHING.
I BASICALLY STARTED LEARNING MASSAGE BECAUSE MY OLDER SISTER ORDERED ME TO.
MASSAGE?
?
AT THE TIME, THERE WAS AN OLD LADY NEXT DOOR WITH BAD HIPS.
WHEN I VISITED HER, I TOOK THE OPPORTUNITY TO PRACTICE MASSAGE.
HI-YAH!
THUMP THUMP THUMP THUMP
THEN...
THANK YOU, CHIAKI.
I FEEL MUCH BETTER.
IT WAS THE FIRST TIME SOMEBODY... THANKED ME.

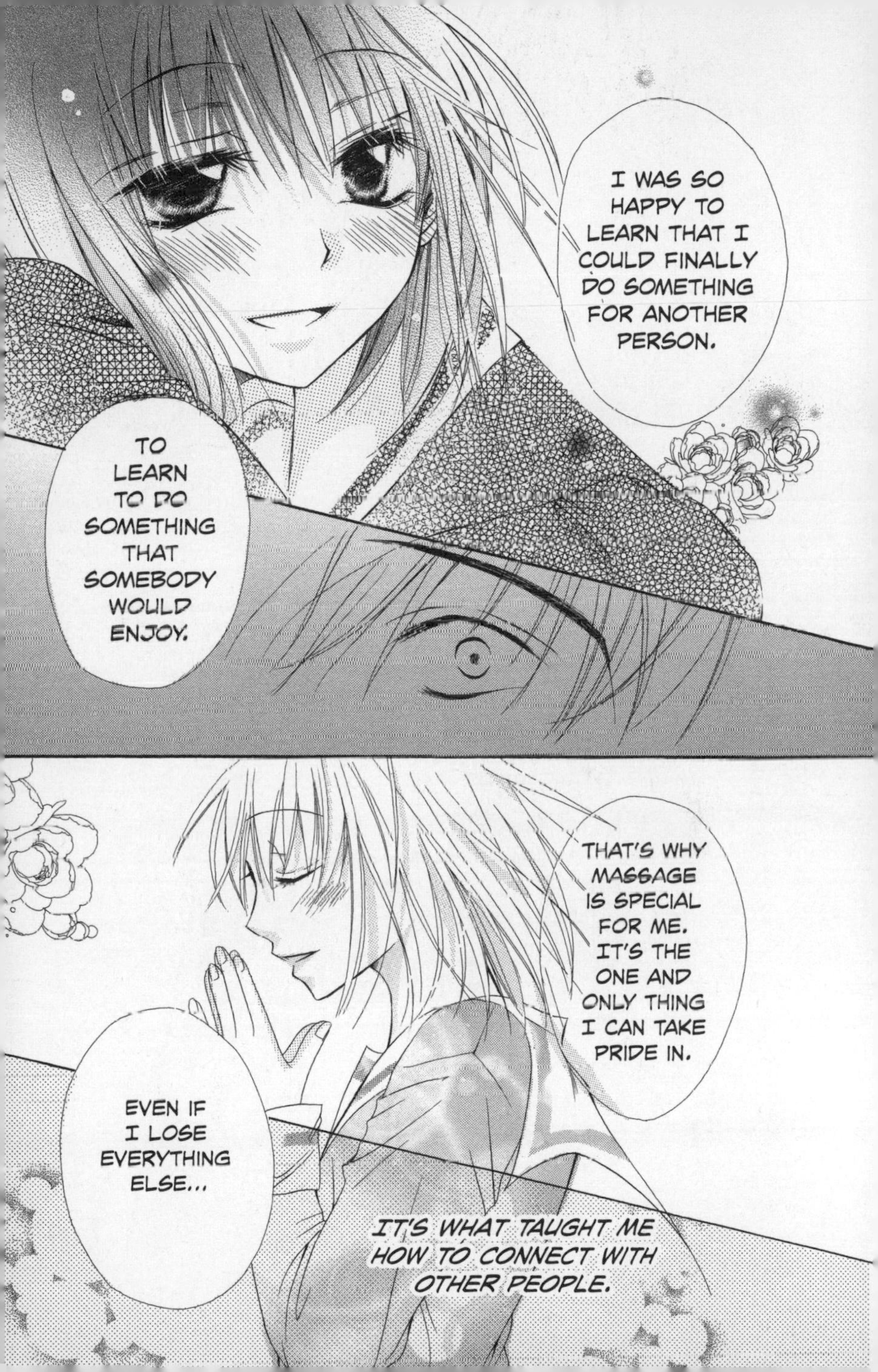
I WAS SO HAPPY TO LEARN THAT I COULD FINALLY DO SOMETHING FOR ANOTHER PERSON.
TO LEARN TO DO SOMETHING THAT SOMEBODY WOULD ENJOY.
THAT'S WHY MASSAGE IS SPECIAL FOR ME. IT'S THE ONE AND ONLY THING I CAN TAKE PRIDE IN.
EVEN IF I LOSE EVERYTHING ELSE...
IT'S WHAT TAUGHT ME HOW TO CONNECT WITH OTHER PEOPLE.

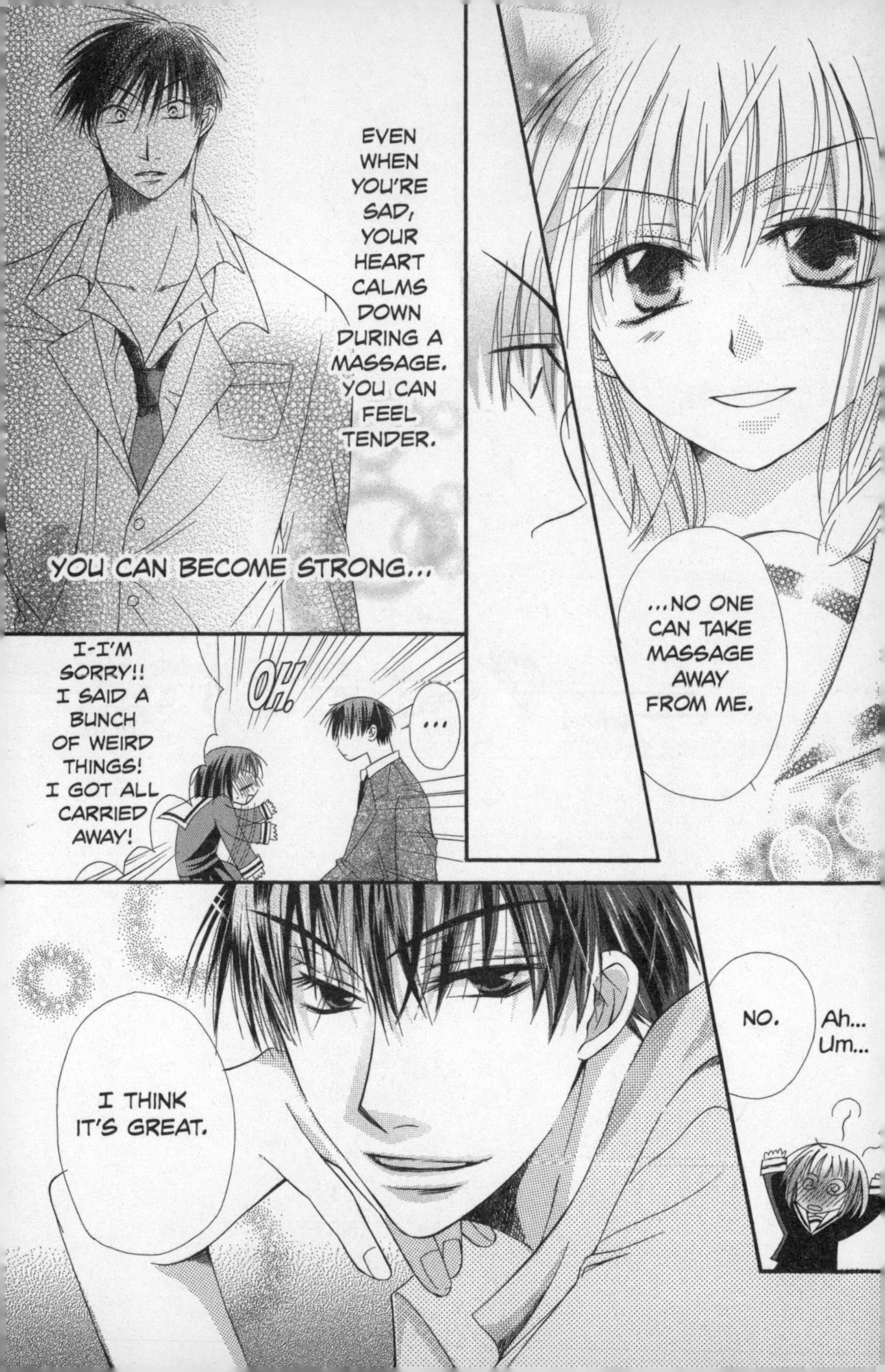
...NO ONE CAN TAKE MASSAGE AWAY FROM ME.
EVEN WHEN YOU'RE SAD, YOUR HEART CALMS DOWN DURING A MASSAGE. YOU CAN FEEL TENDER.
YOU CAN BECOME STRONG...
...
OH!
I-I'M SORRY!! I SAID A BUNCH OF WEIRD THINGS! I GOT ALL CARRIED AWAY!
Ah... Um...
NO.
I THINK IT'S GREAT.

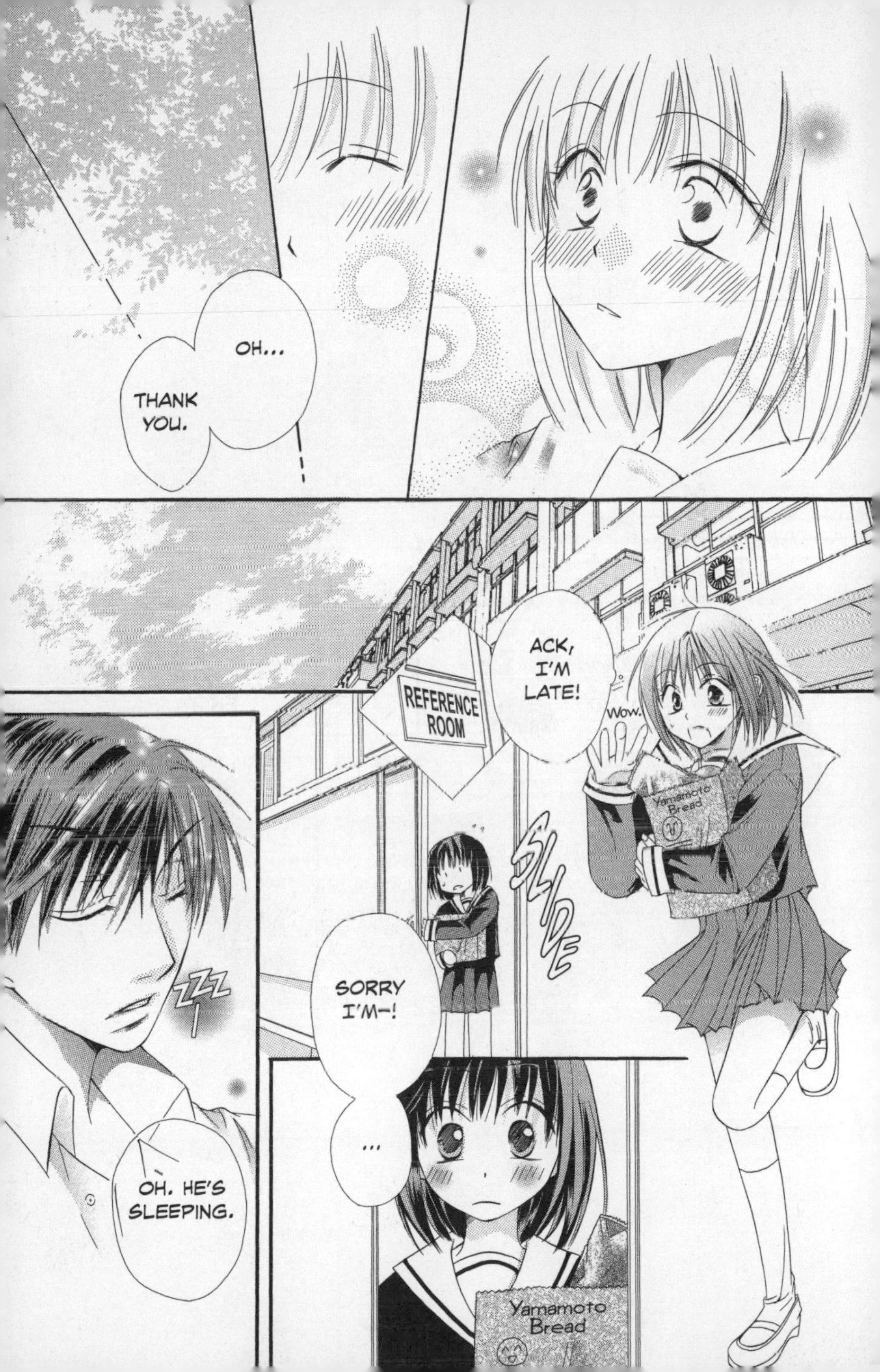
OH...
THANK YOU.
ACK, I'M LATE!
REFERENCE ROOM
Wow.
SLIDE
Yamamoto Bread
SORRY I'M—!
...
Yamamoto Bread
ZZZ
OH. HE'S SLEEPING.

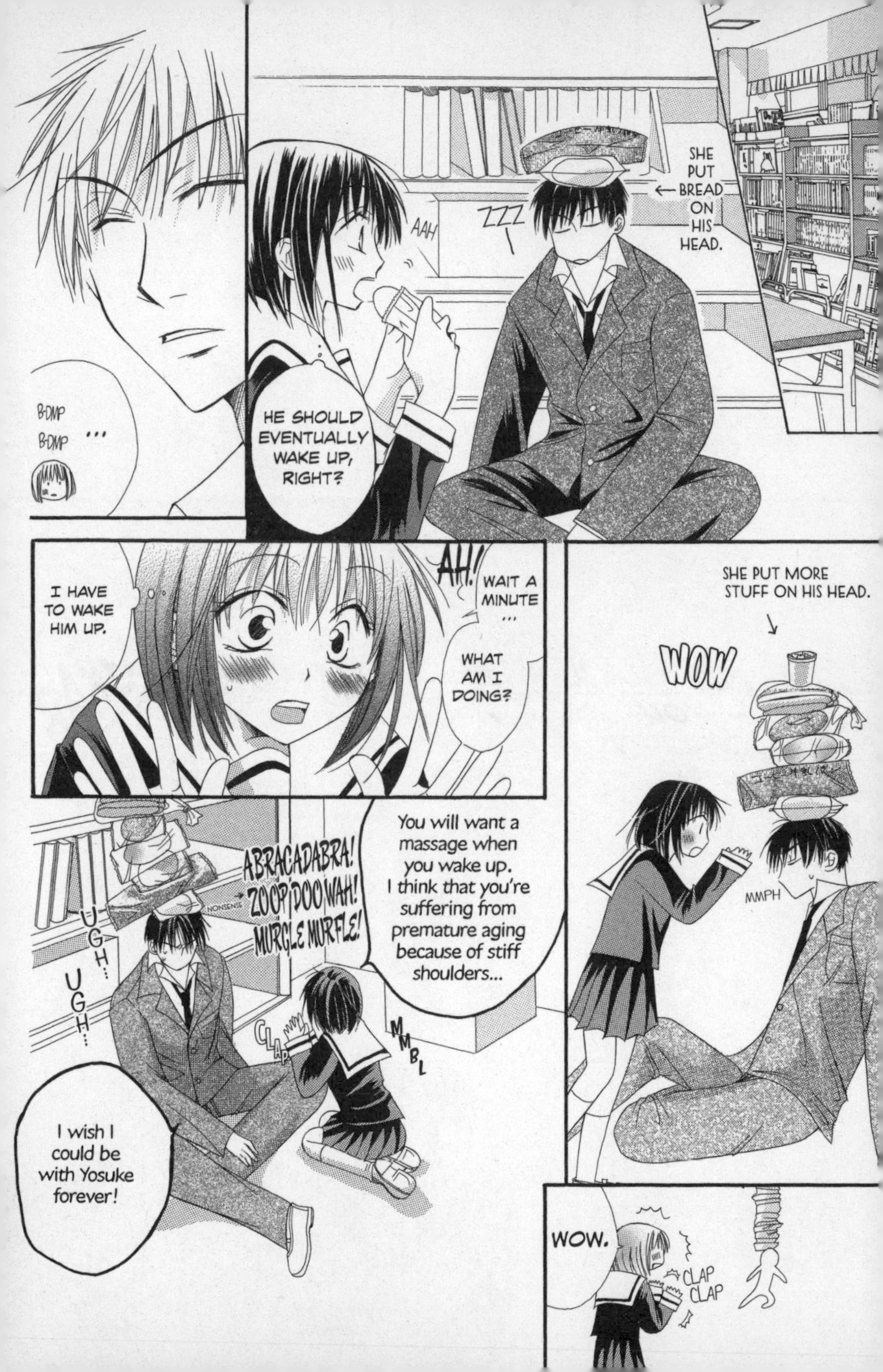
ZZZ
SHE PUT BREAD ON HIS HEAD.
AAH
HE SHOULD EVENTUALLY WAKE UP, RIGHT?
...
B-DMP
B-DMP
SHE PUT MORE STUFF ON HIS HEAD.
WOW
MMPH
WOW.
CLAP CLAP
AH!
WAIT A MINUTE ...
WHAT AM I DOING?
I HAVE TO WAKE HIM UP.
You will want a massage when you wake up. I think that you're suffering from premature aging because of stiff shoulders...
ABRACADABRA! ZOOP DOO WAH! MURGLE MURFLE!
NONSENSE
MMBL
CLAP
UGH...
UGH...
I wish I could be with Yosuke forever!

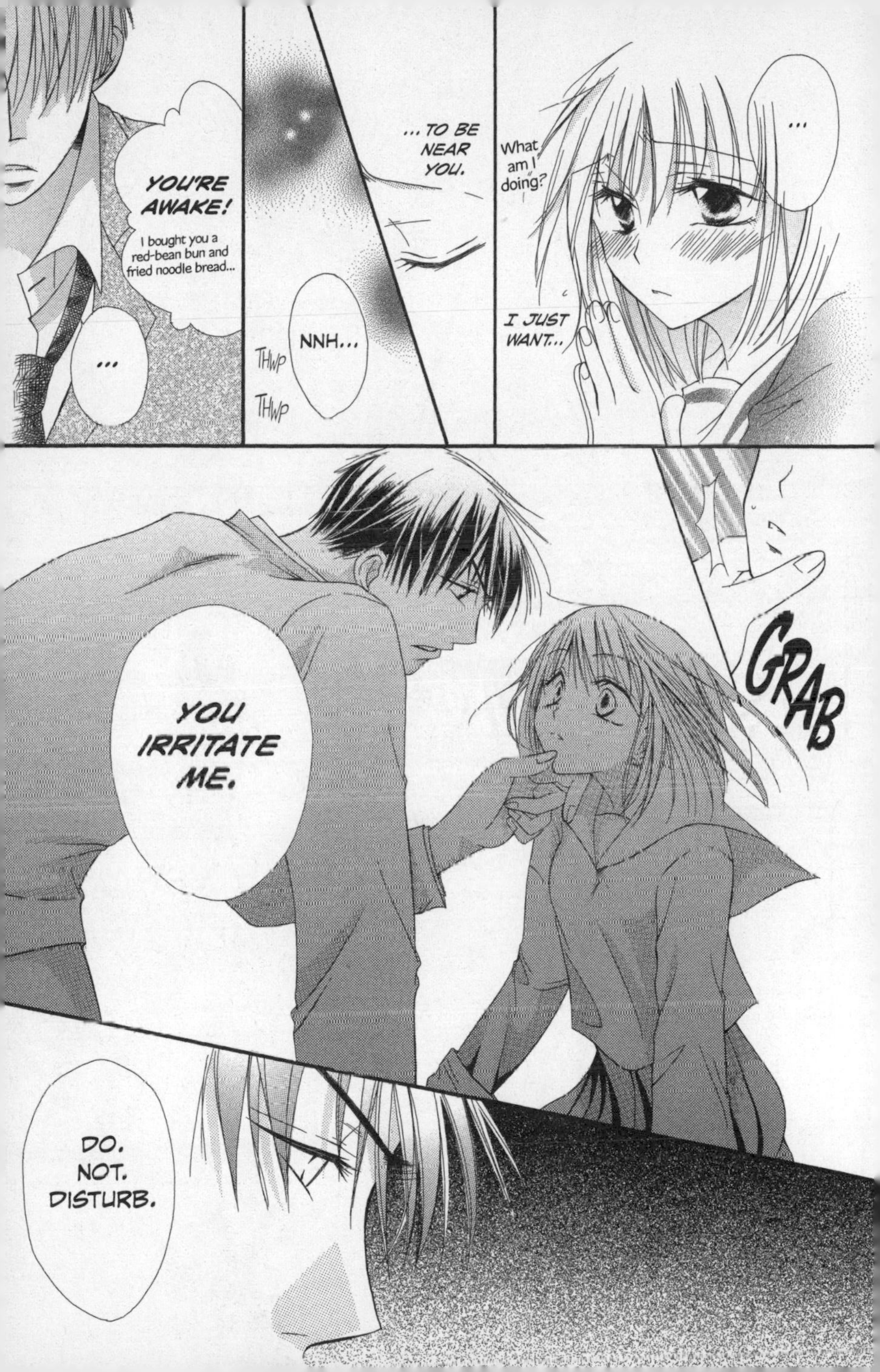
...
What am I doing?
I JUST WANT...
...TO BE NEAR YOU.
NNH...
THWP
THWP
YOU'RE AWAKE!
I bought you a red-bean bun and fried noodle bread...
...
GRAB
YOU IRRITATE ME.
DO. NOT. DISTURB.

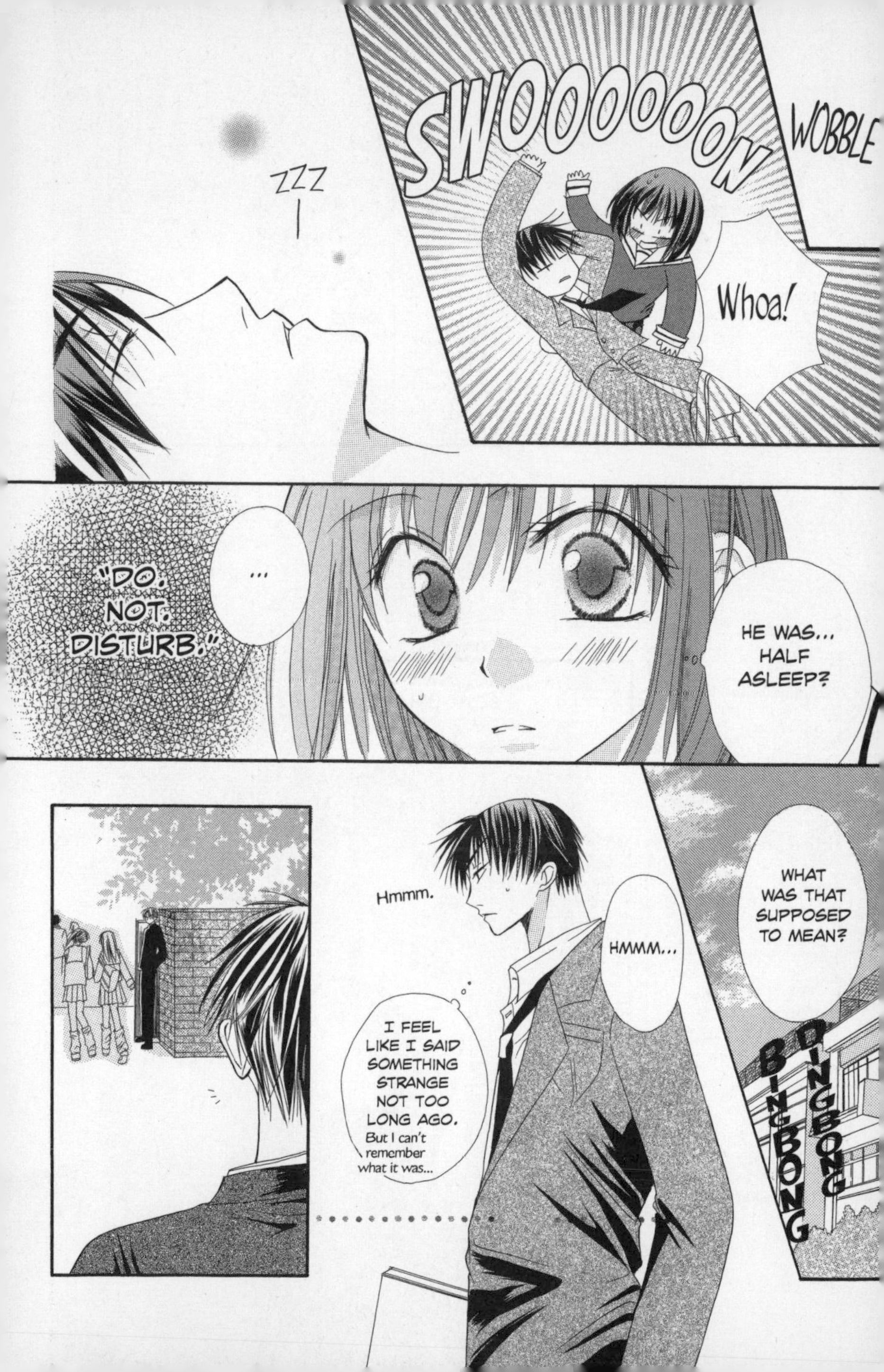
WOBBLE
SWOOOOOON
Whoa!
ZZZ
HE WAS... HALF ASLEEP?
...
"DO. NOT. DISTURB."
WHAT WAS THAT SUPPOSED TO MEAN?
DINGDONG
BINGBONG
HMMM...
Hmmm.
I FEEL LIKE I SAID SOMETHING STRANGE NOT TOO LONG AGO.
But I can't remember what it was...

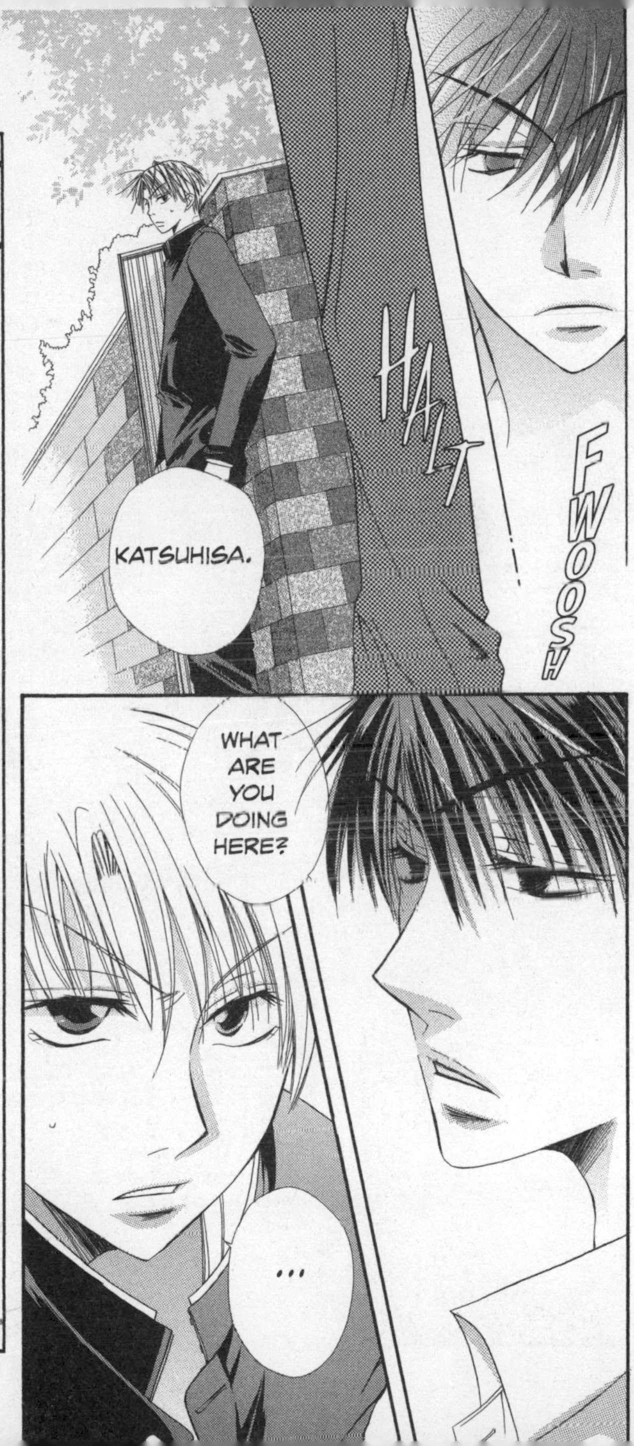
FWOOSH
HALT
KATSUHISA.
WHAT ARE YOU DOING HERE?
...

Massage Is Great!!

Just when I was thinking I needed to get more familiar with the subject, since the story was suddenly serialized... I received a heavenly call from my editor.

"Would you like to go do some research on massage?"

I will go!!

Yes, I will go!!

And that's how I ended up at the massage therapist's! Although it was called research, it was a very pleasant time that involved asking questions while getting a massage.

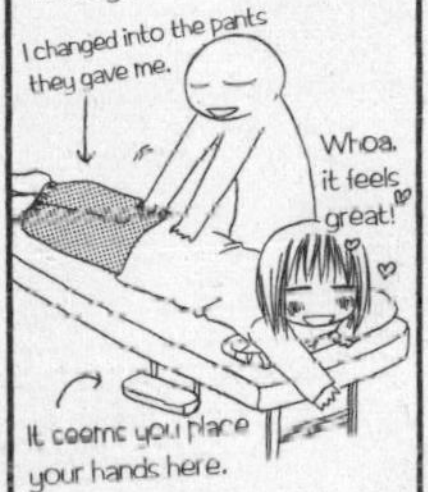
I changed into the pants they gave me.
Whoa, it feels great!
It seems you place your hands here.

During this time, I listened to lots of stories and gathered that there are lots of difficult things about the job. Laws and other things start to get involved.

In reality, it's not legal for high school students to give massages. This is fiction, so please understand that.

I would appreciate it if you read this series with a sense of fancy... like it would be fun if this kind of thing actually happened.

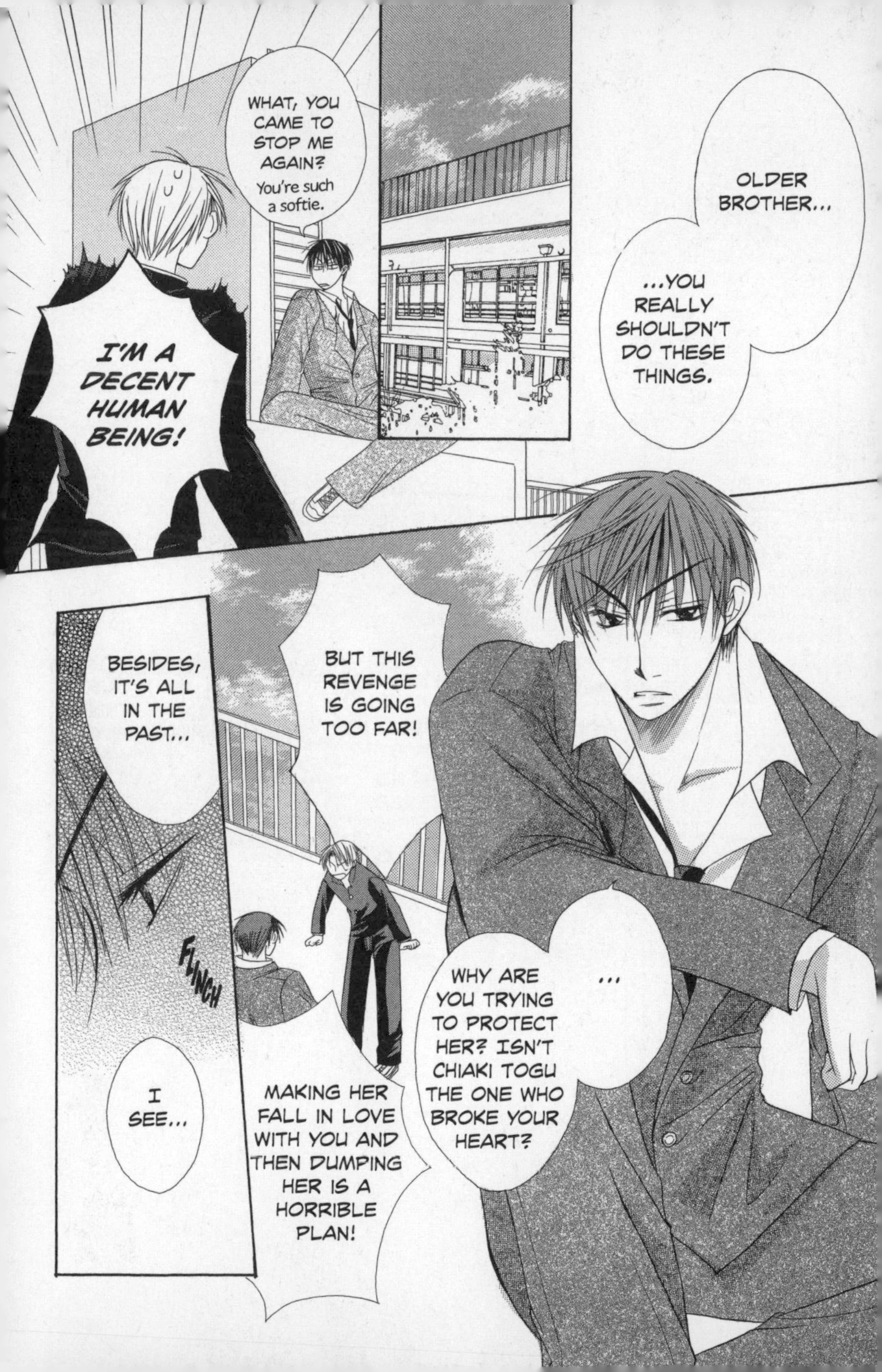
OLDER BROTHER...
...YOU REALLY SHOULDN'T DO THESE THINGS.
WHAT, YOU CAME TO STOP ME AGAIN? You're such a softie.
I'M A DECENT HUMAN BEING!
BUT THIS REVENGE IS GOING TOO FAR!
MAKING HER FALL IN LOVE WITH YOU AND THEN DUMPING HER IS A HORRIBLE PLAN!
WHY ARE YOU TRYING TO PROTECT HER? ISN'T CHIAKI TOGU THE ONE WHO BROKE YOUR HEART?
...
BESIDES, IT'S ALL IN THE PAST...
FLINCH
I SEE...

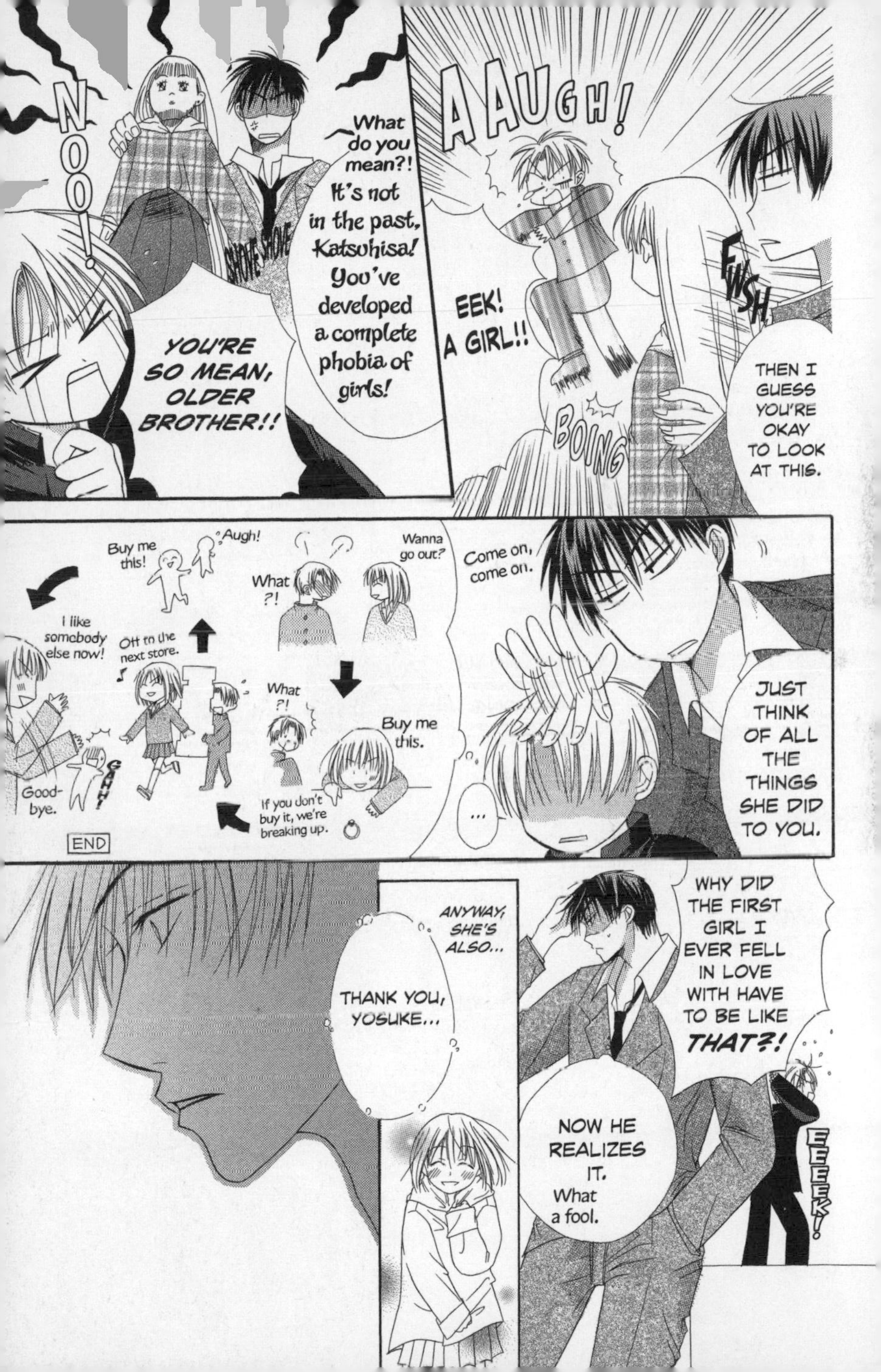
AAUGH!
FWSH
THEN I GUESS YOU'RE OKAY TO LOOK AT THIS.
EEK! A GIRL!!
BOING
What do you mean?! It's not in the past, Katsuhisa! You've developed a complete phobia of girls!
SHOVE SHOVE
NOOO!
YOU'RE SO MEAN, OLDER BROTHER!!
JUST THINK OF ALL THE THINGS SHE DID TO YOU.
Come on, come on.
...
Wanna go out?
What ?!
Buy me this.
What ?!
If you don't buy it, we're breaking up.
Off to the next store.
Buy me this!
Augh!
I like somebody else now!
Good-bye.
GAHH!
END
WHY DID THE FIRST GIRL I EVER FELL IN LOVE WITH HAVE TO BE LIKE THAT?!
EEEEK!
NOW HE REALIZES IT.
What a fool.
ANYWAY, SHE'S ALSO...
THANK YOU, YOSUKE...

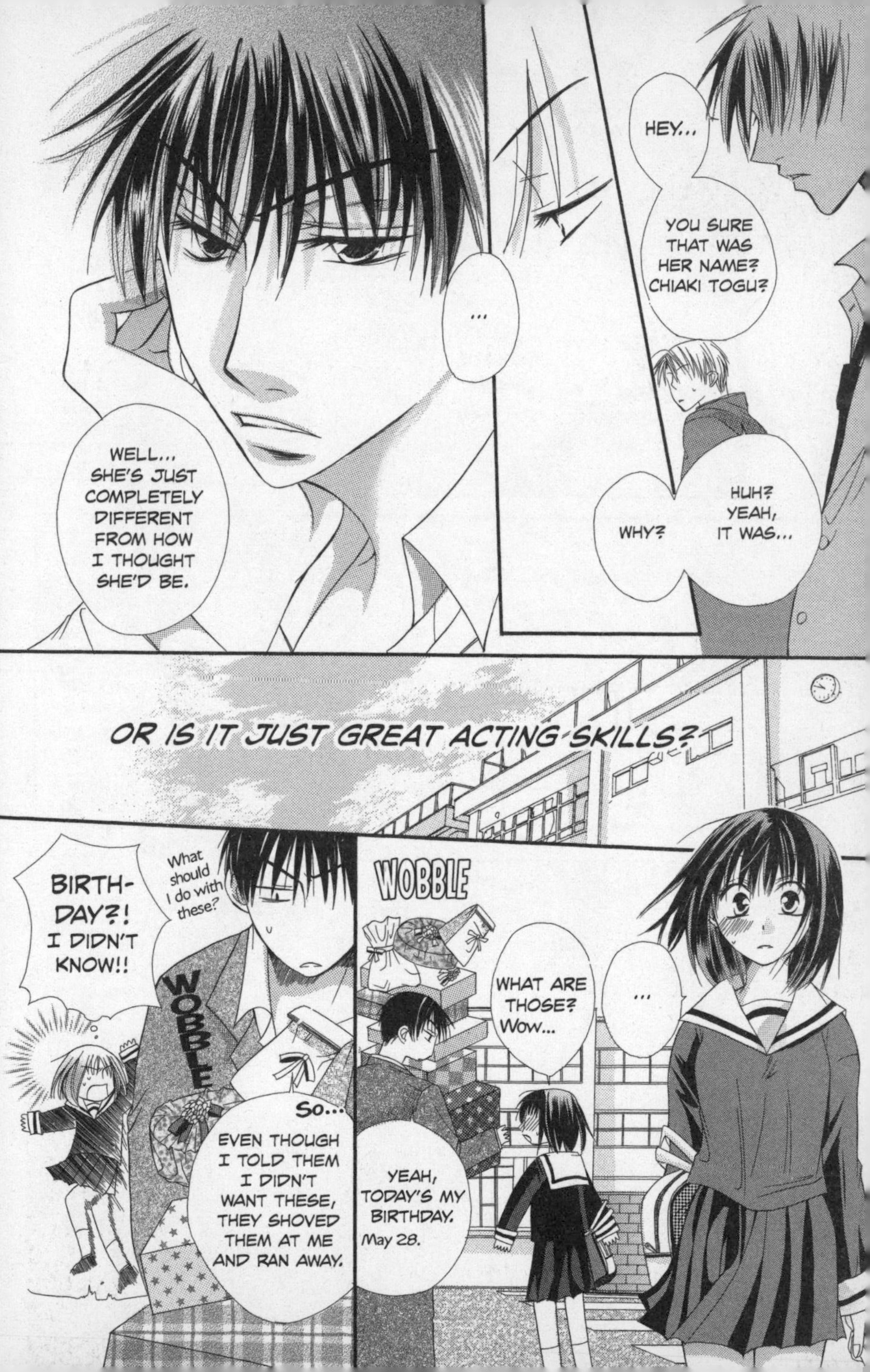
HEY...
YOU SURE THAT WAS HER NAME? CHIAKI TOGU?
HUH? YEAH, IT WAS...
WHY?
...
WELL... SHE'S JUST COMPLETELY DIFFERENT FROM HOW I THOUGHT SHE'D BE.
OR IS IT JUST GREAT ACTING SKILLS?
...
WHAT ARE THOSE? Wow...
WOBBLE
YEAH, TODAY'S MY BIRTHDAY. May 28.
BIRTH-DAY?! I DIDN'T KNOW!!
What should I do with these?
WOBBLE
So...
EVEN THOUGH I TOLD THEM I DIDN'T WANT THESE, THEY SHOVED THEM AT ME AND RAN AWAY.

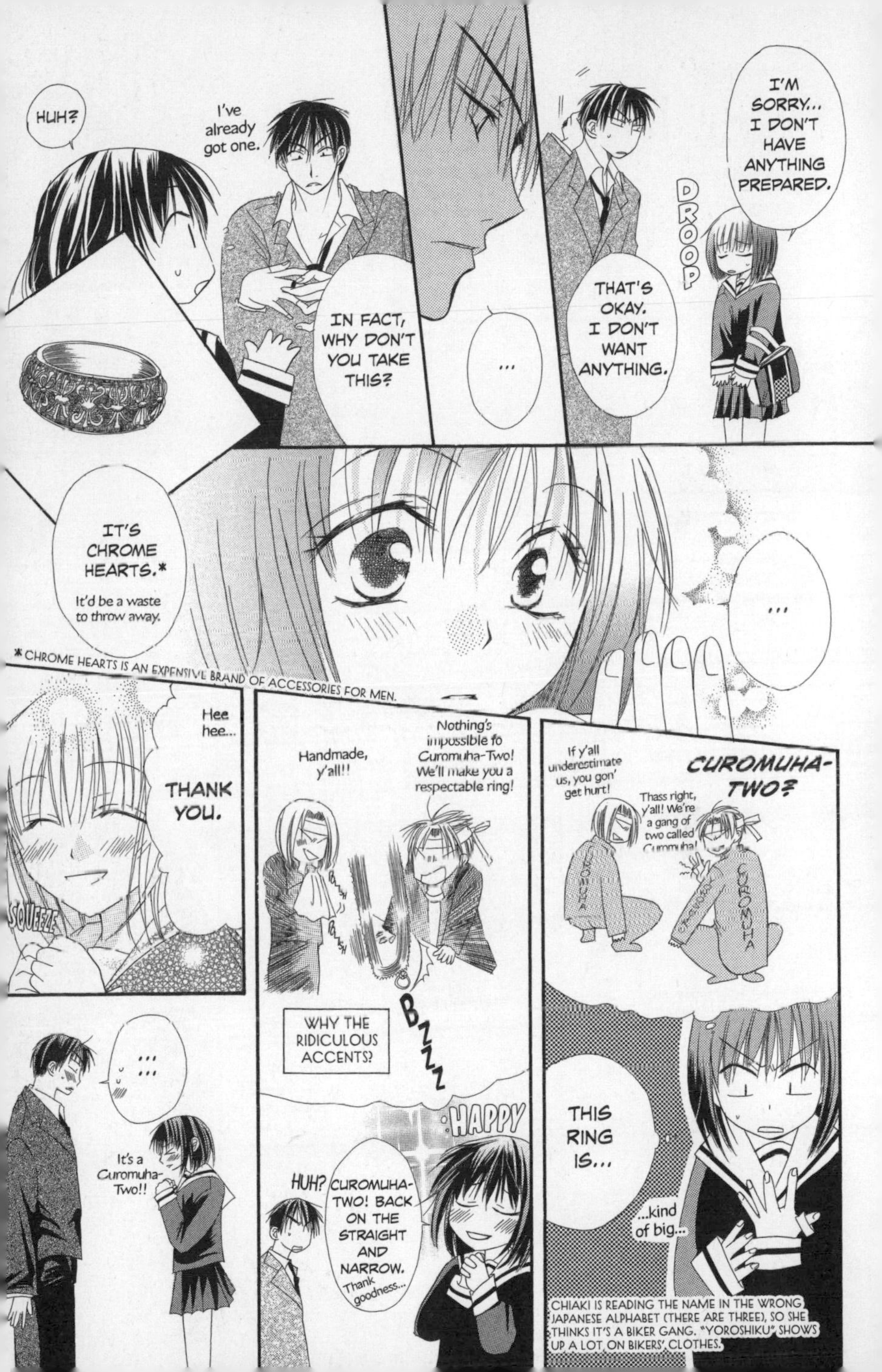
I'M SORRY... I DON'T HAVE ANYTHING PREPARED.
DROOP
THAT'S OKAY. I DON'T WANT ANYTHING.
...
I've already got one.
HUH?
IN FACT, WHY DON'T YOU TAKE THIS?
...
IT'S CHROME HEARTS.* It'd be a waste to throw away.
* CHROME HEARTS IS AN EXPENSIVE BRAND OF ACCESSORIES FOR MEN.
CUROMUHA-TWO?
If y'all underestimate us, you gon' get hurt!
Thass right, y'all! We're a gang of two called Curomuha!
CUROMUHA
CUROMUHA
Nothing's impossible fo Curomuha-Two! We'll make you a respectable ring!
Handmade, y'all!!
POLISH
POLISH
Hee hee...
THANK YOU.
SQUEEZE
THIS RING IS...
...kind of big...
CHIAKI IS READING THE NAME IN THE WRONG JAPANESE ALPHABET (THERE ARE THREE), SO SHE THINKS IT'S A BIKER GANG. "YOROSHIKU" SHOWS UP A LOT ON BIKERS' CLOTHES.
WHY THE RIDICULOUS ACCENTS?
BZZZ
HAPPY
CUROMUHA-TWO! BACK ON THE STRAIGHT AND NARROW. Thank goodness...
HUH?
... ...
It's a Curomuha-Two!!

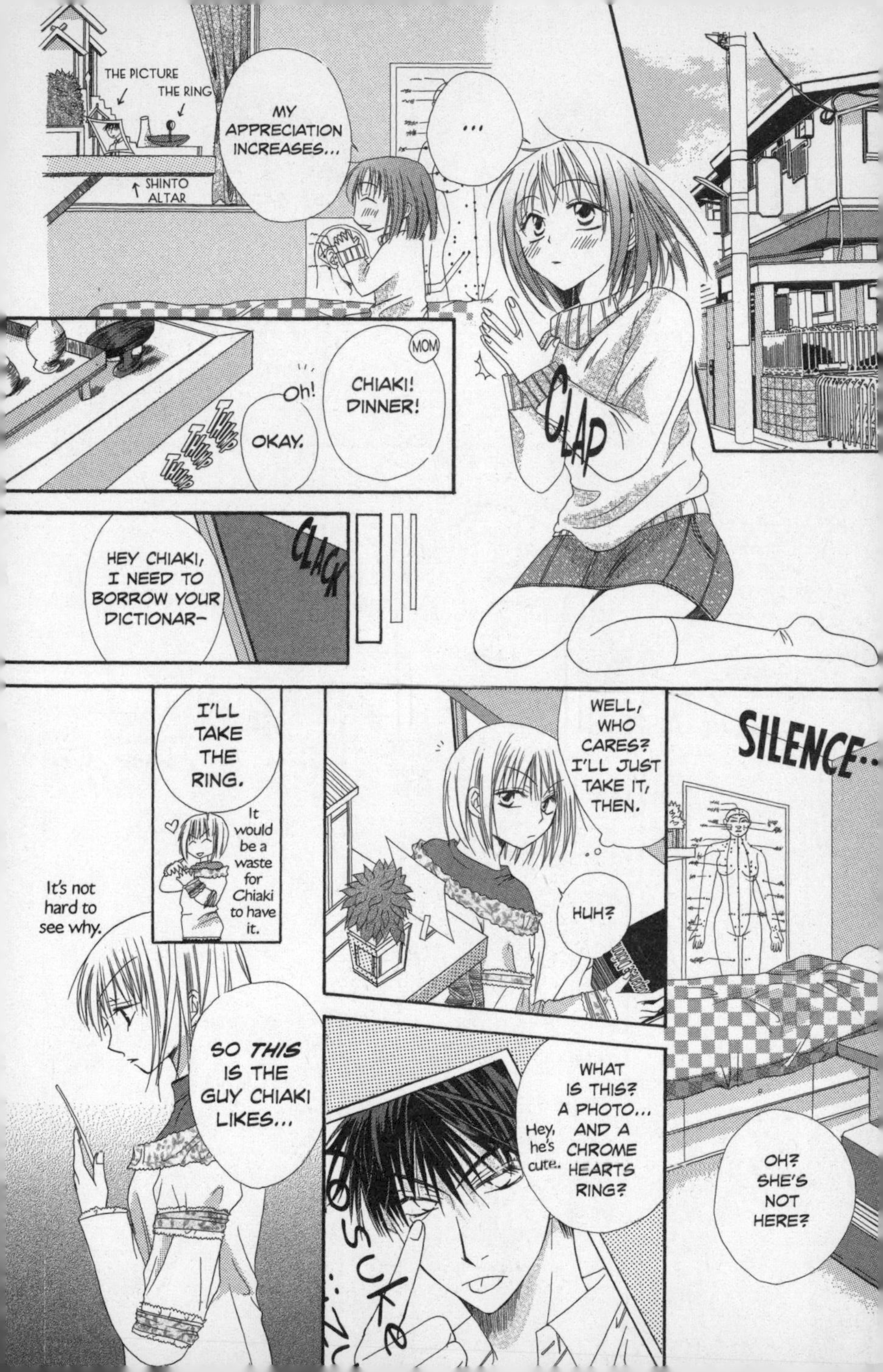
...
MY APPRECIATION INCREASES...
THE PICTURE
THE RING
SHINTO ALTAR
CLAP
MOM
CHIAKI! DINNER!
Oh!
OKAY.
THUMP THUMP THUMP
CLACK
HEY CHIAKI, I NEED TO BORROW YOUR DICTIONAR–
SILENCE...
OH? SHE'S NOT HERE?
HUH?
WELL, WHO CARES? I'LL JUST TAKE IT, THEN.
WHAT IS THIS? A PHOTO... AND A CHROME HEARTS RING?
Hey, he's cute.
I'LL TAKE THE RING.
It would be a waste for Chiaki to have it.
It's not hard to see why.
SO THIS IS THE GUY CHIAKI LIKES...

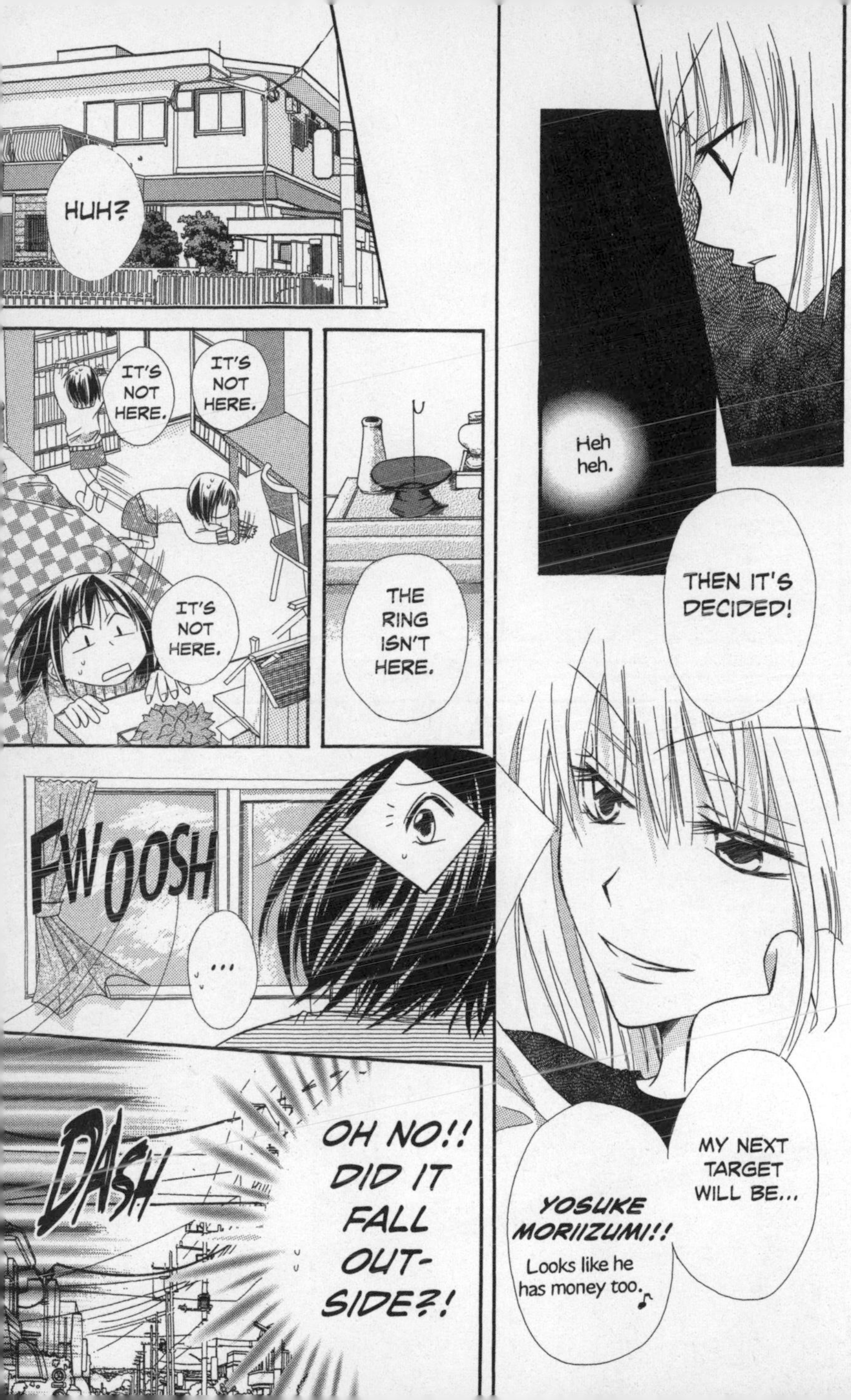
Heh heh.
THEN IT'S DECIDED!
MY NEXT TARGET WILL BE...
YOSUKE MORIIZUMI!!
Looks like he has money too.♪
HUH?
THE RING ISN'T HERE.
IT'S NOT HERE.
IT'S NOT HERE.
IT'S NOT HERE.
FWOOSH
...
OH NO!! DID IT FALL OUT-SIDE?!
DASH

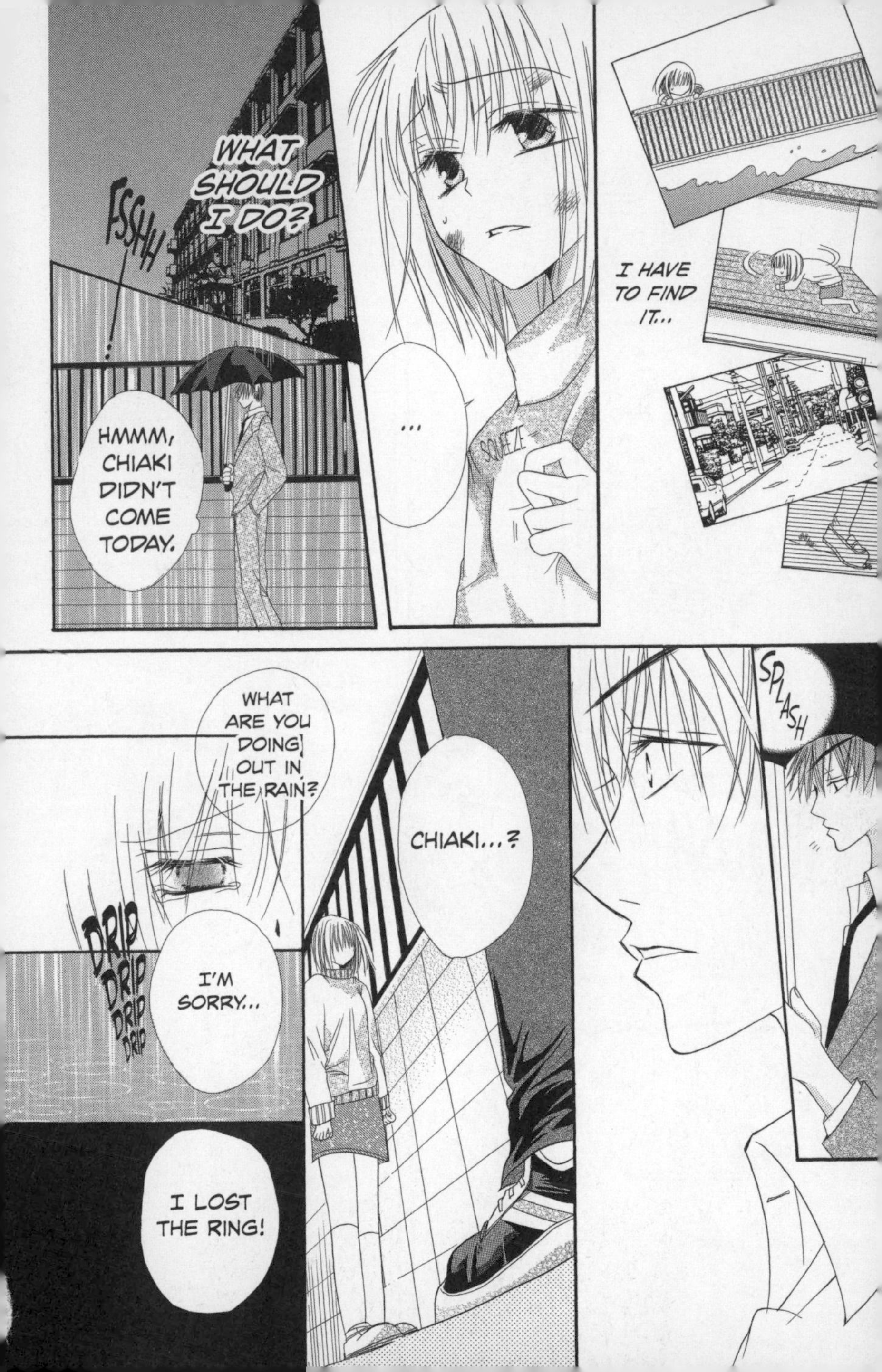
I HAVE TO FIND IT...
...
SQUEEZE
WHAT SHOULD I DO?
FSSHH
HMMM, CHIAKI DIDN'T COME TODAY.
SPLASH
CHIAKI...?
WHAT ARE YOU DOING OUT IN THE RAIN?
DRIP DRIP DRIP DRIP
I'M SORRY...
I LOST THE RING!

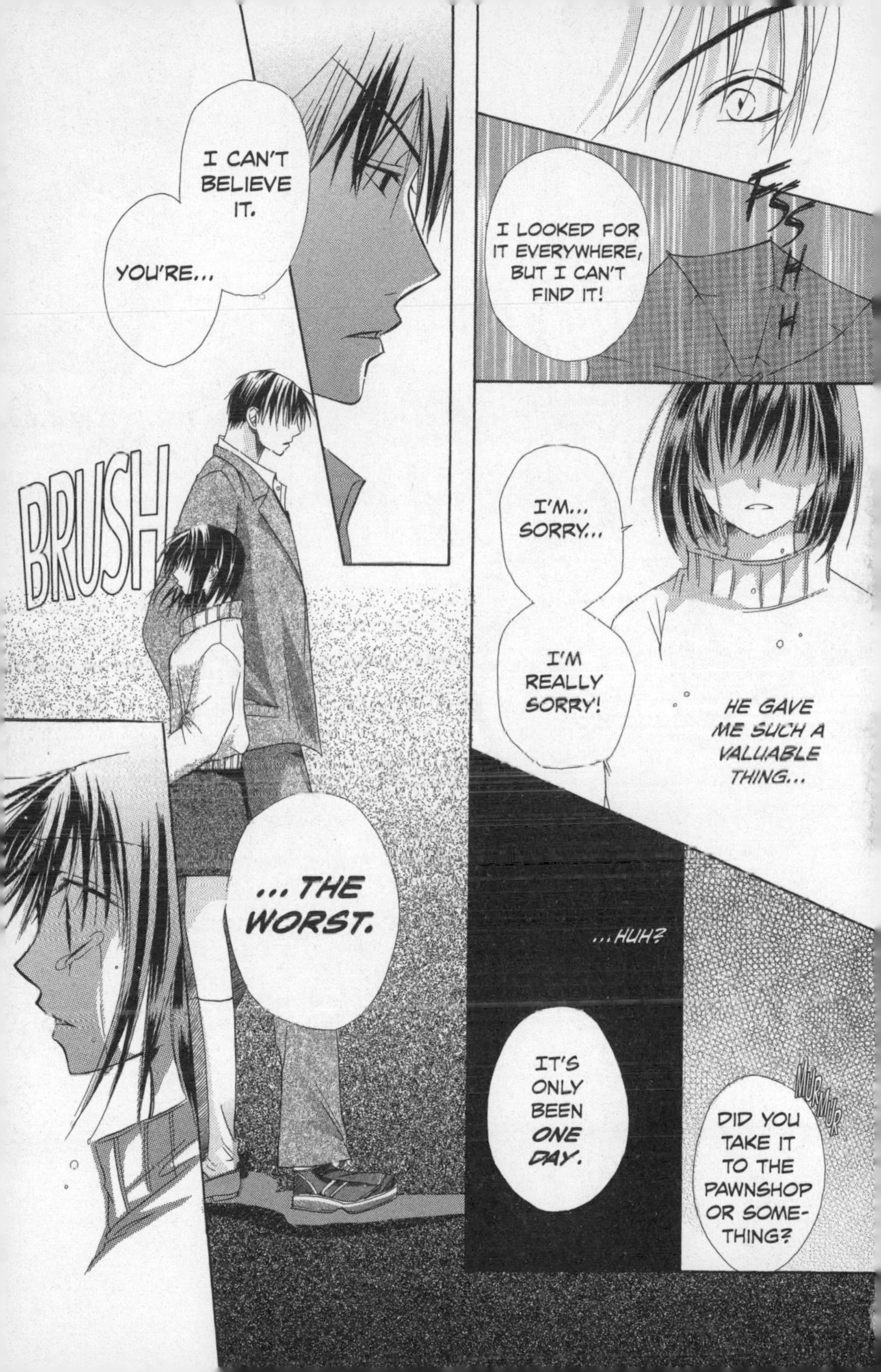
FSSHH
I LOOKED FOR IT EVERYWHERE, BUT I CAN'T FIND IT!
I'M... SORRY...
I'M REALLY SORRY!
HE GAVE ME SUCH A VALUABLE THING...
MURMUR
DID YOU TAKE IT TO THE PAWNSHOP OR SOME-THING?
...HUH?
IT'S ONLY BEEN ONE DAY.
I CAN'T BELIEVE IT.
YOU'RE...
BRUSH
...THE WORST.

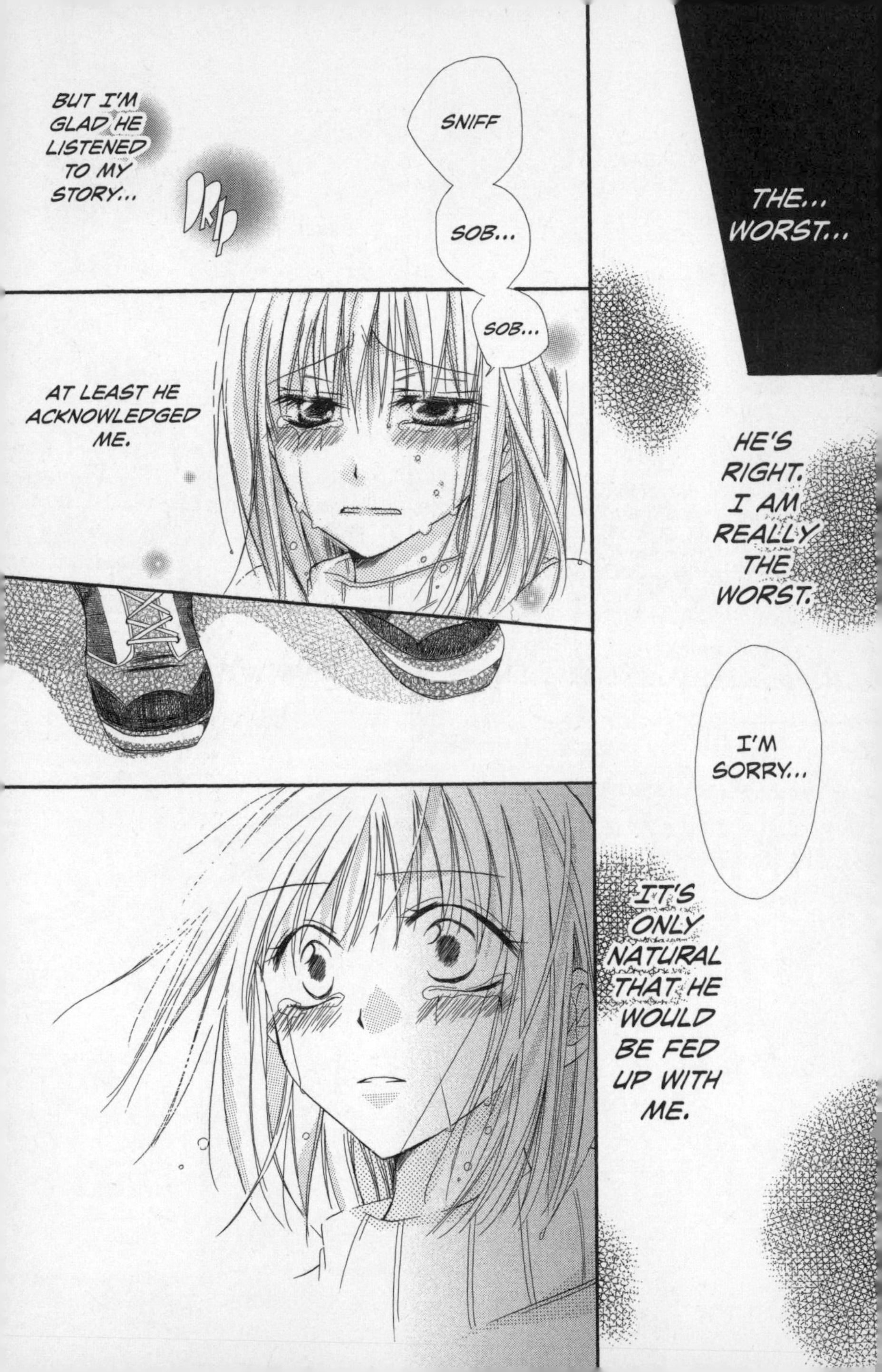
THE... WORST...
HE'S RIGHT. I AM REALLY THE WORST.
I'M SORRY...
IT'S ONLY NATURAL THAT HE WOULD BE FED UP WITH ME.
SNIFF
SOB...
SOB...
BUT I'M GLAD HE LISTENED TO MY STORY...
DRIP
AT LEAST HE ACKNOWLEDGED ME.

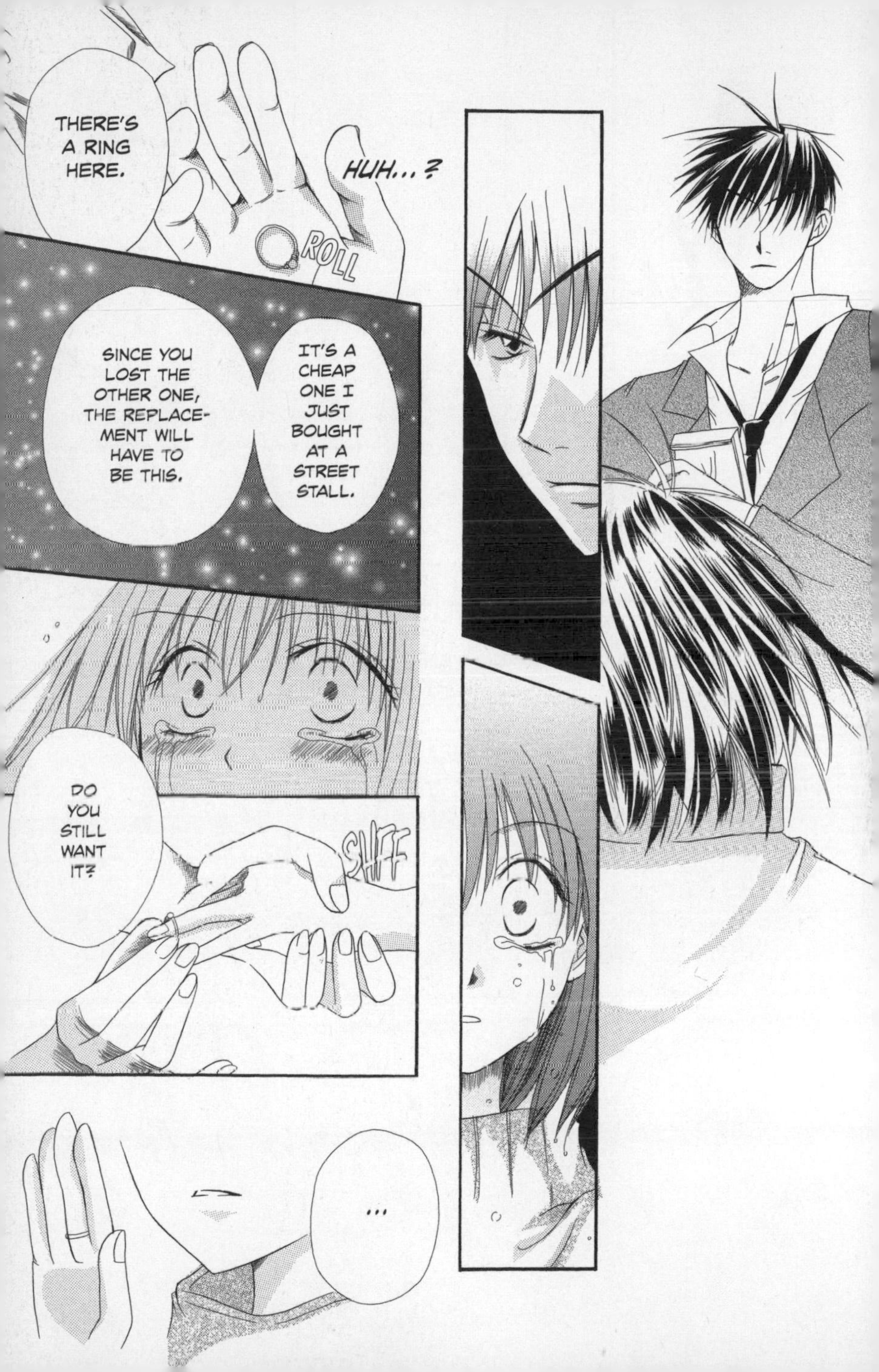
THERE'S A RING HERE.
HUH...?
ROLL
IT'S A CHEAP ONE I JUST BOUGHT AT A STREET STALL.
SINCE YOU LOST THE OTHER ONE, THE REPLACEMENT WILL HAVE TO BE THIS.
DO YOU STILL WANT IT?
SHFF
...

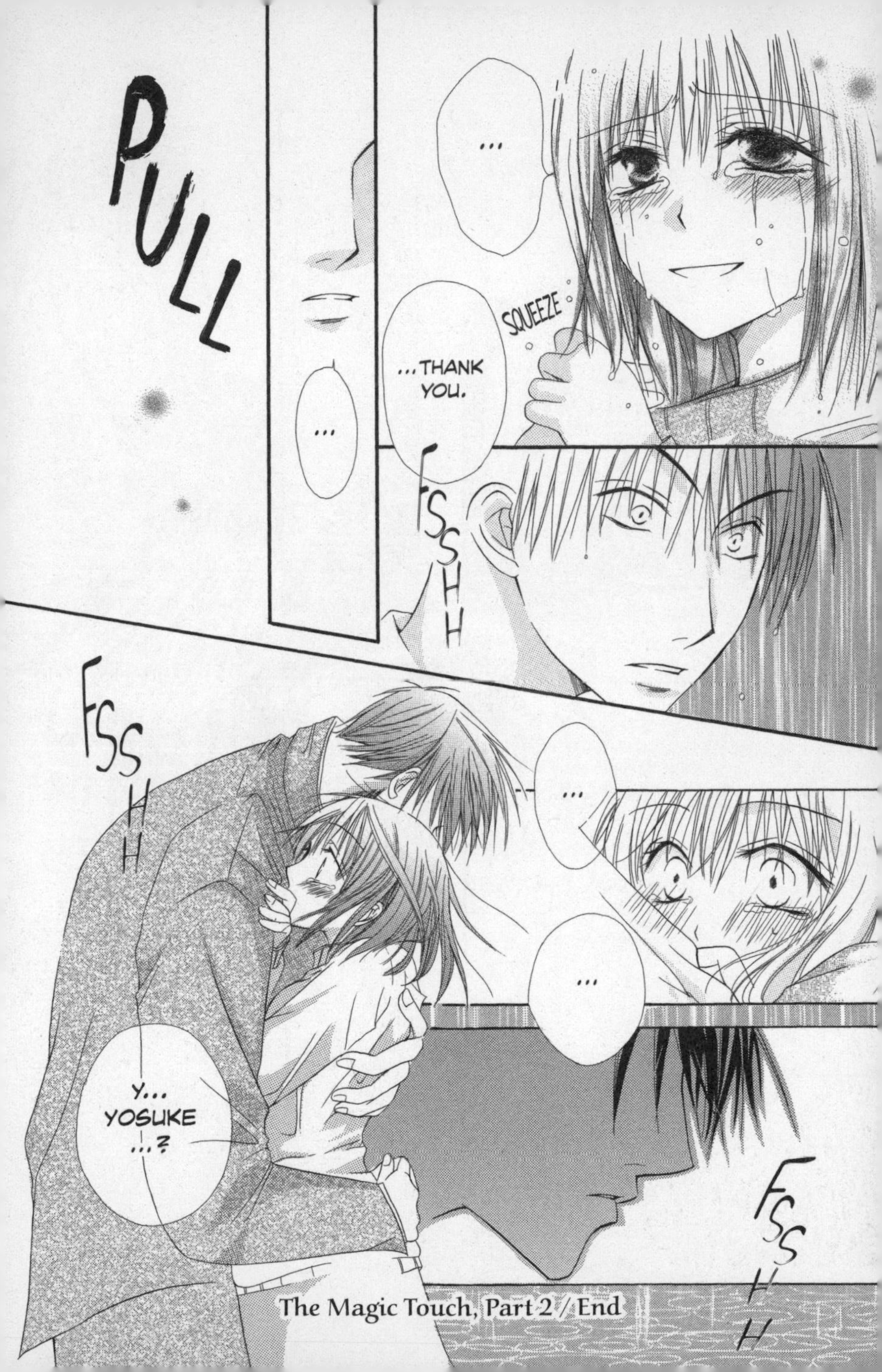
...
SQUEEZE
...THANK YOU.
FSSHH
PULL
...
...
...
FSSHH
FSSHH
Y... YOSUKE ...?

The Magic Touch, Part 2 / End

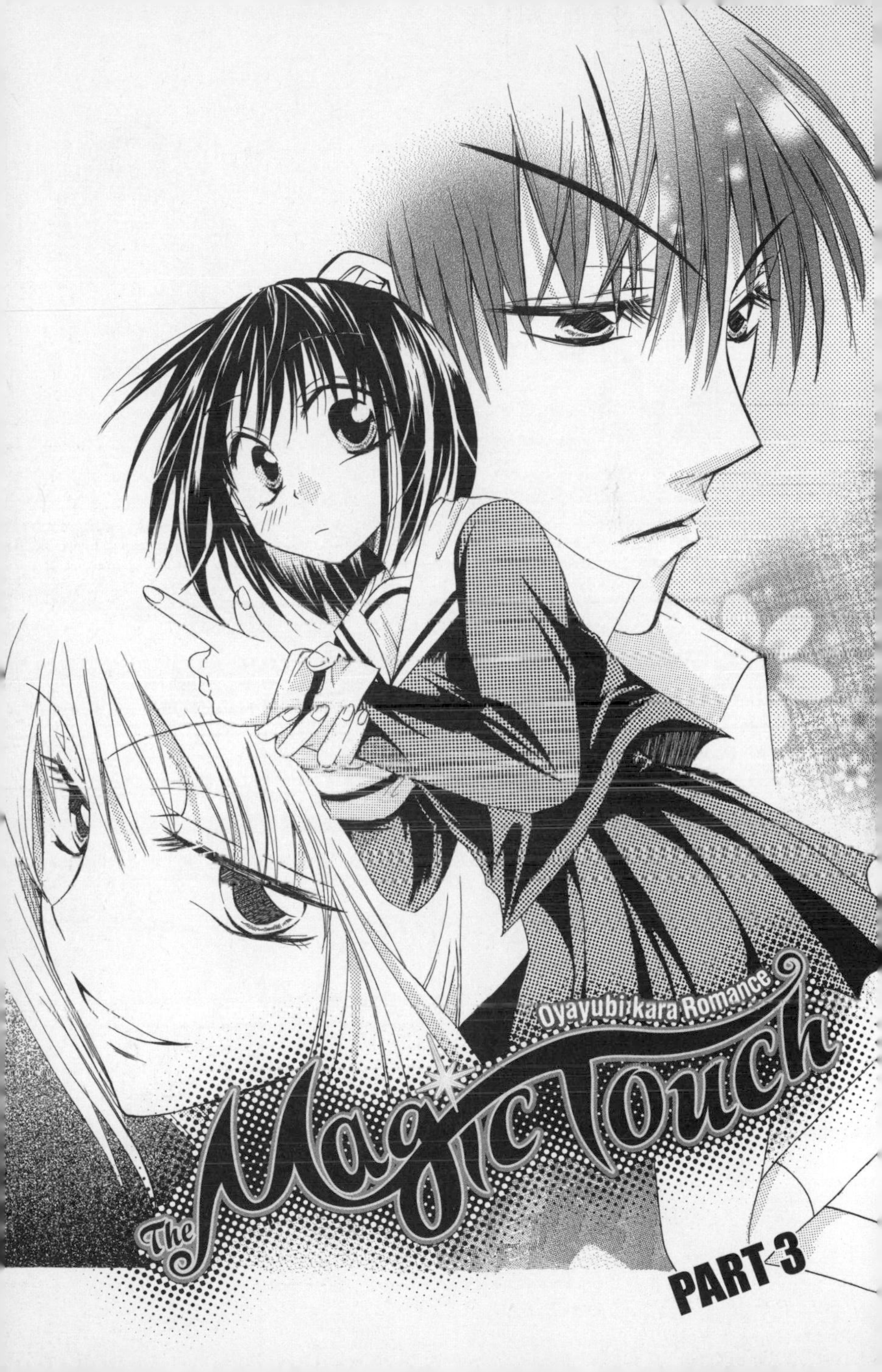
Oyayubi kara Romance
The Magic Touch
PART 3

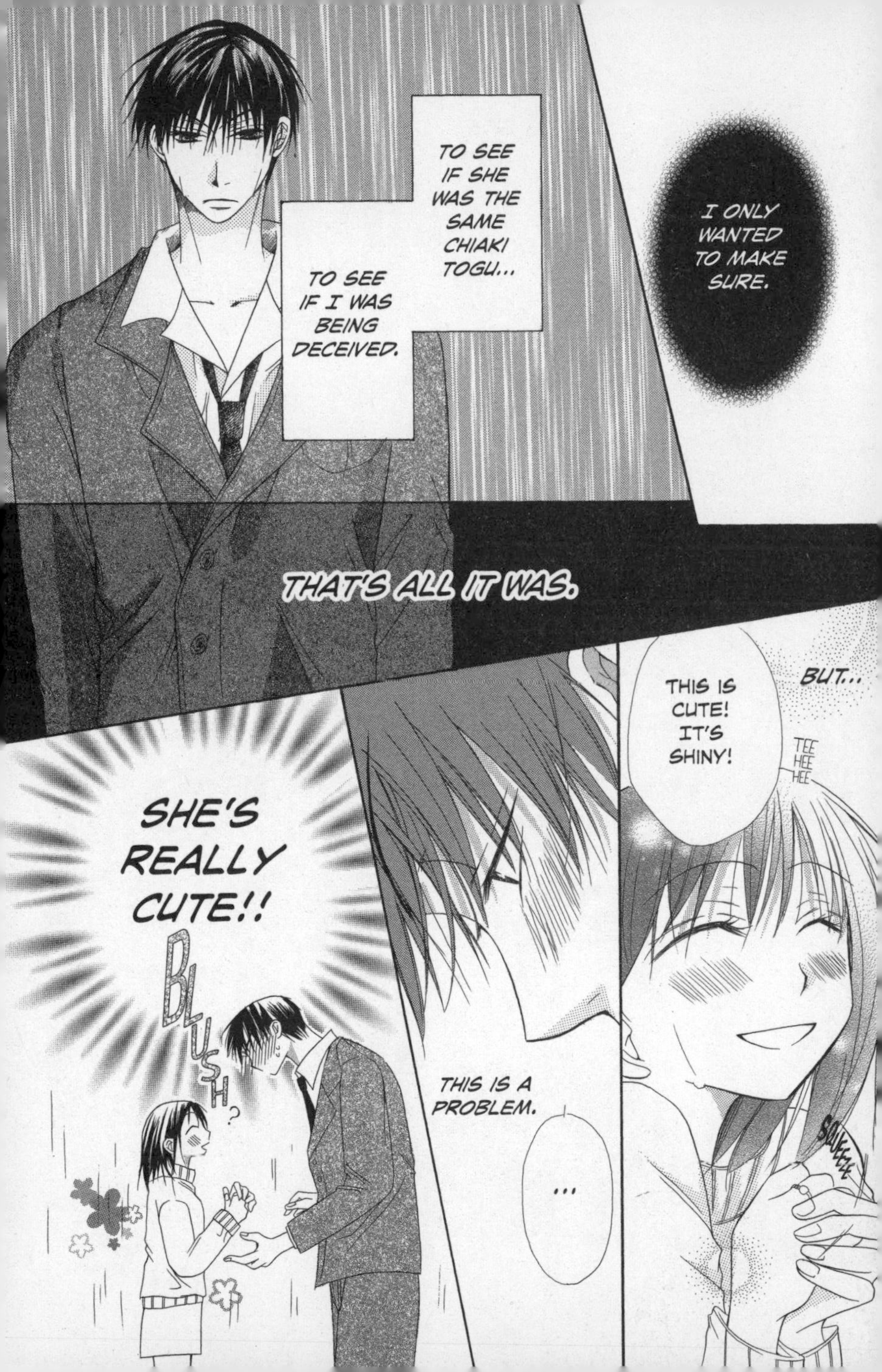
I ONLY WANTED TO MAKE SURE.
TO SEE IF SHE WAS THE SAME CHIAKI TOGU...
TO SEE IF I WAS BEING DECEIVED.
THAT'S ALL IT WAS.
BUT...
THIS IS CUTE! IT'S SHINY!
TEE HEE HEE
SQUEEZE
THIS IS A PROBLEM.
...
SHE'S REALLY CUTE!!
BLUSH
?

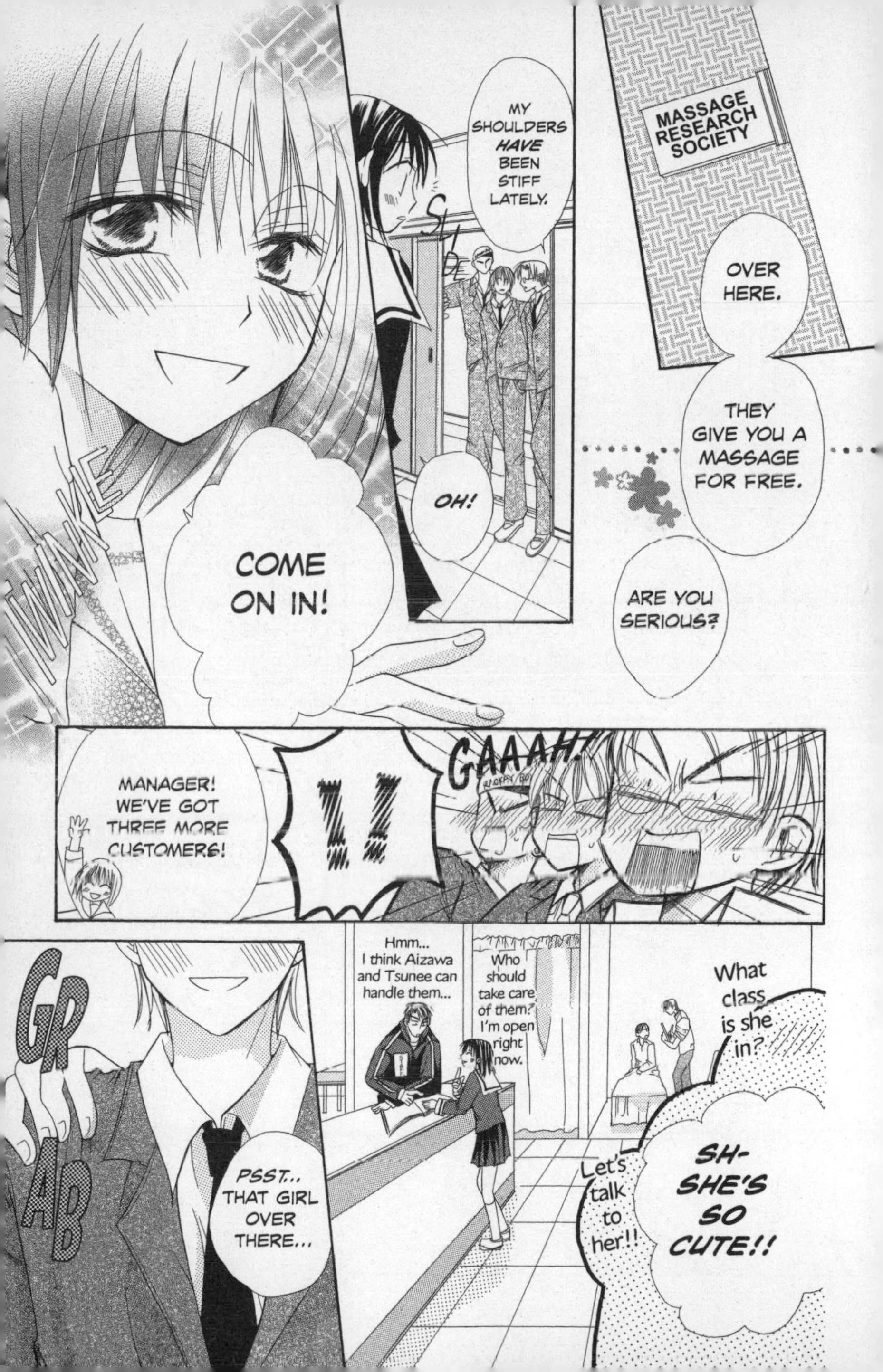
MASSAGE RESEARCH SOCIETY
OVER HERE.
THEY GIVE YOU A MASSAGE FOR FREE.
ARE YOU SERIOUS?
MY SHOULDERS *HAVE* BEEN STIFF LATELY.
SLIDE
OH!
COME ON IN!
TWINKLE
GAAAH!
!!
MANAGER! WE'VE GOT THREE MORE CUSTOMERS!
What class is she in?
SH-SHE'S SO CUTE!!
Let's talk to her!!
Who should take care of them? I'm open right now.
Hmm... I think Aizawa and Tsunee can handle them...
GRAB
PSST... THAT GIRL OVER THERE...

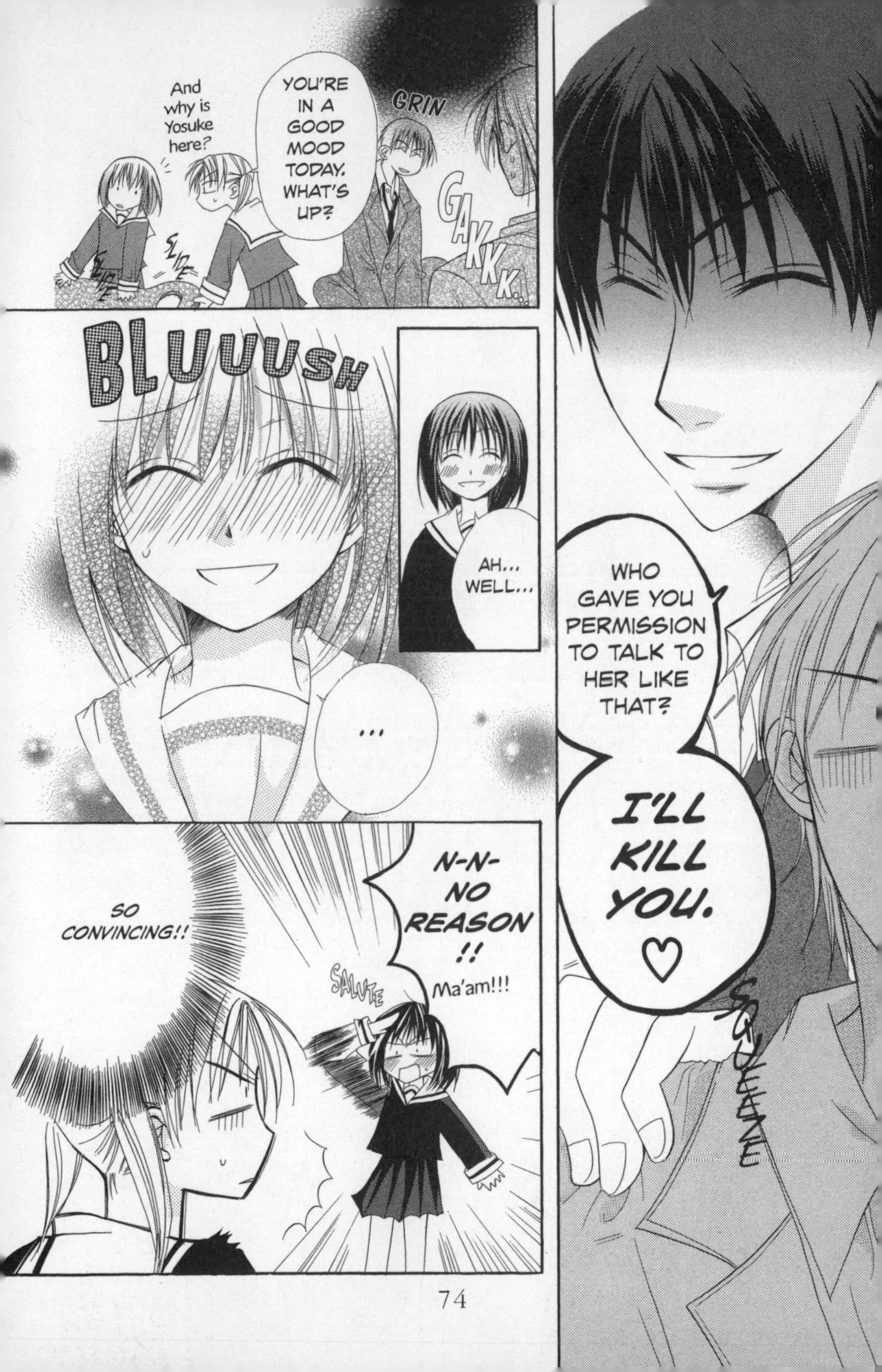
WHO GAVE YOU PERMISSION TO TALK TO HER LIKE THAT?
I'LL KILL YOU. ♥
GRIN
GAKKK..
YOU'RE IN A GOOD MOOD TODAY. WHAT'S UP?
And why is Yosuke here?
AH... WELL...
BLUUUSH
...
N-N-NO REASON!!
Ma'am!!!
SALUTE
SO CONVINCING!!

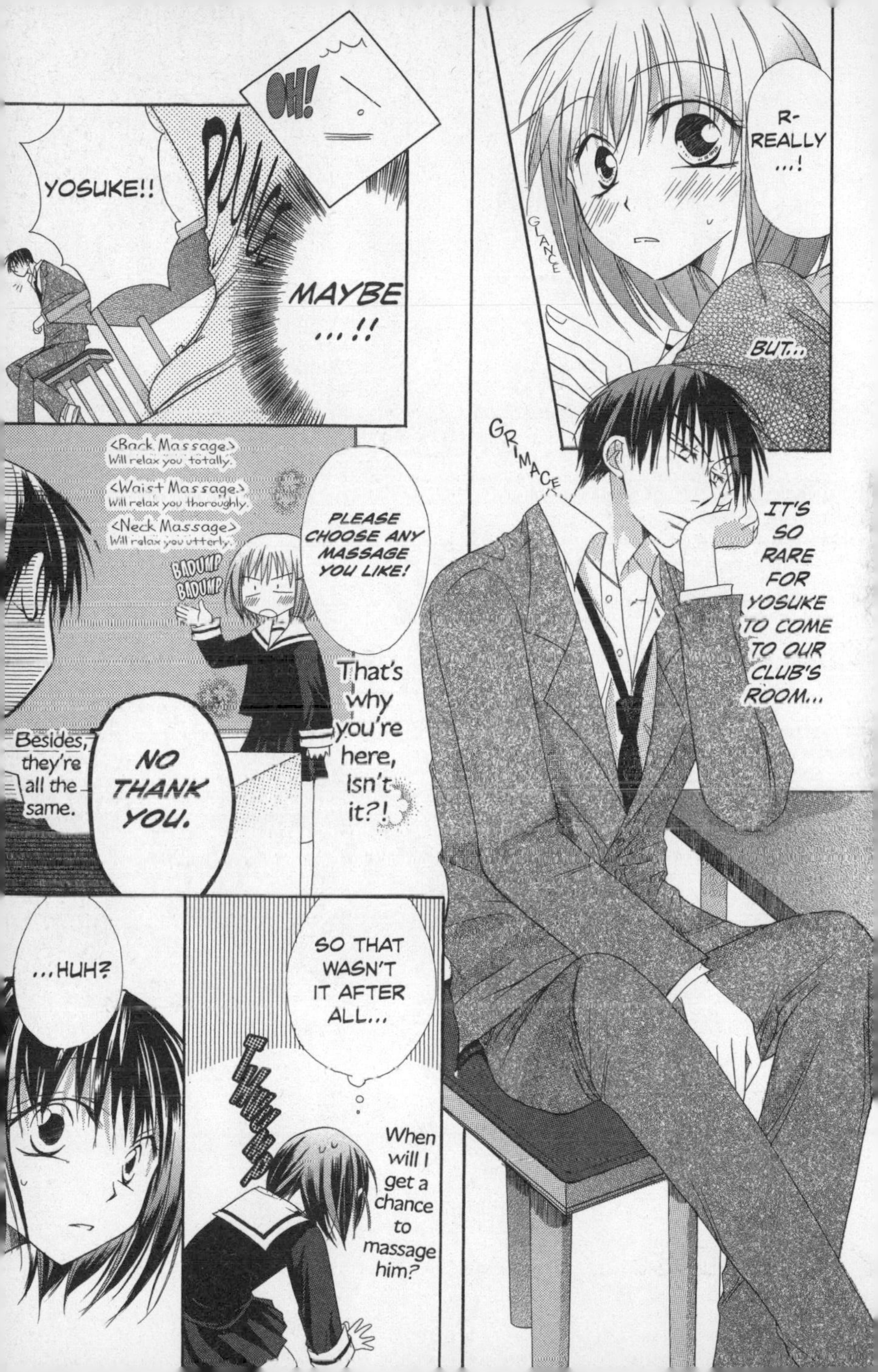
R-REALLY ...!
GLANCE
BUT...
GRIMACE
IT'S SO RARE FOR YOSUKE TO COME TO OUR CLUB'S ROOM...
OH!
YOSUKE!!
MAYBE ...!!
<Back Massage> Will relax you totally.
<Waist Massage> Will relax you thoroughly.
<Neck Massage> Will relax you utterly.
BADUMP BADUMP
PLEASE CHOOSE ANY MASSAGE YOU LIKE!
That's why you're here, isn't it?!
NO THANK YOU.
Besides, they're all the same.
SO THAT WASN'T IT AFTER ALL...
When will I get a chance to massage him?
...HUH?

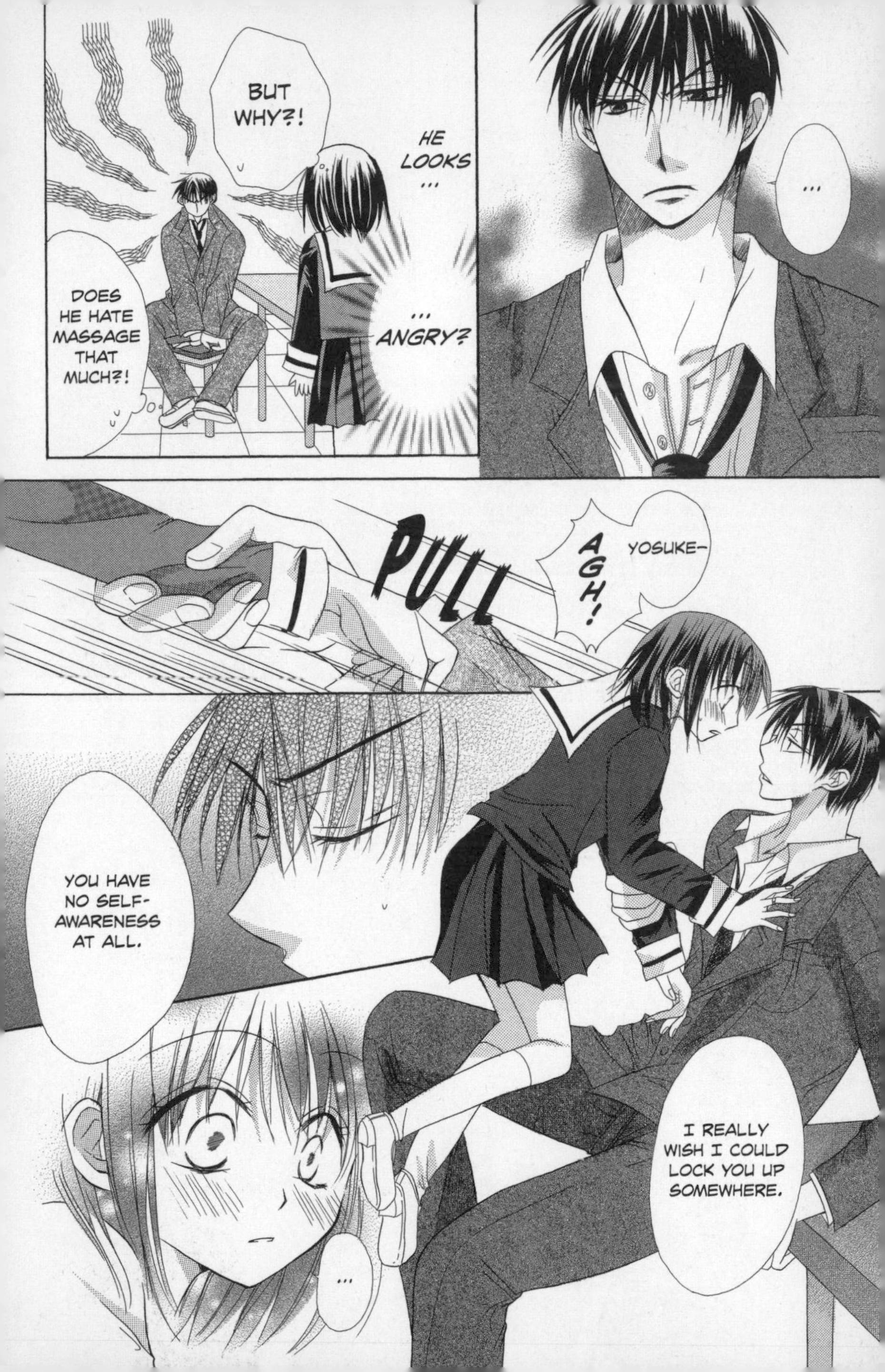
...
BUT WHY?!
HE LOOKS ...
... ANGRY?
DOES HE HATE MASSAGE THAT MUCH?!
PULL
AGH!
YOSUKE-
YOU HAVE NO SELF-AWARENESS AT ALL.
I REALLY WISH I COULD LOCK YOU UP SOMEWHERE.
...

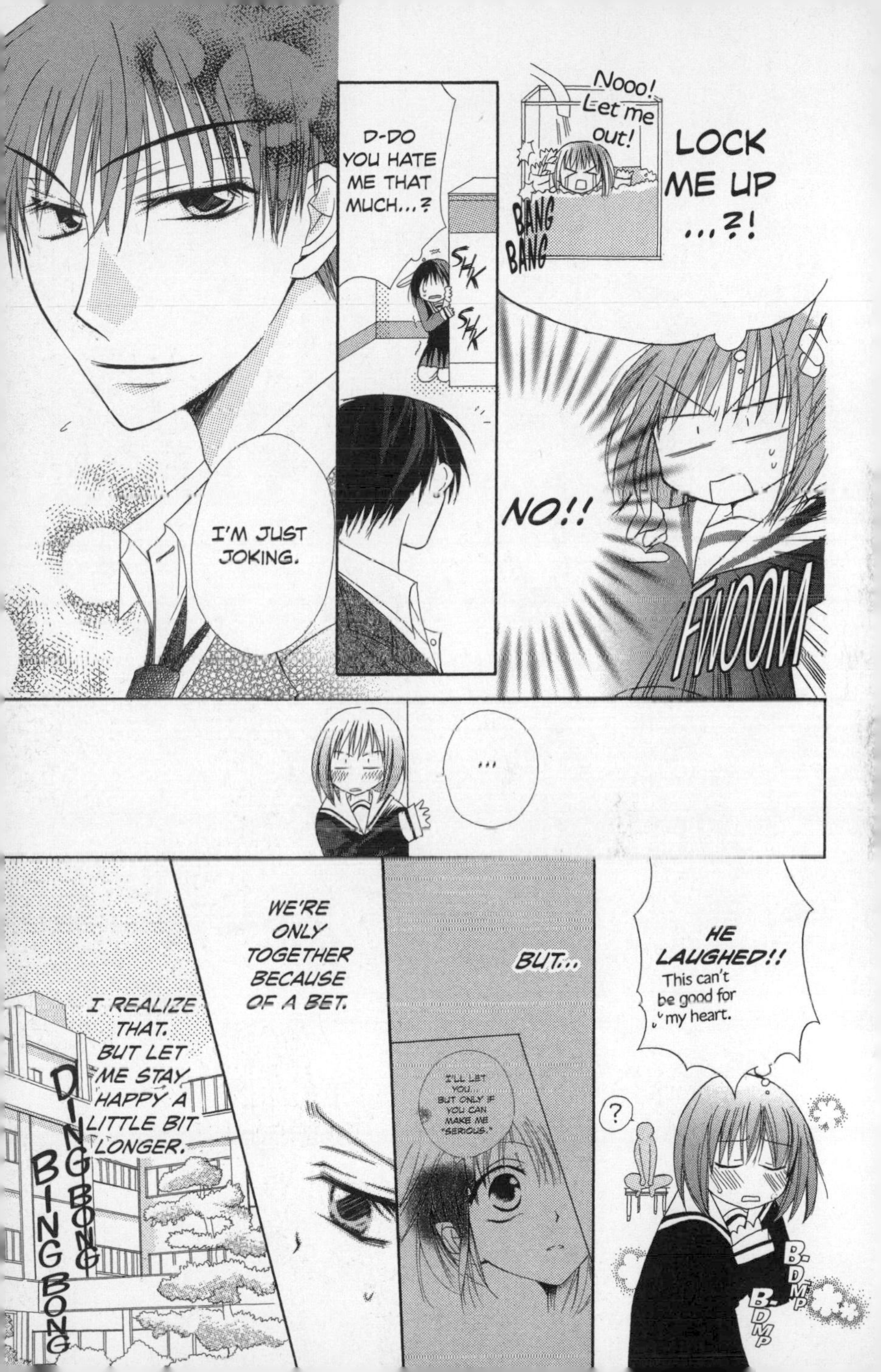
LOCK ME UP ...?!
Nooo! Let me out!
BANG BANG
NO!!
FWOOM
D-DO YOU HATE ME THAT MUCH...?
SHK SHK
I'M JUST JOKING.
...
HE LAUGHED!!
This can't be good for my heart.
?
B-BDMP B-BDMP
BUT...
I'LL LET YOU... BUT ONLY IF YOU CAN MAKE ME "SERIOUS."
WE'RE ONLY TOGETHER BECAUSE OF A BET.
I REALIZE THAT. BUT LET ME STAY HAPPY A LITTLE BIT LONGER.
DING BONG
BING BONG

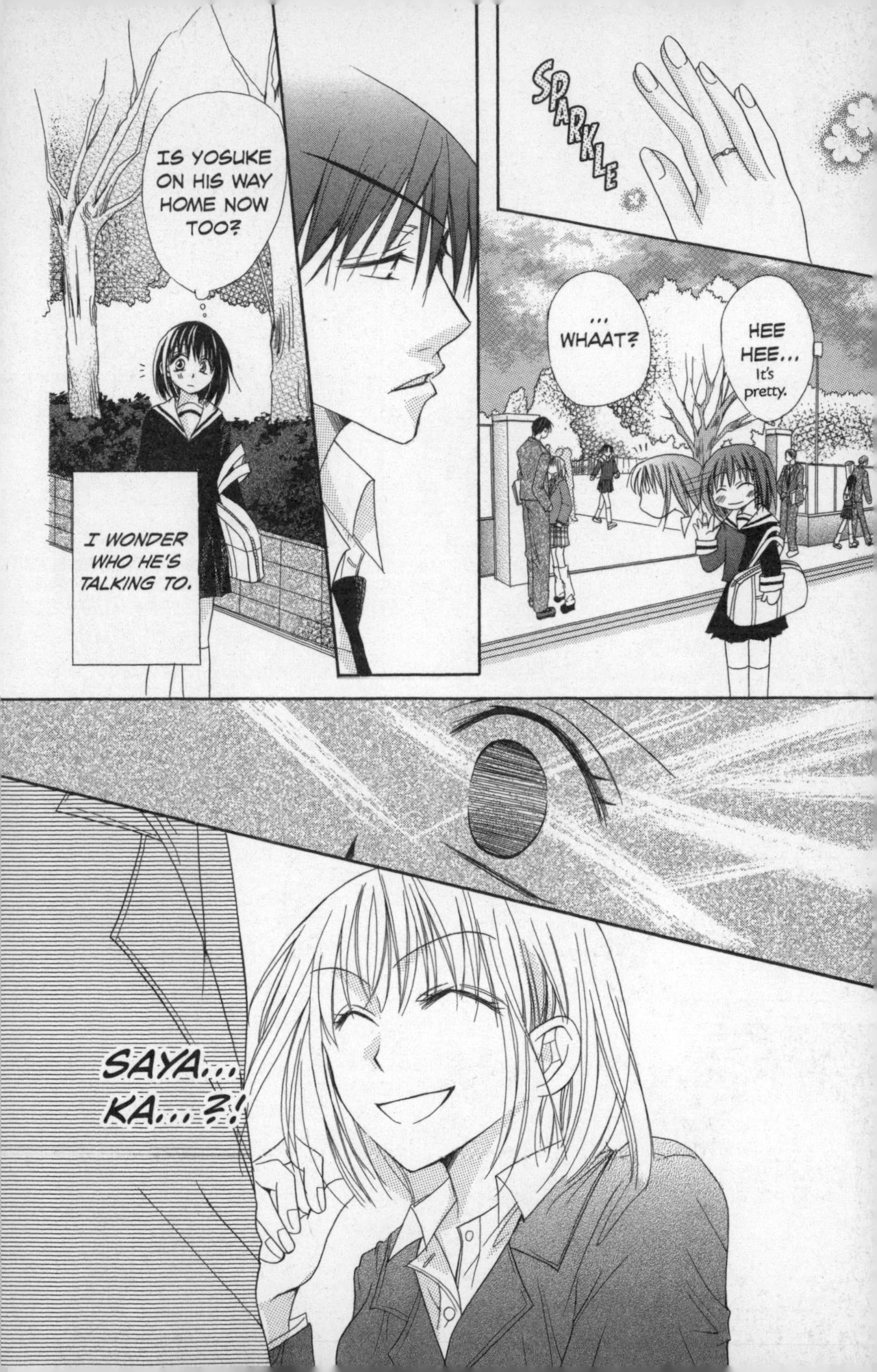
SPARKLE
HEE HEE... It's pretty.
... WHAAT?
IS YOSUKE ON HIS WAY HOME NOW TOO?
I WONDER WHO HE'S TALKING TO.
SAYA... KA... ?!

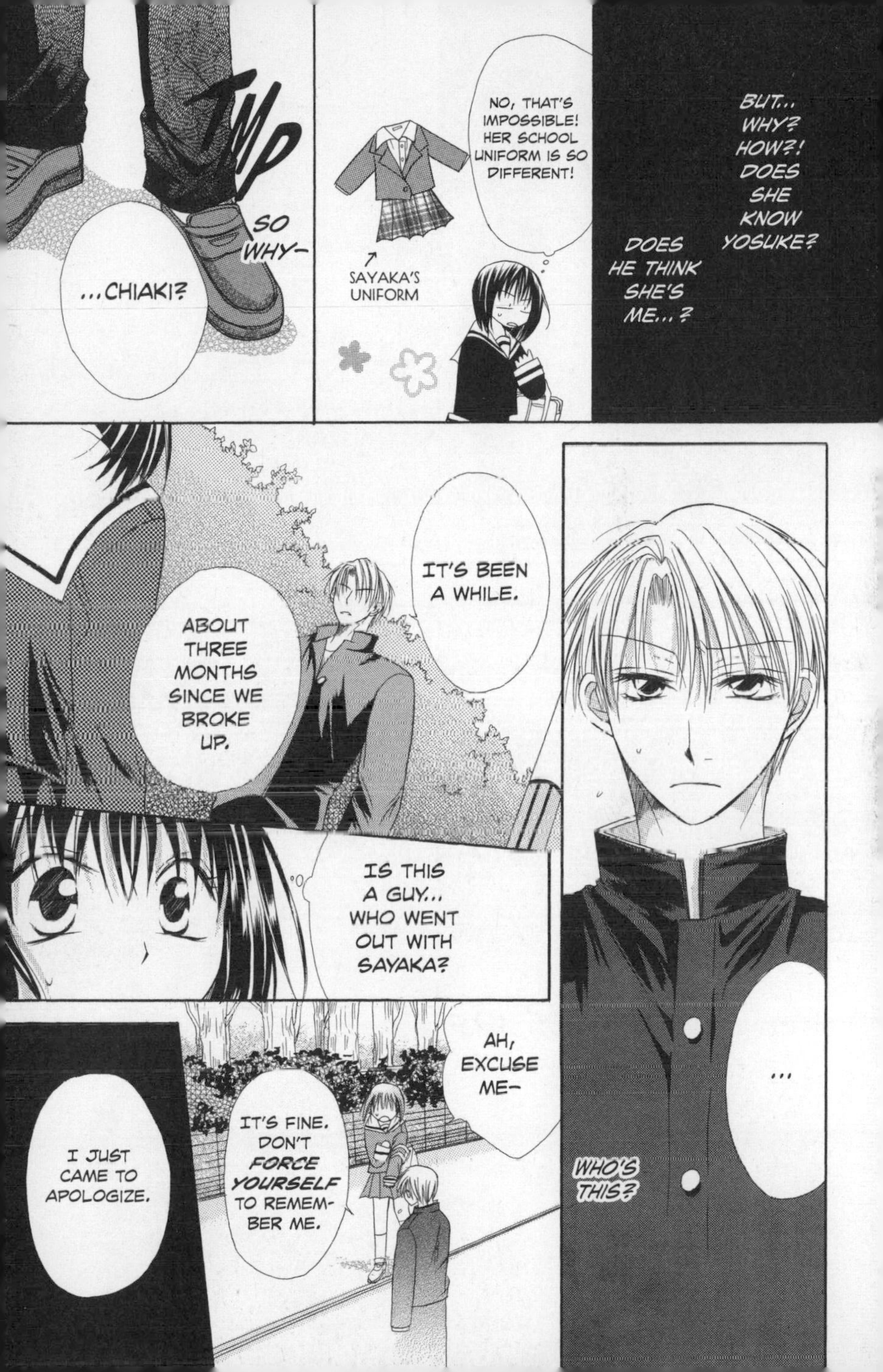
BUT... WHY? HOW?! DOES SHE KNOW YOSUKE?
DOES HE THINK SHE'S ME...?
NO, THAT'S IMPOSSIBLE! HER SCHOOL UNIFORM IS SO DIFFERENT!
SAYAKA'S UNIFORM
TMP
SO WHY—
...CHIAKI?
...
WHO'S THIS?
IT'S BEEN A WHILE.
ABOUT THREE MONTHS SINCE WE BROKE UP.
IS THIS A GUY... WHO WENT OUT WITH SAYAKA?
AH, EXCUSE ME—
IT'S FINE. DON'T *FORCE YOURSELF* TO REMEMBER ME.
I JUST CAME TO APOLOGIZE.

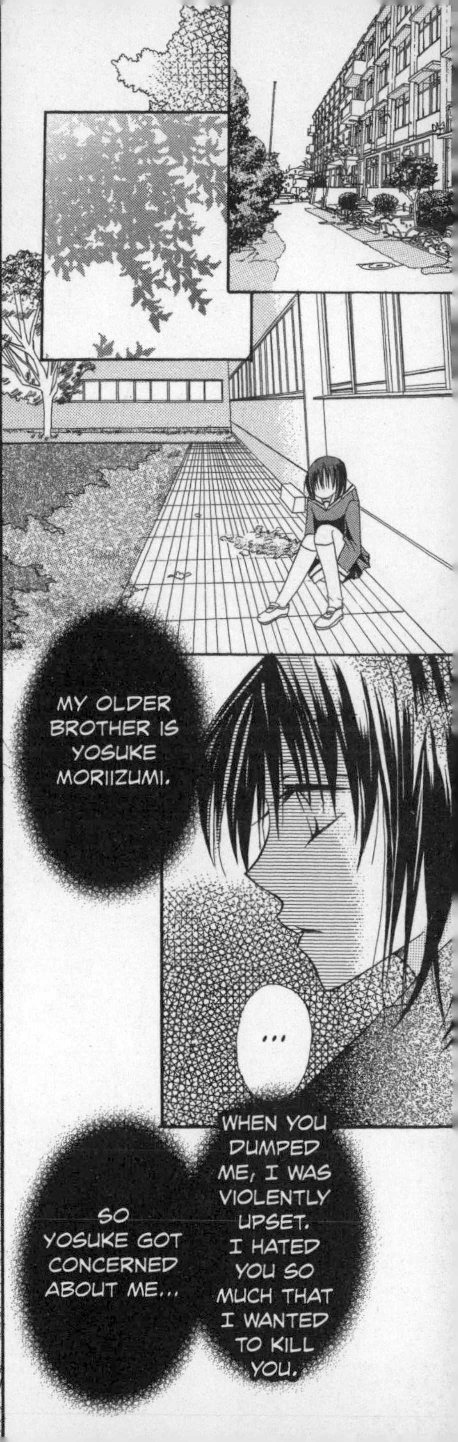
MY OLDER BROTHER IS YOSUKE MORIIZUMI.
...
WHEN YOU DUMPED ME, I WAS VIOLENTLY UPSET. I HATED YOU SO MUCH THAT I WANTED TO KILL YOU.
SO YOSUKE GOT CONCERNED ABOUT ME...

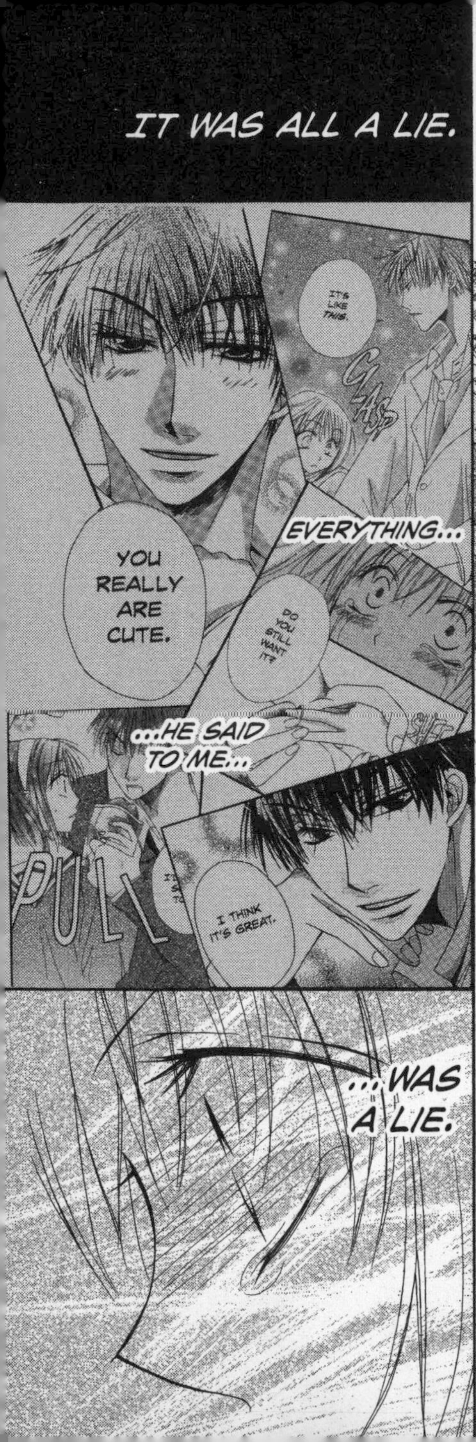
IT WAS ALL A LIE.
IT'S LIKE THIS.
CLASP
YOU REALLY ARE CUTE.
EVERYTHING...
DO YOU STILL WANT IT?
...HE SAID TO ME...
I THINK IT'S GREAT.
PULL
...WAS A LIE.

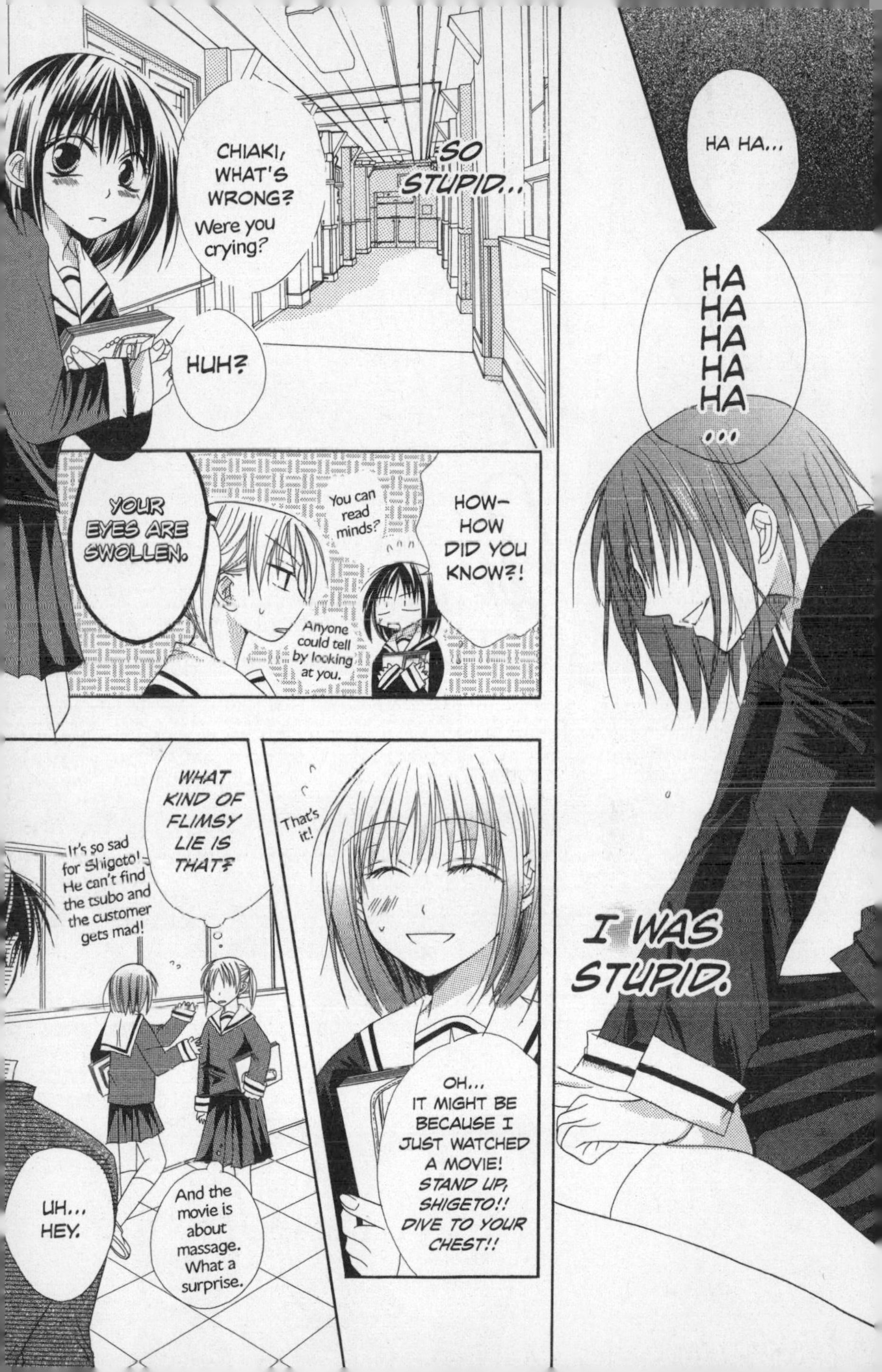
HA HA...
HA HA HA HA HA...
I WAS STUPID.
SO STUPID...
CHIAKI, WHAT'S WRONG? Were you crying?
HUH?
HOW-HOW DID YOU KNOW?!
You can read minds?
YOUR EYES ARE SWOLLEN.
Anyone could tell by looking at you.
That's it!
OH... IT MIGHT BE BECAUSE I JUST WATCHED A MOVIE! STAND UP, SHIGETO!! DIVE TO YOUR CHEST!!
WHAT KIND OF FLIMSY LIE IS THAT?
It's so sad for Shigeto! He can't find the tsubo and the customer gets mad!
And the movie is about massage. What a surprise.
UH... HEY.

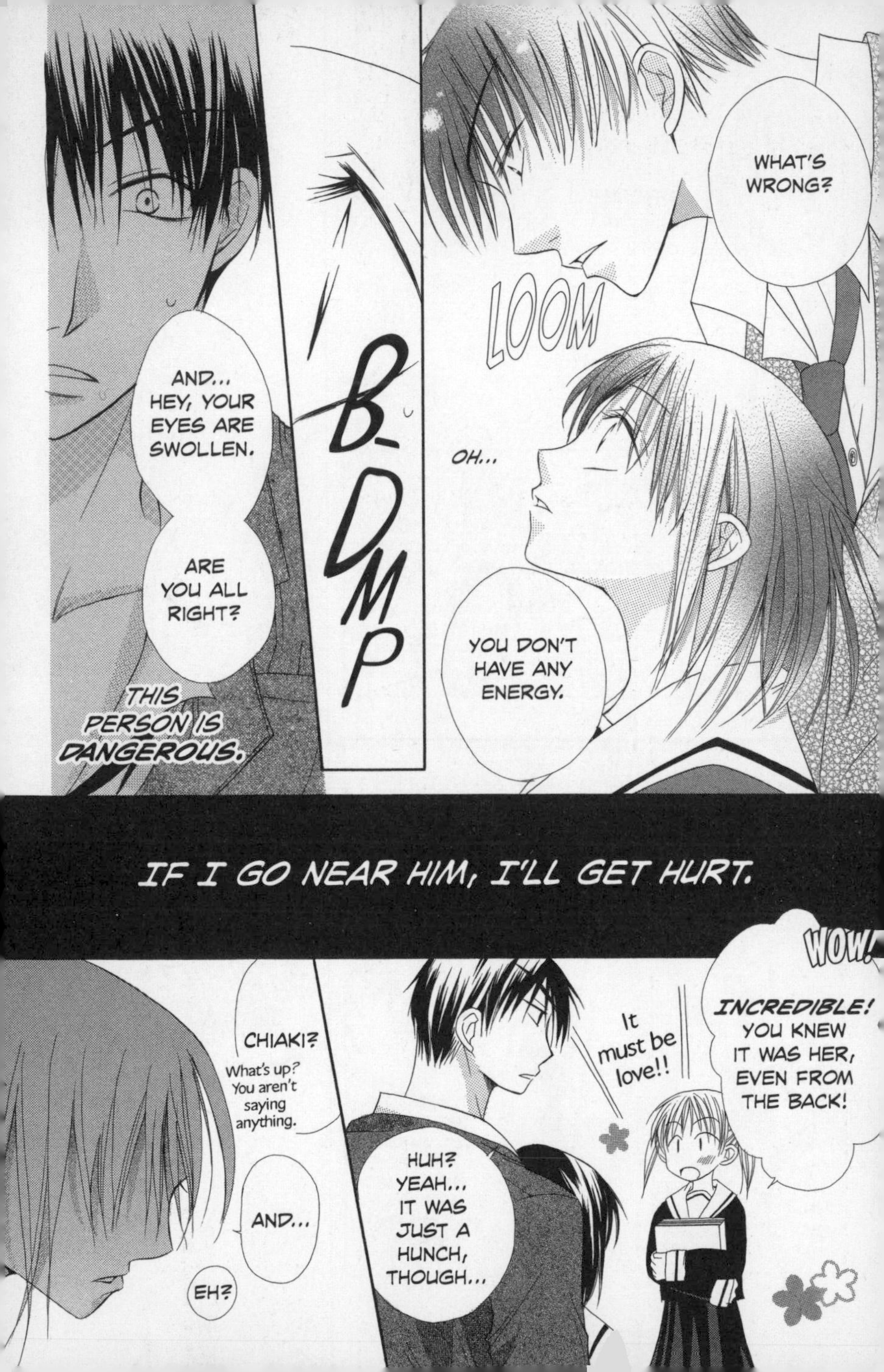
WHAT'S WRONG?
LOOM
OH...
YOU DON'T HAVE ANY ENERGY.
B-DMP
AND... HEY, YOUR EYES ARE SWOLLEN.
ARE YOU ALL RIGHT?
THIS PERSON IS DANGEROUS.
IF I GO NEAR HIM, I'LL GET HURT.
WOW!
INCREDIBLE! YOU KNEW IT WAS HER, EVEN FROM THE BACK!
It must be love!!
HUH? YEAH... IT WAS JUST A HUNCH, THOUGH...
CHIAKI?
What's up? You aren't saying anything.
AND...
EH?

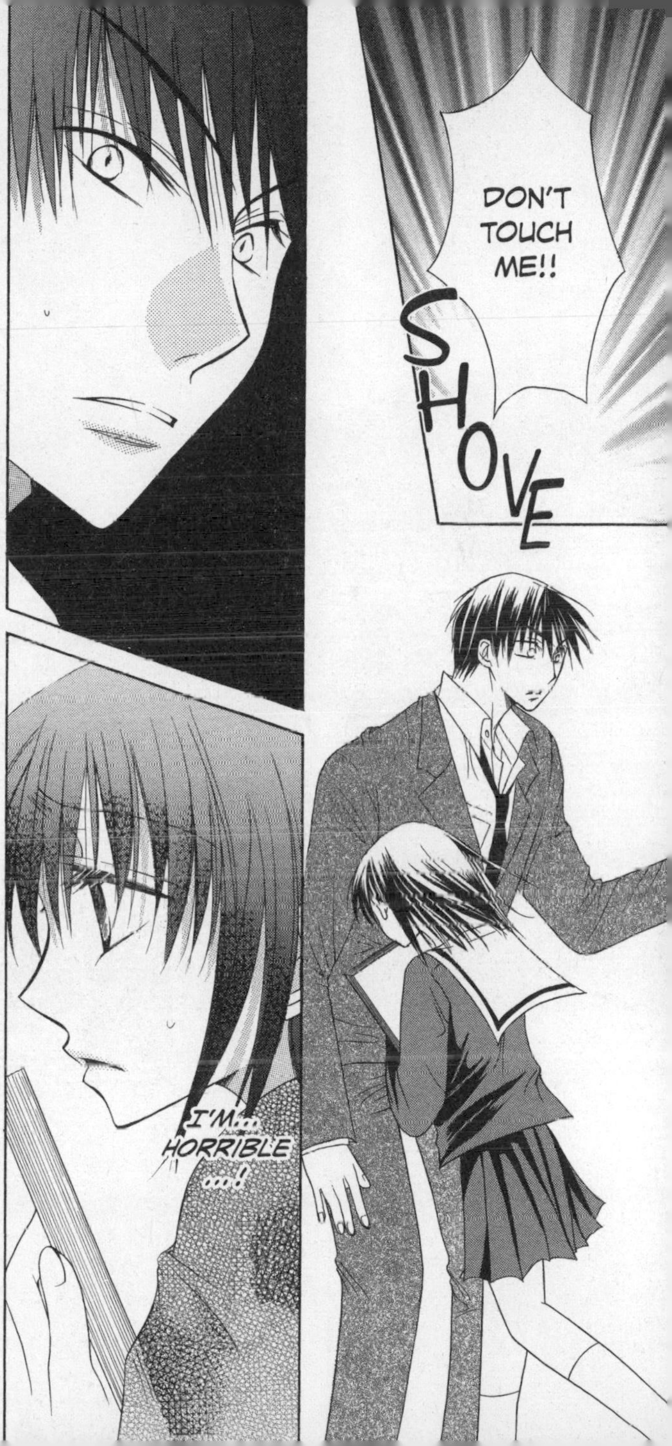
DON'T TOUCH ME!!
SHOVE
I'M... HORRIBLE ...!

Making the Manga, Part 1

<The Magic Touch>

Maybe because the hero in my previous series that won the award was plain, my editor asked me to draw a "handsome boy" when I was making this story. Wh-what's handsome? Since I had no clue about what meets the standard of "handsomeness" in our society, I thought, "I see!! A show-off!!" So that's how Yosuke started out.

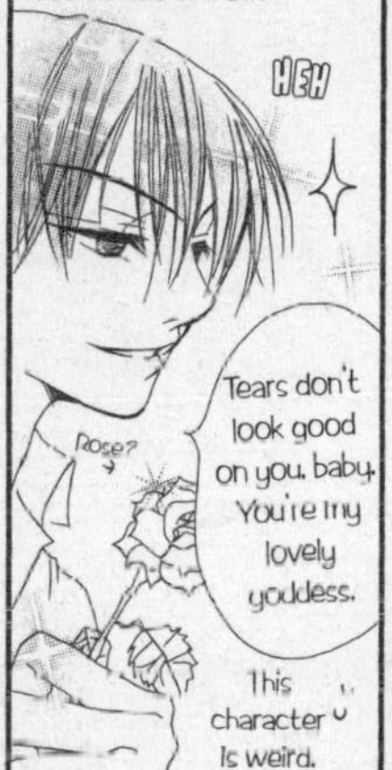
HEH
Rose?
Tears don't look good on you, baby. You're my lovely goddess.
This character is weird.

And then...

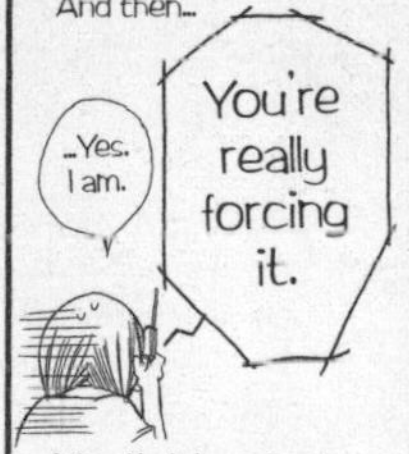
You're really forcing it.
...Yes. I am.

After that, I received a 30-minute lecture from my editor on what handsomeness is. And with that, today's Yosuke was born. I hope he looks handsome now.

I'M SORRY. I CAN'T PRETEND NOT TO KNOW.
I WANT TO BELIEVE. I WANT TO BELIEVE IN YOU, YOSUKE.
BUT I CAN'T...
...BECAUSE IT ALL MAKES TOO MUCH SENSE.
"IF YOU CAN MAKE ME FALL IN LOVE WITH YOU."
"WHY DO YOU THINK?"
"YOU IRRITATE ME."
THAT WAS THE STORY THEN...
AND...
...HE CHOSE SAYAKA.
HE CHOSE SAYAKA OVER ME.
THUMP
SAYAKA ...

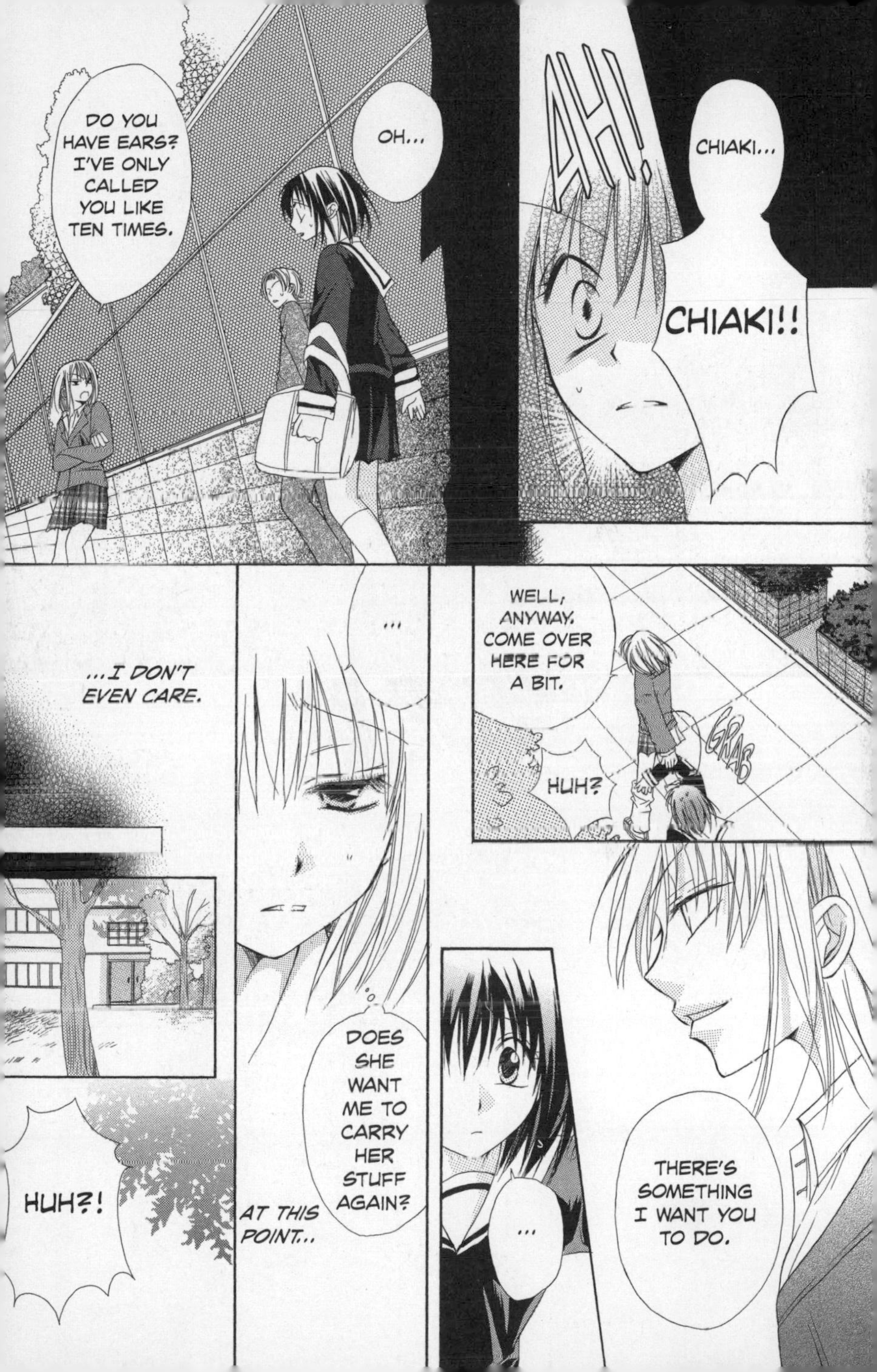
CHIAKI...
CHIAKI!!
AH!
OH...
DO YOU HAVE EARS? I'VE ONLY CALLED YOU LIKE TEN TIMES.
WELL, ANYWAY. COME OVER HERE FOR A BIT.
GRAB
HUH?
THERE'S SOMETHING I WANT YOU TO DO.
...
...
DOES SHE WANT ME TO CARRY HER STUFF AGAIN?
AT THIS POINT...
...I DON'T EVEN CARE.
HUH?!

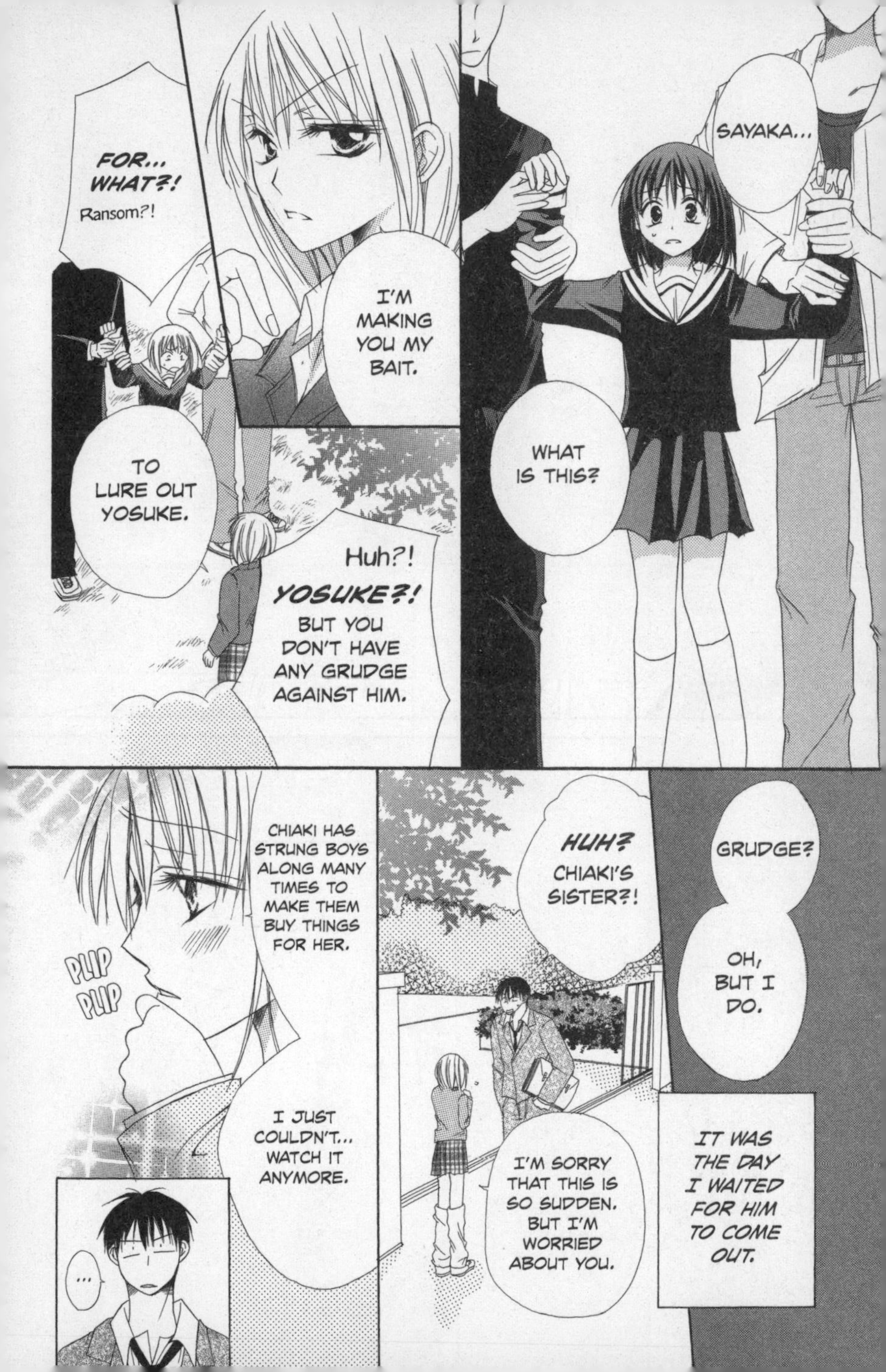
SAYAKA...
WHAT IS THIS?
FOR... WHAT?!
Ransom?!
I'M MAKING YOU MY BAIT.
TO LURE OUT YOSUKE.
Huh?!
YOSUKE?!
BUT YOU DON'T HAVE ANY GRUDGE AGAINST HIM.
GRUDGE?
OH, BUT I DO.
IT WAS THE DAY I WAITED FOR HIM TO COME OUT.
HUH? CHIAKI'S SISTER?!
I'M SORRY THAT THIS IS SO SUDDEN. BUT I'M WORRIED ABOUT YOU.
CHIAKI HAS STRUNG BOYS ALONG MANY TIMES TO MAKE THEM BUY THINGS FOR HER.
PLIP PLIP
I JUST COULDN'T... WATCH IT ANYMORE.
...

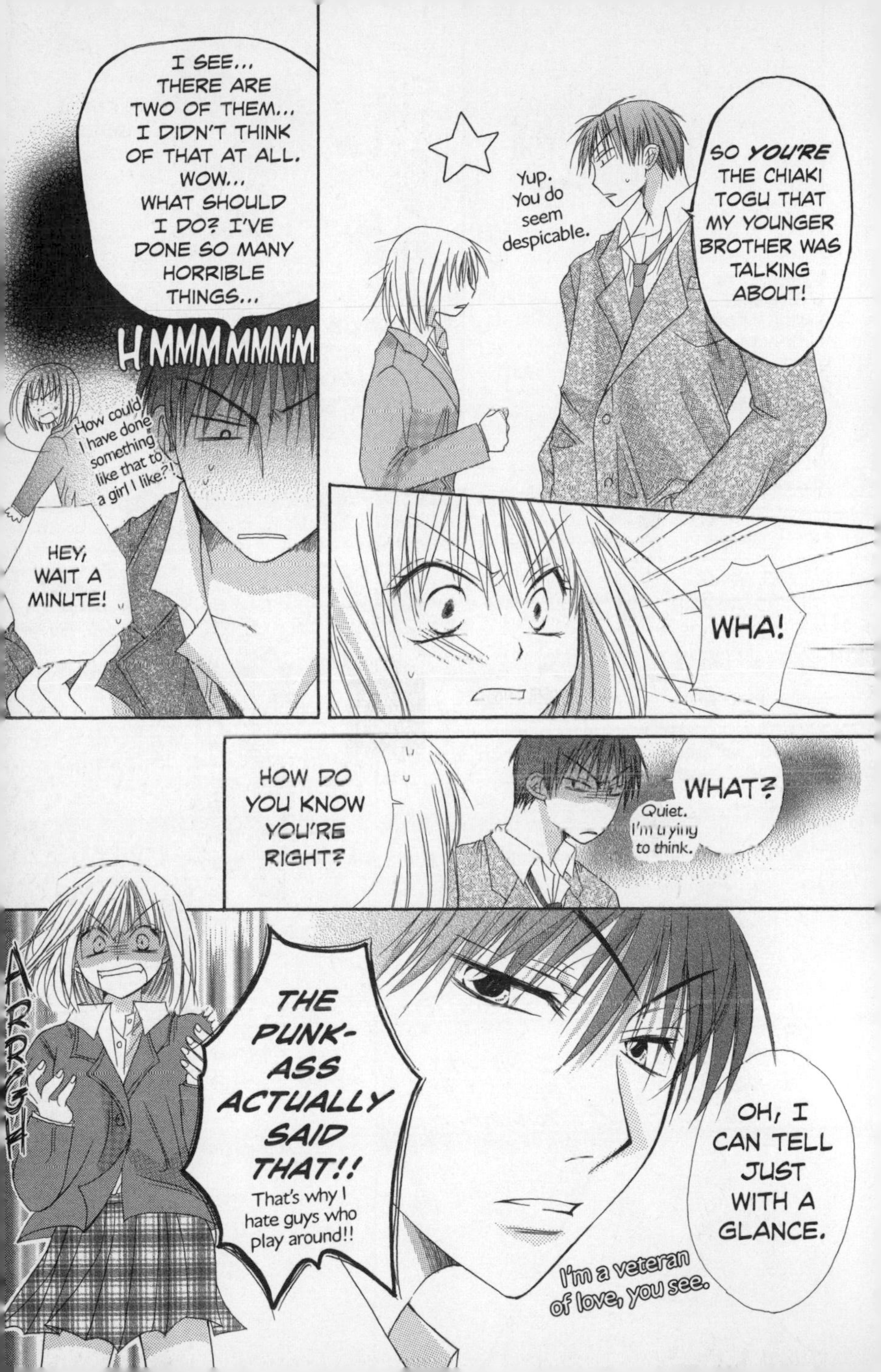
SO YOU'RE THE CHIAKI TOGU THAT MY YOUNGER BROTHER WAS TALKING ABOUT!
Yup. You do seem despicable.
WHA!
I SEE... THERE ARE TWO OF THEM... I DIDN'T THINK OF THAT AT ALL. WOW... WHAT SHOULD I DO? I'VE DONE SO MANY HORRIBLE THINGS...
H MMM MMMM
How could I have done something like that to a girl I like?!
HEY, WAIT A MINUTE!
WHAT?
Quiet. I'm trying to think.
HOW DO YOU KNOW YOU'RE RIGHT?
OH, I CAN TELL JUST WITH A GLANCE.
I'm a veteran of love, you see.
THE PUNK-ASS ACTUALLY SAID THAT!!
That's why I hate guys who play around!!
ARRGH

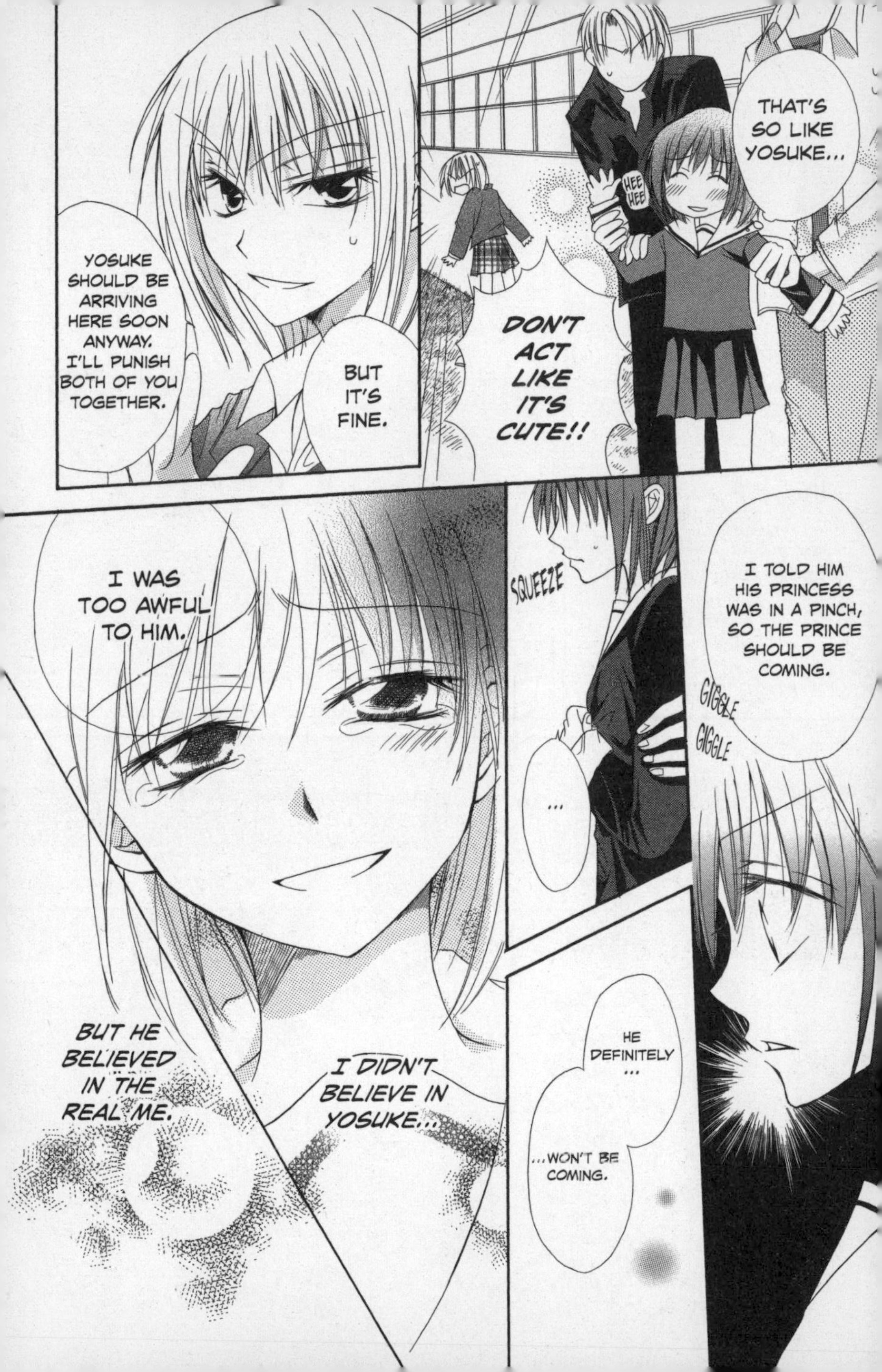
THAT'S SO LIKE YOSUKE...
HEE HEE
DON'T ACT LIKE IT'S CUTE!!
BUT IT'S FINE.
YOSUKE SHOULD BE ARRIVING HERE SOON ANYWAY. I'LL PUNISH BOTH OF YOU TOGETHER.
I TOLD HIM HIS PRINCESS WAS IN A PINCH, SO THE PRINCE SHOULD BE COMING.
GIGGLE GIGGLE
SQUEEZE
...
HE DEFINITELY...
...WON'T BE COMING.
I WAS TOO AWFUL TO HIM.
I DIDN'T BELIEVE IN YOSUKE...
BUT HE BELIEVED IN THE REAL ME.

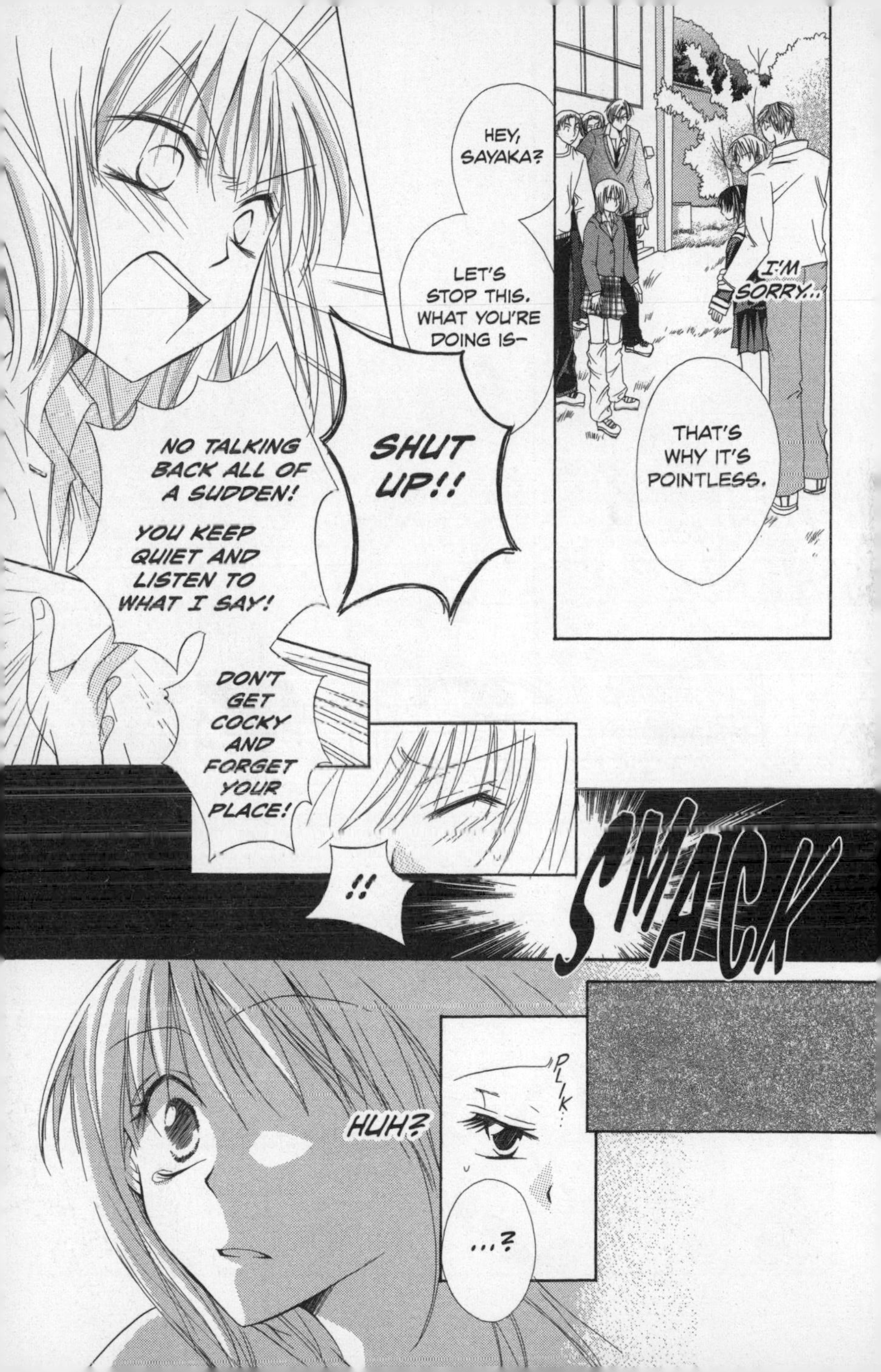
I'M SORRY...
THAT'S WHY IT'S POINTLESS.
HEY, SAYAKA?
LET'S STOP THIS. WHAT YOU'RE DOING IS–
SHUT UP!!
NO TALKING BACK ALL OF A SUDDEN!
YOU KEEP QUIET AND LISTEN TO WHAT I SAY!
DON'T GET COCKY AND FORGET YOUR PLACE!
!!
SMACK
PLIK..
...?
HUH?

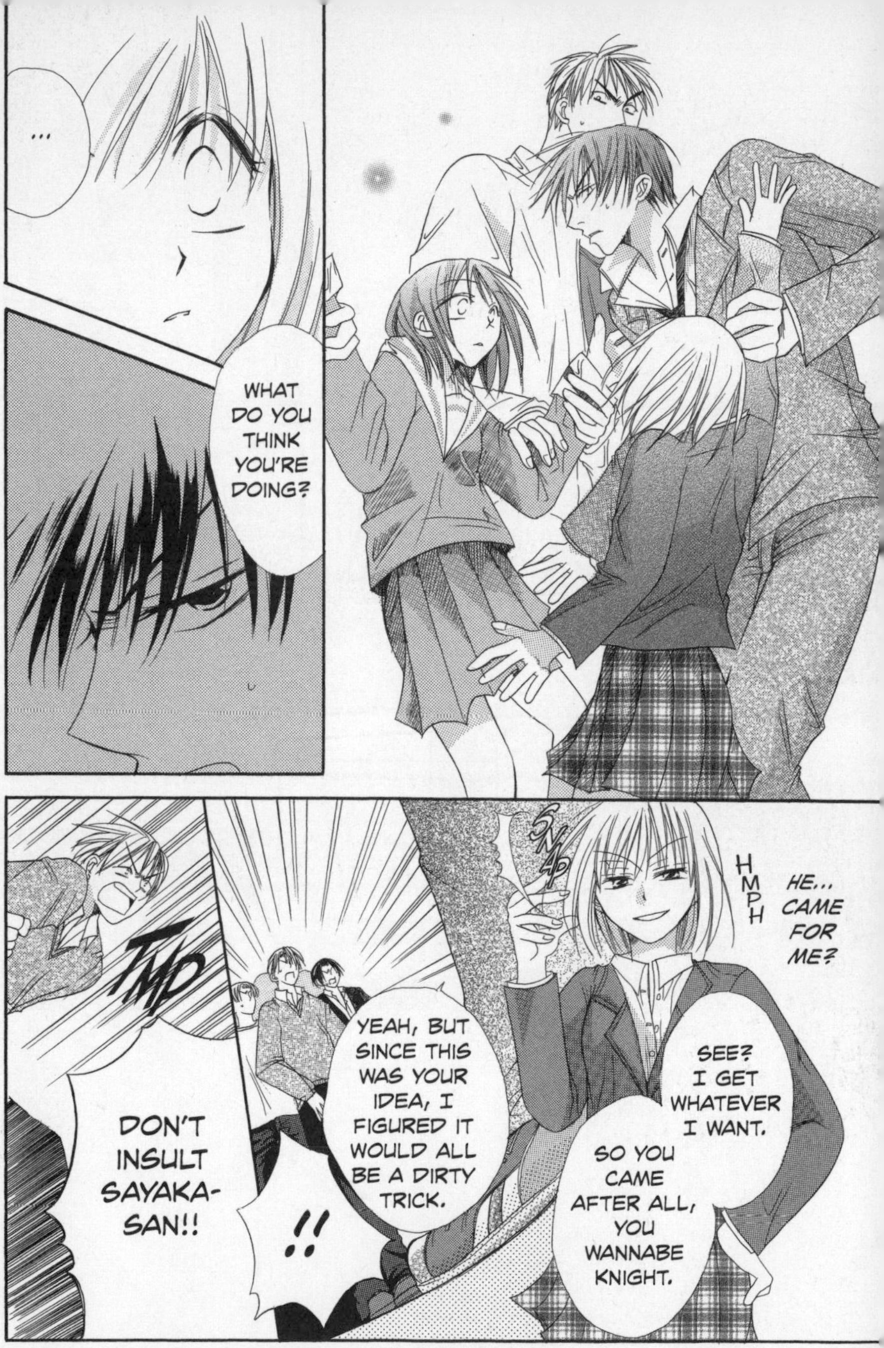
...
WHAT DO YOU THINK YOU'RE DOING?
SNAP
HMPH
HE... CAME FOR ME?
SEE? I GET WHATEVER I WANT.
SO YOU CAME AFTER ALL, YOU WANNABE KNIGHT.
YEAH, BUT SINCE THIS WAS YOUR IDEA, I FIGURED IT WOULD ALL BE A DIRTY TRICK.
!!
TMP
DON'T INSULT SAYAKA-SAN!!

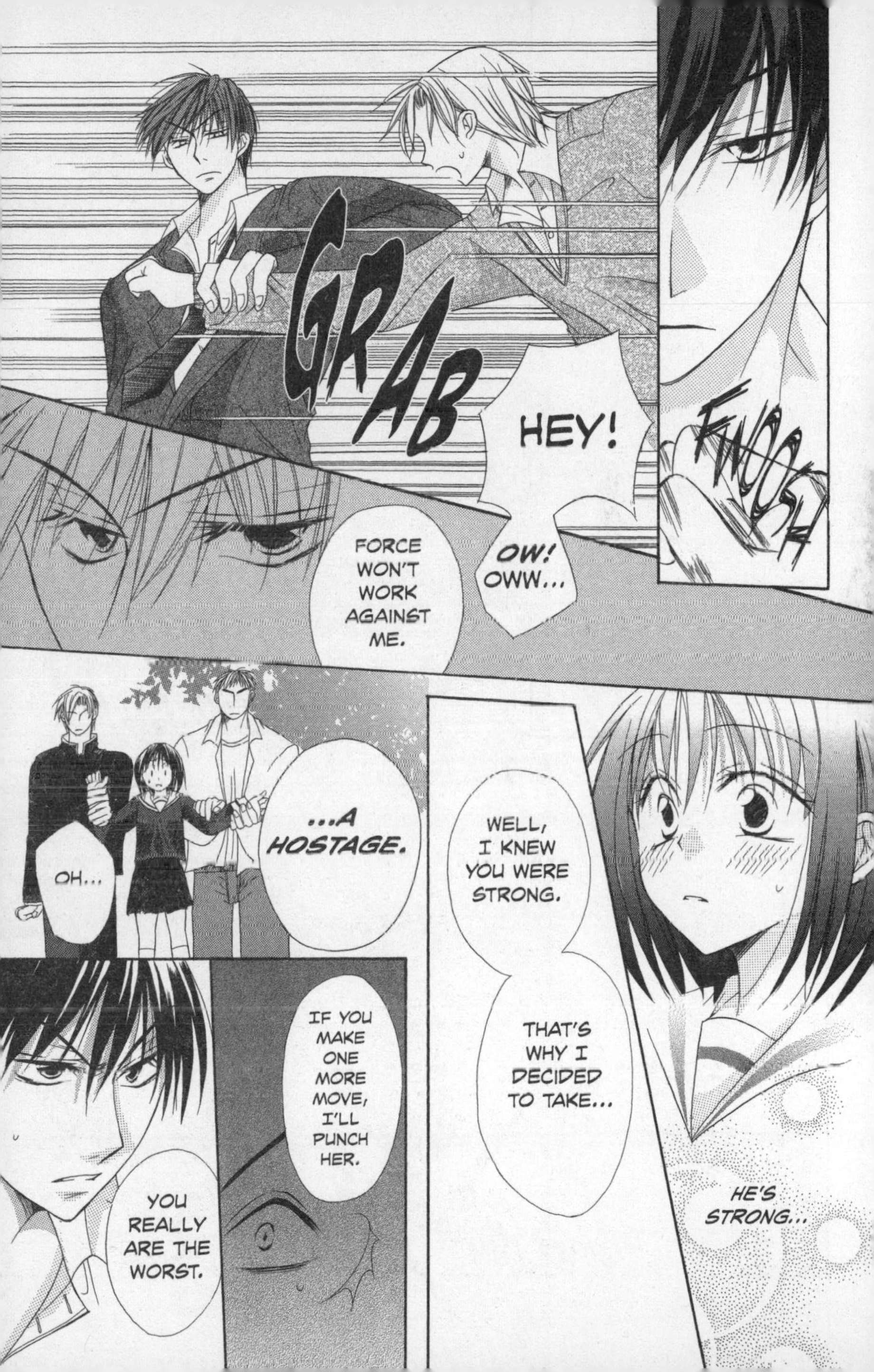
FWOOSH
GRAB
HEY!
OW! OWW...
FORCE WON'T WORK AGAINST ME.
WELL, I KNEW YOU WERE STRONG.
THAT'S WHY I DECIDED TO TAKE...
HE'S STRONG...
...A HOSTAGE.
OH...
IF YOU MAKE ONE MORE MOVE, I'LL PUNCH HER.
YOU REALLY ARE THE WORST.

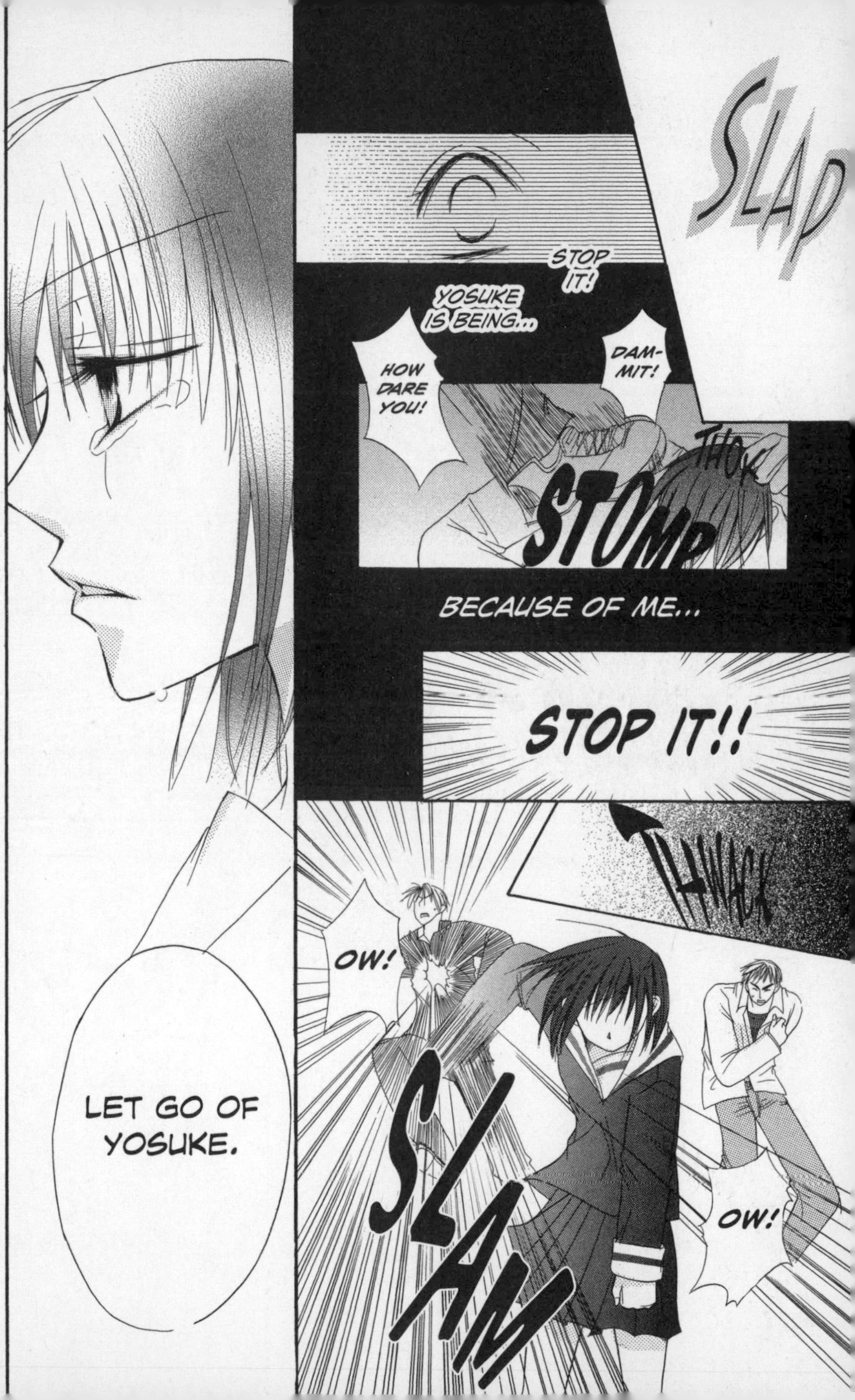
SLAP
STOP IT!
YOSUKE IS BEING...
DAM-MIT!
HOW DARE YOU!
THOK
STOMP
BECAUSE OF ME...
STOP IT!!
THWACK
OW!
SLAM
OW!
LET GO OF YOSUKE.

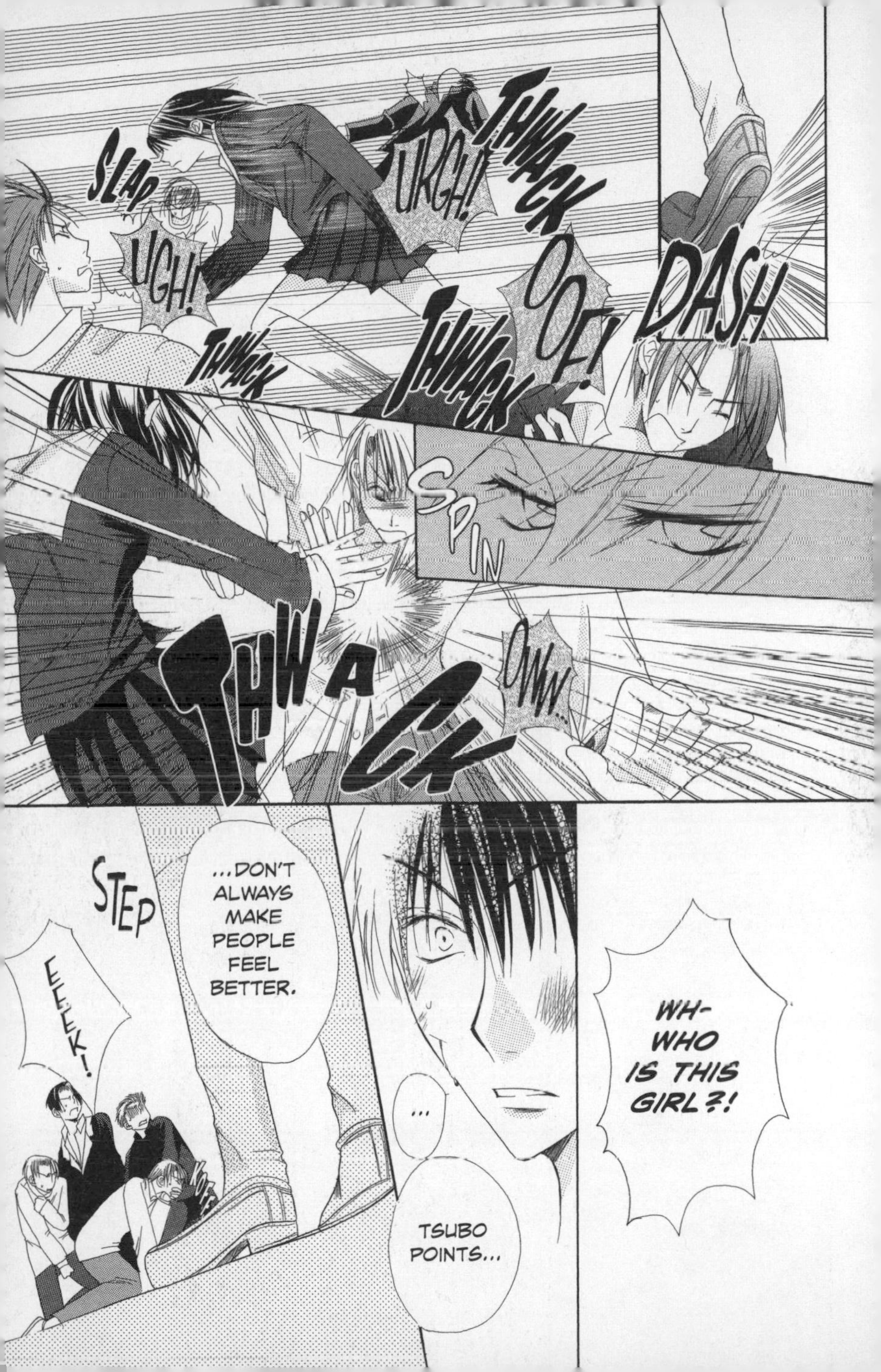
DASH
THWACK
URGH!
SLAP
UGH!
OOF!
THWACK
THWACK
SPIN
THWACK
OWW...
WH-WHO IS THIS GIRL?!
...
TSUBO POINTS...
...DON'T ALWAYS MAKE PEOPLE FEEL BETTER.
STEP
EEEEK!

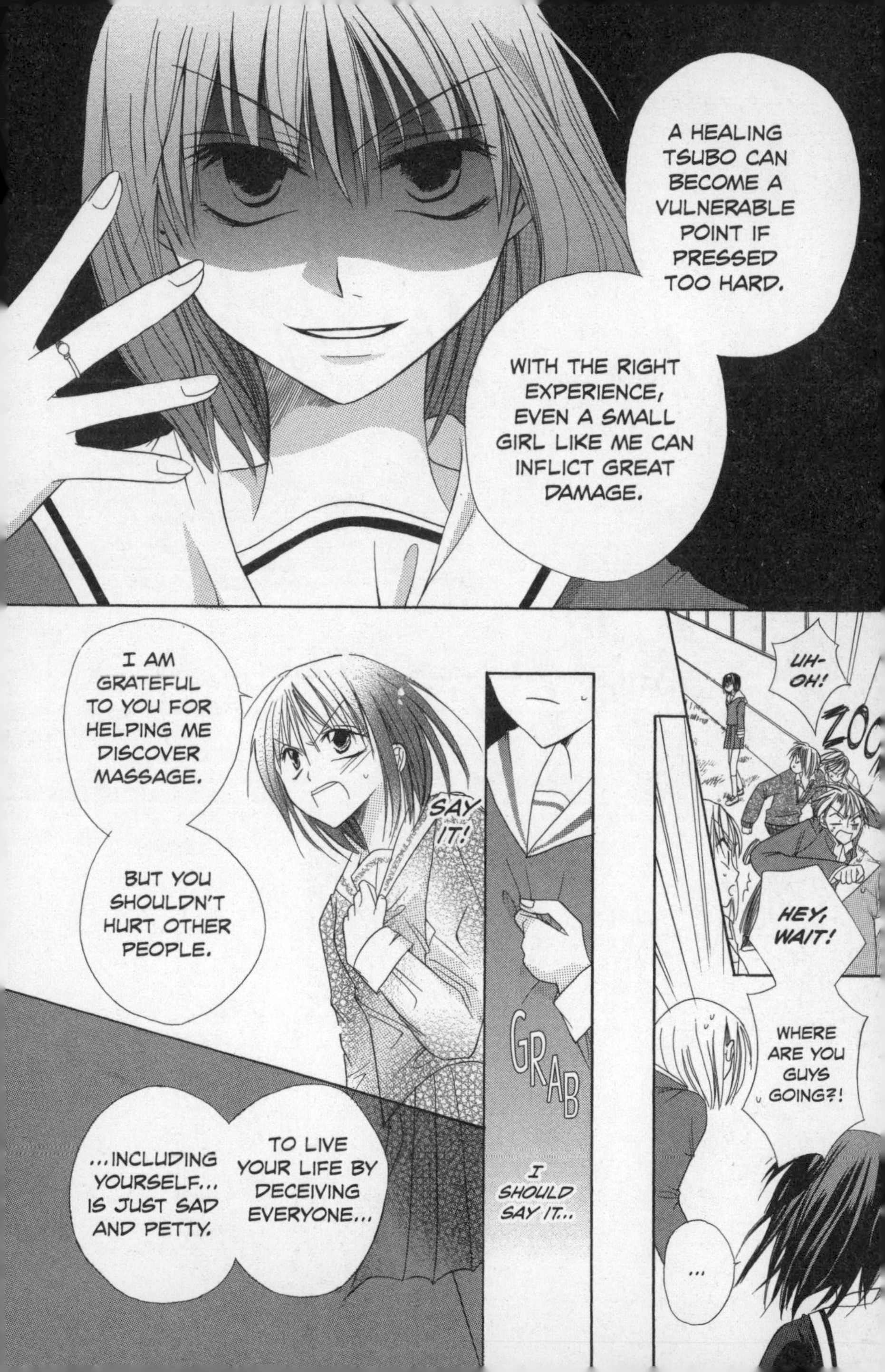
A HEALING TSUBO CAN BECOME A VULNERABLE POINT IF PRESSED TOO HARD.
WITH THE RIGHT EXPERIENCE, EVEN A SMALL GIRL LIKE ME CAN INFLICT GREAT DAMAGE.
UH-OH!
ZOO
HEY, WAIT!
WHERE ARE YOU GUYS GOING?!
...
GRAB
I SHOULD SAY IT...
SAY IT!
I AM GRATEFUL TO YOU FOR HELPING ME DISCOVER MASSAGE.
BUT YOU SHOULDN'T HURT OTHER PEOPLE.
TO LIVE YOUR LIFE BY DECEIVING EVERYONE...
...INCLUDING YOURSELF... IS JUST SAD AND PETTY.

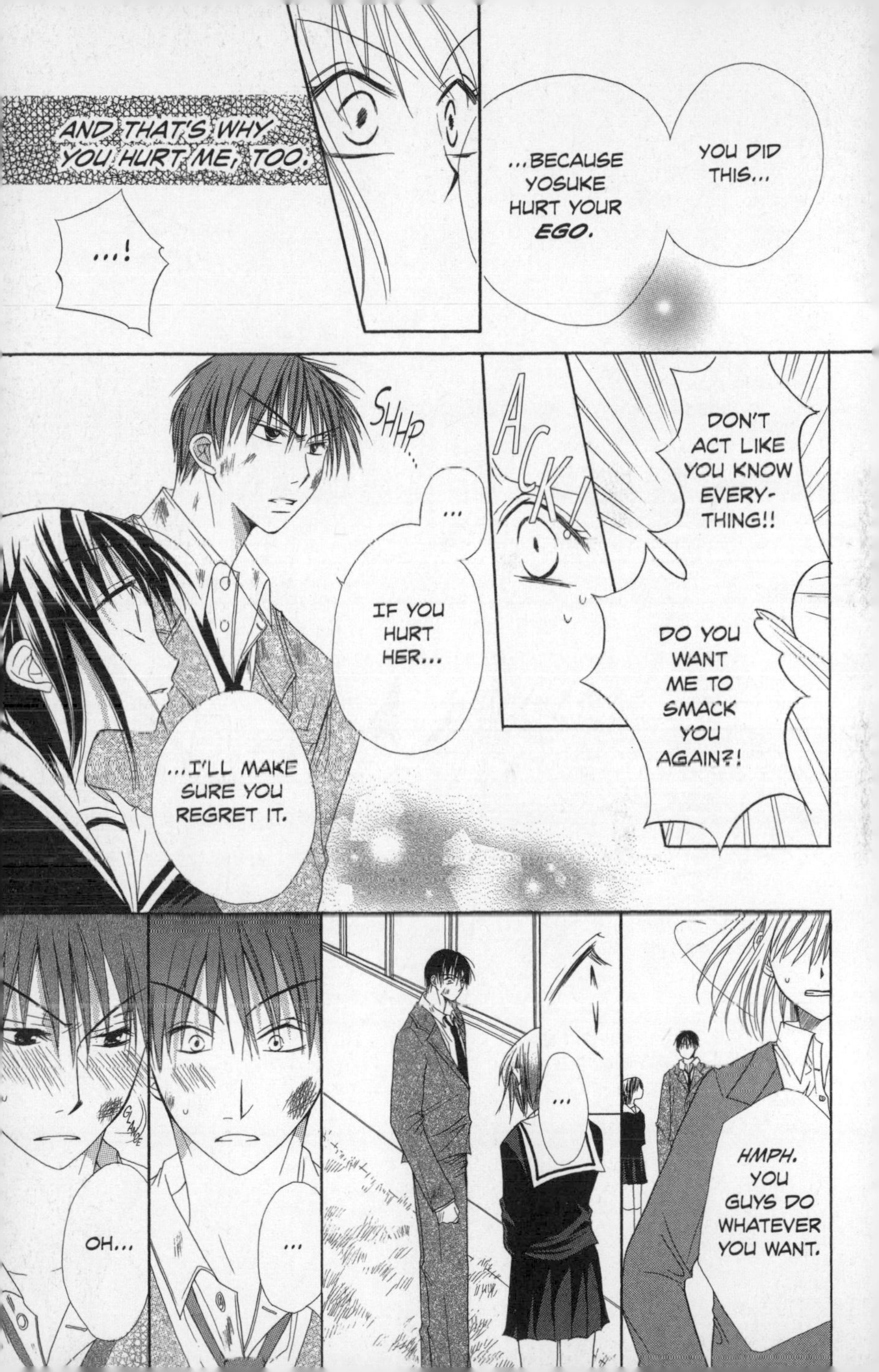
YOU DID THIS...
...BECAUSE YOSUKE HURT YOUR EGO.
AND THAT'S WHY YOU HURT ME, TOO.
...!
ACK!
DON'T ACT LIKE YOU KNOW EVERY-THING!!
DO YOU WANT ME TO SMACK YOU AGAIN?!
SHHP...
...
IF YOU HURT HER...
...I'LL MAKE SURE YOU REGRET IT.
HMPH. YOU GUYS DO WHATEVER YOU WANT.
...
...
GLANCE
OH...

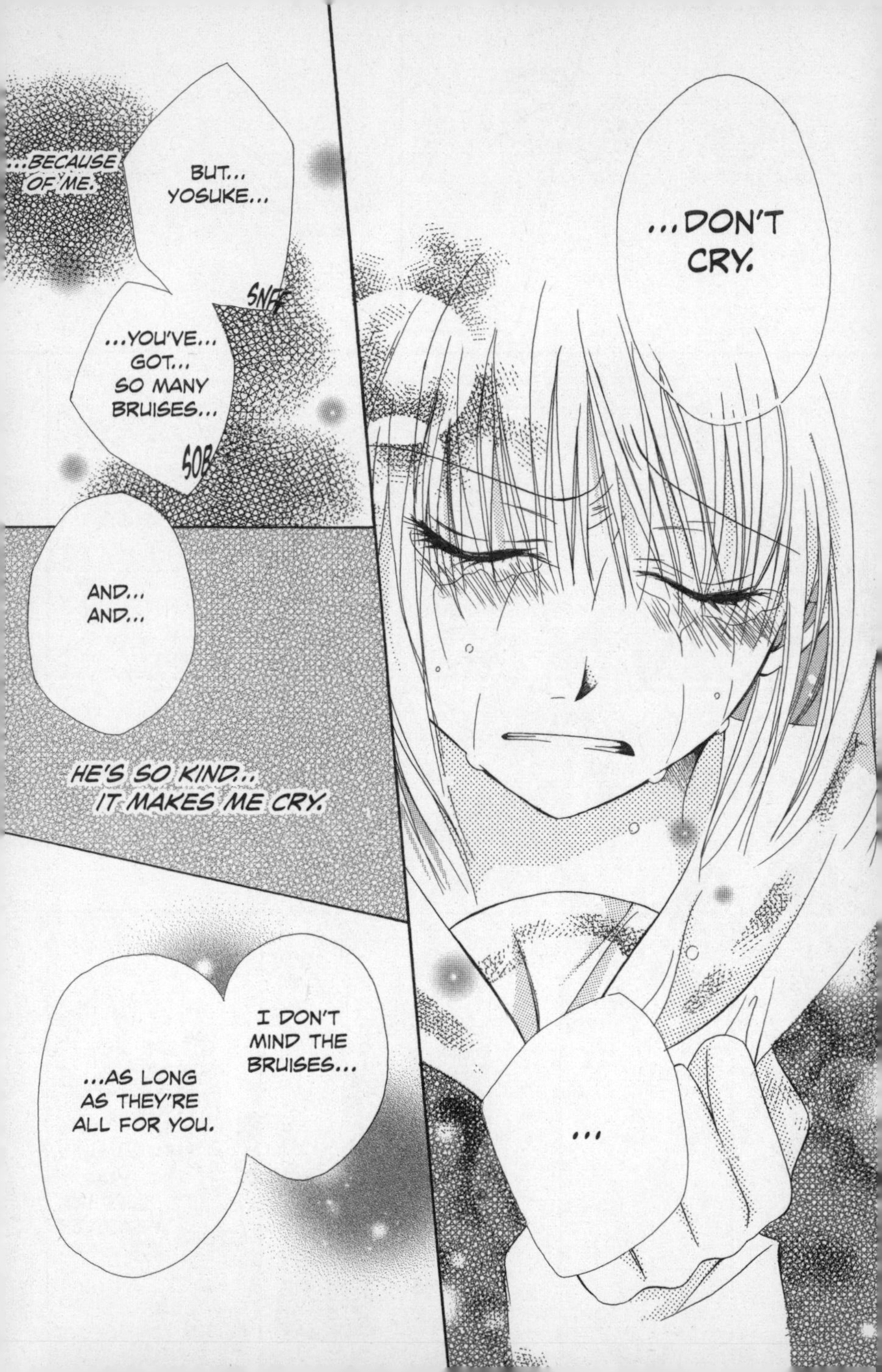
...DON'T CRY.
...
BUT... YOSUKE...
...BECAUSE OF ME.
SNFF
...YOU'VE... GOT... SO MANY BRUISES...
SOB
AND... AND...
HE'S SO KIND... IT MAKES ME CRY.
I DON'T MIND THE BRUISES...
...AS LONG AS THEY'RE ALL FOR YOU.

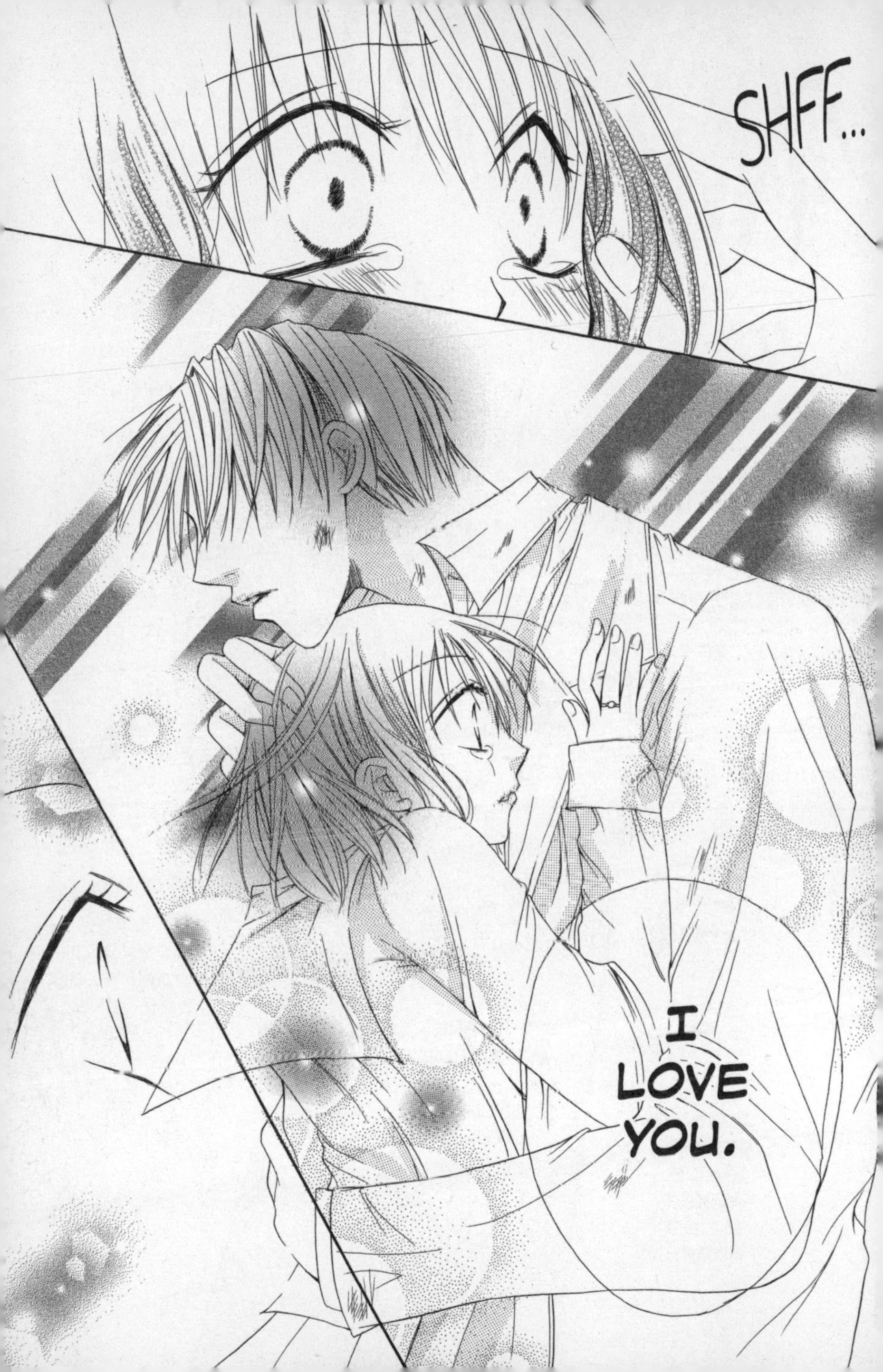
SHFF...
I LOVE YOU.

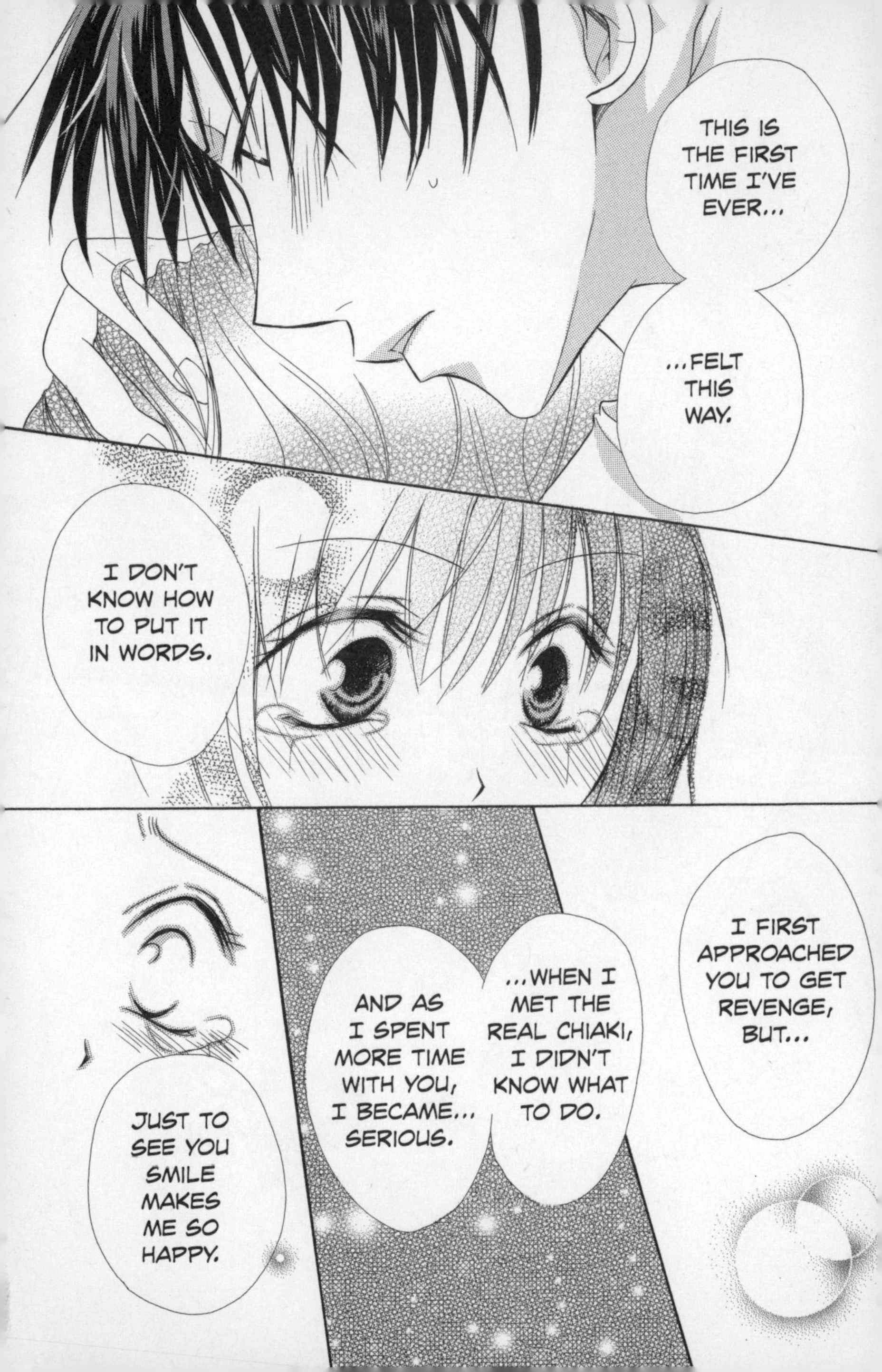
THIS IS THE FIRST TIME I'VE EVER...
...FELT THIS WAY.
I DON'T KNOW HOW TO PUT IT IN WORDS.
I FIRST APPROACHED YOU TO GET REVENGE, BUT...
...WHEN I MET THE REAL CHIAKI, I DIDN'T KNOW WHAT TO DO.
AND AS I SPENT MORE TIME WITH YOU, I BECAME... SERIOUS.
JUST TO SEE YOU SMILE MAKES ME SO HAPPY.

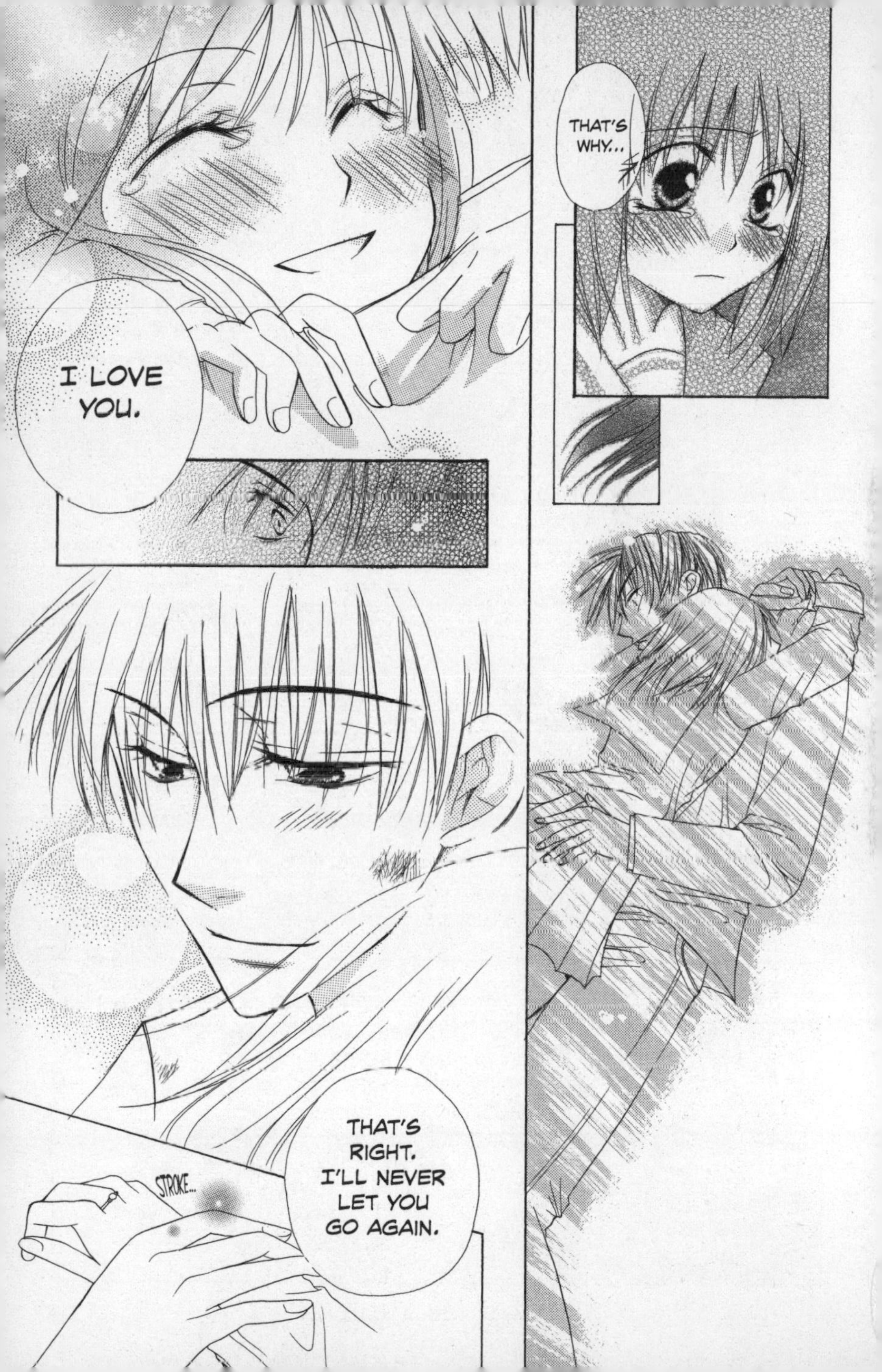
THAT'S WHY...
I LOVE YOU.
THAT'S RIGHT. I'LL NEVER LET YOU GO AGAIN.
STROKE...

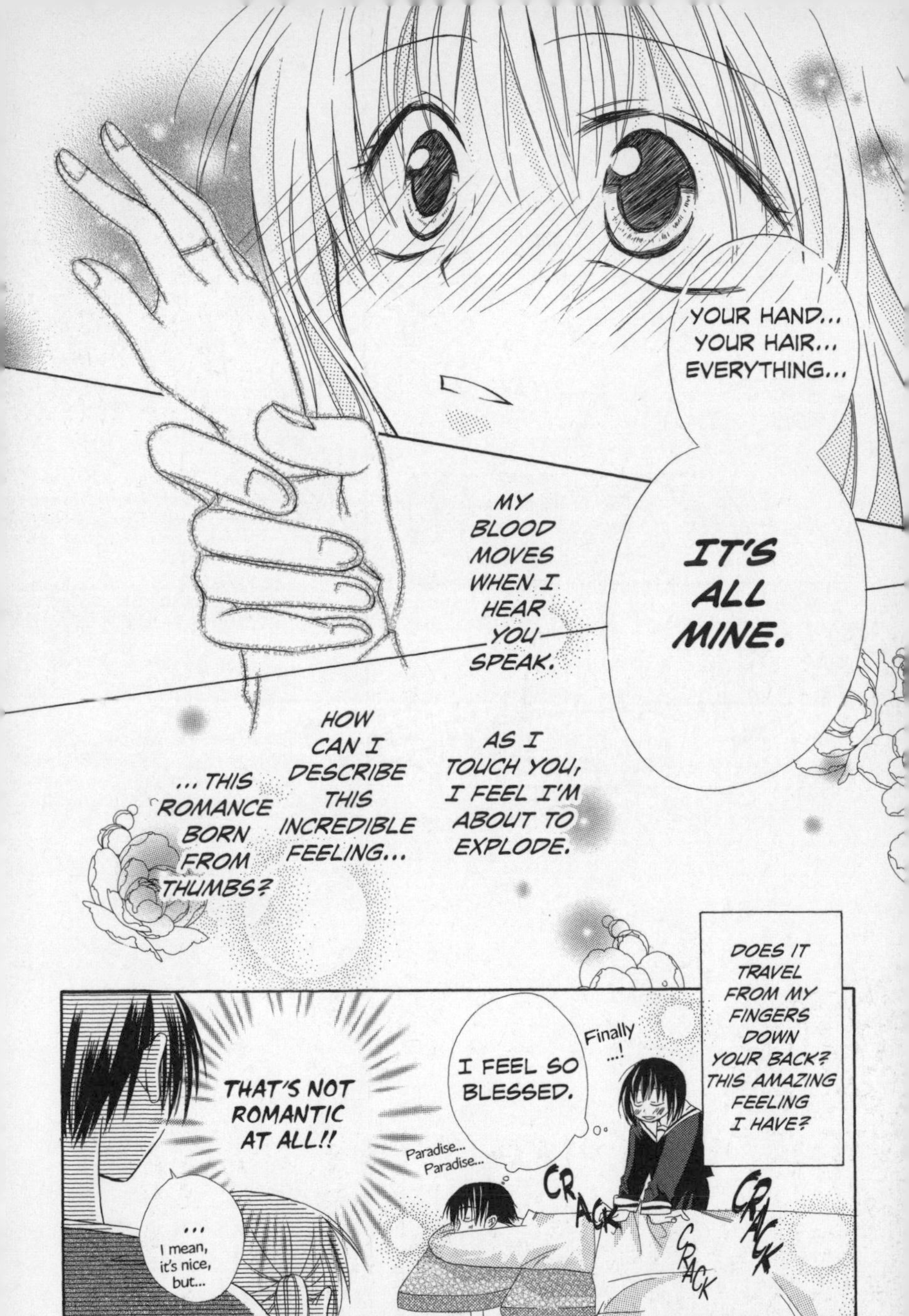
YOUR HAND... YOUR HAIR... EVERYTHING...
IT'S ALL MINE.
MY BLOOD MOVES WHEN I HEAR YOU SPEAK.
AS I TOUCH YOU, I FEEL I'M ABOUT TO EXPLODE.
HOW CAN I DESCRIBE THIS INCREDIBLE FEELING...
...THIS ROMANCE BORN FROM THUMBS?
DOES IT TRAVEL FROM MY FINGERS DOWN YOUR BACK? THIS AMAZING FEELING I HAVE?
Finally ...!
I FEEL SO BLESSED.
CRACK
CRACK
CRACK
Paradise... Paradise...
THAT'S NOT ROMANTIC AT ALL!!
... I mean, it's nice, but...

The Magic Touch, Part 3 / End

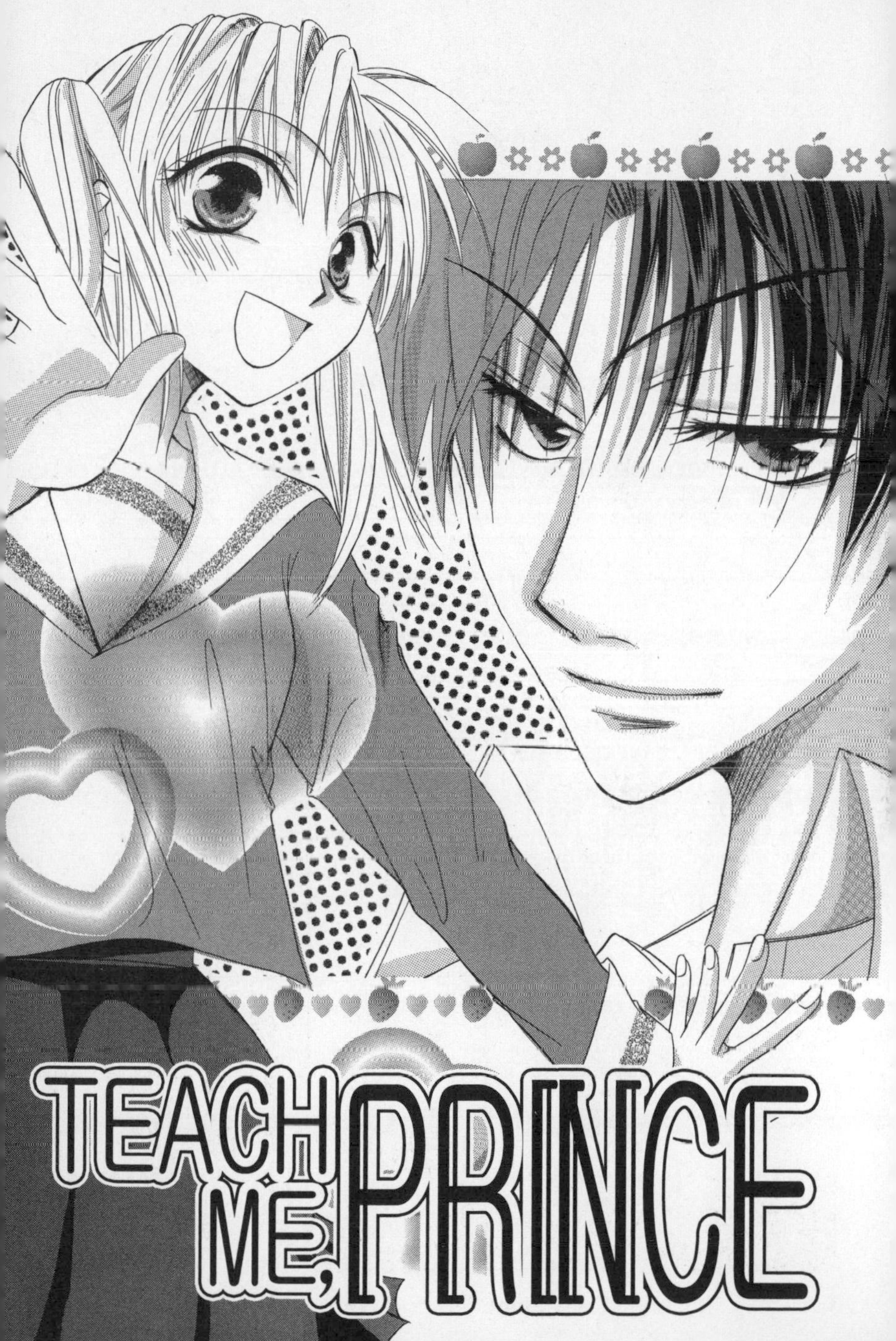
TEACH ME, PRINCE

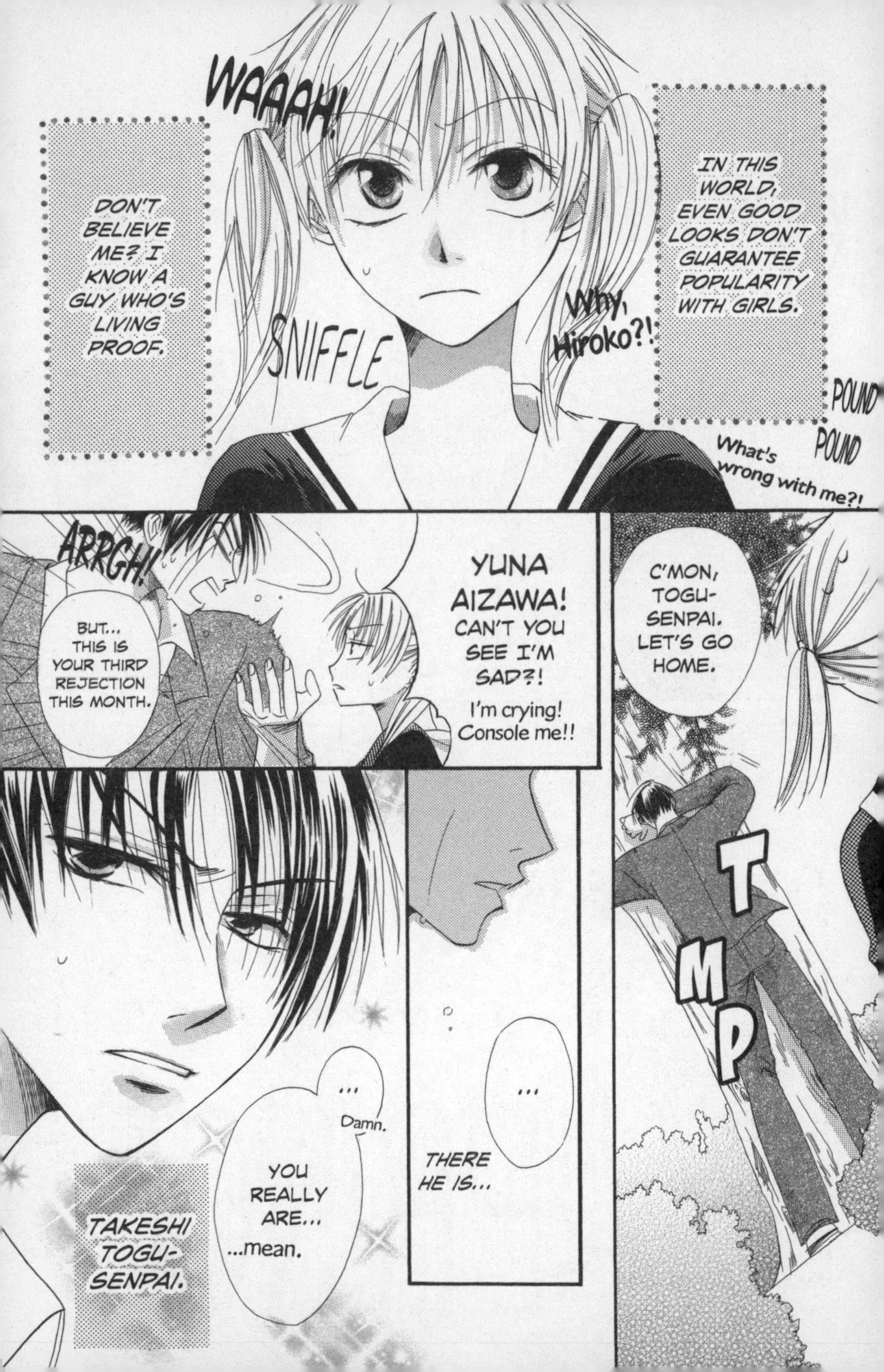
IN THIS WORLD, EVEN GOOD LOOKS DON'T GUARANTEE POPULARITY WITH GIRLS.
POUND
POUND
What's wrong with me?!
Why, Hiroko?!
SNIFFLE
WAAAH!
DON'T BELIEVE ME? I KNOW A GUY WHO'S LIVING PROOF.
C'MON, TOGU-SENPAI. LET'S GO HOME.
TMP
YUNA AIZAWA! CAN'T YOU SEE I'M SAD?!
I'm crying! Console me!!
ARRGH!
BUT... THIS IS YOUR THIRD REJECTION THIS MONTH.
...
THERE HE IS...
...
Damn.
YOU REALLY ARE...
...mean.
TAKESHI TOGU-SENPAI.

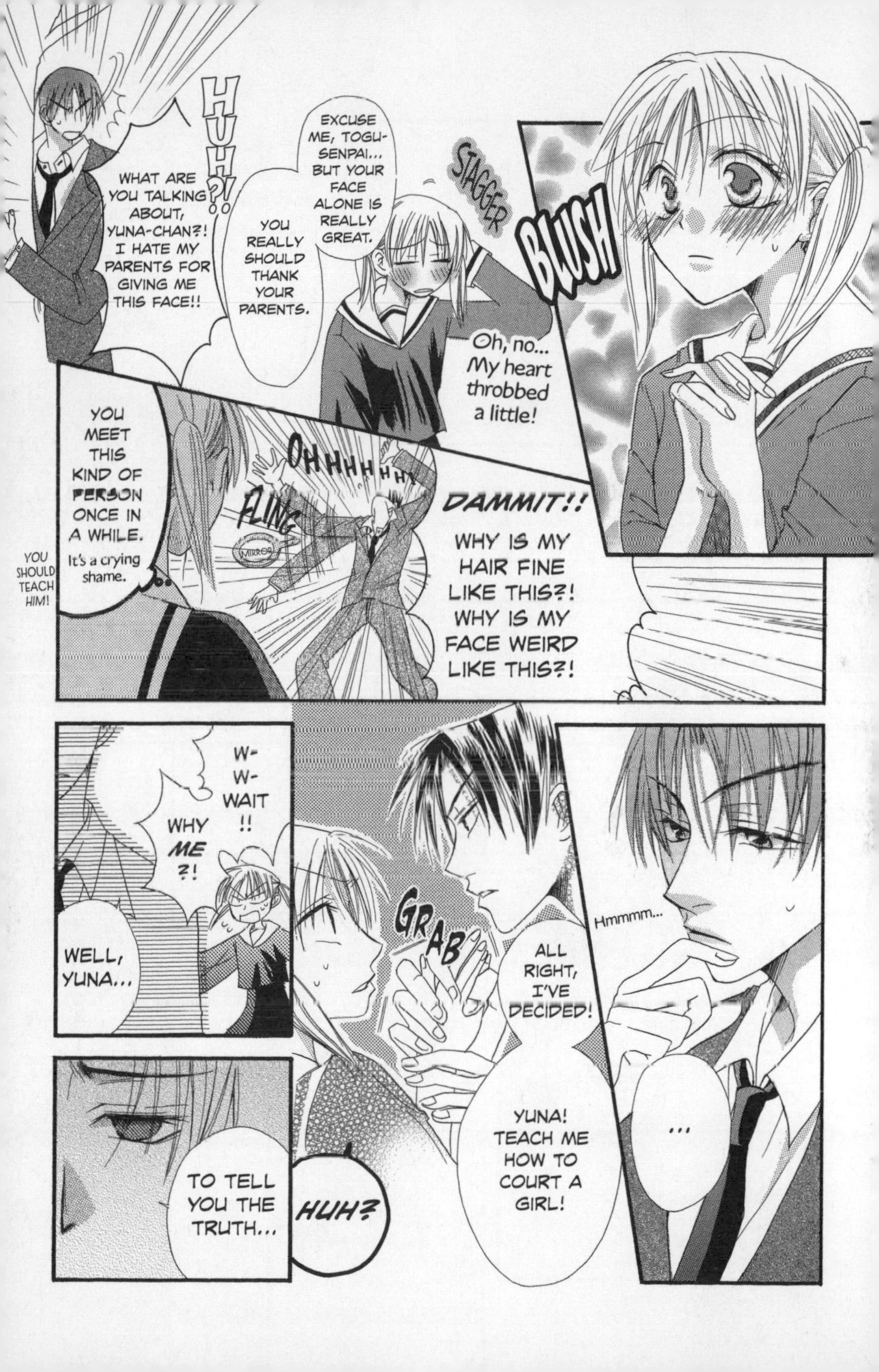
STAGGER
BLUSH
Oh, no... My heart throbbed a little!
EXCUSE ME, TOGU-SENPAI... BUT YOUR FACE ALONE IS REALLY GREAT.
YOU REALLY SHOULD THANK YOUR PARENTS.
HUH?!
WHAT ARE YOU TALKING ABOUT, YUNA-CHAN?! I HATE MY PARENTS FOR GIVING ME THIS FACE!!
DAMMIT!!
WHY IS MY HAIR FINE LIKE THIS?! WHY IS MY FACE WEIRD LIKE THIS?!
OHHHHHHH
FLING
MIRROR
YOU MEET THIS KIND OF PERSON ONCE IN A WHILE.
It's a crying shame.
YOU SHOULD TEACH HIM!
Hmmmm...
...
ALL RIGHT, I'VE DECIDED!
GRAB
YUNA! TEACH ME HOW TO COURT A GIRL!
W-W-WAIT!!
WHY ME?!
WELL, YUNA...
HUH?
TO TELL YOU THE TRUTH...

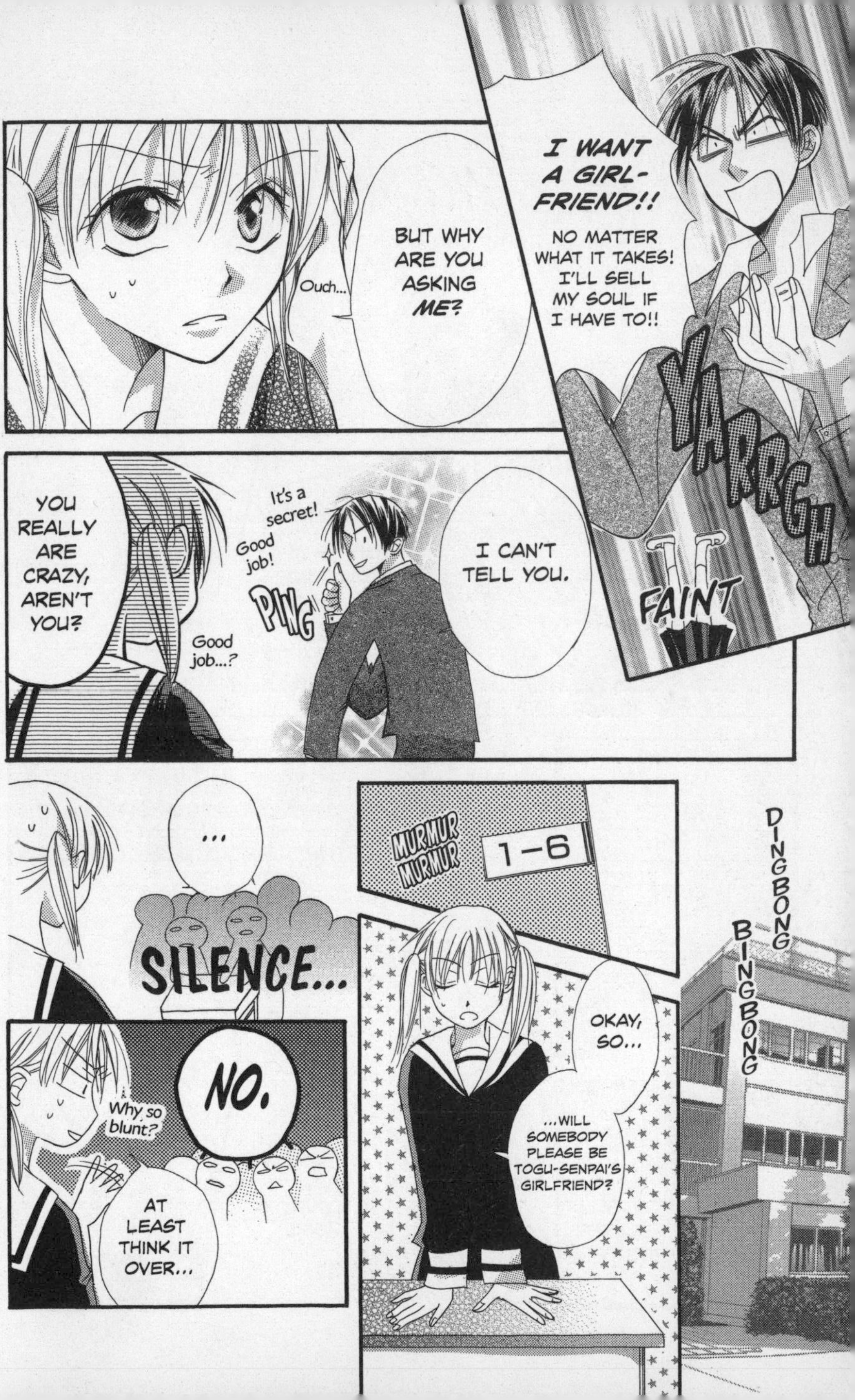
I WANT A GIRL-FRIEND!!
NO MATTER WHAT IT TAKES! I'LL SELL MY SOUL IF I HAVE TO!!
YARRGH
FAINT
BUT WHY ARE YOU ASKING ME?
Ouch...
I CAN'T TELL YOU.
It's a secret!
Good job!
PING
YOU REALLY ARE CRAZY, AREN'T YOU?
Good job...?
DINGBONG
BINGBONG
MURMUR MURMUR
1-6
OKAY, SO...
...WILL SOMEBODY PLEASE BE TOGU-SENPAI'S GIRLFRIEND?
...
SILENCE...
NO.
Why so blunt?
AT LEAST THINK IT OVER...

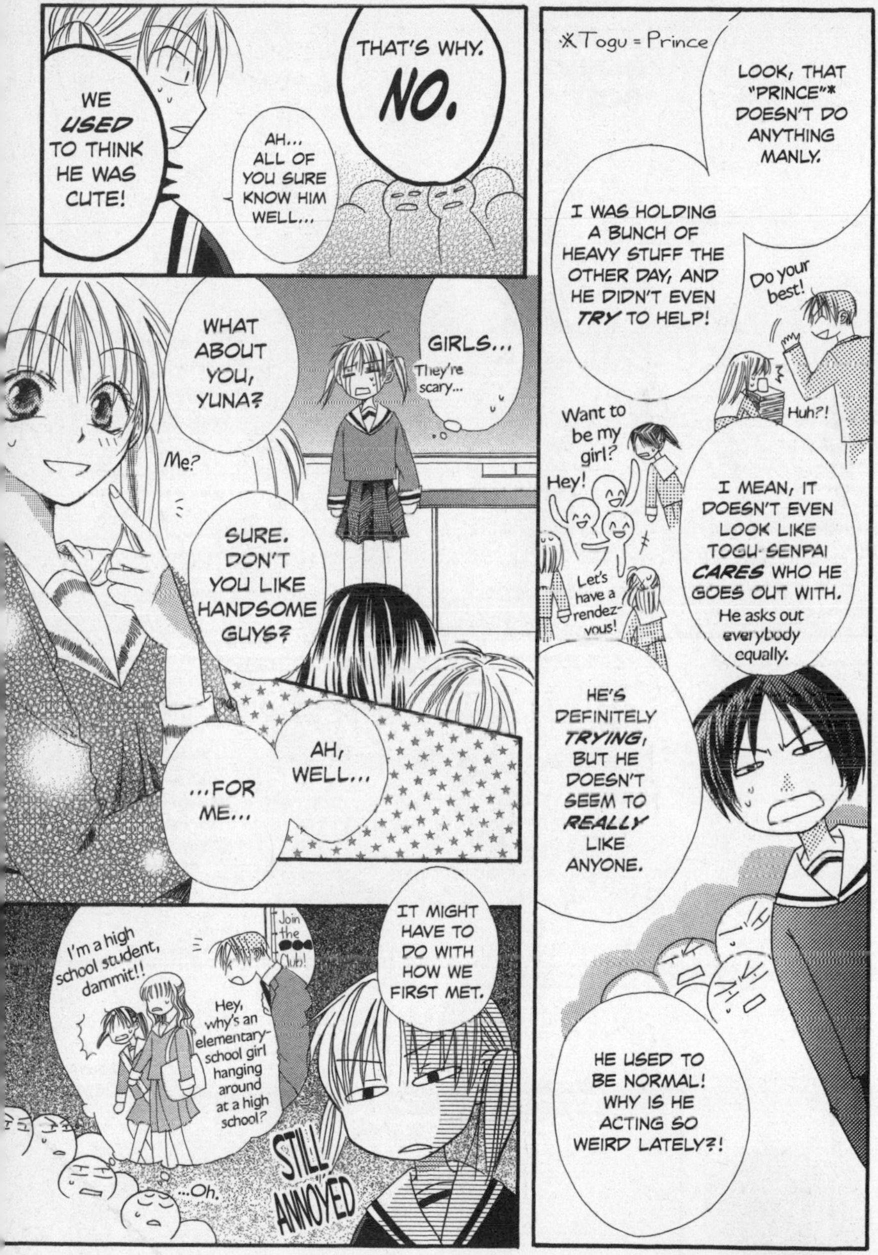
※Togu = Prince
LOOK, THAT "PRINCE"* DOESN'T DO ANYTHING MANLY.
I WAS HOLDING A BUNCH OF HEAVY STUFF THE OTHER DAY, AND HE DIDN'T EVEN TRY TO HELP!
Do your best!
Huh?!
Want to be my girl?
Hey!
Let's have a rendezvous!
I MEAN, IT DOESN'T EVEN LOOK LIKE TOGU-SENPAI CARES WHO HE GOES OUT WITH. He asks out everybody equally.
HE'S DEFINITELY TRYING, BUT HE DOESN'T SEEM TO REALLY LIKE ANYONE.
HE USED TO BE NORMAL! WHY IS HE ACTING SO WEIRD LATELY?!
THAT'S WHY. NO.
WE USED TO THINK HE WAS CUTE!
AH... ALL OF YOU SURE KNOW HIM WELL...
GIRLS...
They're scary...
WHAT ABOUT YOU, YUNA?
Me?
SURE. DON'T YOU LIKE HANDSOME GUYS?
AH, WELL...
...FOR ME...
IT MIGHT HAVE TO DO WITH HOW WE FIRST MET.
Join the
Club!
I'm a high school student, dammit!!
Hey, why's an elementary-school girl hanging around at a high school?
STILL ANNOYED
...Oh.

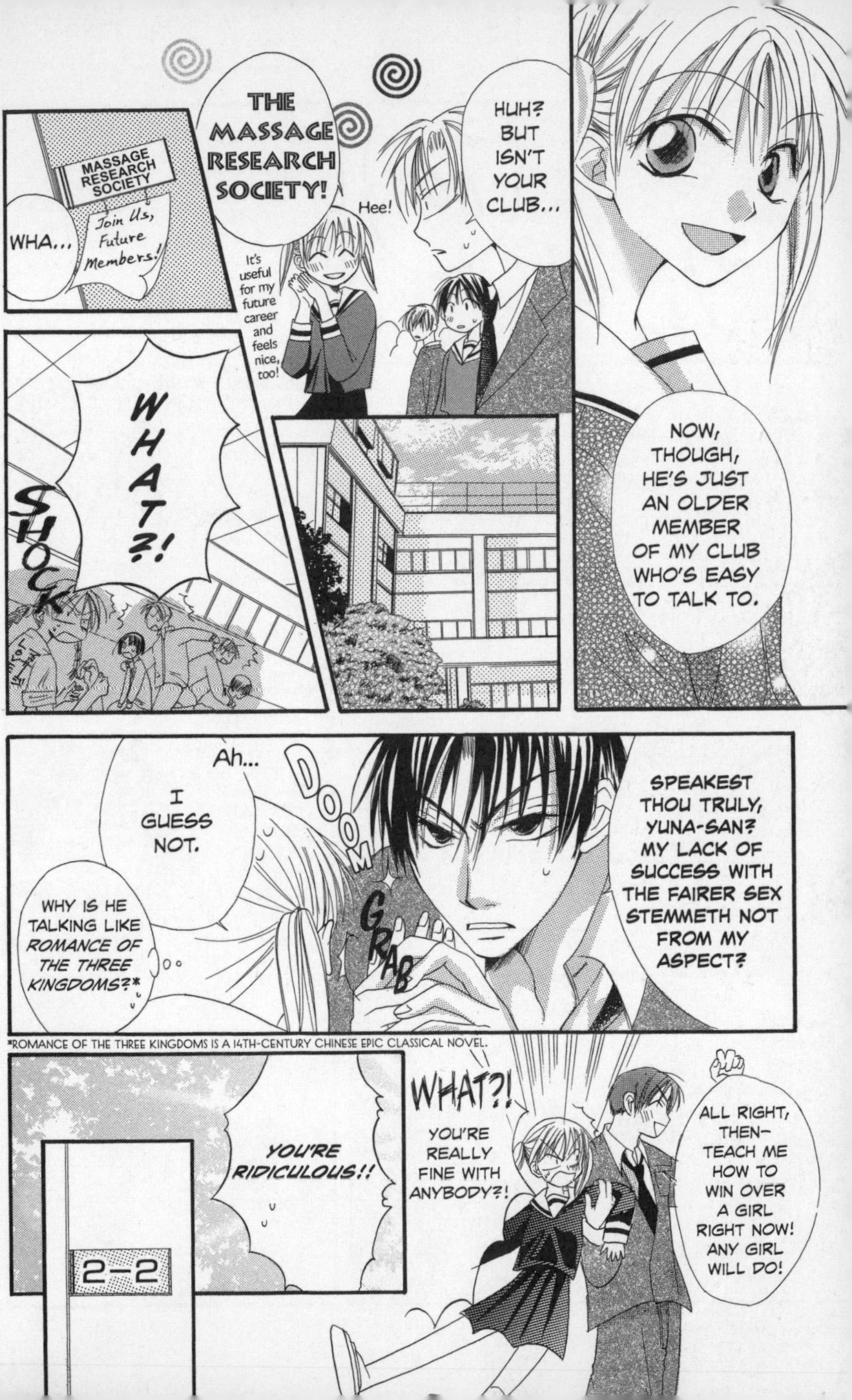
NOW, THOUGH, HE'S JUST AN OLDER MEMBER OF MY CLUB WHO'S EASY TO TALK TO.
HUH? BUT ISN'T YOUR CLUB...
THE MASSAGE RESEARCH SOCIETY!
Hee!
It's useful for my future career and feels nice, too!
MASSAGE RESEARCH SOCIETY
Join Us, Future Members!
WHA...
WHAT?!
SHOCK
SPEAKEST THOU TRULY, YUNA-SAN? MY LACK OF SUCCESS WITH THE FAIRER SEX STEMMETH NOT FROM MY ASPECT?
GRAB
DOOM
Ah...
I GUESS NOT.
WHY IS HE TALKING LIKE *ROMANCE OF THE THREE KINGDOMS*?*
ALL RIGHT, THEN—TEACH ME HOW TO WIN OVER A GIRL RIGHT NOW! ANY GIRL WILL DO!
WHAT?!
YOU'RE REALLY FINE WITH ANYBODY?!
YOU'RE RIDICULOUS!!
2-2

*ROMANCE OF THE THREE KINGDOMS IS A 14TH-CENTURY CHINESE EPIC CLASSICAL NOVEL.

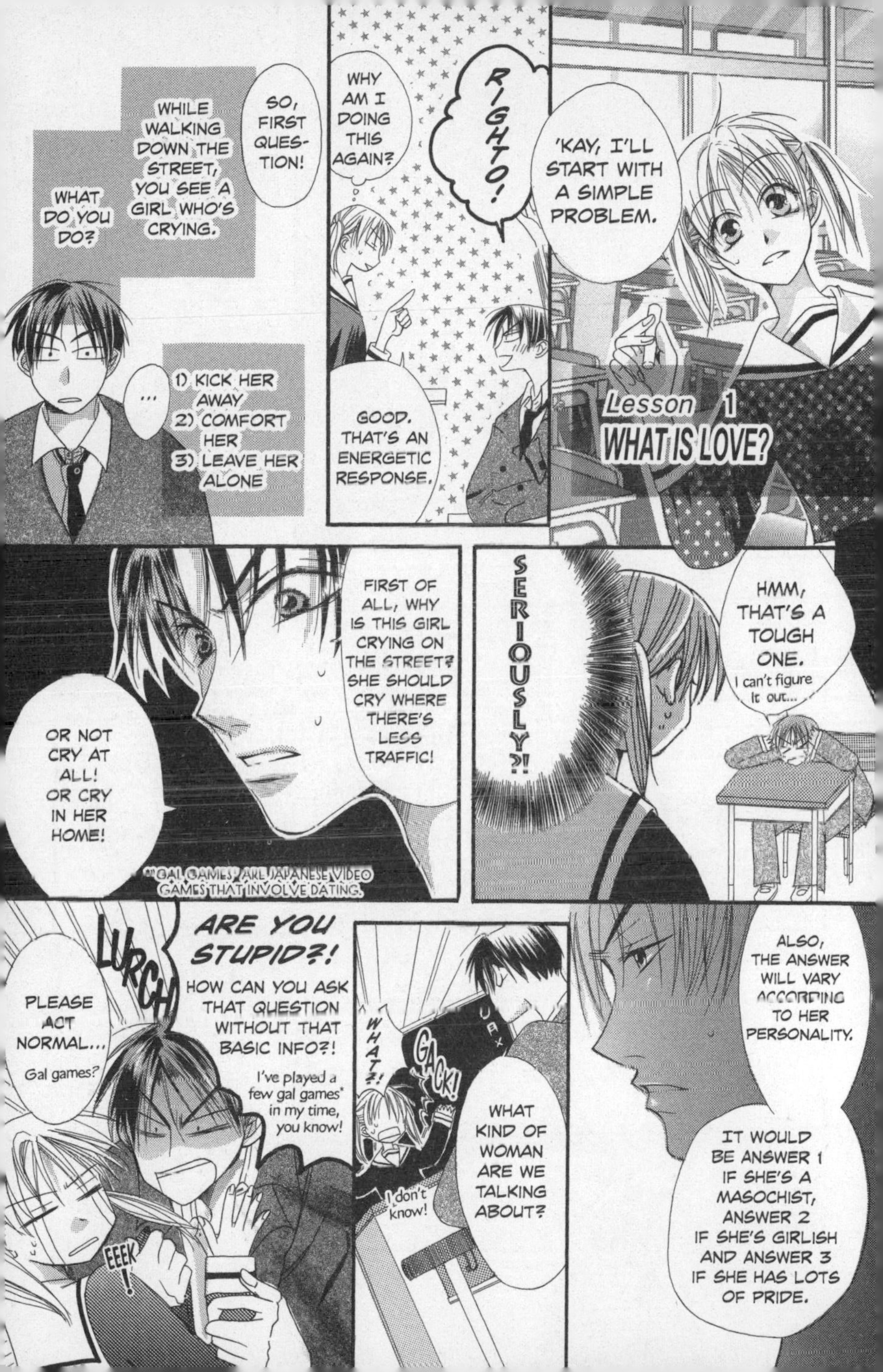
'KAY, I'LL START WITH A SIMPLE PROBLEM.
Lesson 1
WHAT IS LOVE?
RIGHTO!
WHY AM I DOING THIS AGAIN?
GOOD. THAT'S AN ENERGETIC RESPONSE.
SO, FIRST QUESTION!
WHILE WALKING DOWN THE STREET, YOU SEE A GIRL WHO'S CRYING.
WHAT DO YOU DO?
1) KICK HER AWAY
2) COMFORT HER
3) LEAVE HER ALONE
...
SERIOUSLY?!
HMM, THAT'S A TOUGH ONE.
I can't figure it out...
FIRST OF ALL, WHY IS THIS GIRL CRYING ON THE STREET? SHE SHOULD CRY WHERE THERE'S LESS TRAFFIC!
OR NOT CRY AT ALL! OR CRY IN HER HOME!
*GAL GAMES ARE JAPANESE VIDEO GAMES THAT INVOLVE DATING.
ALSO, THE ANSWER WILL VARY ACCORDING TO HER PERSONALITY.
IT WOULD BE ANSWER 1 IF SHE'S A MASOCHIST, ANSWER 2 IF SHE'S GIRLISH AND ANSWER 3 IF SHE HAS LOTS OF PRIDE.
WHAT KIND OF WOMAN ARE WE TALKING ABOUT?
WHAT?!
GACK!
I don't know!
ARE YOU STUPID?!
HOW CAN YOU ASK THAT QUESTION WITHOUT THAT BASIC INFO?!
I've played a few gal games* in my time, you know!
LURCH
PLEASE ACT NORMAL...
Gal games?
EEEK!

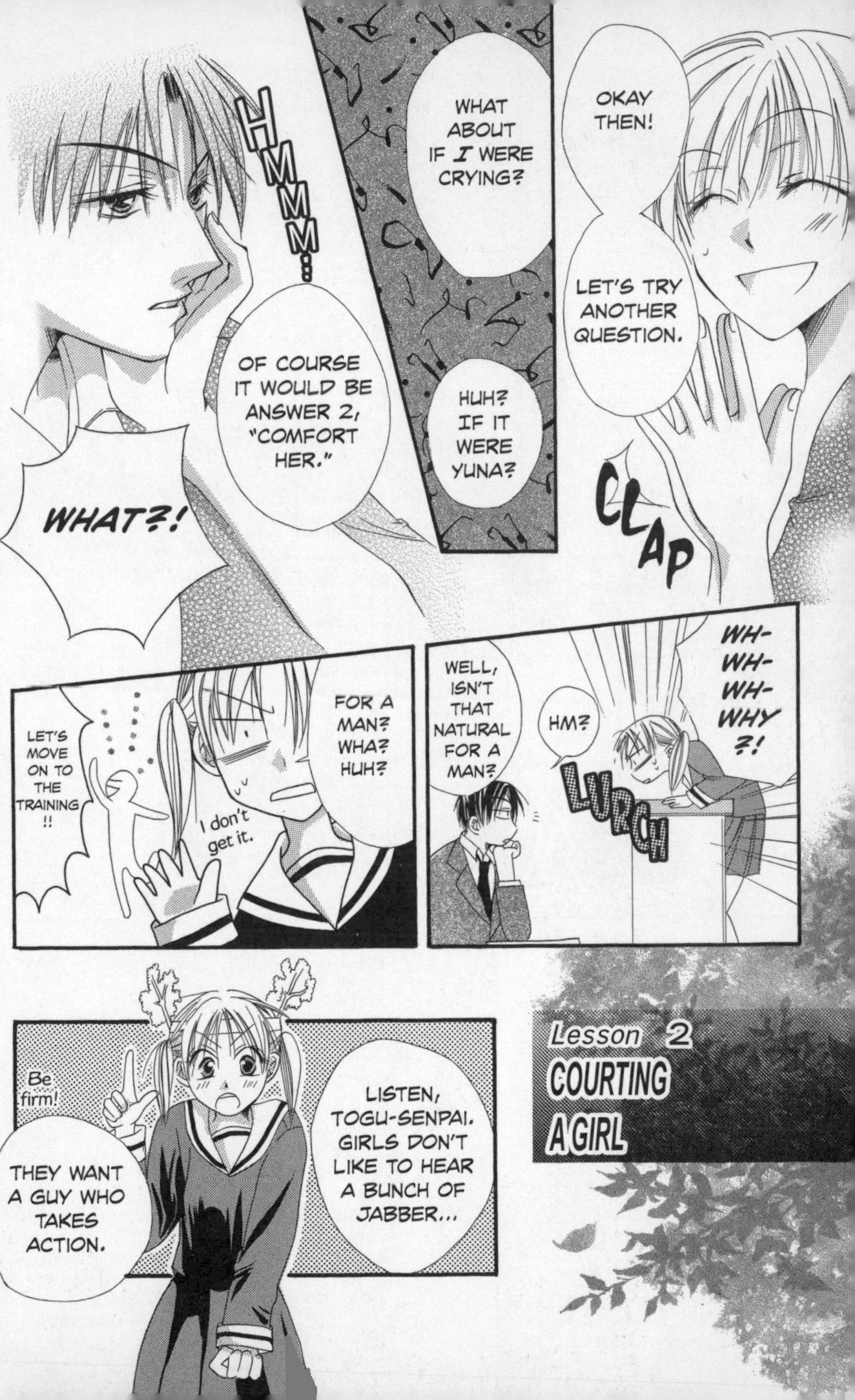
OKAY THEN!
LET'S TRY ANOTHER QUESTION.
CLAP
WHAT ABOUT IF *I* WERE CRYING?
HUH? IF IT WERE YUNA?
HMMM..
OF COURSE IT WOULD BE ANSWER 2, "COMFORT HER."
WHAT?!
WH-WH-WH-WHY?!
HM?
LURCH
WELL, ISN'T THAT NATURAL FOR A MAN?
FOR A MAN? WHA? HUH?
I don't get it.
LET'S MOVE ON TO THE TRAINING!!
Lesson 2
COURTING A GIRL
LISTEN, TOGU-SENPAI. GIRLS DON'T LIKE TO HEAR A BUNCH OF JABBER...
Be firm!
THEY WANT A GUY WHO TAKES ACTION.

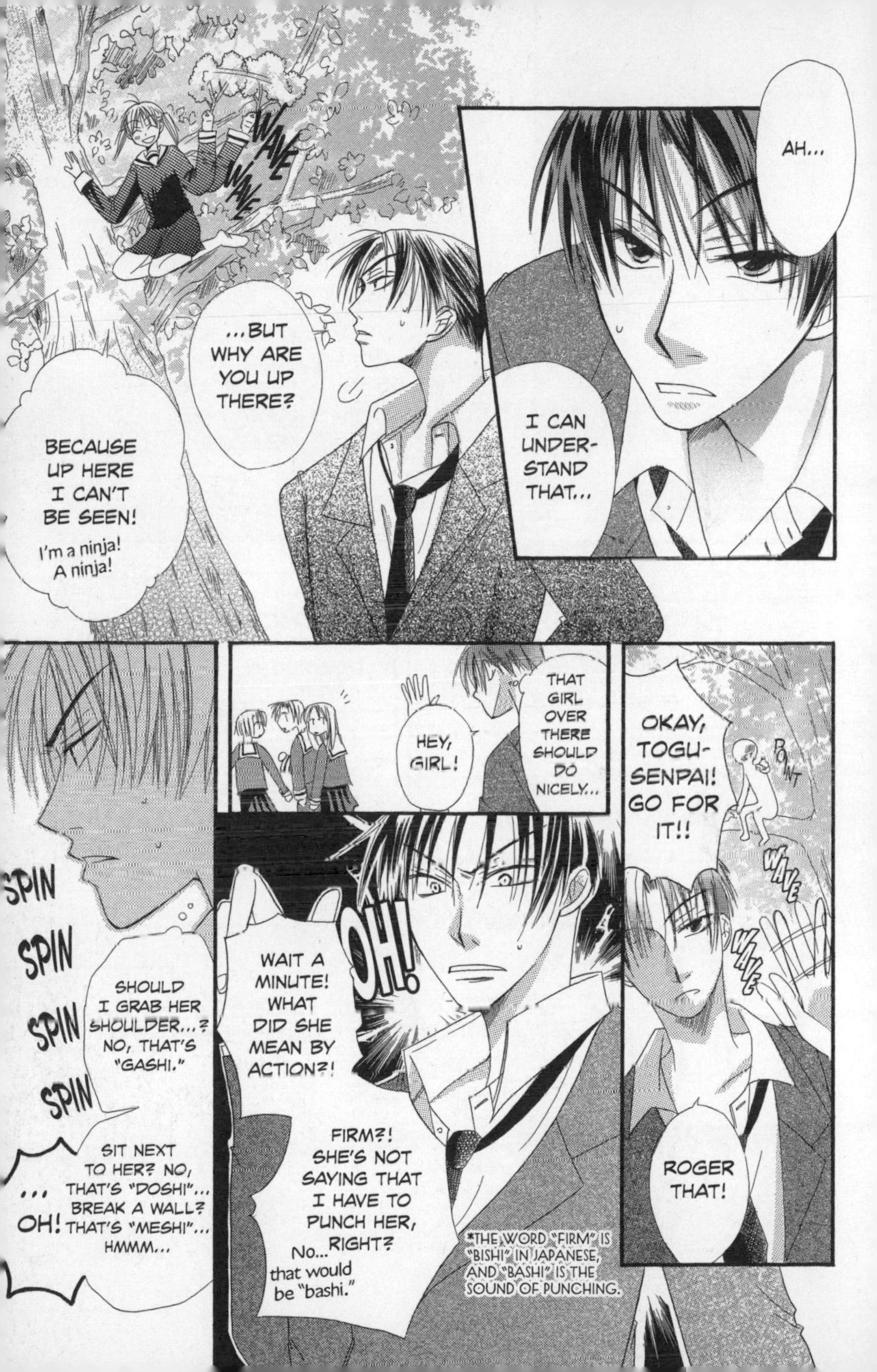
AH...
I CAN UNDER-STAND THAT...
WAVE WAVE
...BUT WHY ARE YOU UP THERE?
BECAUSE UP HERE I CAN'T BE SEEN!
I'm a ninja! A ninja!
OKAY, TOGU-SENPAI! GO FOR IT!!
POINT
WAVE
WAVE
ROGER THAT!
THAT GIRL OVER THERE SHOULD DO NICELY...
HEY, GIRL!
OH!
WAIT A MINUTE! WHAT DID SHE MEAN BY ACTION?!
FIRM?! SHE'S NOT SAYING THAT I HAVE TO PUNCH HER, RIGHT?
No... that would be "bashi."
*THE WORD "FIRM" IS "BISHI" IN JAPANESE, AND "BASHI" IS THE SOUND OF PUNCHING.
SPIN
SPIN
SPIN
SPIN
SHOULD I GRAB HER SHOULDER...? NO, THAT'S "GASHI."
SIT NEXT TO HER? NO, THAT'S "DOSHI"... BREAK A WALL? THAT'S "MESHI"... HMMM...
...OH!

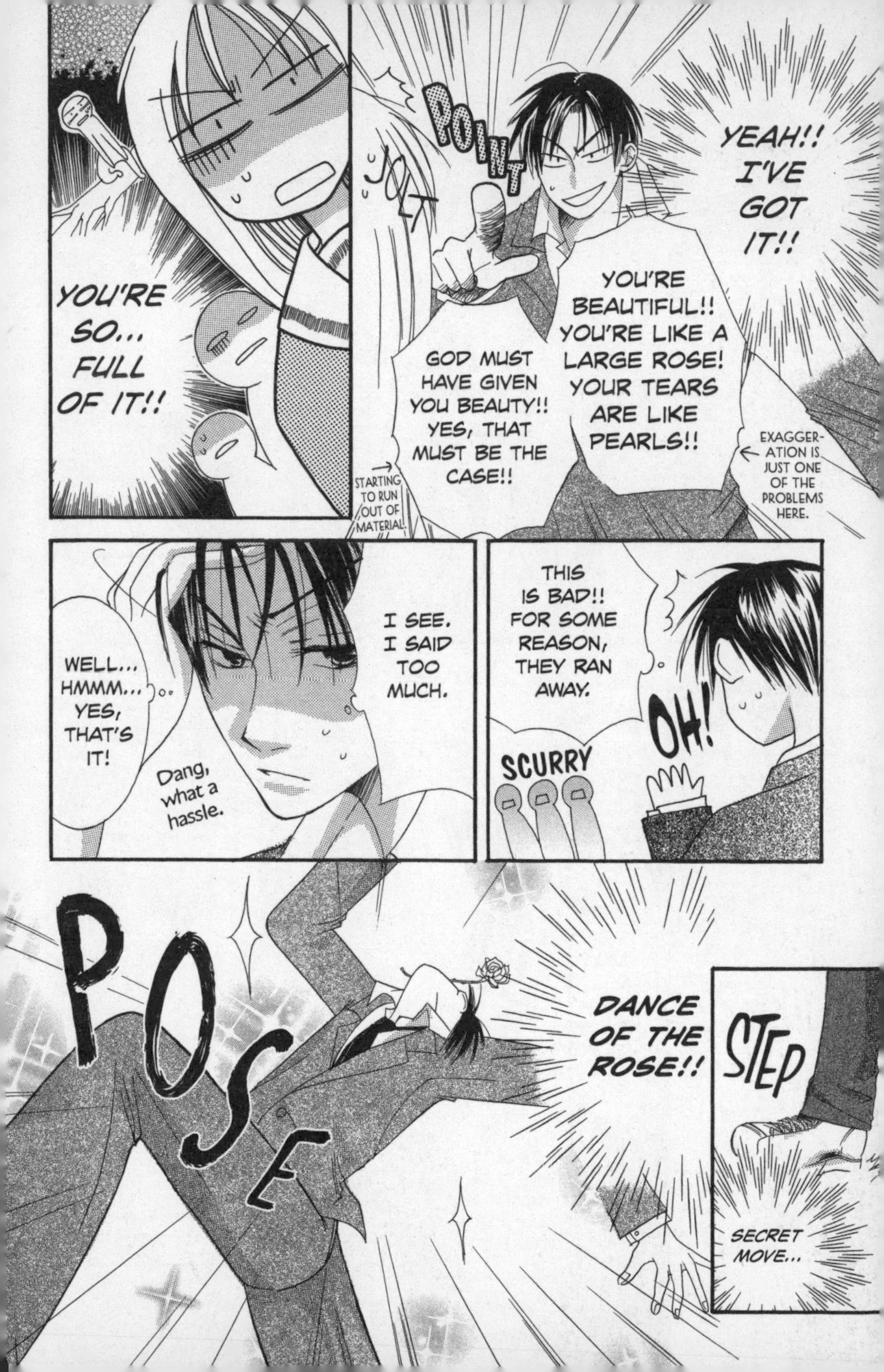
YEAH!! I'VE GOT IT!!
POINT
JOLT
YOU'RE BEAUTIFUL!! YOU'RE LIKE A LARGE ROSE! YOUR TEARS ARE LIKE PEARLS!!
EXAGGERATION IS JUST ONE OF THE PROBLEMS HERE.
GOD MUST HAVE GIVEN YOU BEAUTY!! YES, THAT MUST BE THE CASE!!
STARTING TO RUN OUT OF MATERIAL.
YOU'RE SO... FULL OF IT!!
THIS IS BAD!! FOR SOME REASON, THEY RAN AWAY.
OH!
SCURRY
I SEE. I SAID TOO MUCH.
WELL... HMMM... YES, THAT'S IT!
Dang, what a hassle.
STEP
SECRET MOVE...
DANCE OF THE ROSE!!
POSE

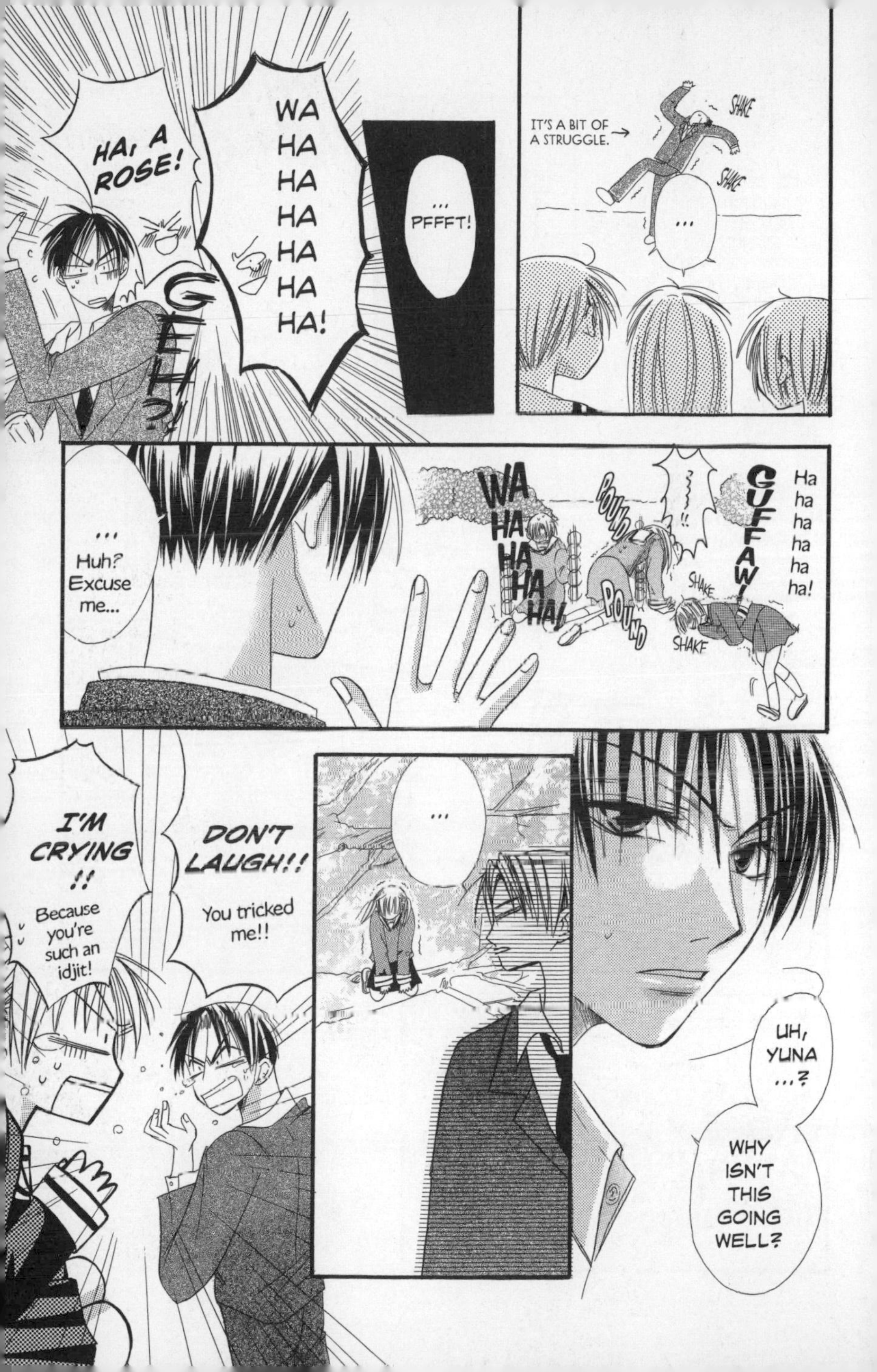
IT'S A BIT OF A STRUGGLE.
SHAKE
SHAKE
...
... PFFFT!
WA HA HA HA HA HA HA!
HA, A ROSE!
GEH?!
Ha ha ha ha ha ha!
GUFFAW!
SHAKE
SHAKE
!!
POUND
POUND
WA HA HA HA HA!
... Huh? Excuse me...
UH, YUNA...?
WHY ISN'T THIS GOING WELL?
...
DON'T LAUGH!!
You tricked me!!
I'M CRYING!!
Because you're such an idjit!

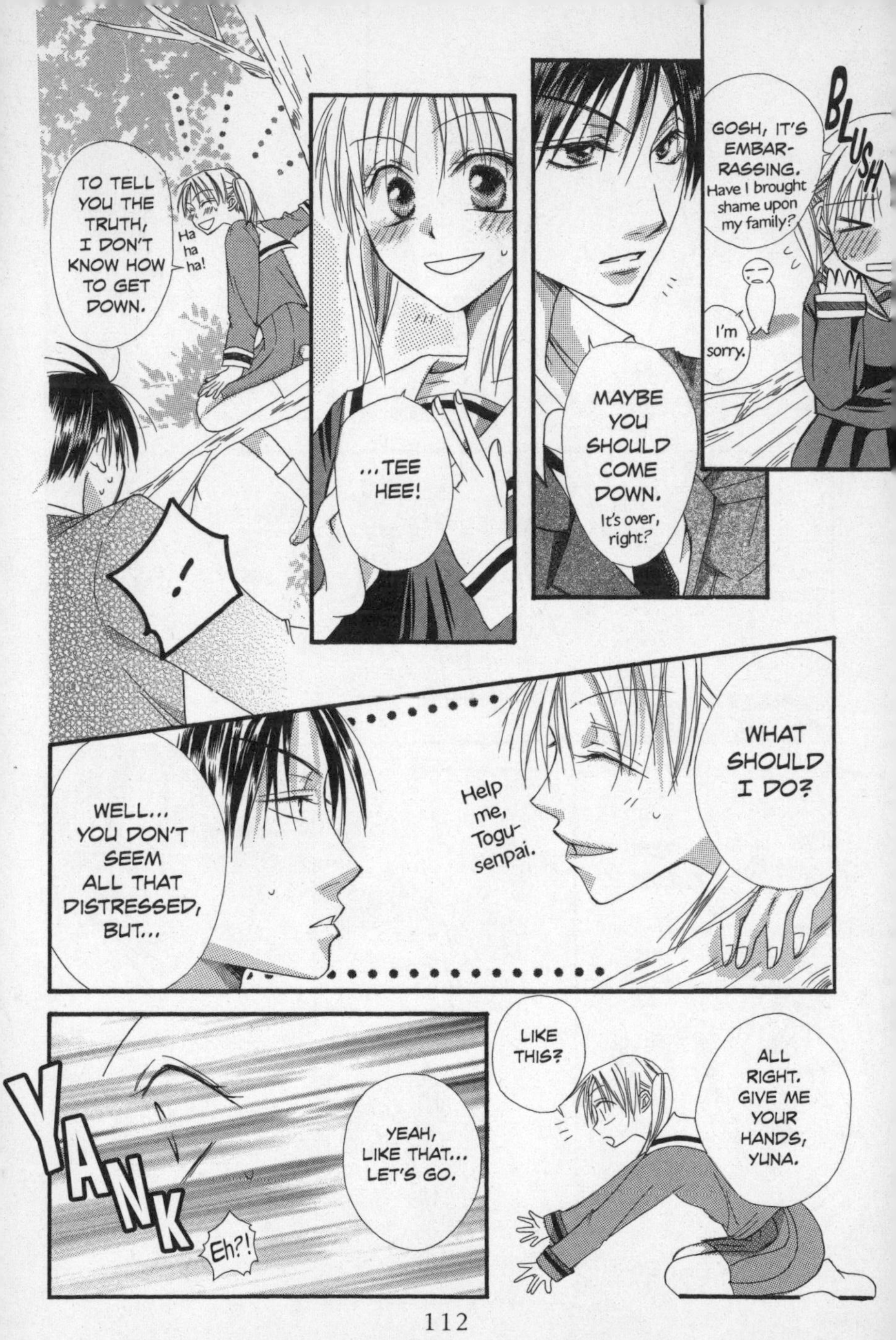
BLUSH
GOSH, IT'S EMBARRASSING. Have I brought shame upon my family?
I'm sorry.
MAYBE YOU SHOULD COME DOWN. It's over, right?
...TEE HEE!
TO TELL YOU THE TRUTH, I DON'T KNOW HOW TO GET DOWN.
Ha ha ha!
!
WHAT SHOULD I DO?
Help me, Togu-senpai.
WELL... YOU DON'T SEEM ALL THAT DISTRESSED, BUT...
ALL RIGHT. GIVE ME YOUR HANDS, YUNA.
LIKE THIS?
YEAH, LIKE THAT... LET'S GO.
YANK
Eh?!

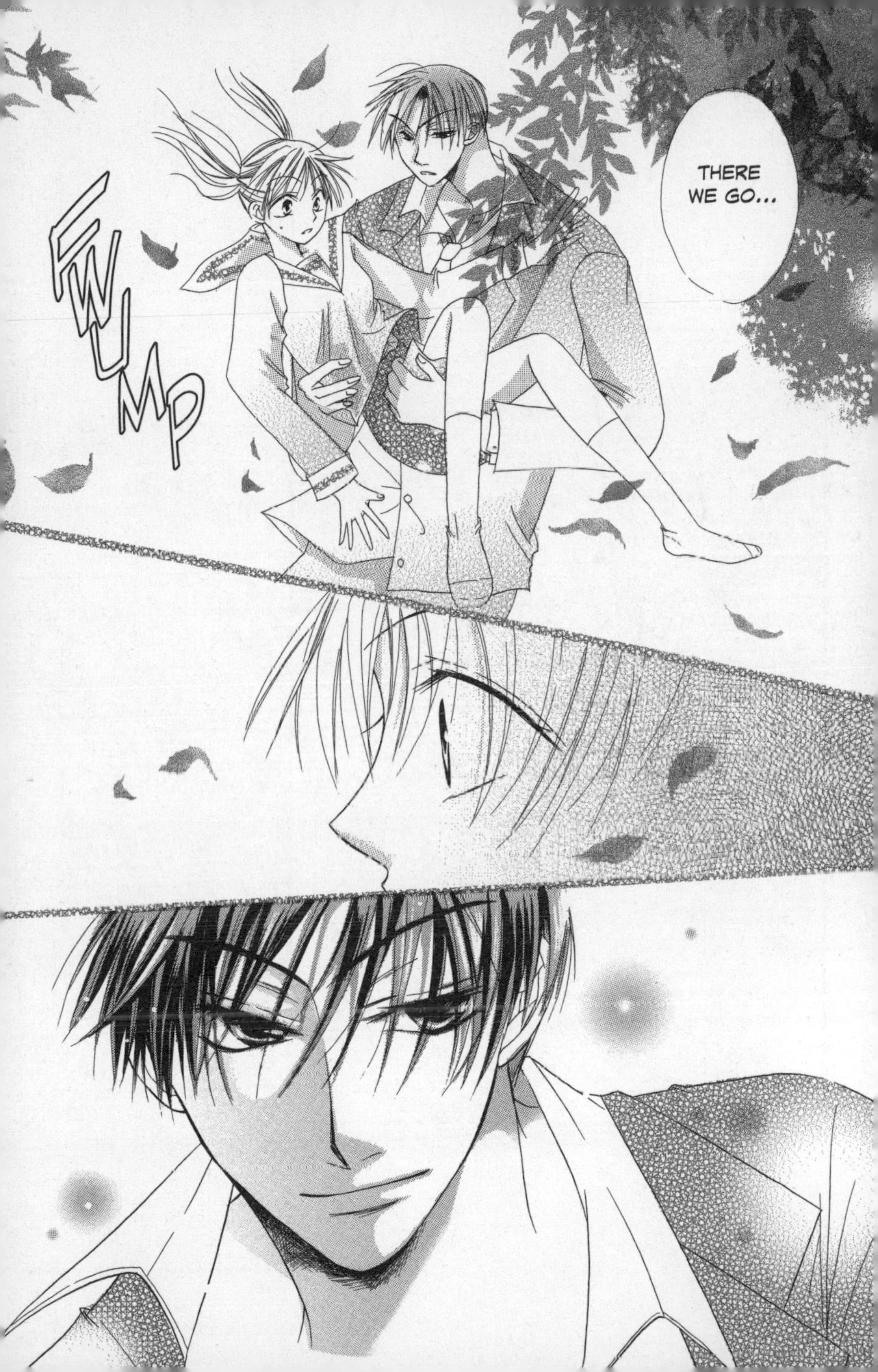
THERE WE GO...
FWUMP

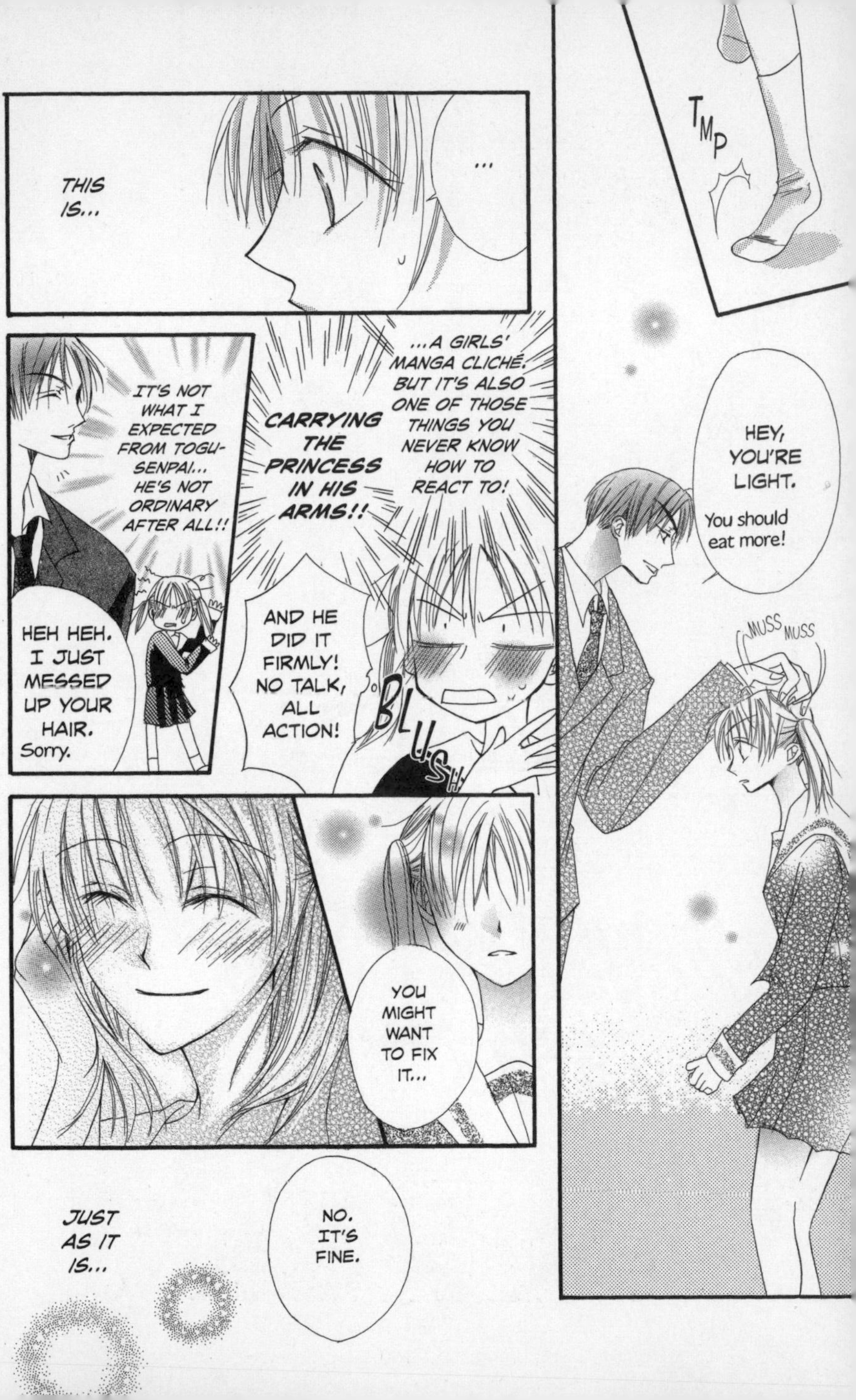
TMP
HEY, YOU'RE LIGHT. You should eat more!
MUSS MUSS
...
THIS IS...
...A GIRLS' MANGA CLICHÉ. BUT IT'S ALSO ONE OF THOSE THINGS YOU NEVER KNOW HOW TO REACT TO!
CARRYING THE PRINCESS IN HIS ARMS!!
AND HE DID IT FIRMLY! NO TALK, ALL ACTION!
BLUSH
IT'S NOT WHAT I EXPECTED FROM TOGU-SENPAI... HE'S NOT ORDINARY AFTER ALL!!
HEH HEH. I JUST MESSED UP YOUR HAIR. Sorry.
YOU MIGHT WANT TO FIX IT...
NO. IT'S FINE.
JUST AS IT IS...

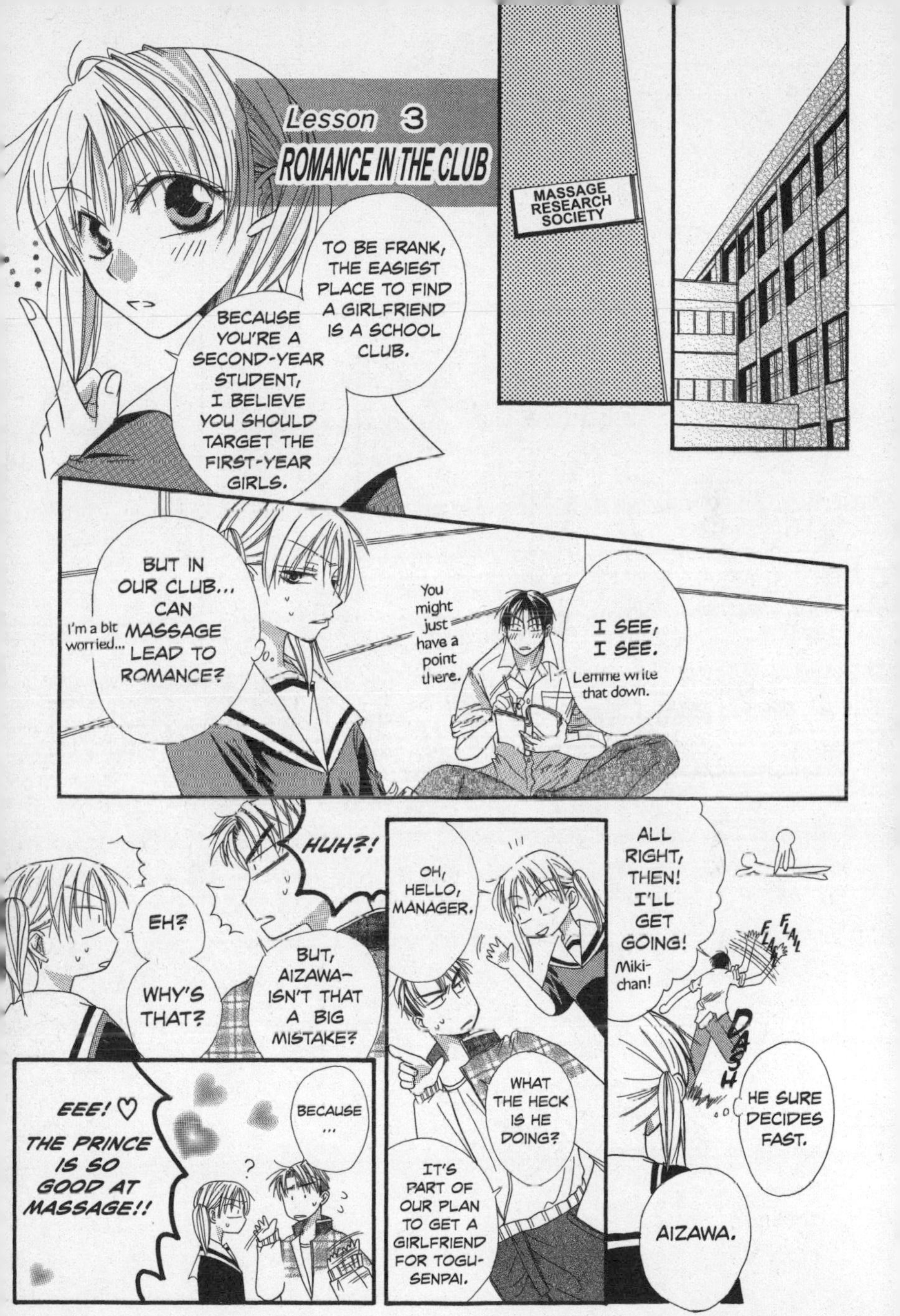
MASSAGE RESEARCH SOCIETY
Lesson 3
ROMANCE IN THE CLUB
TO BE FRANK, THE EASIEST PLACE TO FIND A GIRLFRIEND IS A SCHOOL CLUB.
BECAUSE YOU'RE A SECOND-YEAR STUDENT, I BELIEVE YOU SHOULD TARGET THE FIRST-YEAR GIRLS.
I SEE, I SEE.
Lemme write that down.
You might just have a point there.
BUT IN OUR CLUB... CAN MASSAGE LEAD TO ROMANCE?
I'm a bit worried...
ALL RIGHT, THEN! I'LL GET GOING!
Miki-chan!
FLAIL FLAIL
DASH
HE SURE DECIDES FAST.
AIZAWA.
OH, HELLO, MANAGER.
WHAT THE HECK IS HE DOING?
IT'S PART OF OUR PLAN TO GET A GIRLFRIEND FOR TOGU-SENPAI.
HUH?!
BUT, AIZAWA-ISN'T THAT A BIG MISTAKE?
EH?
WHY'S THAT?
BECAUSE ...
EEE! ♡ THE PRINCE IS SO GOOD AT MASSAGE!!

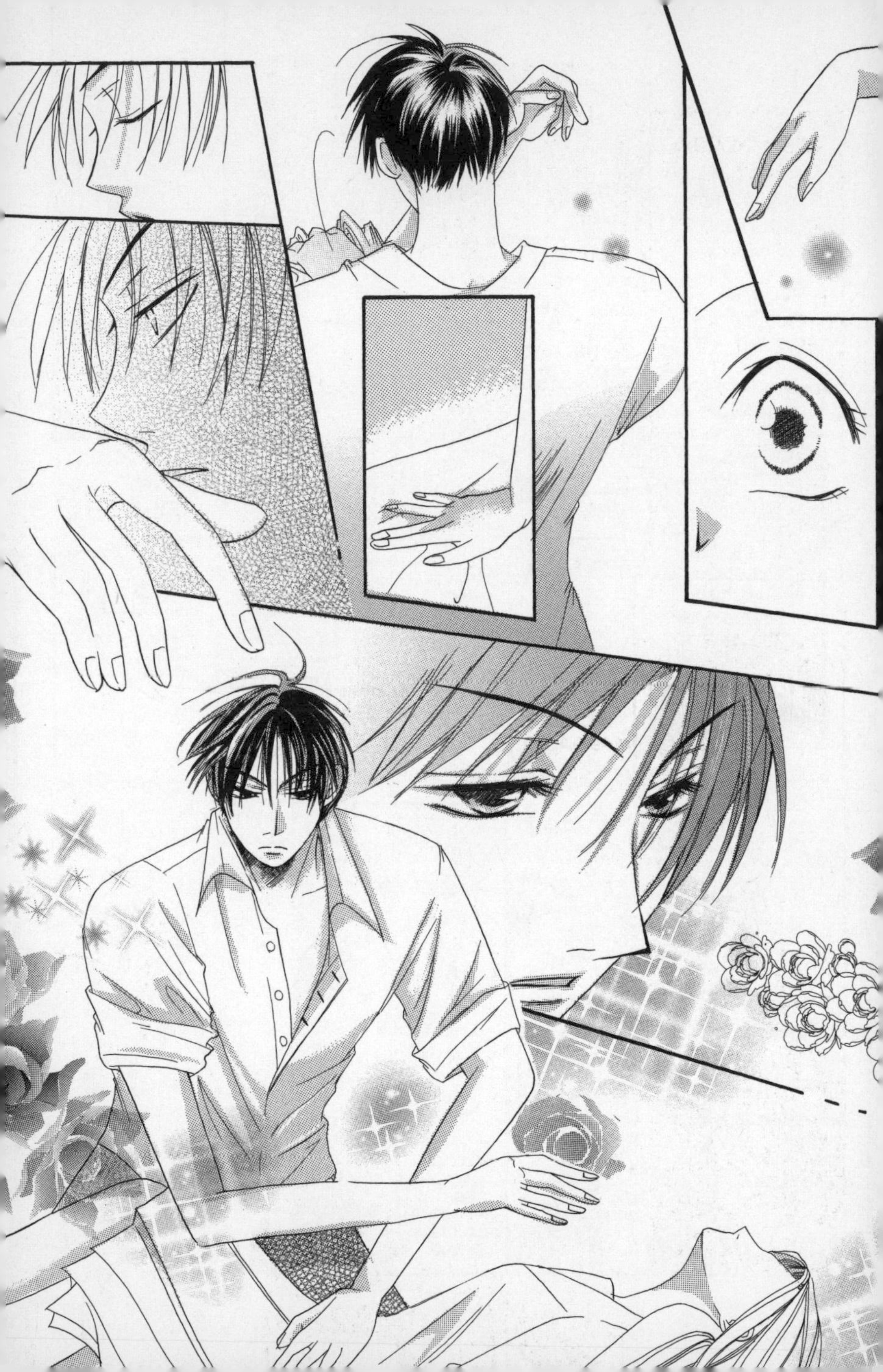

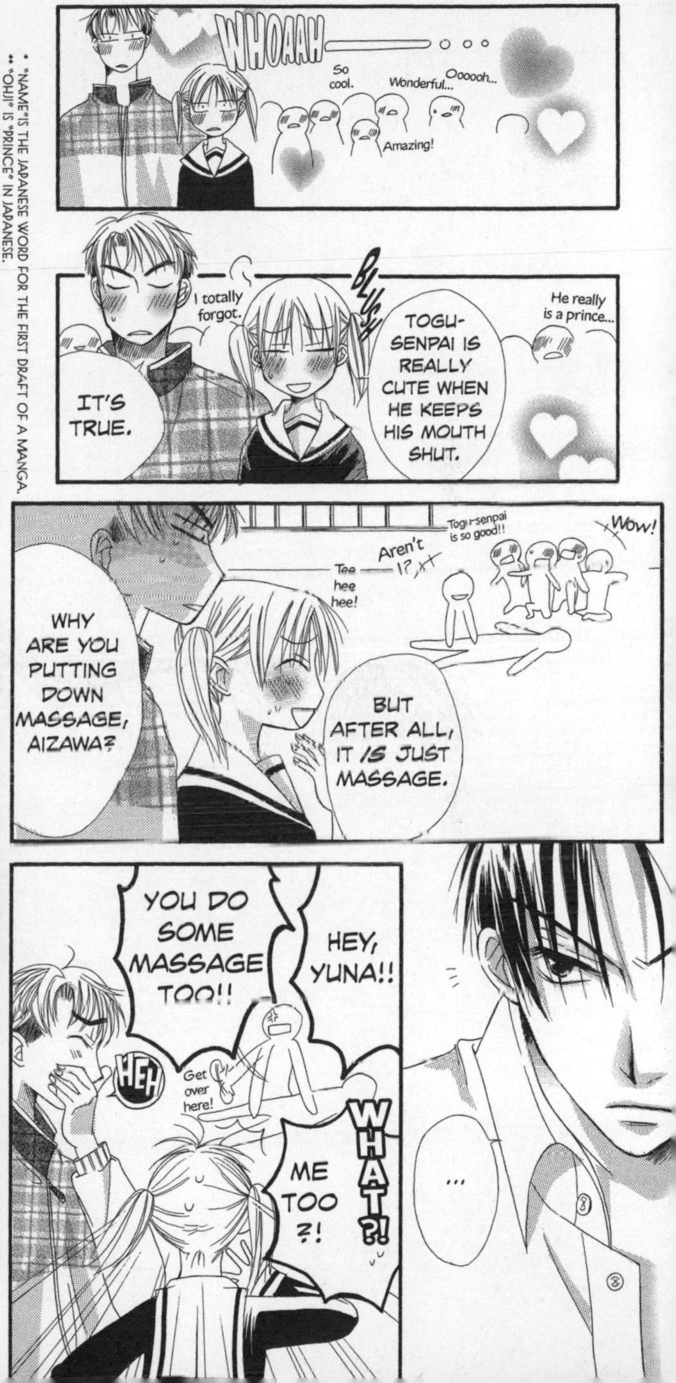
WHOAAH
Ooooh...
Wonderful...
So cool.
Amazing!
He really is a prince...
BLUSH
TOGU-SENPAI IS REALLY CUTE WHEN HE KEEPS HIS MOUTH SHUT.
I totally forgot.
IT'S TRUE.
Wow!
Togu-senpai is so good!!
Aren't I?
Tee hee hee!
BUT AFTER ALL, IT *IS* JUST MASSAGE.
WHY ARE YOU PUTTING DOWN MASSAGE, AIZAWA?
...
HEY, YUNA!!
YOU DO SOME MASSAGE TOO!!
WHAT?!
ME TOO?!
HEH
Get over here!

Making the Manga, -Part 2

<Teach Me, Prince>

It took me six hours to produce the name.* It was a story I thought of quickly, so please read it quickly. I had written a different story before this, but since it felt too gloomy and I didn't like it, I wrote a new one immediately. I gave him his last name, Togu, because I wanted it to go along with the title of "Prince." My train of thought was:

Prince → Ohji** → Prince from the Heian Period → Togu.

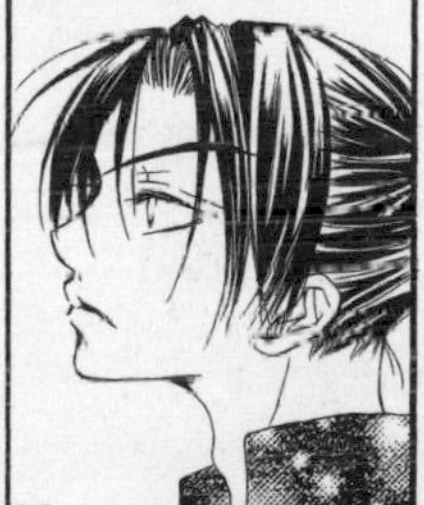
TAKESHI TOGU
His hair grew.

* "NAME" IS THE JAPANESE WORD FOR THE FIRST DRAFT OF A MANGA.
** "OHJI" IS "PRINCE" IN JAPANESE.

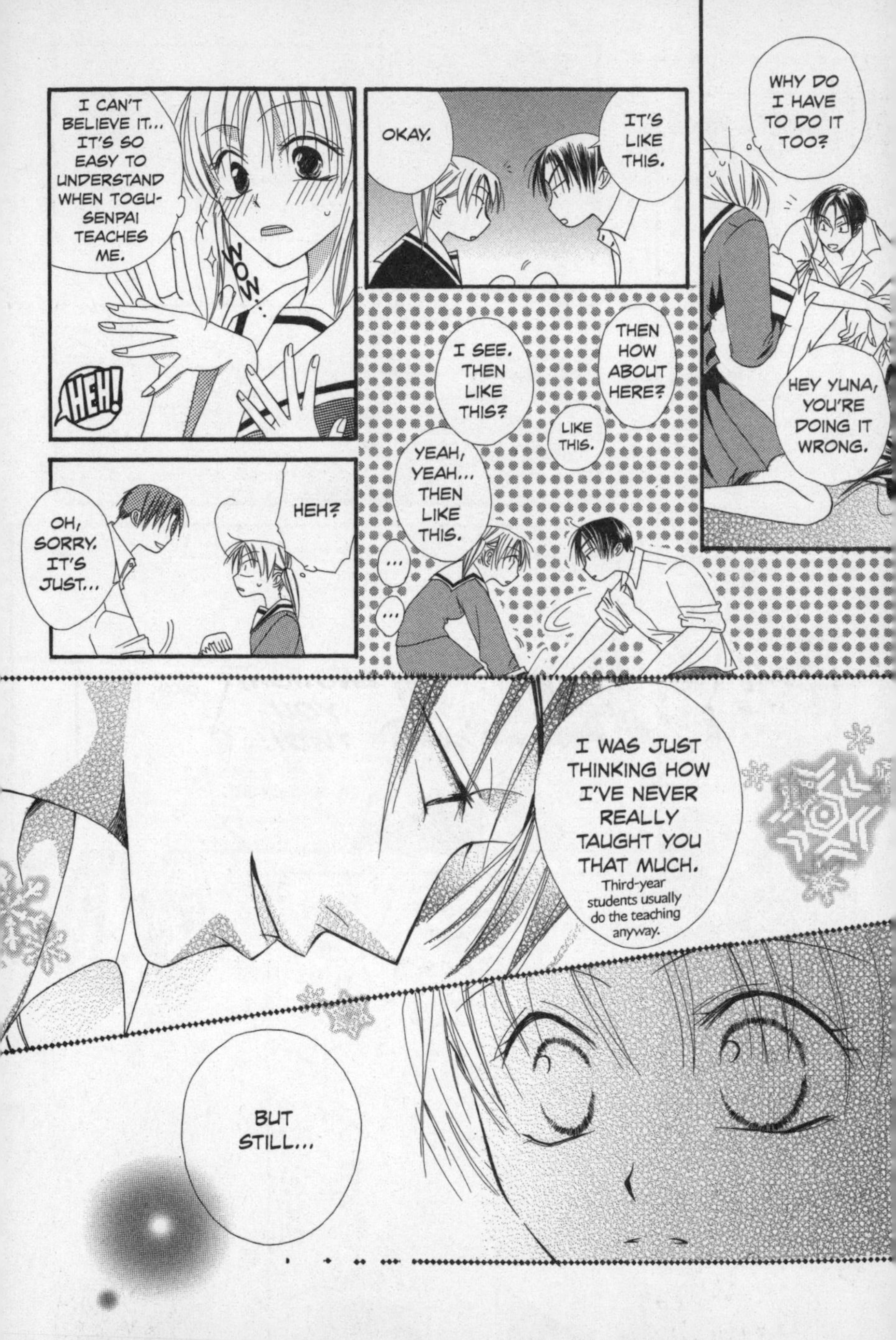
WHY DO I HAVE TO DO IT TOO?
HEY YUNA, YOU'RE DOING IT WRONG.
IT'S LIKE THIS.
OKAY.
THEN HOW ABOUT HERE?
LIKE THIS.
I SEE. THEN LIKE THIS?
YEAH, YEAH... THEN LIKE THIS.
...
...
I CAN'T BELIEVE IT... IT'S SO EASY TO UNDERSTAND WHEN TOGU-SENPAI TEACHES ME.
WOW...
HEH!
HEH?
OH, SORRY. IT'S JUST...
I WAS JUST THINKING HOW I'VE NEVER REALLY TAUGHT YOU THAT MUCH.
Third-year students usually do the teaching anyway.
BUT STILL...

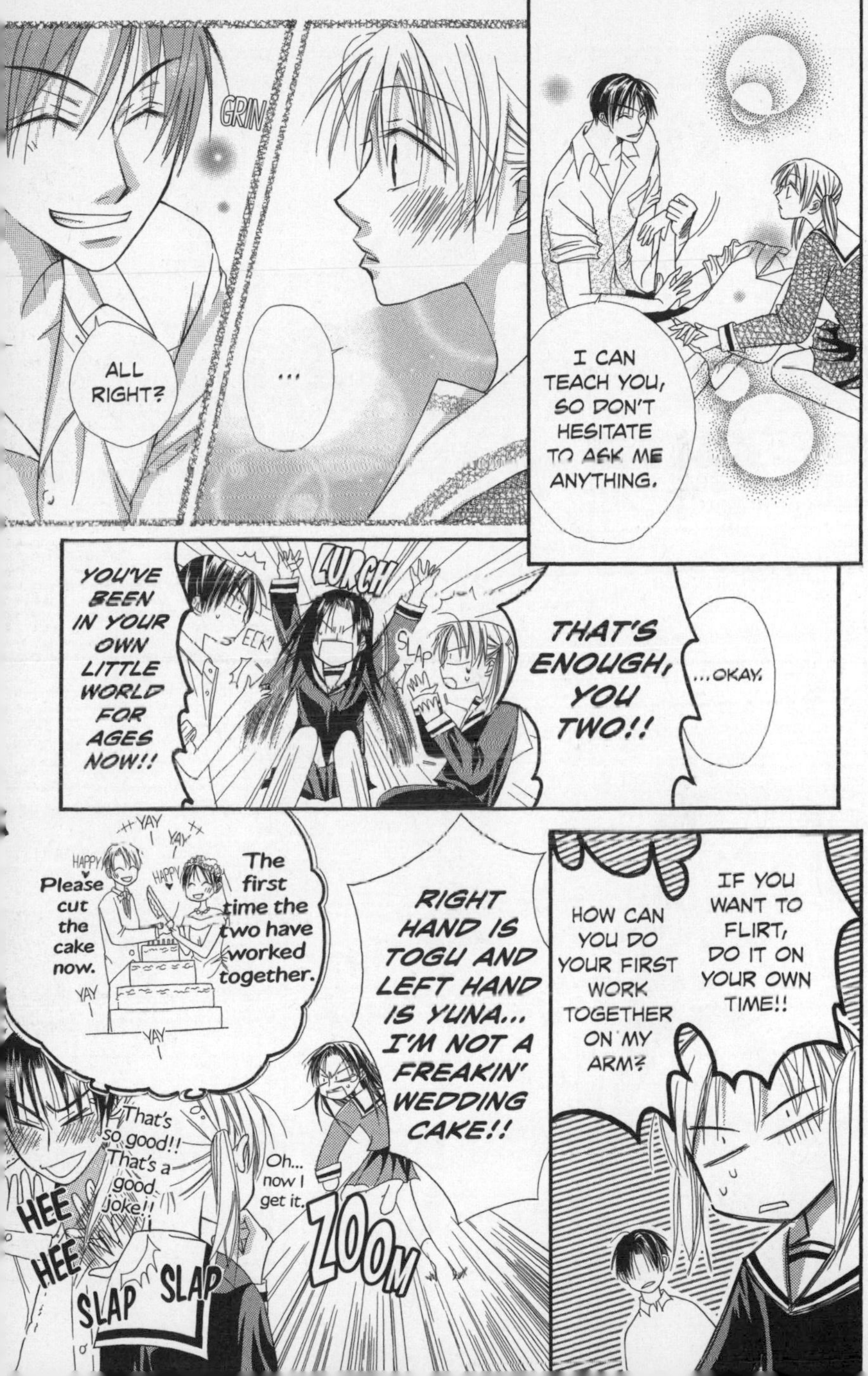
I CAN TEACH YOU, SO DON'T HESITATE TO ASK ME ANYTHING.
...
GRIN
ALL RIGHT?
...OKAY.
THAT'S ENOUGH, YOU TWO!!
ZURCH
SLAP
EEK!
YOU'VE BEEN IN YOUR OWN LITTLE WORLD FOR AGES NOW!!
IF YOU WANT TO FLIRT, DO IT ON YOUR OWN TIME!!
HOW CAN YOU DO YOUR FIRST WORK TOGETHER ON MY ARM?
RIGHT HAND IS TOGU AND LEFT HAND IS YUNA... I'M NOT A FREAKIN' WEDDING CAKE!!
The first time the two have worked together.
YAY
YAY
HAPPY
HAPPY
Please cut the cake now.
YAY
YAY
ZOOM
Oh... now I get it.
That's so good!! That's a good joke!!
HEE
HEE
SLAP
SLAP

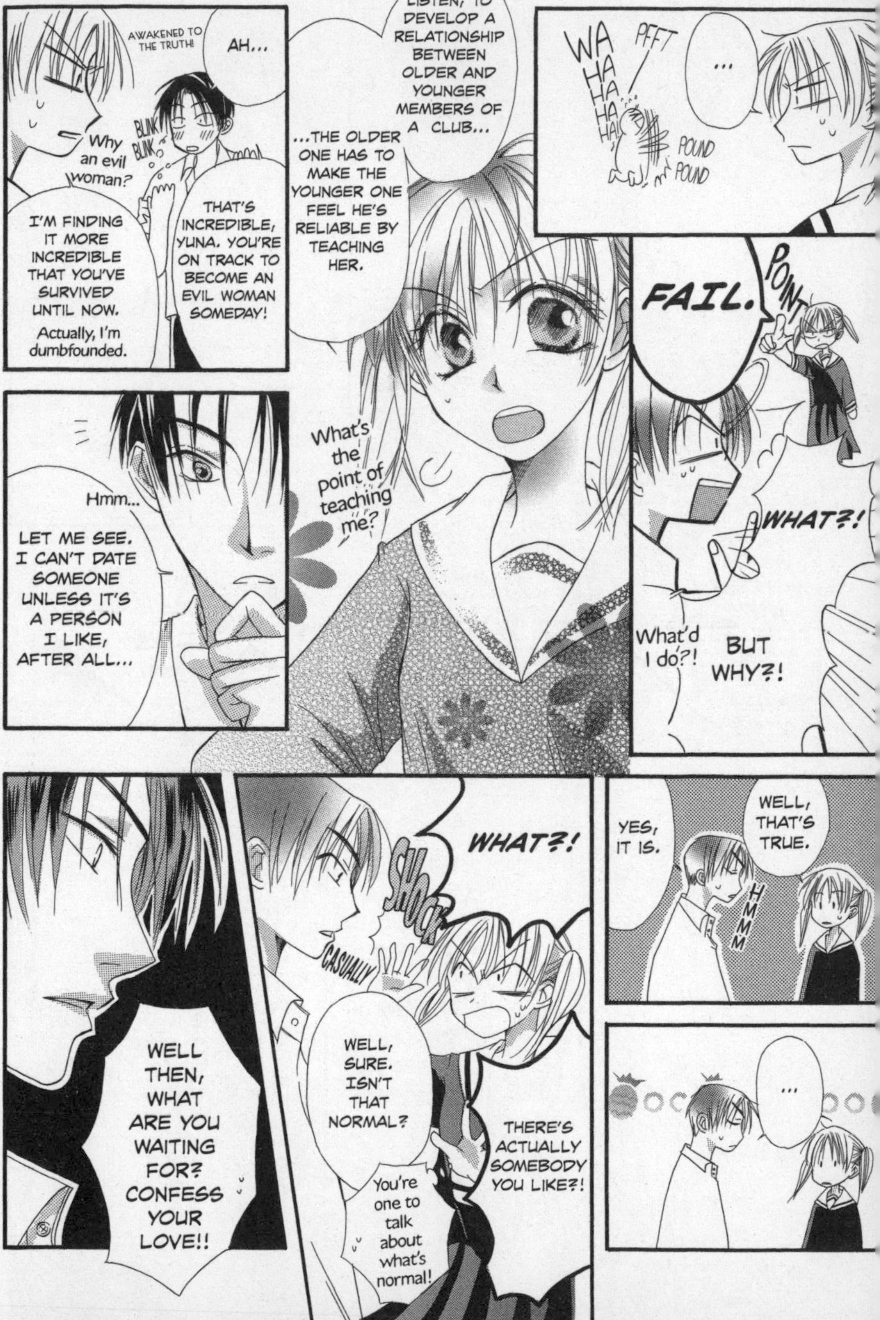
WA HA HA HA HA HA!
PFFT
POUND POUND
...
LISTEN, TO DEVELOP A RELATIONSHIP BETWEEN OLDER AND YOUNGER MEMBERS OF A CLUB...
...THE OLDER ONE HAS TO MAKE THE YOUNGER ONE FEEL HE'S RELIABLE BY TEACHING HER.
What's the point of teaching me?
AH...
AWAKENED TO THE TRUTH!
BLINK BLINK
THAT'S INCREDIBLE, YUNA. YOU'RE ON TRACK TO BECOME AN EVIL WOMAN SOMEDAY!
Why an evil woman?
I'M FINDING IT MORE INCREDIBLE THAT YOU'VE SURVIVED UNTIL NOW.
Actually, I'm dumbfounded.
POINT
FAIL.
WHAT?!
BUT WHY?!
What'd I do?!
Hmm...
LET ME SEE. I CAN'T DATE SOMEONE UNLESS IT'S A PERSON I LIKE, AFTER ALL...
WELL, THAT'S TRUE.
YES, IT IS.
HMMM
...
WHAT?!
SHOCK
CASUALLY
THERE'S ACTUALLY SOMEBODY YOU LIKE?!
WELL, SURE. ISN'T THAT NORMAL?
You're one to talk about what's normal!
WELL THEN, WHAT ARE YOU WAITING FOR? CONFESS YOUR LOVE!!

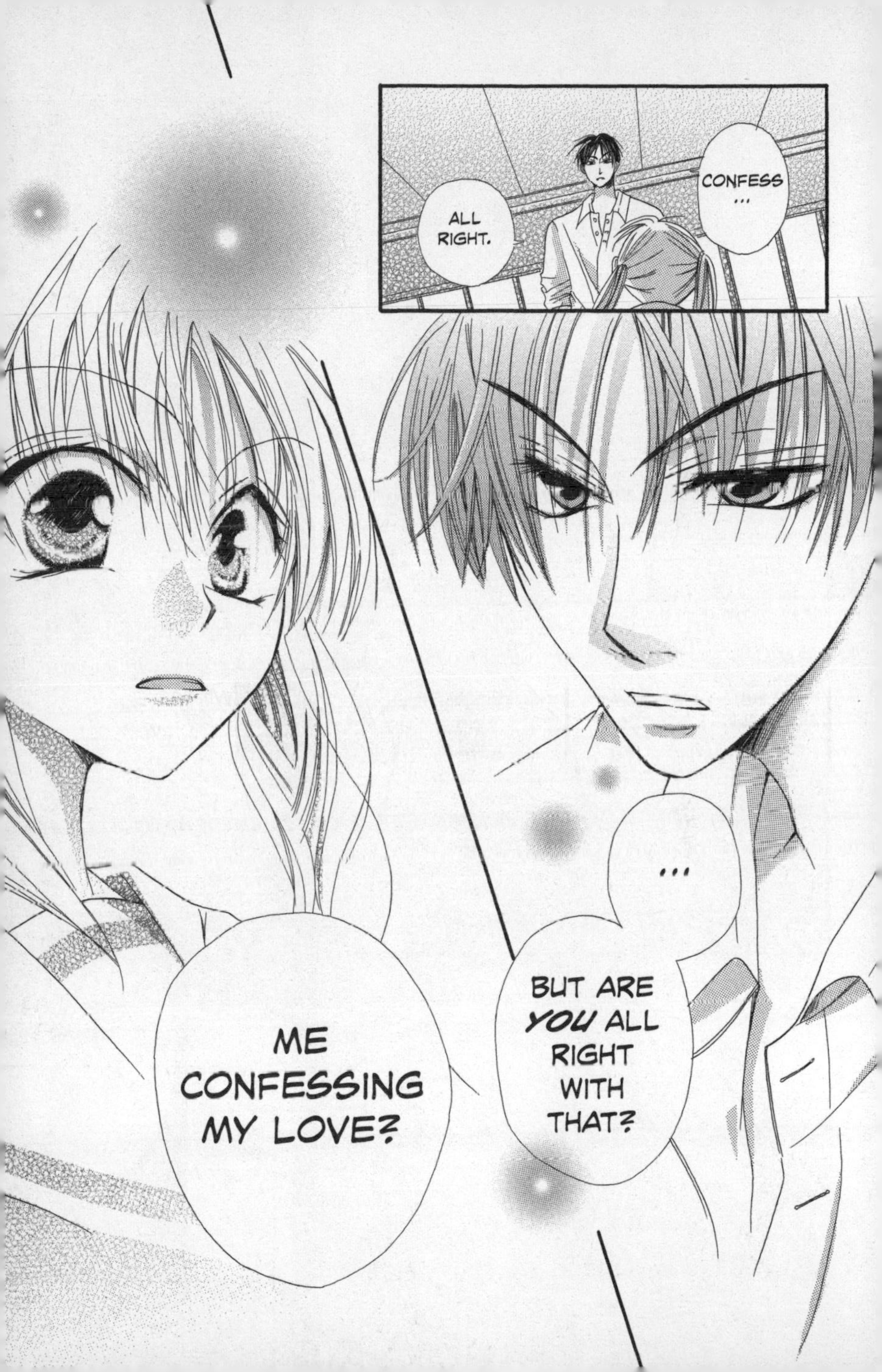
CONFESS...
ALL RIGHT.
...
BUT ARE *YOU* ALL RIGHT WITH THAT?
ME CONFESSING MY LOVE?

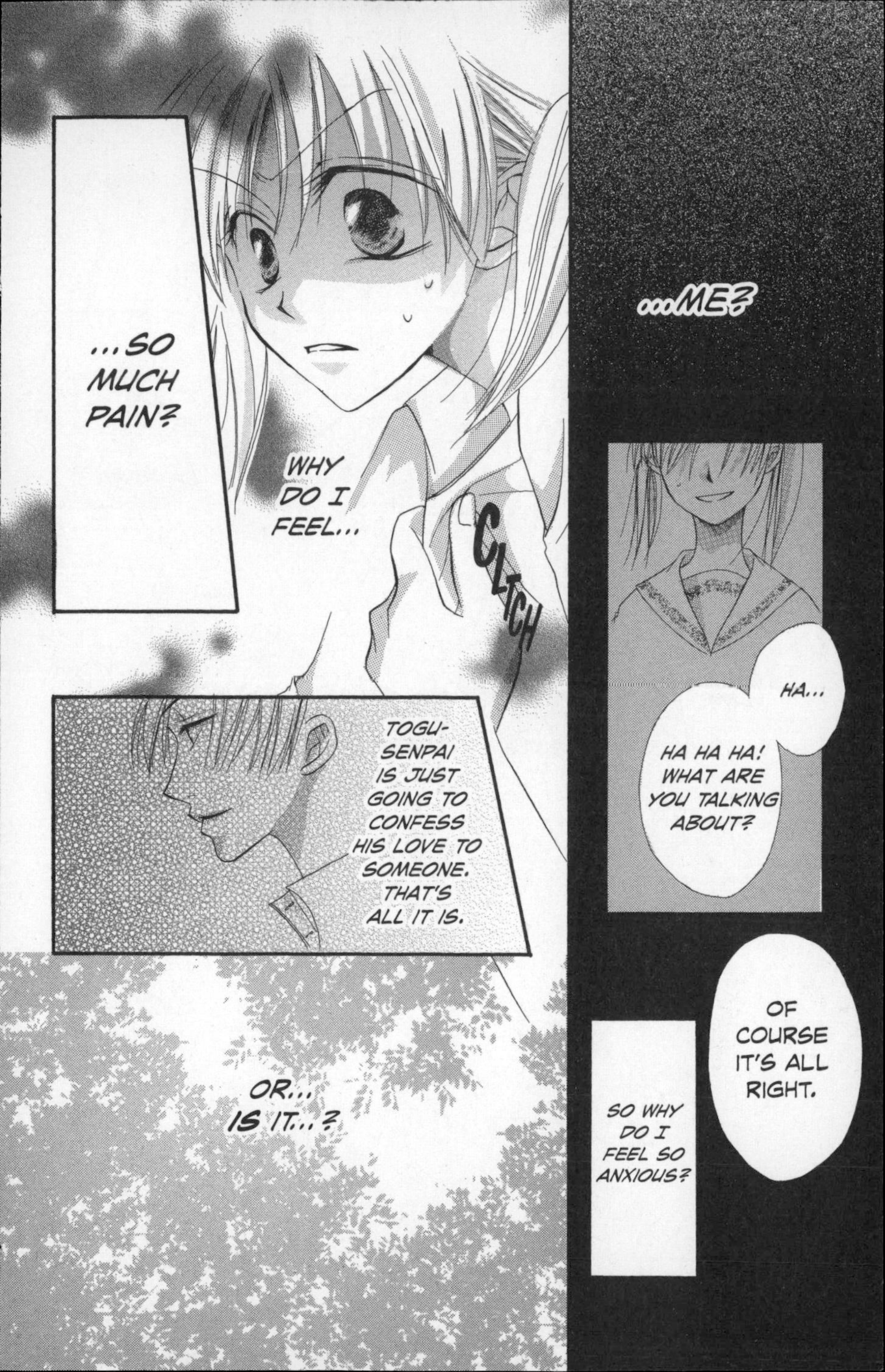
...ME?
HA...
HA HA HA! WHAT ARE YOU TALKING ABOUT?
OF COURSE IT'S ALL RIGHT.
SO WHY DO I FEEL SO ANXIOUS?
CLTCH
WHY DO I FEEL...
...SO MUCH PAIN?
TOGU-SENPAI IS JUST GOING TO CONFESS HIS LOVE TO SOMEONE. THAT'S ALL IT IS.
OR... IS IT...?

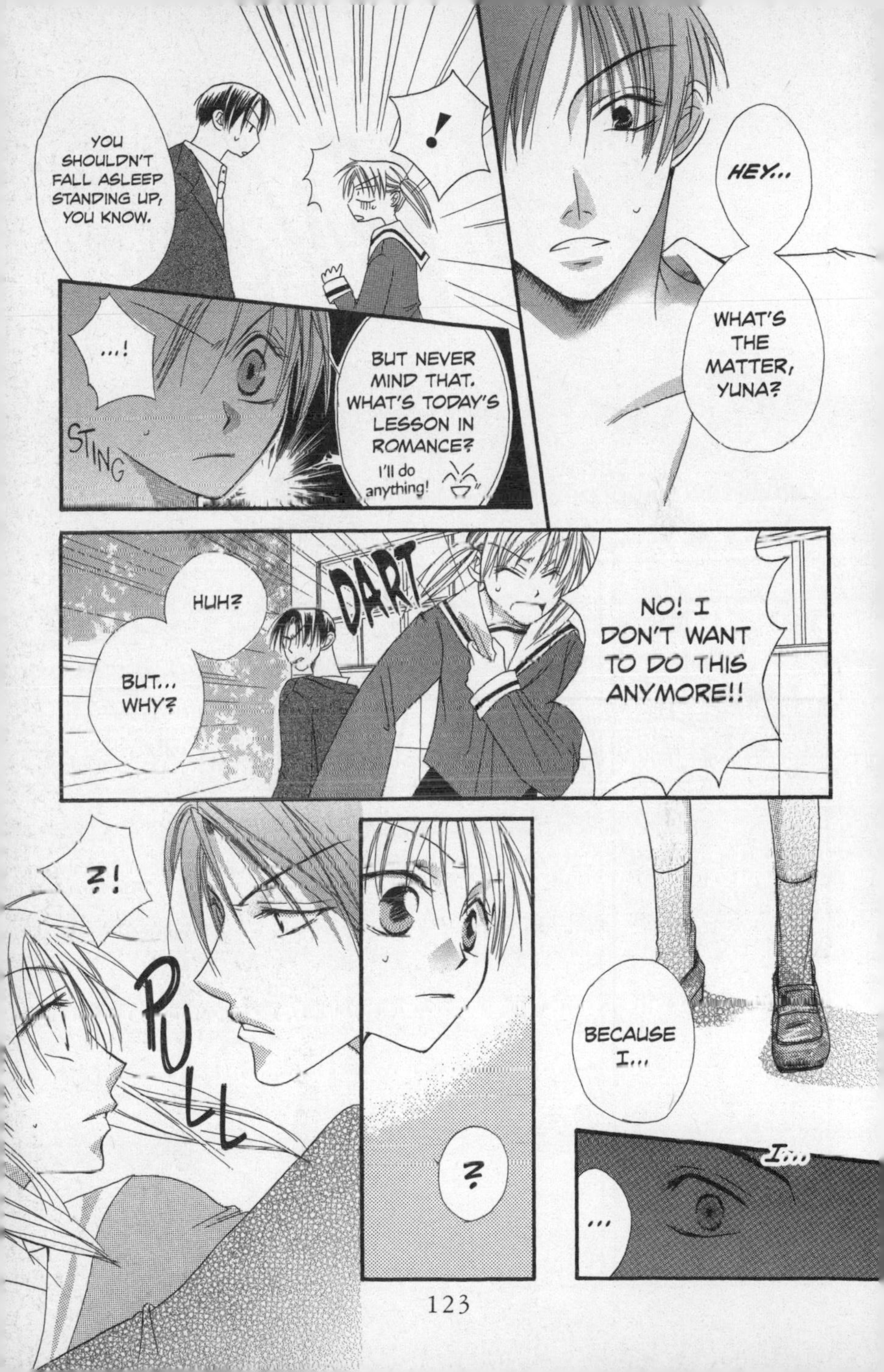
HEY...
WHAT'S THE MATTER, YUNA?
!
YOU SHOULDN'T FALL ASLEEP STANDING UP, YOU KNOW.
BUT NEVER MIND THAT. WHAT'S TODAY'S LESSON IN ROMANCE?
I'll do anything!
...!
STING
NO! I DON'T WANT TO DO THIS ANYMORE!!
DART
HUH?
BUT... WHY?
BECAUSE I...
I...
...
?
?!
PULL

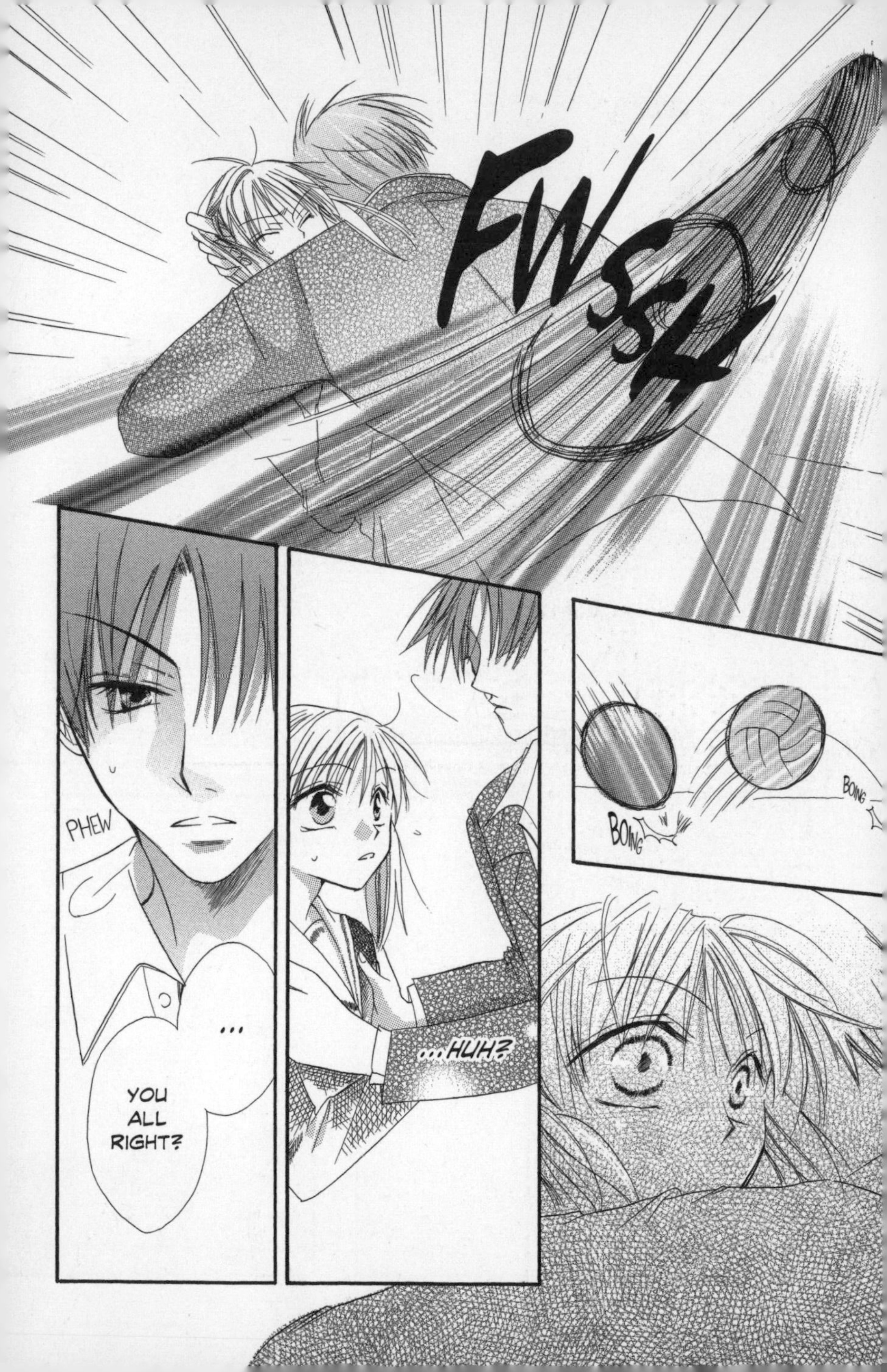
FWSH
BOING
BOING
...HUH?
PHEW
...
YOU ALL RIGHT?

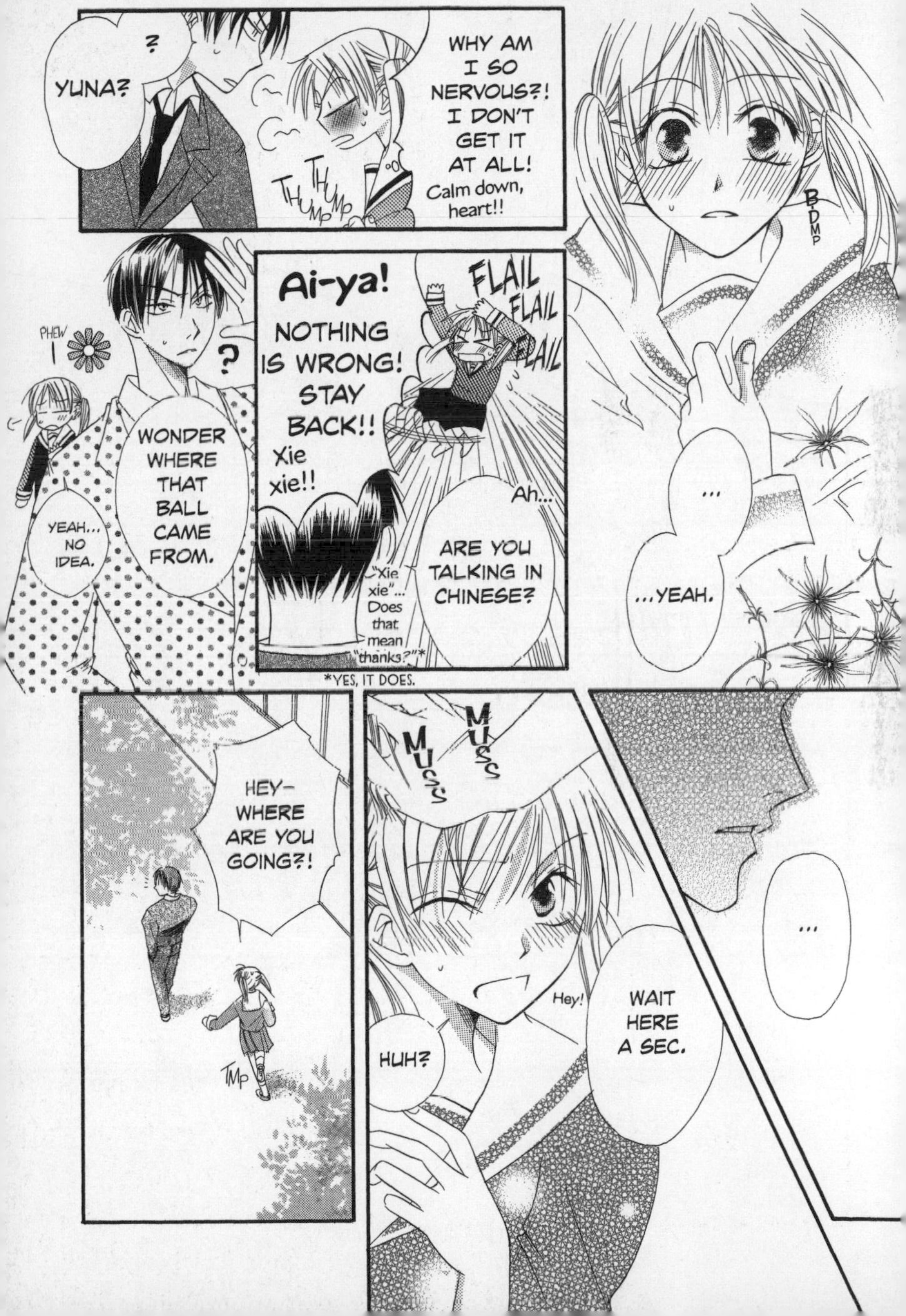

B-DMP
...
...YEAH.
WHY AM I SO NERVOUS?! I DON'T GET IT AT ALL!
Calm down, heart!!
THUMP THUMP
?
YUNA?
FLAIL FLAIL FLAIL
Ai-ya! NOTHING IS WRONG! STAY BACK!!
Xie xie!!
Ah...
ARE YOU TALKING IN CHINESE?
"Xie xie"... Does that mean "thanks?"*
*YES, IT DOES.
?
WONDER WHERE THAT BALL CAME FROM.
PHEW
YEAH... NO IDEA.
...
MUSS MUSS
Hey!
WAIT HERE A SEC.
HUH?
HEY— WHERE ARE YOU GOING?!
TMP

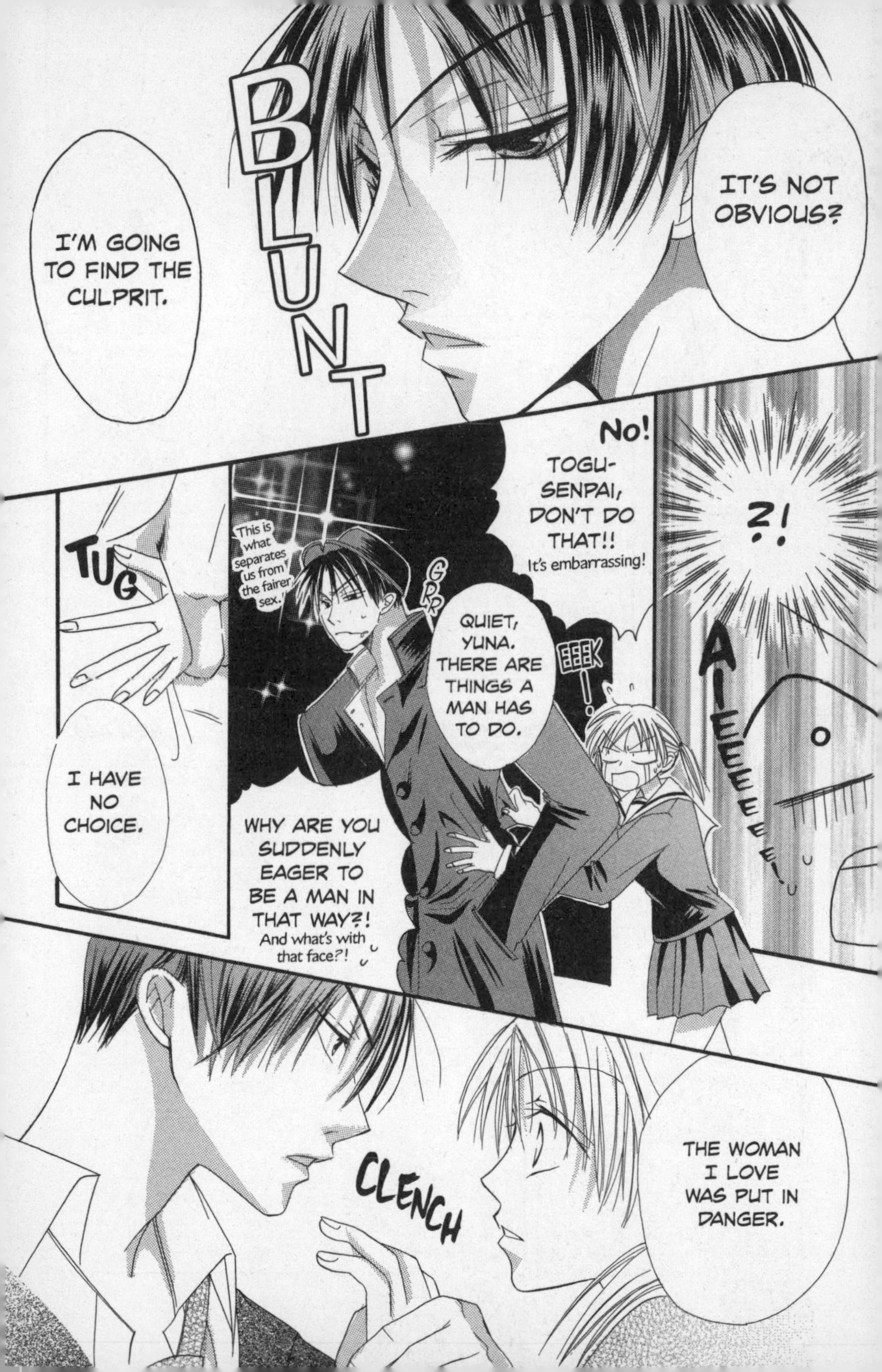
IT'S NOT OBVIOUS?
BLUNT
I'M GOING TO FIND THE CULPRIT.
?!
AIEEEEEE!
No!
TOGU-SENPAI, DON'T DO THAT!!
It's embarrassing!
QUIET, YUNA. THERE ARE THINGS A MAN HAS TO DO.
EEEK!
GRR
This is what separates us from the fairer sex.
WHY ARE YOU SUDDENLY EAGER TO BE A MAN IN THAT WAY?!
And what's with that face?!
TUG
I HAVE NO CHOICE.
THE WOMAN I LOVE WAS PUT IN DANGER.
CLENCH

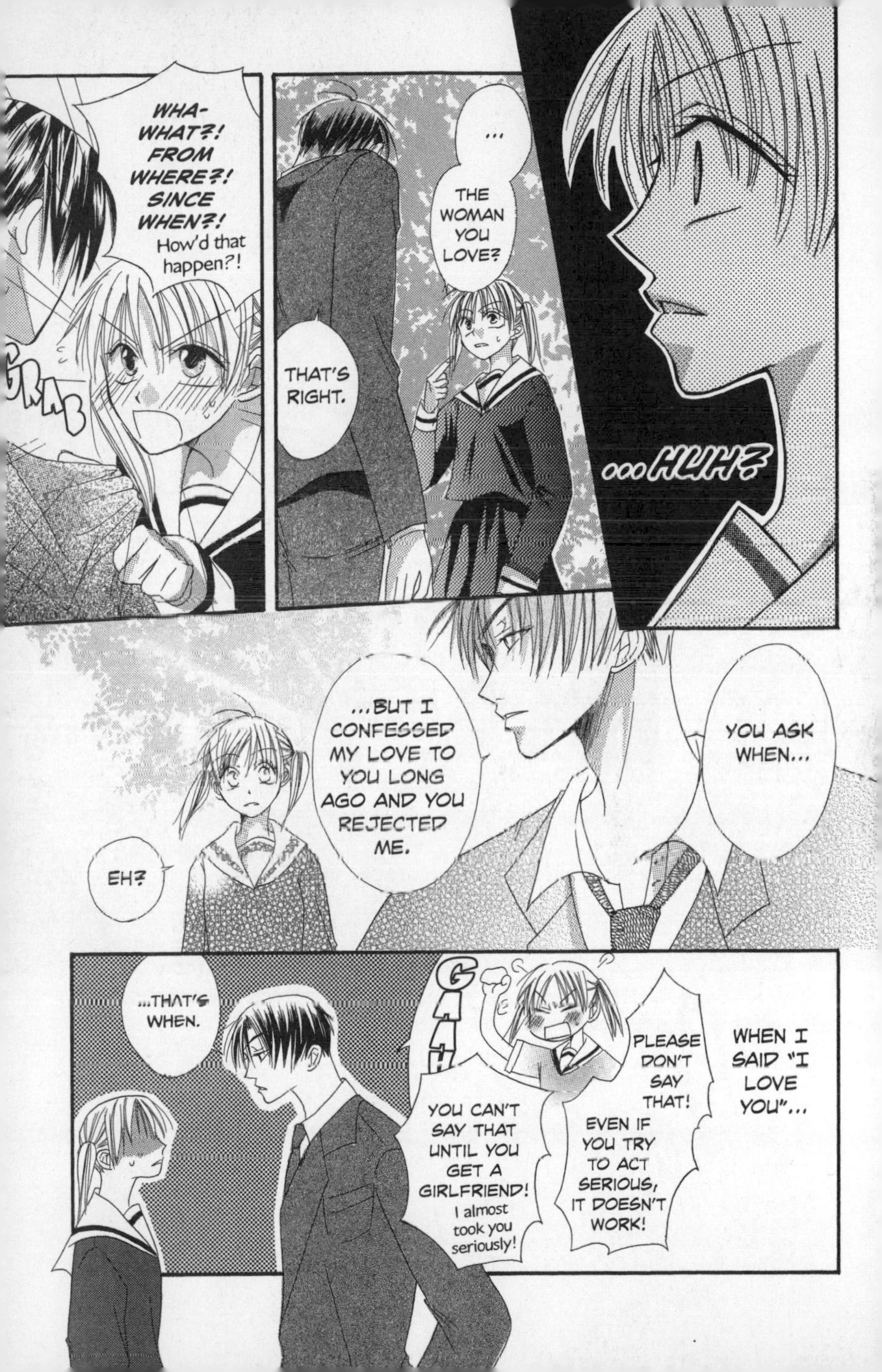
...HUH?
...
THE WOMAN YOU LOVE?
THAT'S RIGHT.
WHA-WHAT?! FROM WHERE?! SINCE WHEN?!
How'd that happen?!
GRAB
YOU ASK WHEN...
...BUT I CONFESSED MY LOVE TO YOU LONG AGO AND YOU REJECTED ME.
EH?
WHEN I SAID "I LOVE YOU"...
...THAT'S WHEN.
PLEASE DON'T SAY THAT!
EVEN IF YOU TRY TO ACT SERIOUS, IT DOESN'T WORK!
GAAH
YOU CAN'T SAY THAT UNTIL YOU GET A GIRLFRIEND!
I almost took you seriously!

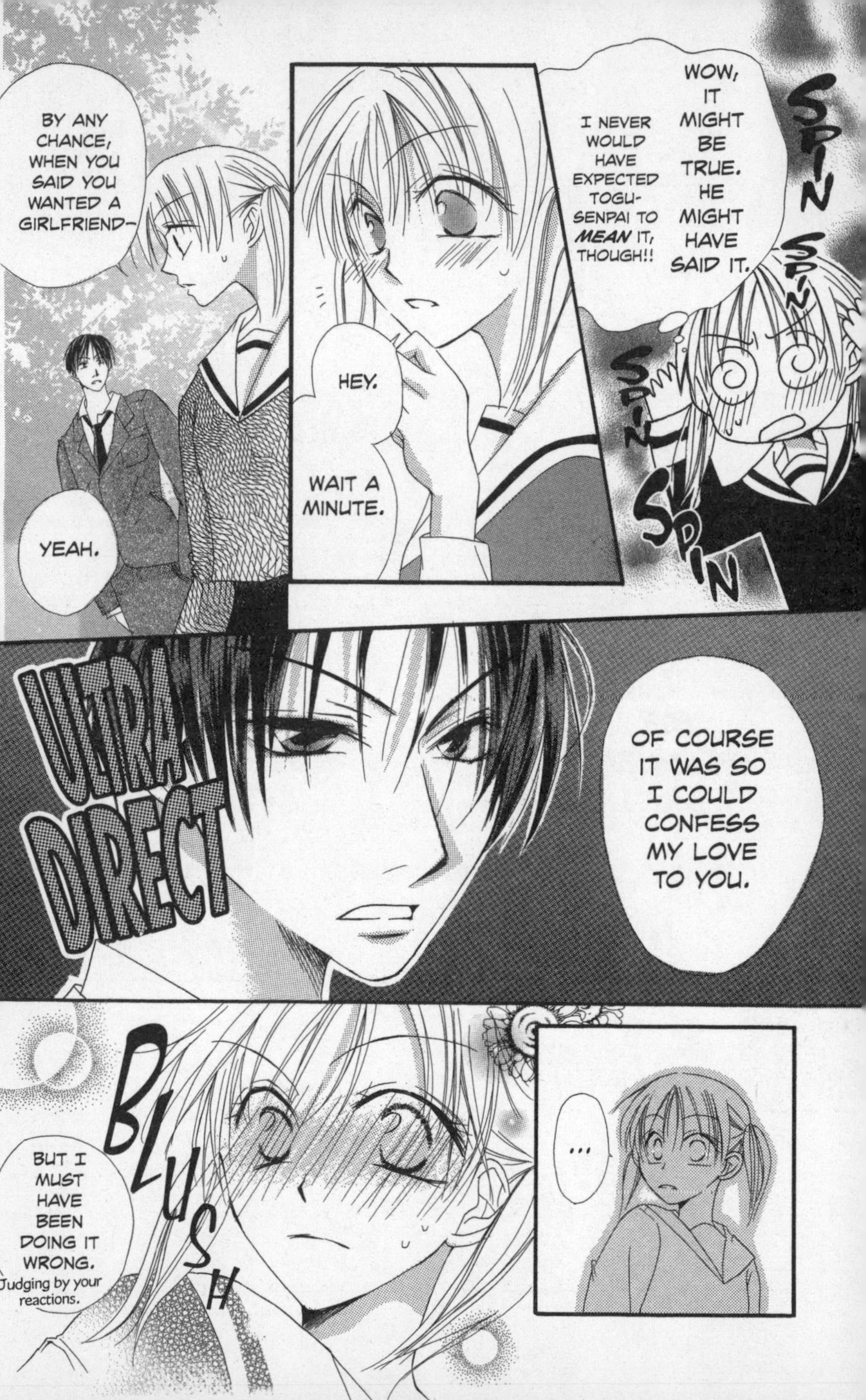
WOW, IT MIGHT BE TRUE. HE MIGHT HAVE SAID IT.
I NEVER WOULD HAVE EXPECTED TOGU-SENPAI TO *MEAN* IT, THOUGH!!
SPIN
SPIN
SPIN
SPIN
HEY.
WAIT A MINUTE.
BY ANY CHANCE, WHEN YOU SAID YOU WANTED A GIRLFRIEND—
YEAH.
OF COURSE IT WAS SO I COULD CONFESS MY LOVE TO YOU.
ULTRA DIRECT
...
BLUSH
BUT I MUST HAVE BEEN DOING IT WRONG.
Judging by your reactions.

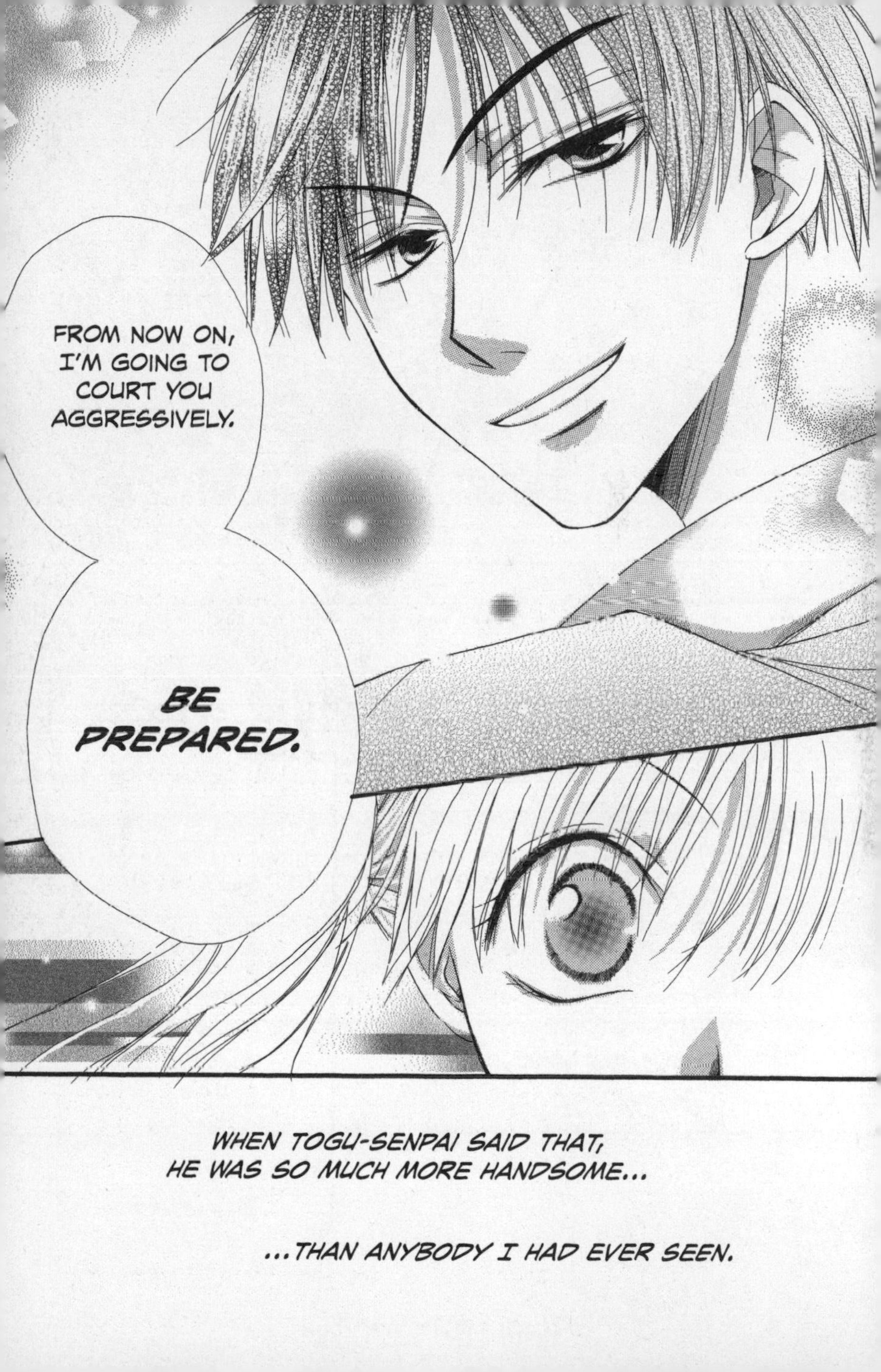
FROM NOW ON, I'M GOING TO COURT YOU AGGRESSIVELY.
BE PREPARED.
WHEN TOGU-SENPAI SAID THAT, HE WAS SO MUCH MORE HANDSOME...
...THAN ANYBODY I HAD EVER SEEN.

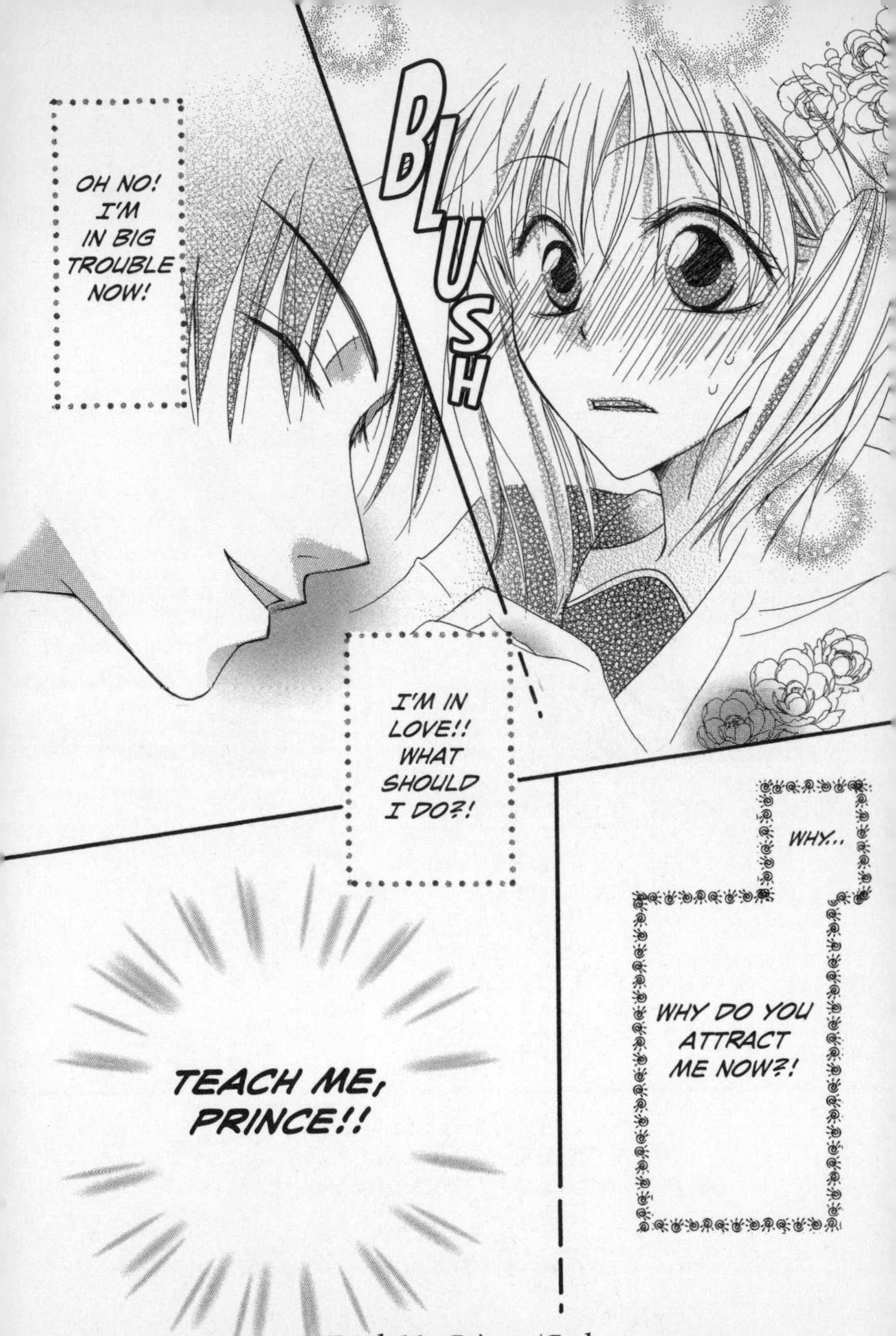
BLUSH
OH NO! I'M IN BIG TROUBLE NOW!
I'M IN LOVE!! WHAT SHOULD I DO?!
WHY...
WHY DO YOU ATTRACT ME NOW?!
TEACH ME, PRINCE!!

Teach Me, Prince / End

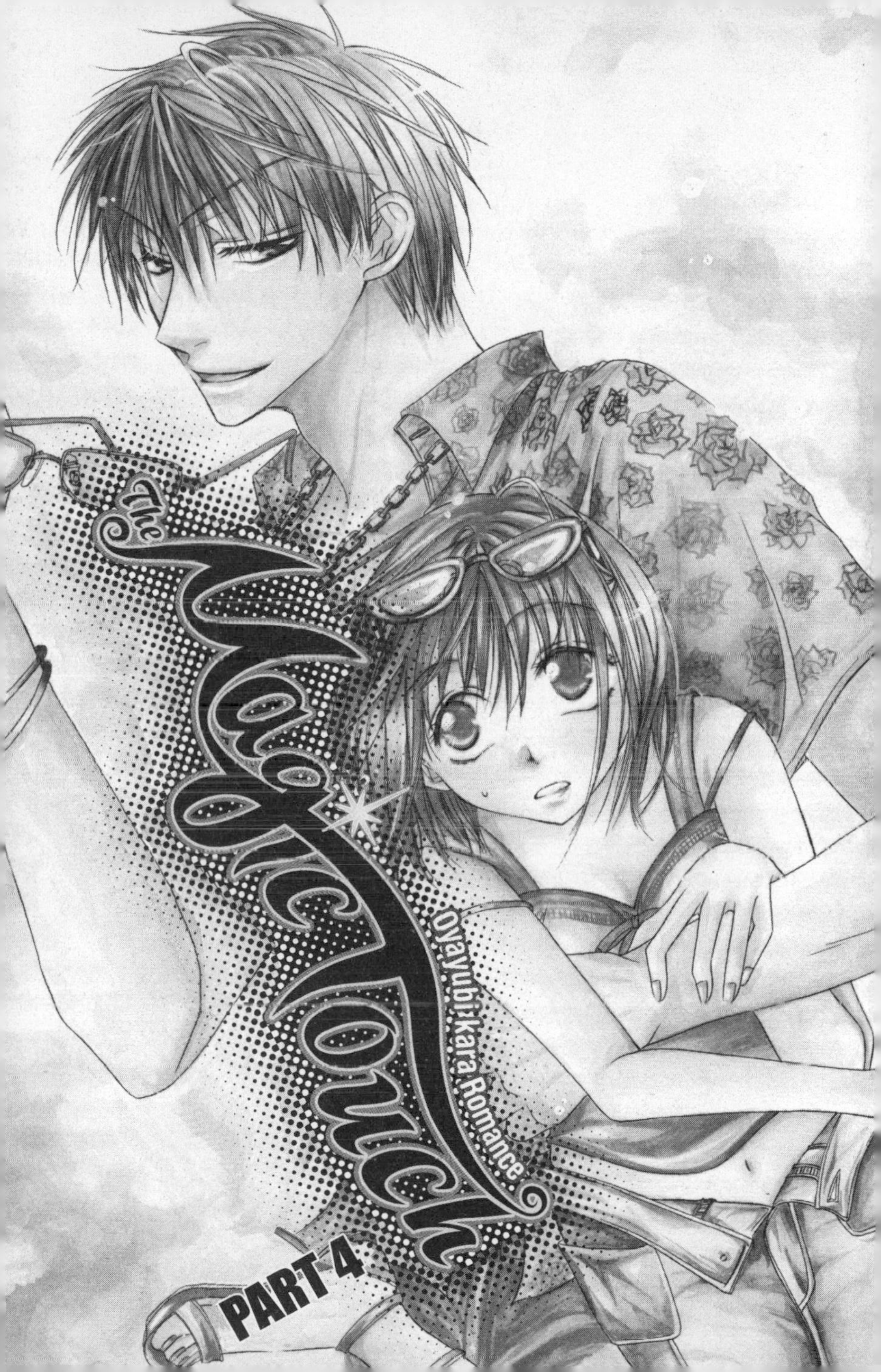
The Magic Touch
Oyayubi kara Romance
PART 4

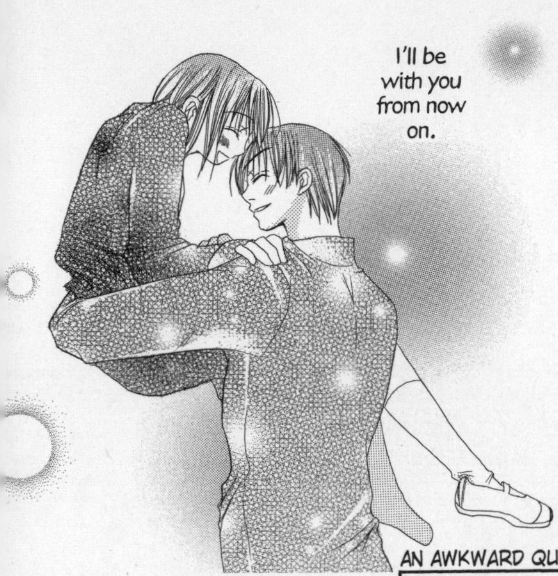
I'll be with you from now on.

A MISCOMMUNICATION

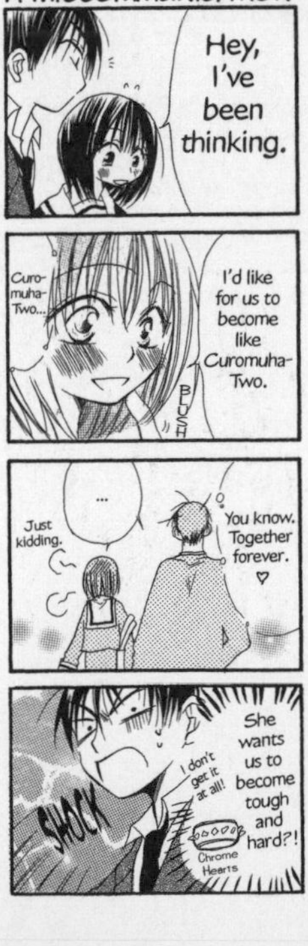
Hey, I've been thinking.
I'd like for us to become like Curomuha-Two.
Curomuha-Two...
BLUSH
You know. Together forever. ♡
...
Just kidding.
She wants us to become tough and hard?!
I don't get it at all!
SHOCK
Chrome Hearts

AN AWKWARD QUESTION

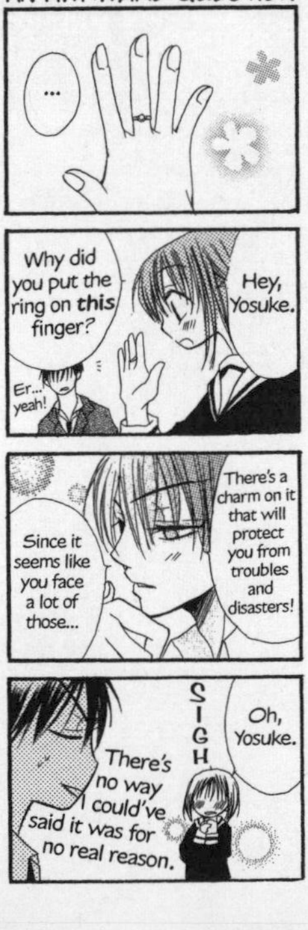
...
Hey, Yosuke.
Why did you put the ring on **this** finger?
Er... yeah!
There's a charm on it that will protect you from troubles and disasters!
Since it seems like you face a lot of those...
Oh, Yosuke.
SIGH
There's no way I could've said it was for no real reason.

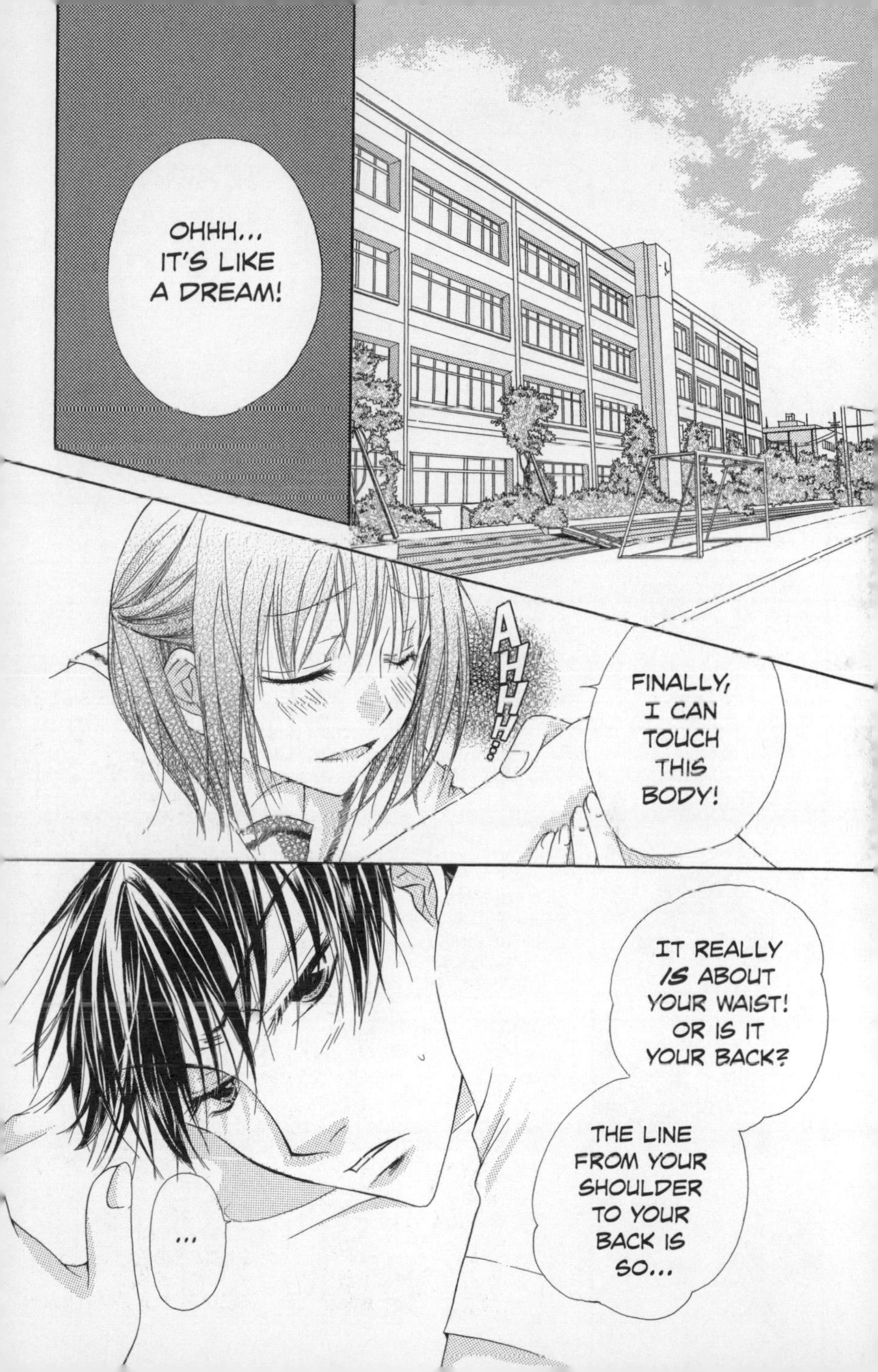
OHHH... IT'S LIKE A DREAM!
AHHH...
FINALLY, I CAN TOUCH THIS BODY!
IT REALLY *IS* ABOUT YOUR WAIST! OR IS IT YOUR BACK?
THE LINE FROM YOUR SHOULDER TO YOUR BACK IS SO...
...

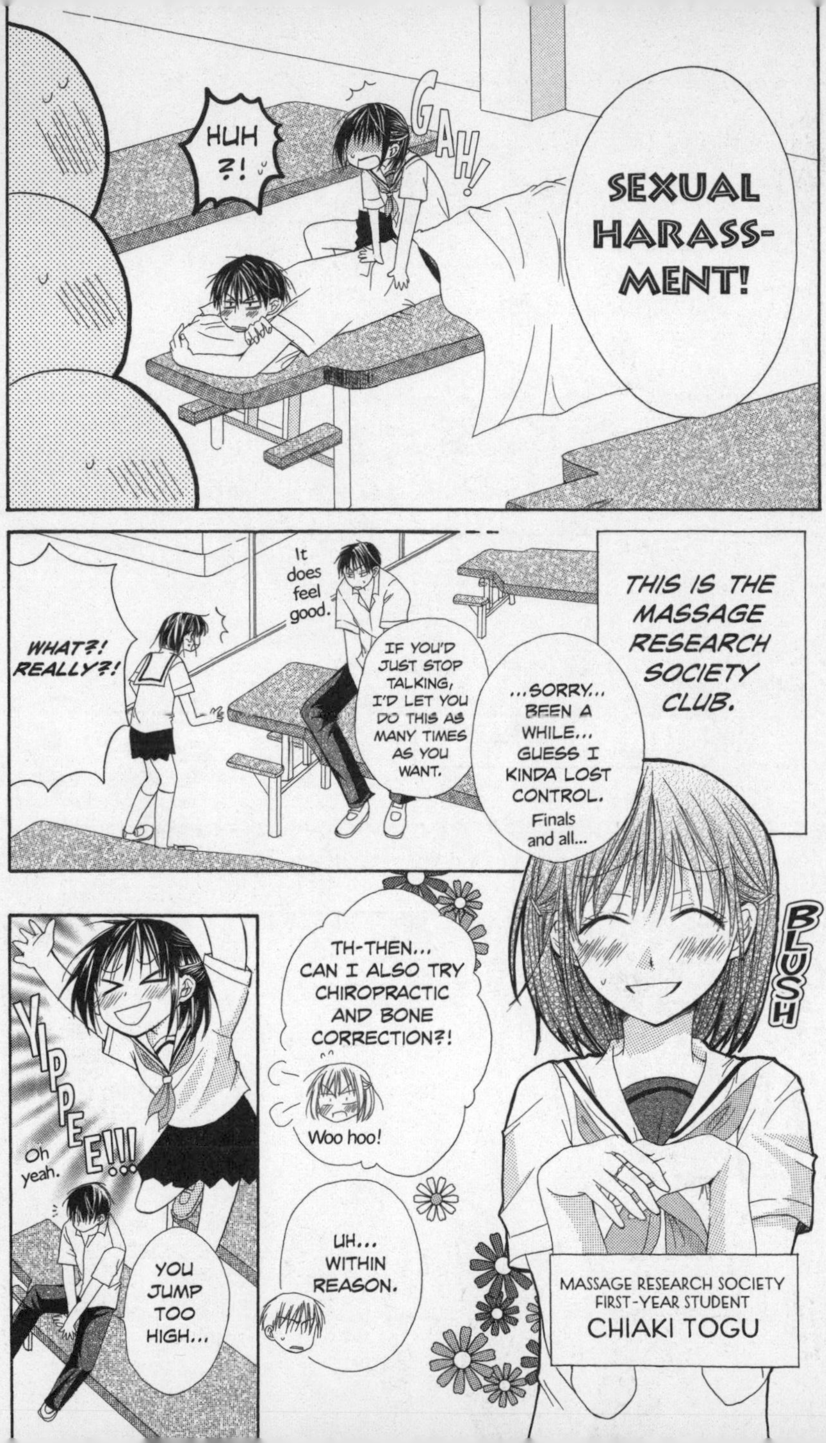
SEXUAL HARASS-MENT!
GAH!
HUH ?!
THIS IS THE MASSAGE RESEARCH SOCIETY CLUB.
It does feel good.
IF YOU'D JUST STOP TALKING, I'D LET YOU DO THIS AS MANY TIMES AS YOU WANT.
WHAT?! REALLY?!
BLUSH
...SORRY... BEEN A WHILE... GUESS I KINDA LOST CONTROL.
Finals and all...
TH-THEN... CAN I ALSO TRY CHIROPRACTIC AND BONE CORRECTION?!
Woo hoo!
UH... WITHIN REASON.
MASSAGE RESEARCH SOCIETY
FIRST-YEAR STUDENT
CHIAKI TOGU
YIPPEE!!!
Oh yeah.
YOU JUMP TOO HIGH...

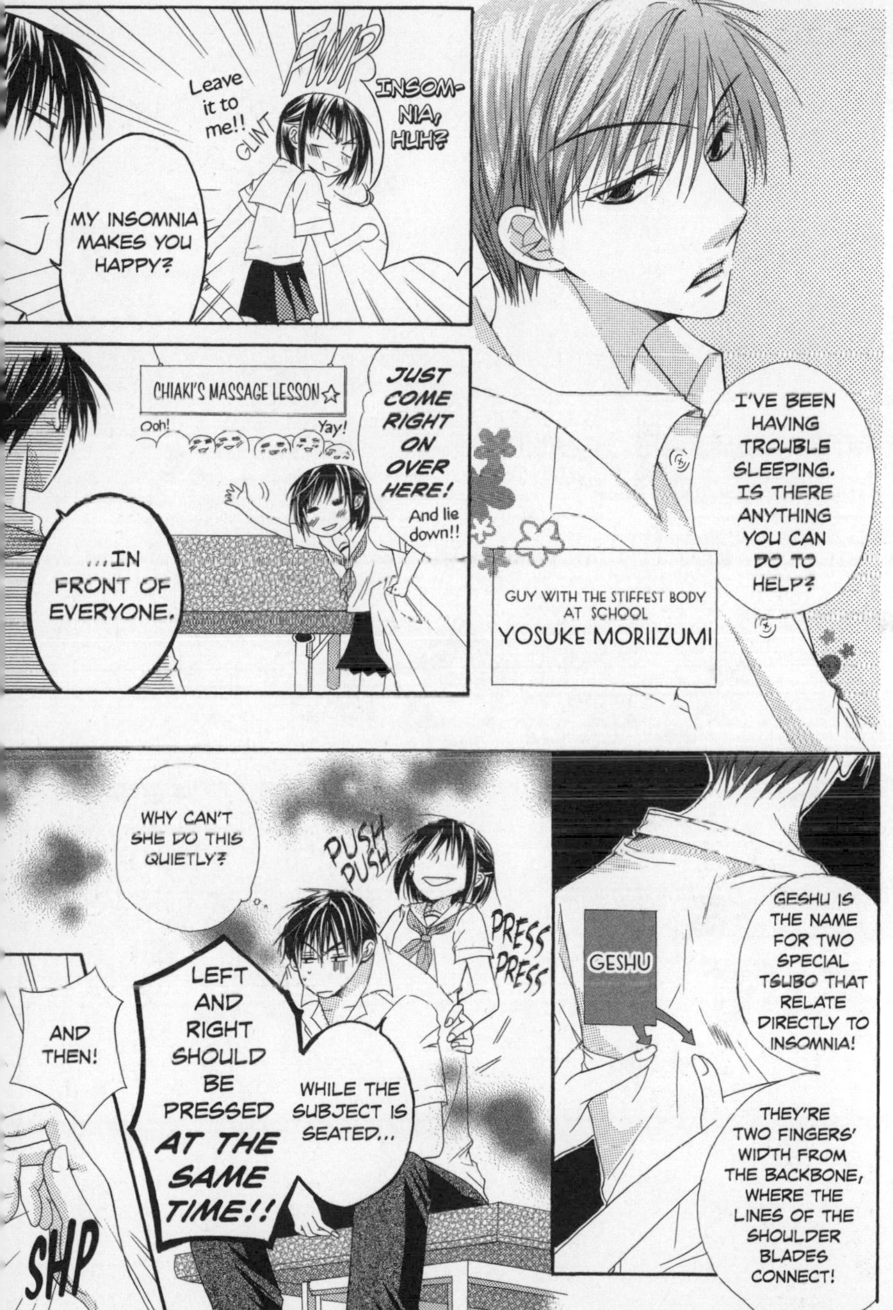
I'VE BEEN HAVING TROUBLE SLEEPING. IS THERE ANYTHING YOU CAN DO TO HELP?
GUY WITH THE STIFFEST BODY AT SCHOOL
YOSUKE MORIIZUMI
FWIP
INSOMNIA, HUH?
Leave it to me!!
GLINT
MY INSOMNIA MAKES YOU HAPPY?
JUST COME RIGHT ON OVER HERE!
And lie down!!
CHIAKI'S MASSAGE LESSON☆
Yay!
Ooh!
...IN FRONT OF EVERYONE.
GESHU IS THE NAME FOR TWO SPECIAL TSUBO THAT RELATE DIRECTLY TO INSOMNIA!
GESHU
THEY'RE TWO FINGERS' WIDTH FROM THE BACKBONE, WHERE THE LINES OF THE SHOULDER BLADES CONNECT!
PUSH PUSH
PRESS PRESS
WHY CAN'T SHE DO THIS QUIETLY?
WHILE THE SUBJECT IS SEATED...
LEFT AND RIGHT SHOULD BE PRESSED AT THE SAME TIME!!
AND THEN!
SHP

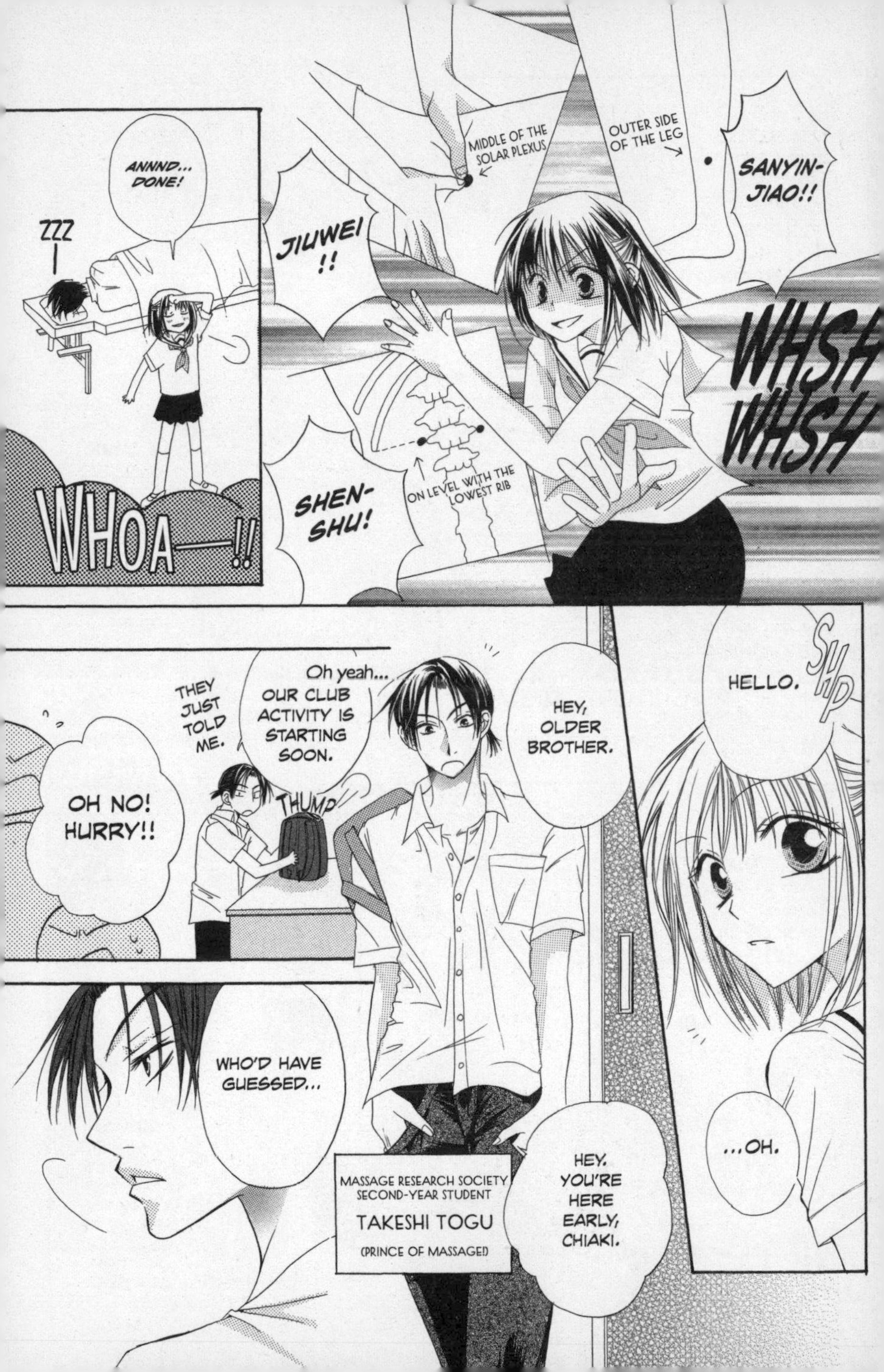
SANYIN-JIAO!!
OUTER SIDE OF THE LEG
MIDDLE OF THE SOLAR PLEXUS
JIUWEI !!
WHSH WHSH
ON LEVEL WITH THE LOWEST RIB
SHEN-SHU!
ANNND... DONE!
ZZZ
WHOA—!!
HELLO.
SHP
...OH.
HEY, OLDER BROTHER.
Oh yeah...
OUR CLUB ACTIVITY IS STARTING SOON.
THEY JUST TOLD ME.
OH NO! HURRY!!
THUMP
MASSAGE RESEARCH SOCIETY SECOND-YEAR STUDENT
TAKESHI TOGU
(PRINCE OF MASSAGE!)
HEY. YOU'RE HERE EARLY, CHIAKI.
WHO'D HAVE GUESSED...

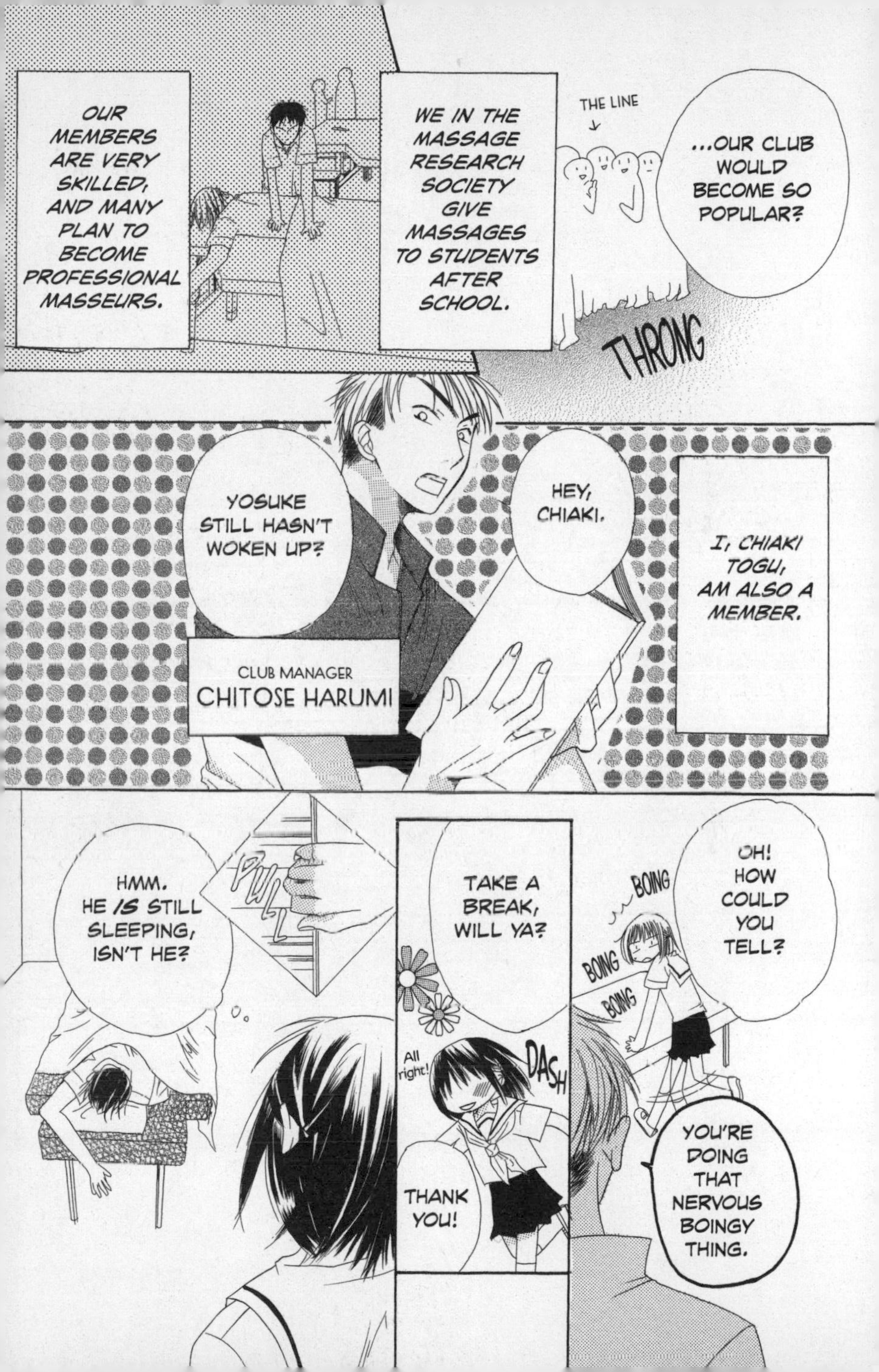
THE LINE
...OUR CLUB WOULD BECOME SO POPULAR?
THRONG
WE IN THE MASSAGE RESEARCH SOCIETY GIVE MASSAGES TO STUDENTS AFTER SCHOOL.
OUR MEMBERS ARE VERY SKILLED, AND MANY PLAN TO BECOME PROFESSIONAL MASSEURS.
I, CHIAKI TOGU, AM ALSO A MEMBER.
HEY, CHIAKI.
YOSUKE STILL HASN'T WOKEN UP?
CLUB MANAGER
CHITOSE HARUMI
OH! HOW COULD YOU TELL?
BOING
BOING
BOING
YOU'RE DOING THAT NERVOUS BOINGY THING.
TAKE A BREAK, WILL YA?
All right!
DASH
THANK YOU!
HMM. HE *IS* STILL SLEEPING, ISN'T HE?
PULL

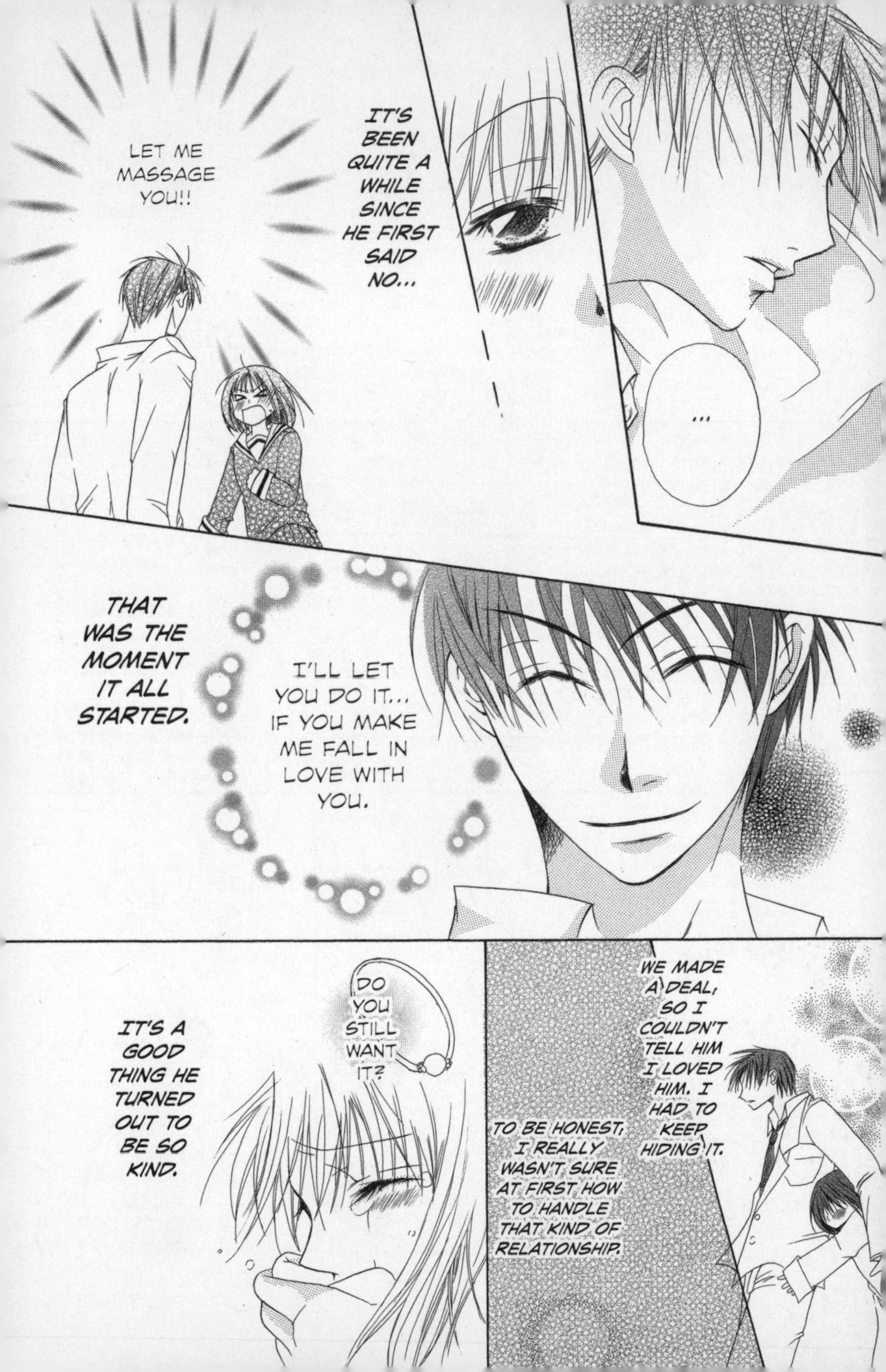
...
IT'S BEEN QUITE A WHILE SINCE HE FIRST SAID NO...
LET ME MASSAGE YOU!!
I'LL LET YOU DO IT... IF YOU MAKE ME FALL IN LOVE WITH YOU.
THAT WAS THE MOMENT IT ALL STARTED.
WE MADE A DEAL, SO I COULDN'T TELL HIM I LOVED HIM. I HAD TO KEEP HIDING IT.
TO BE HONEST, I REALLY WASN'T SURE AT FIRST HOW TO HANDLE THAT KIND OF RELATIONSHIP.
DO YOU STILL WANT IT?
IT'S A GOOD THING HE TURNED OUT TO BE SO KIND.

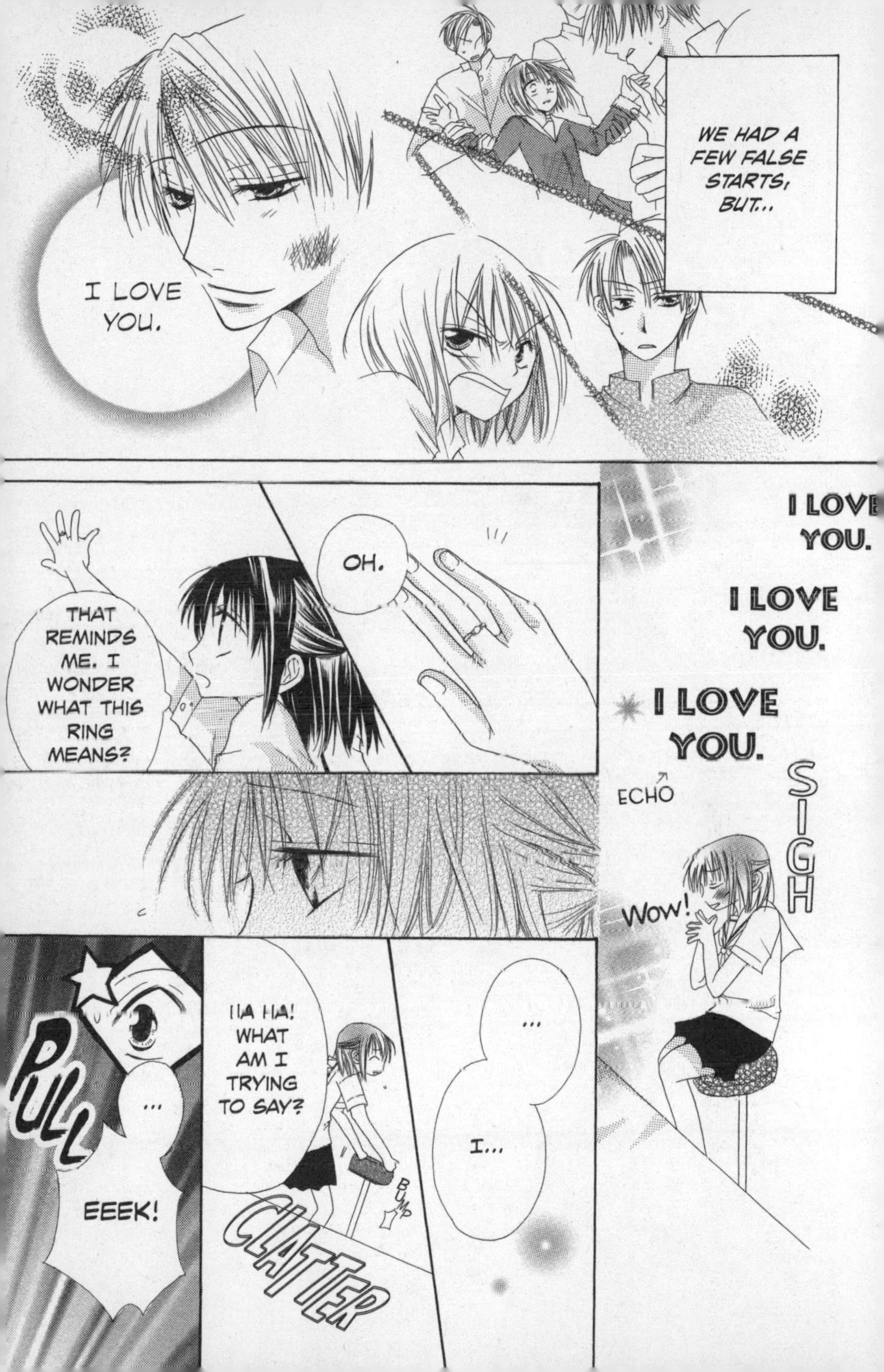
WE HAD A FEW FALSE STARTS, BUT...
I LOVE YOU.
I LOVE YOU.
I LOVE YOU.
I LOVE YOU.
ECHO
SIGH
WOW!
OH.
THAT REMINDS ME. I WONDER WHAT THIS RING MEANS?
...
I...
HA HA! WHAT AM I TRYING TO SAY?
BUMP
CLATTER
...
EEEK!
PULL

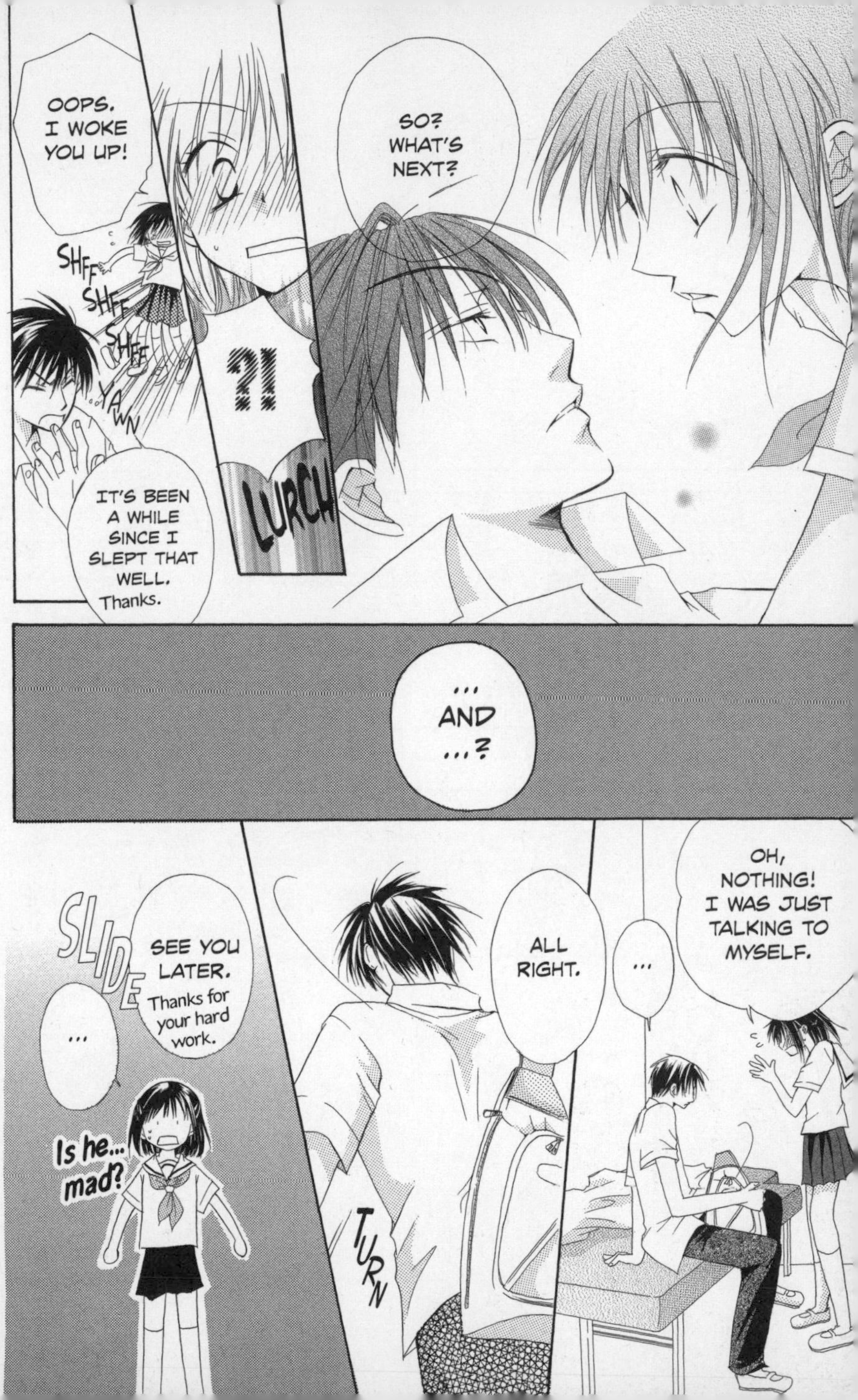
SO? WHAT'S NEXT?
?!
LURCH
OOPS. I WOKE YOU UP!
SHFF
SHFF
SHFF
...YAWN
IT'S BEEN A WHILE SINCE I SLEPT THAT WELL. Thanks.
... AND ...?
OH, NOTHING! I WAS JUST TALKING TO MYSELF.
...
ALL RIGHT.
TURN
SLIDE
SEE YOU LATER. Thanks for your hard work.
...
Is he... mad?

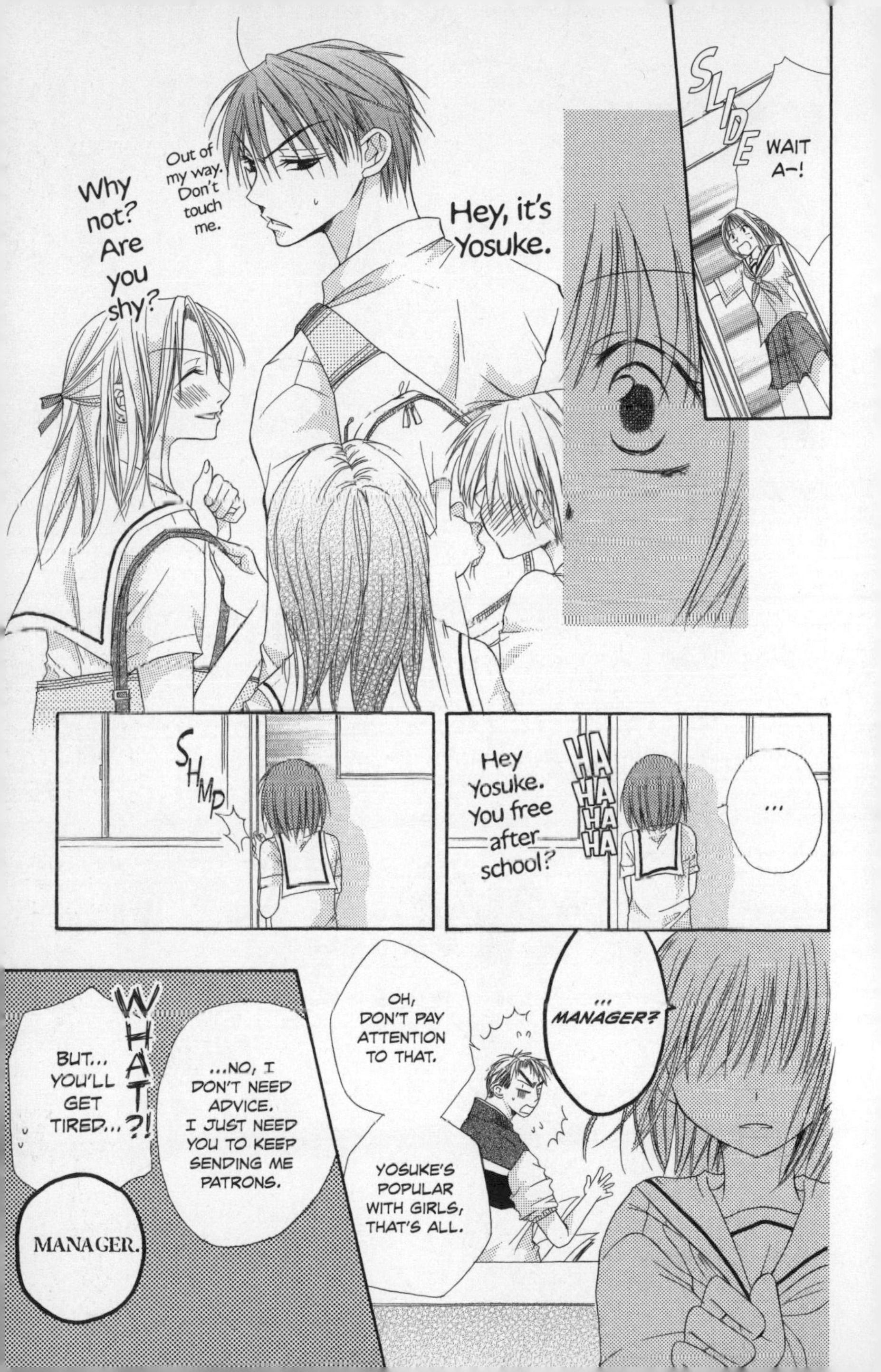
SLIDE
WAIT A–!
Hey, it's Yosuke.
Out of my way. Don't touch me.
Why not? Are you shy?
...
Hey Yosuke. You free after school?
HAHAHAHAHA
SHMP
...MANAGER?
OH, DON'T PAY ATTENTION TO THAT.
YOSUKE'S POPULAR WITH GIRLS, THAT'S ALL.
...NO, I DON'T NEED ADVICE. I JUST NEED YOU TO KEEP SENDING ME PATRONS.
WHAT?!
BUT... YOU'LL GET TIRED...
MANAGER.

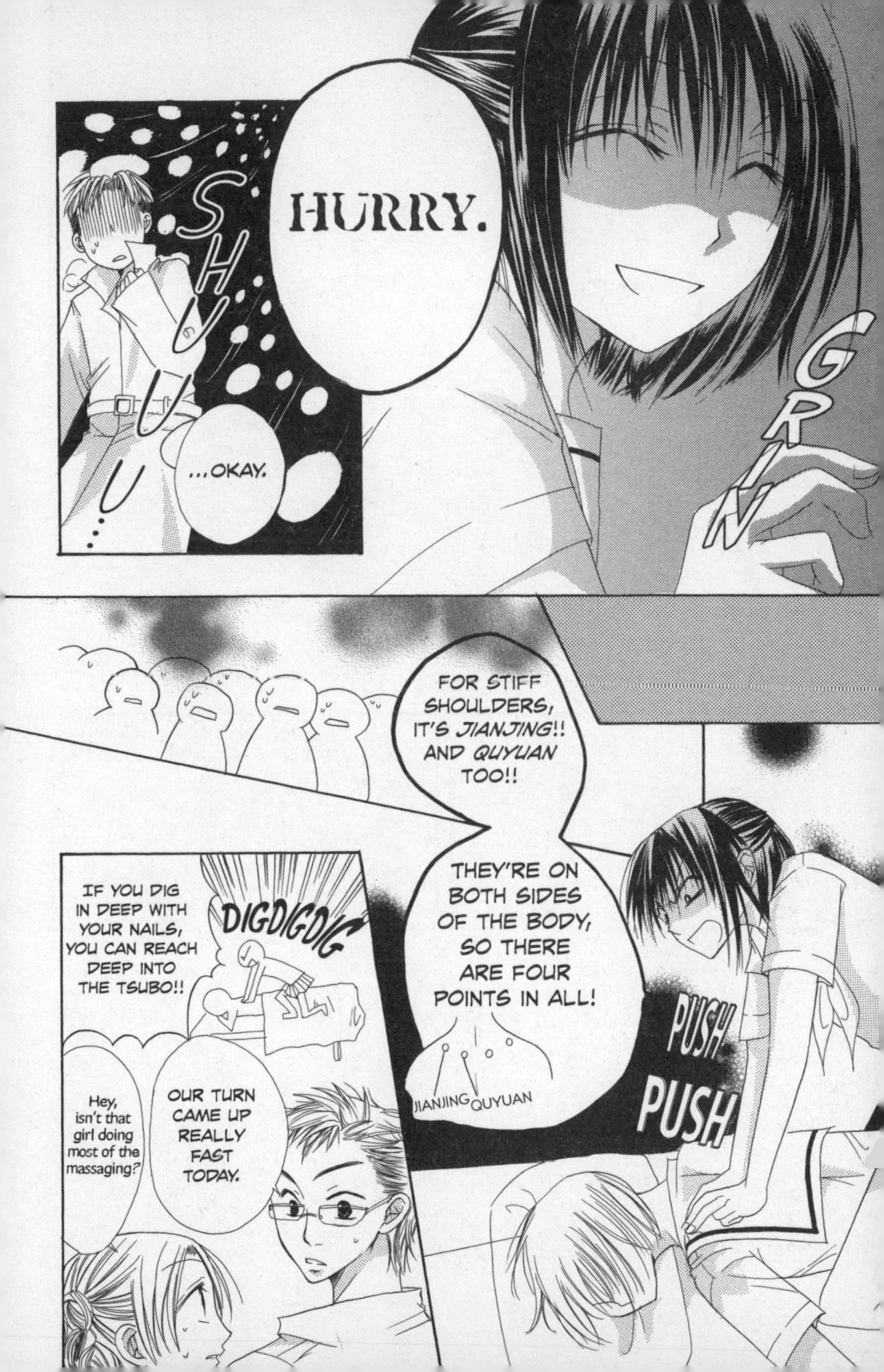
HURRY.
GRIN
SHUUUU...
...OKAY.
FOR STIFF SHOULDERS, IT'S *JIANJING*!! AND *QUYUAN* TOO!!
THEY'RE ON BOTH SIDES OF THE BODY, SO THERE ARE FOUR POINTS IN ALL!
JIANJING
QUYUAN
PUSH PUSH
IF YOU DIG IN DEEP WITH YOUR NAILS, YOU CAN REACH DEEP INTO THE TSUBO!!
DIGDIGDIG
OUR TURN CAME UP REALLY FAST TODAY.
Hey, isn't that girl doing most of the massaging?

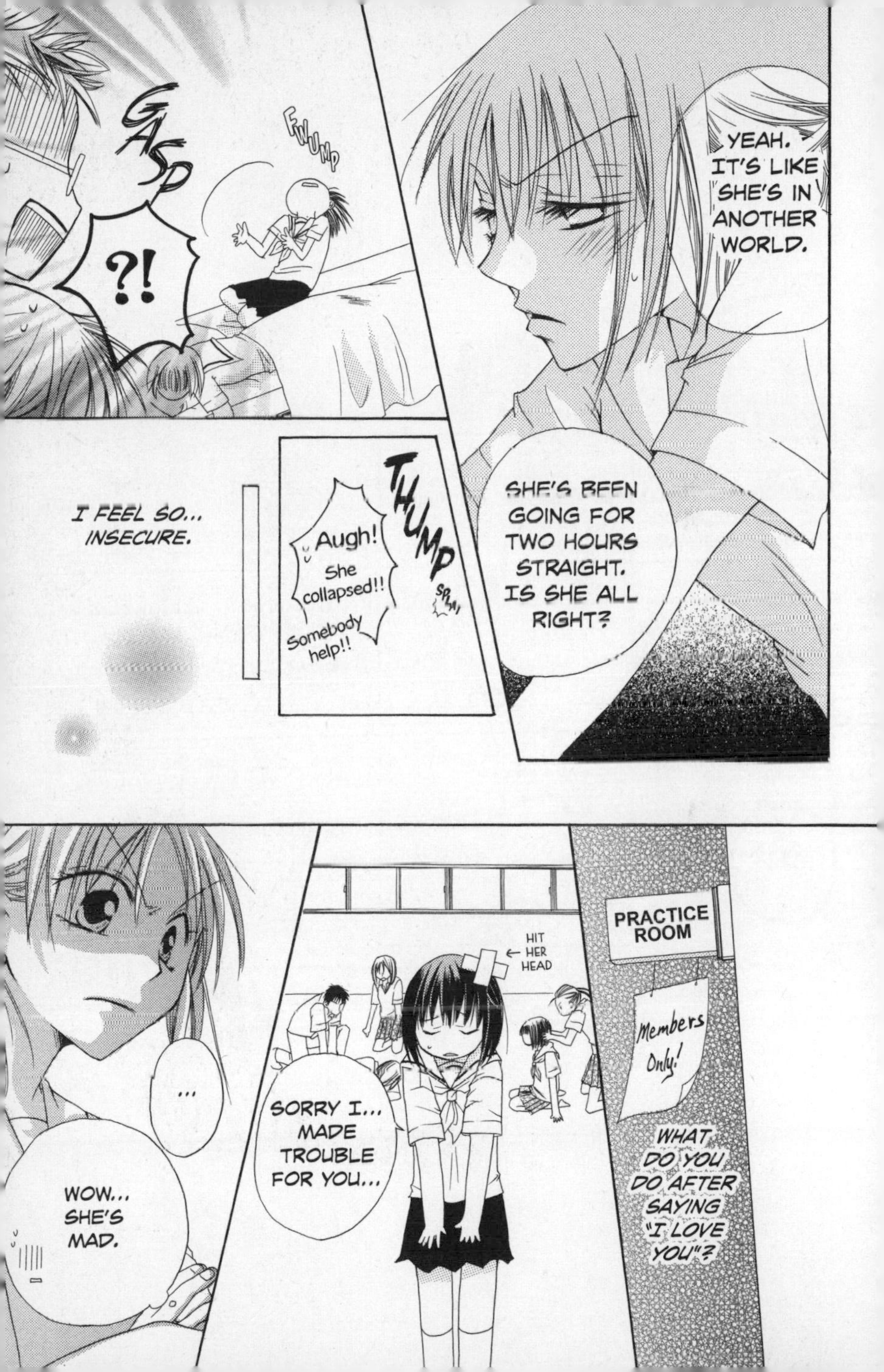
YEAH. IT'S LIKE SHE'S IN ANOTHER WORLD.
SHE'S BEEN GOING FOR TWO HOURS STRAIGHT. IS SHE ALL RIGHT?
GASP
?!
FWUMP
THUMP
Augh! She collapsed!! Somebody help!!
I FEEL SO... INSECURE.
PRACTICE ROOM
Members Only!
WHAT DO YOU DO AFTER SAYING "I LOVE YOU"?
HIT HER HEAD
SORRY I... MADE TROUBLE FOR YOU...
...
WOW... SHE'S MAD.

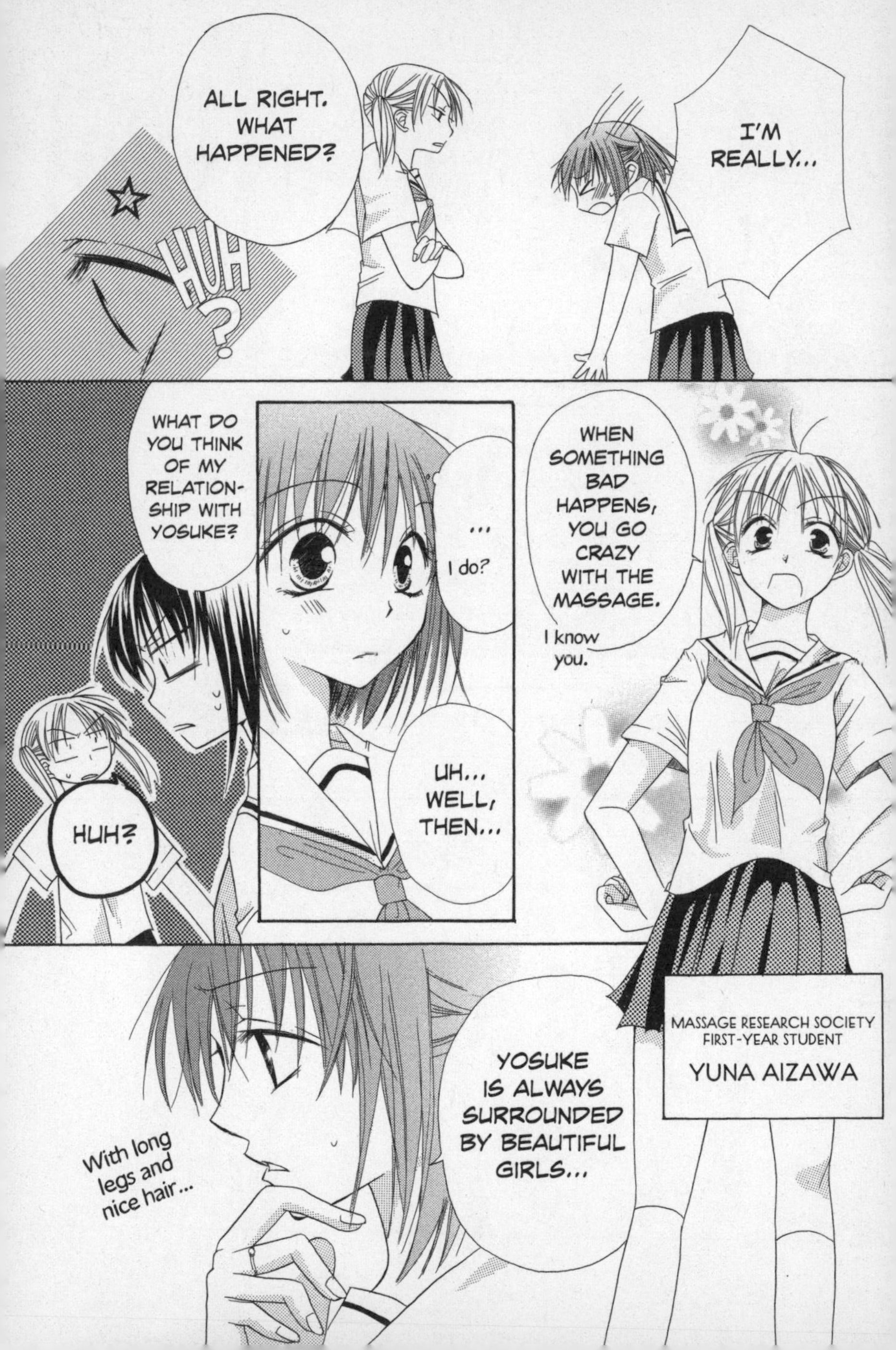
I'M REALLY...
ALL RIGHT. WHAT HAPPENED?
HUH ?
WHEN SOMETHING BAD HAPPENS, YOU GO CRAZY WITH THE MASSAGE.
I know you.
...
I do?
UH... WELL, THEN...
WHAT DO YOU THINK OF MY RELATIONSHIP WITH YOSUKE?
HUH?
MASSAGE RESEARCH SOCIETY FIRST-YEAR STUDENT
YUNA AIZAWA
YOSUKE IS ALWAYS SURROUNDED BY BEAUTIFUL GIRLS...
With long legs and nice hair...

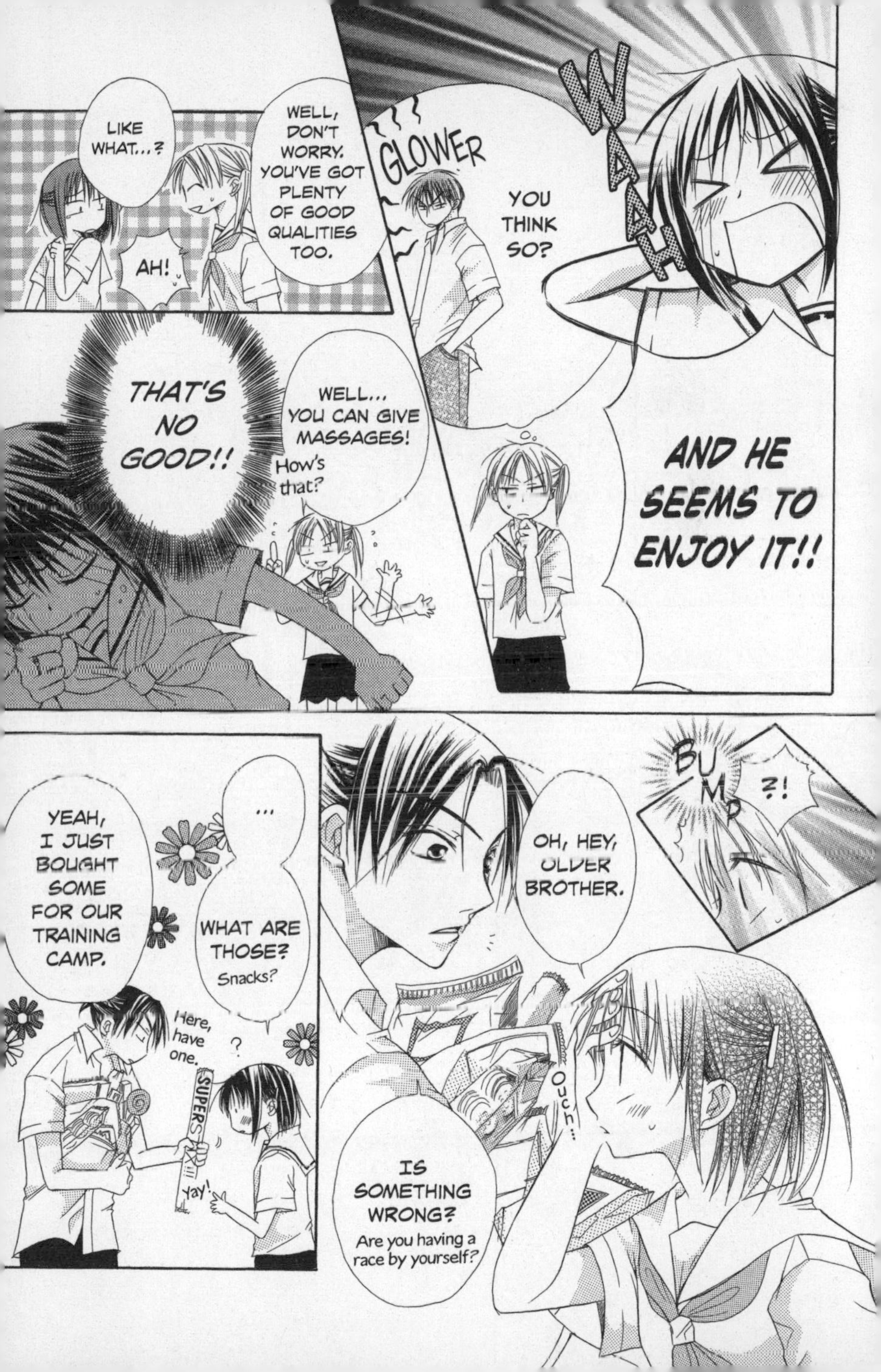
WAAH
GLOWER
YOU THINK SO?
AND HE SEEMS TO ENJOY IT!!
WELL, DON'T WORRY. YOU'VE GOT PLENTY OF GOOD QUALITIES TOO.
LIKE WHAT...?
AH!
WELL... YOU CAN GIVE MASSAGES!
How's that?
THAT'S NO GOOD!!
BUMP
?!
Ouch...
OH, HEY, OLDER BROTHER.
IS SOMETHING WRONG?
Are you having a race by yourself?
...
WHAT ARE THOSE?
Snacks?
YEAH, I JUST BOUGHT SOME FOR OUR TRAINING CAMP.
Here, have one.
?
SUPERS
yay!

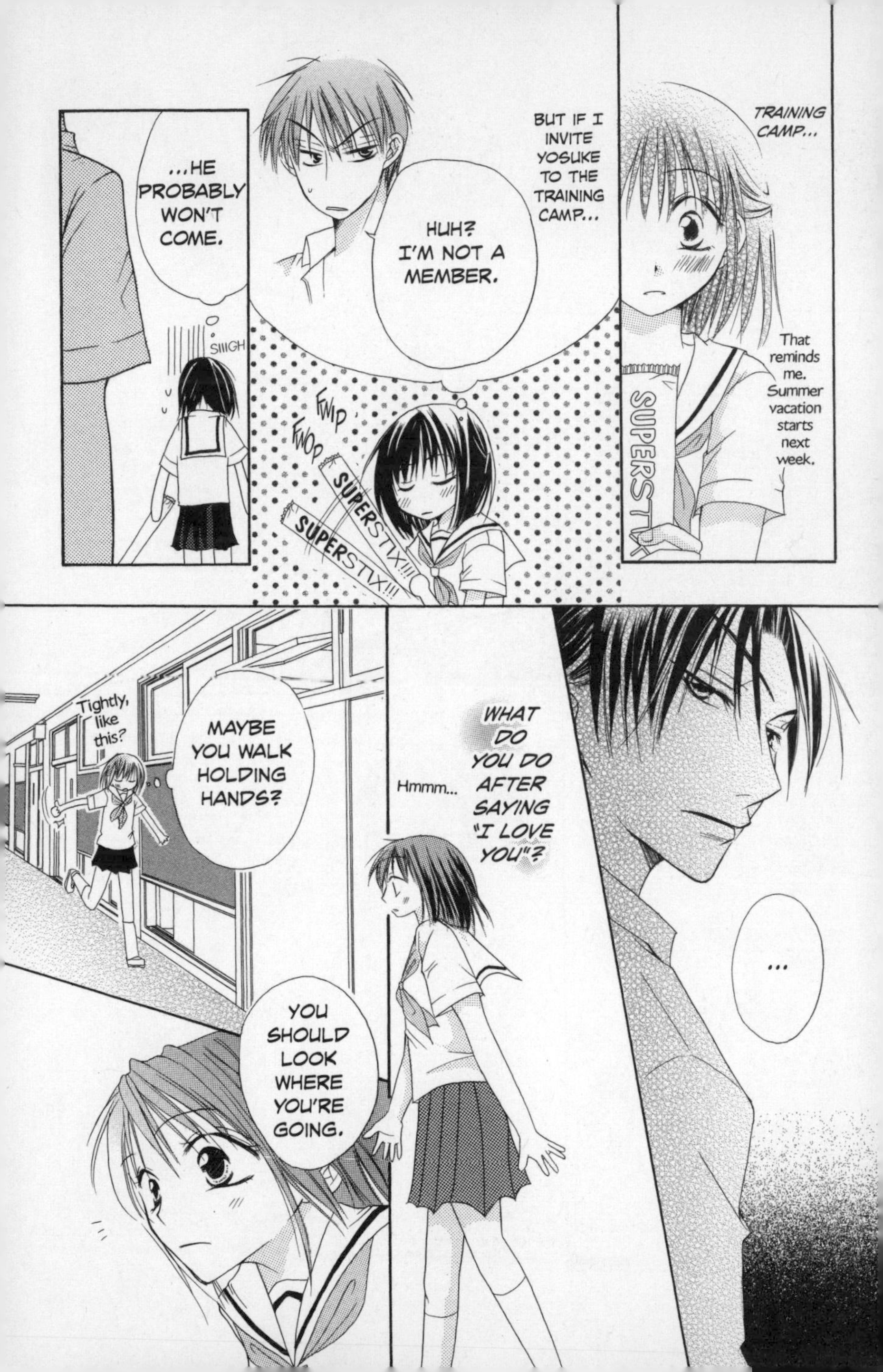
TRAINING CAMP...
That reminds me. Summer vacation starts next week.
SUPERSTIX
BUT IF I INVITE YOSUKE TO THE TRAINING CAMP...
HUH? I'M NOT A MEMBER.
FWIP
FWOP
SUPERSTIX!!!
SUPERSTIX!!!
...HE PROBABLY WON'T COME.
SIIIGH
...
WHAT DO YOU DO AFTER SAYING "I LOVE YOU"?
Hmmm...
MAYBE YOU WALK HOLDING HANDS?
Tightly, like this?
YOU SHOULD LOOK WHERE YOU'RE GOING.

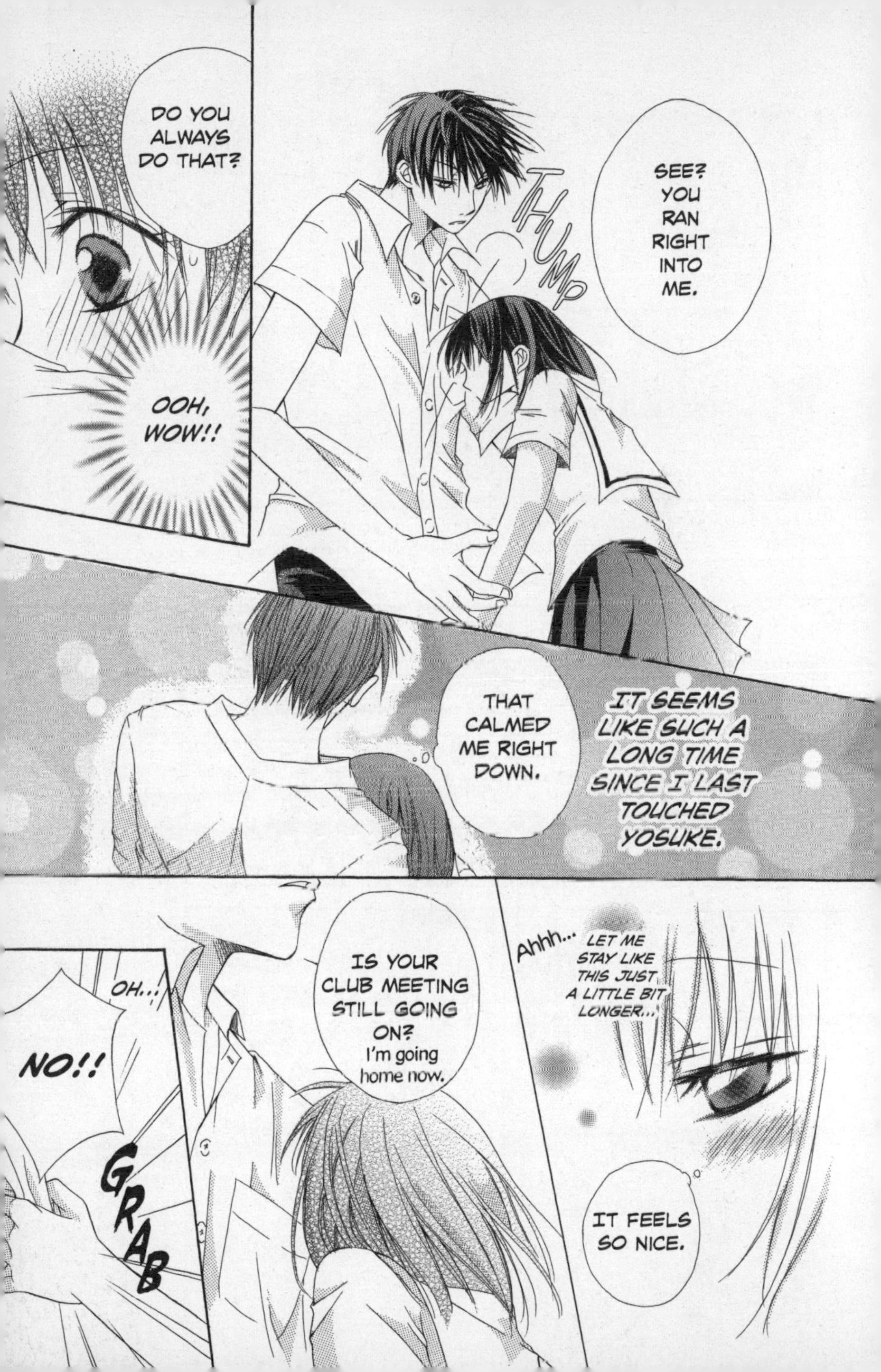
THUMP
SEE? YOU RAN RIGHT INTO ME.
DO YOU ALWAYS DO THAT?
OOH, WOW!!
IT SEEMS LIKE SUCH A LONG TIME SINCE I LAST TOUCHED YOSUKE.
THAT CALMED ME RIGHT DOWN.
Ahhh...
LET ME STAY LIKE THIS JUST A LITTLE BIT LONGER...
IT FEELS SO NICE.
IS YOUR CLUB MEETING STILL GOING ON? I'm going home now.
OH...
NO!!
GRAB

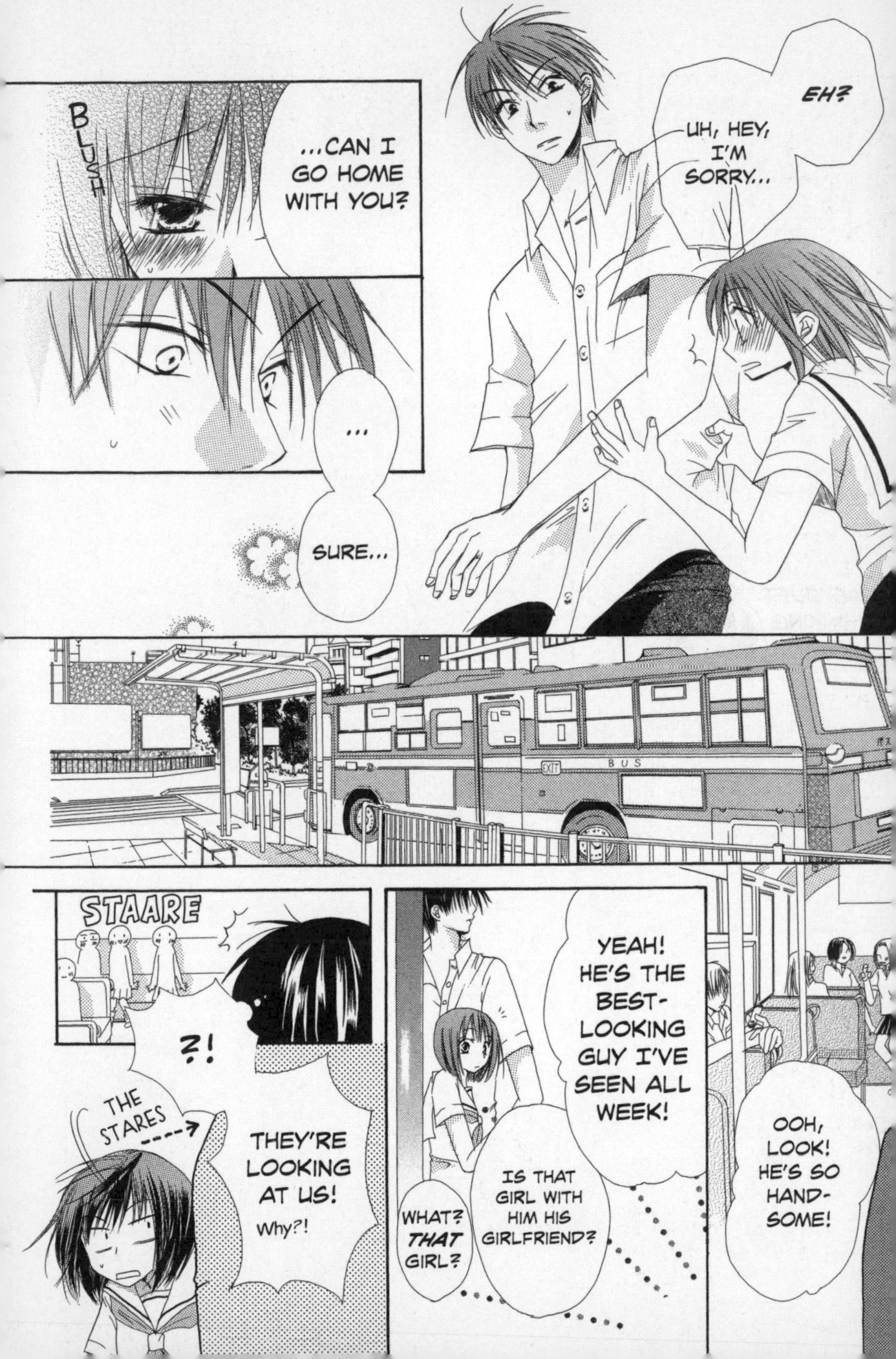
EH?
UH, HEY, I'M SORRY...
BLUSH
...CAN I GO HOME WITH YOU?
...
SURE...
EXIT
BUS
OOH, LOOK! HE'S SO HAND-SOME!
YEAH! HE'S THE BEST-LOOKING GUY I'VE SEEN ALL WEEK!
IS THAT GIRL WITH HIM HIS GIRLFRIEND?
WHAT? THAT GIRL?
STAARE
?!
THEY'RE LOOKING AT US!
Why?!
THE STARES

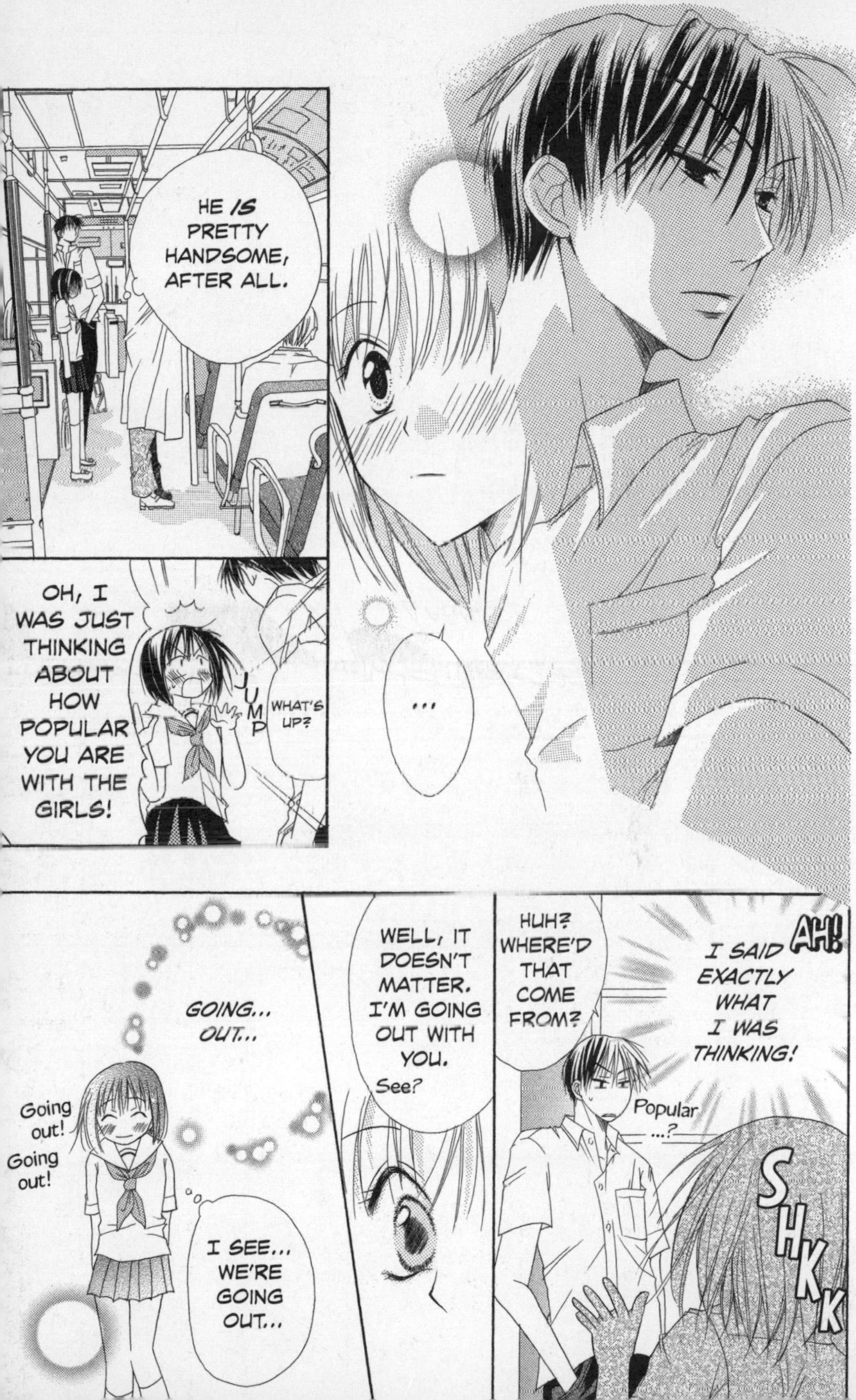
...
HE IS PRETTY HANDSOME, AFTER ALL.
WHAT'S UP?
JUMP
OH, I WAS JUST THINKING ABOUT HOW POPULAR YOU ARE WITH THE GIRLS!
AH!
I SAID EXACTLY WHAT I WAS THINKING!
HUH? WHERE'D THAT COME FROM?
Popular ...?
SHKK
WELL, IT DOESN'T MATTER. I'M GOING OUT WITH YOU.
See?
GOING... OUT...
Going out! Going out!
I SEE... WE'RE GOING OUT...

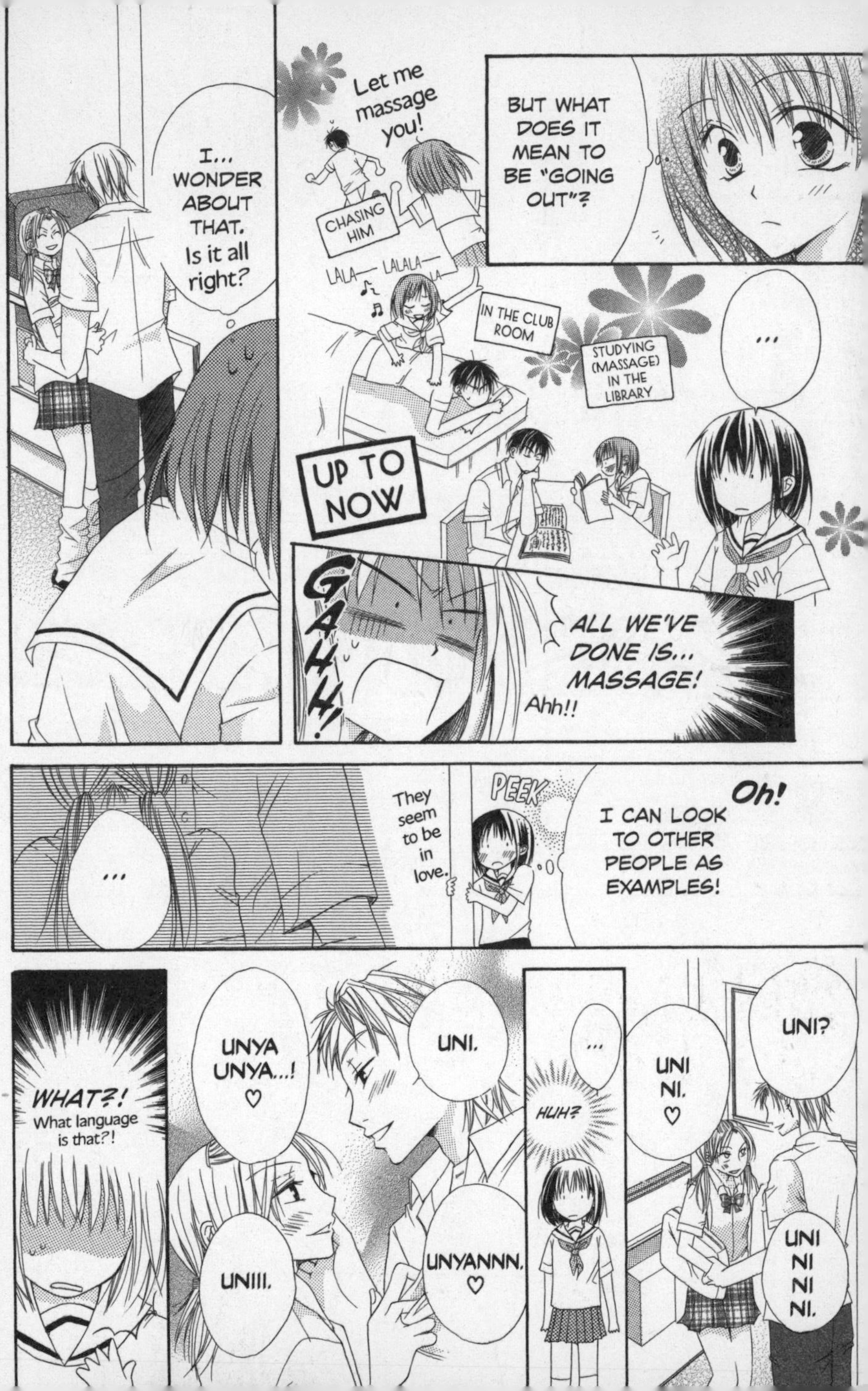
BUT WHAT DOES IT MEAN TO BE "GOING OUT"?
Let me massage you!
CHASING HIM
LALA— LALALA— LA
IN THE CLUB ROOM
STUDYING (MASSAGE) IN THE LIBRARY
...
UP TO NOW
ALL WE'VE DONE IS... MASSAGE!
Ahh!!
GAHH!
I... WONDER ABOUT THAT. Is it all right?
Oh!
I CAN LOOK TO OTHER PEOPLE AS EXAMPLES!
PEEK
They seem to be in love.
...
UNI?
UNI NI NI NI.
UNI NI. ♡
...
HUH?
UNI.
UNYA UNYA...! ♡
UNYANN. ♡
UNIII.
WHAT?! What language is that?!

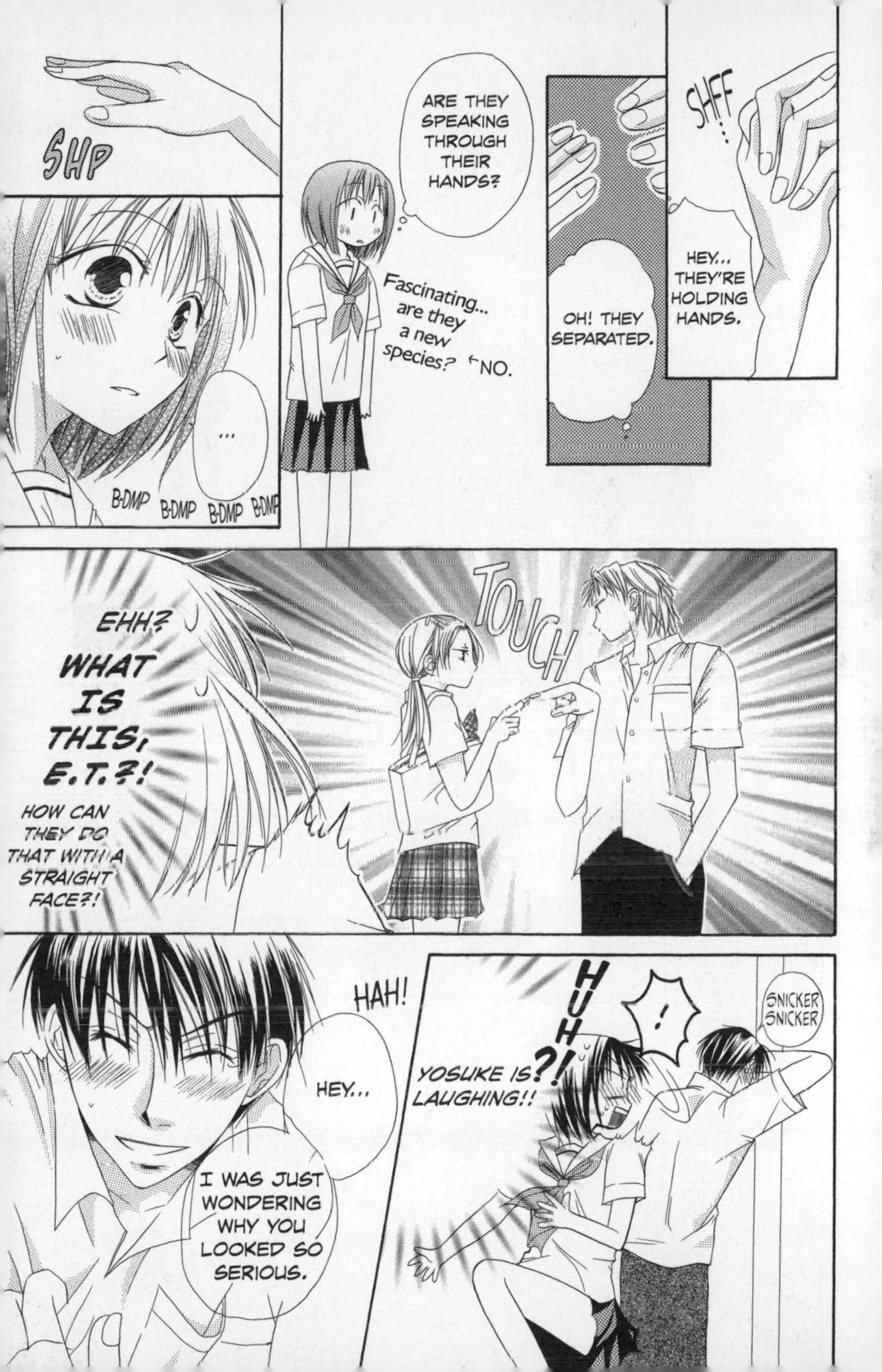
SHFF...
HEY... THEY'RE HOLDING HANDS.
OH! THEY SEPARATED.
ARE THEY SPEAKING THROUGH THEIR HANDS?
Fascinating... are they a new species?
←NO.
SHP
...
B-DMP B-DMP B-DMP B-DMP
TOUCH
EHH? WHAT IS THIS, E.T.?!
HOW CAN THEY DO THAT WITH A STRAIGHT FACE?!
SNICKER SNICKER
HUH?!
!
YOSUKE IS LAUGHING!!
HAH!
HEY...
I WAS JUST WONDERING WHY YOU LOOKED SO SERIOUS.

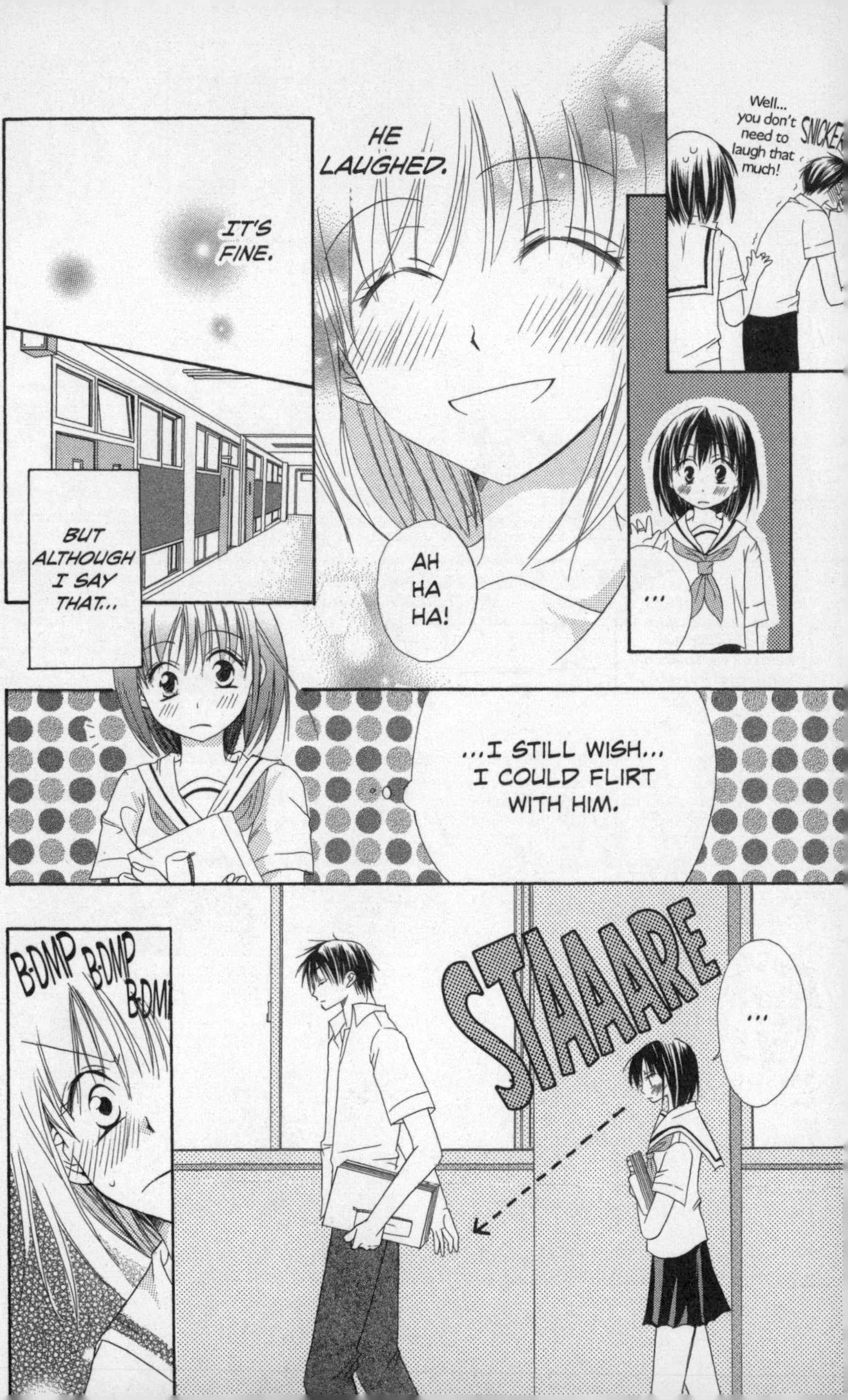
Well... you don't need to laugh that much!
SNICKER
...
HE LAUGHED.
AH HA HA!
IT'S FINE.
BUT ALTHOUGH I SAY THAT...
...I STILL WISH... I COULD FLIRT WITH HIM.
STAAARE
...
B-DMP B-DMP

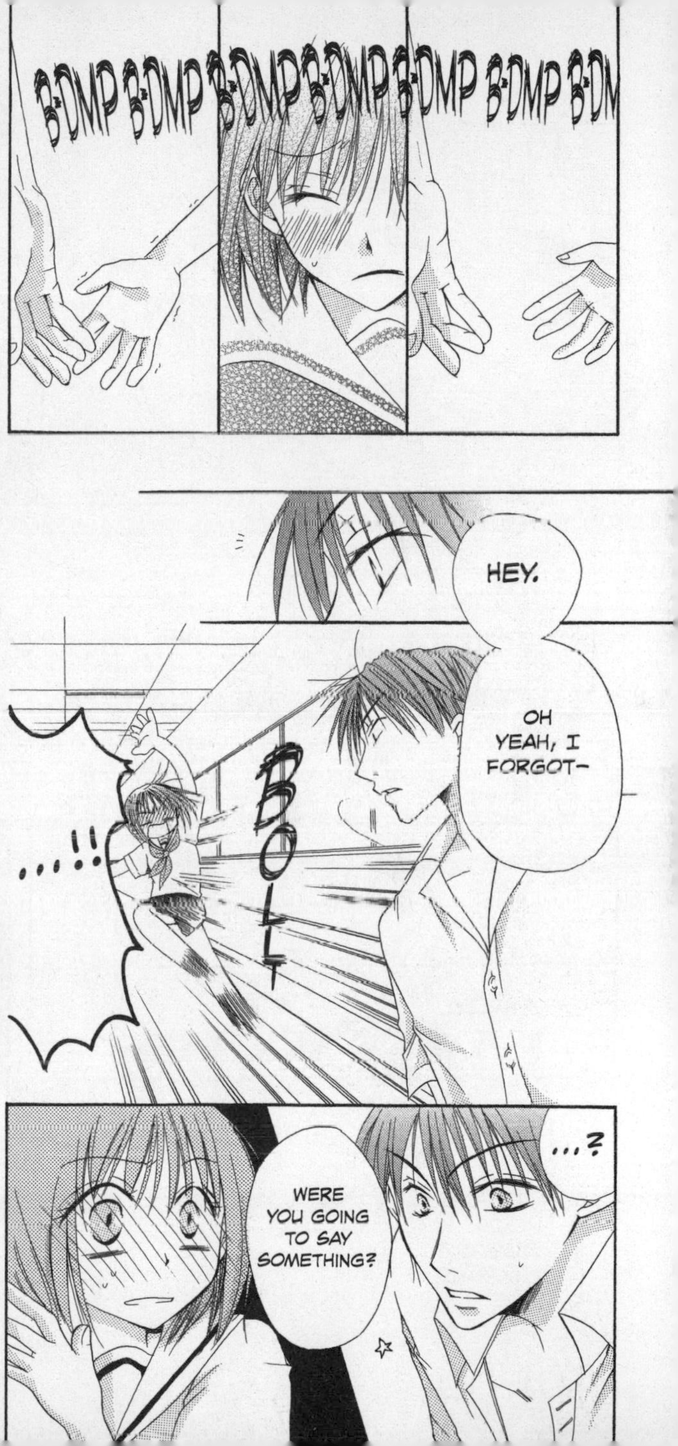
B-DMP B-DMP B-DMP B-DMP B-DMP B-DMP B-DM
HEY.
OH YEAH, I FORGOT-
BOLT
...!!
...?
WERE YOU GOING TO SAY SOMETHING?

The Manager Is a Sweat Suit Junkie

His heart leaps when he sees a new sweat suit! He needs to possess every new suit he sees! As long as there's money, his collection will grow!!!!

Yes, this is Harumi, the sweat suit junkie!!

Burn, Sweat Suit Soul!! Do your best, blood type A!!* (?)

Thus, we establish that the Manager in the story secretly loves sweat suits. See for yourself—he wears a sweat suit every single time he appears!

✿ At first this was going to be the official sweat suit for the Massage Club. But because it was *so* uncool, it was rejected immediately.

⇩

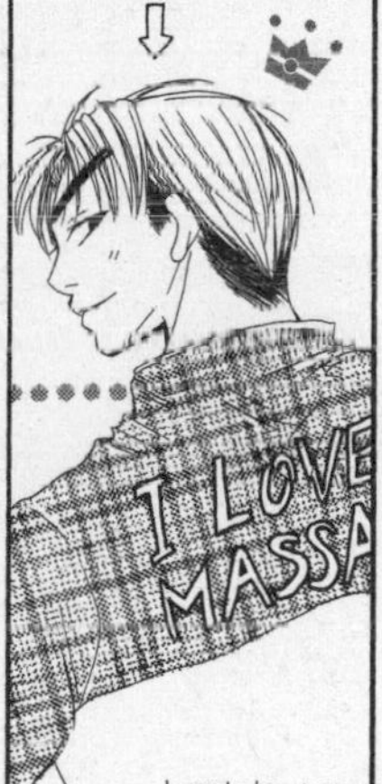
I LOVE MASSA
I wonder how many people actually knew the Manager's name.

*SOME JAPANESE PEOPLE BELIEVE THAT BLOOD TYPE DETERMINES PERSONALITY. TYPE A PEOPLE ARE TYPICALLY REGARDED AS EARNEST AND FASTIDIOUS.

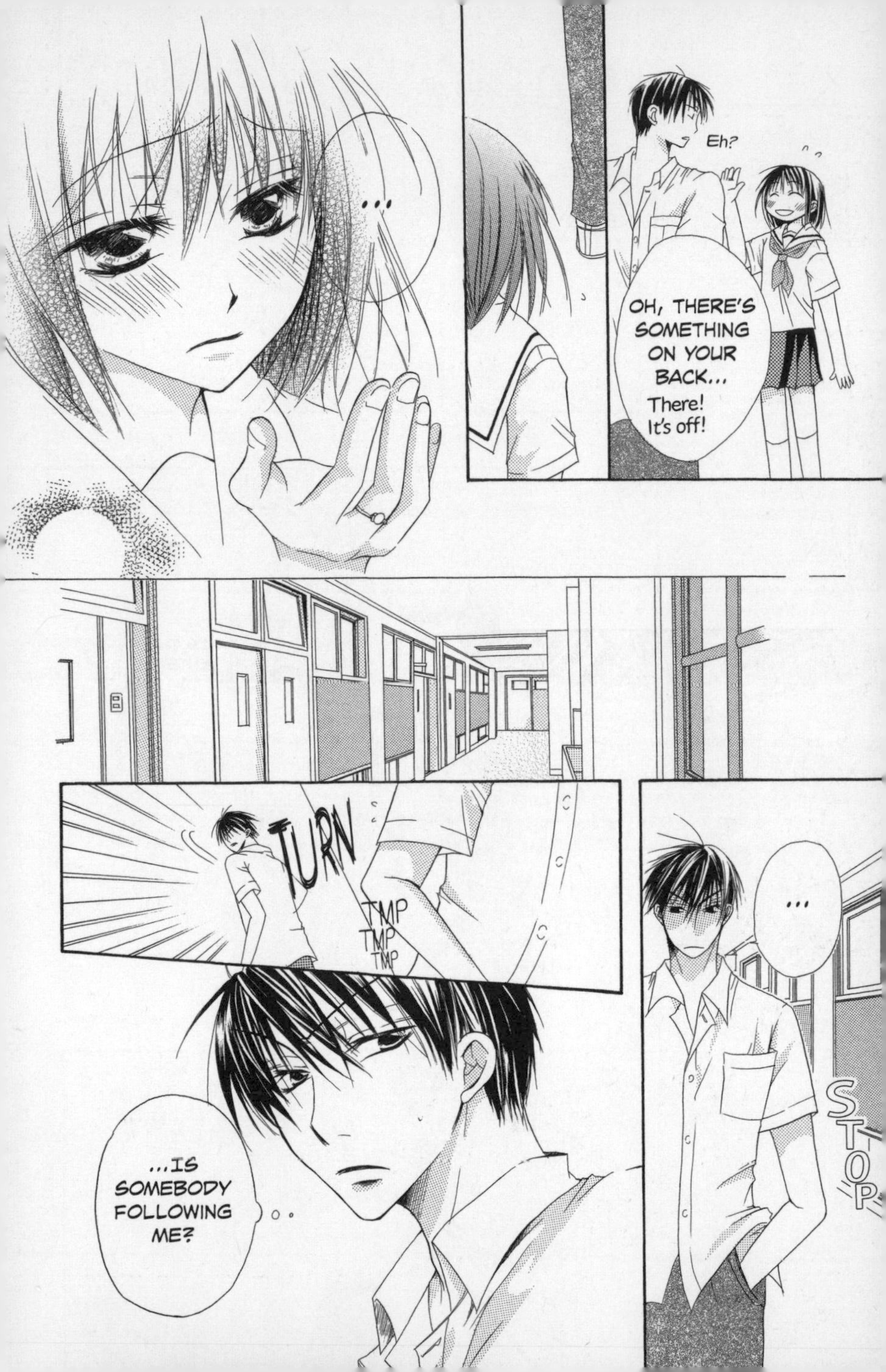
Eh?
OH, THERE'S SOMETHING ON YOUR BACK... There! It's off!
...
...
STOP
TURN
TMP TMP TMP
...IS SOMEBODY FOLLOWING ME?

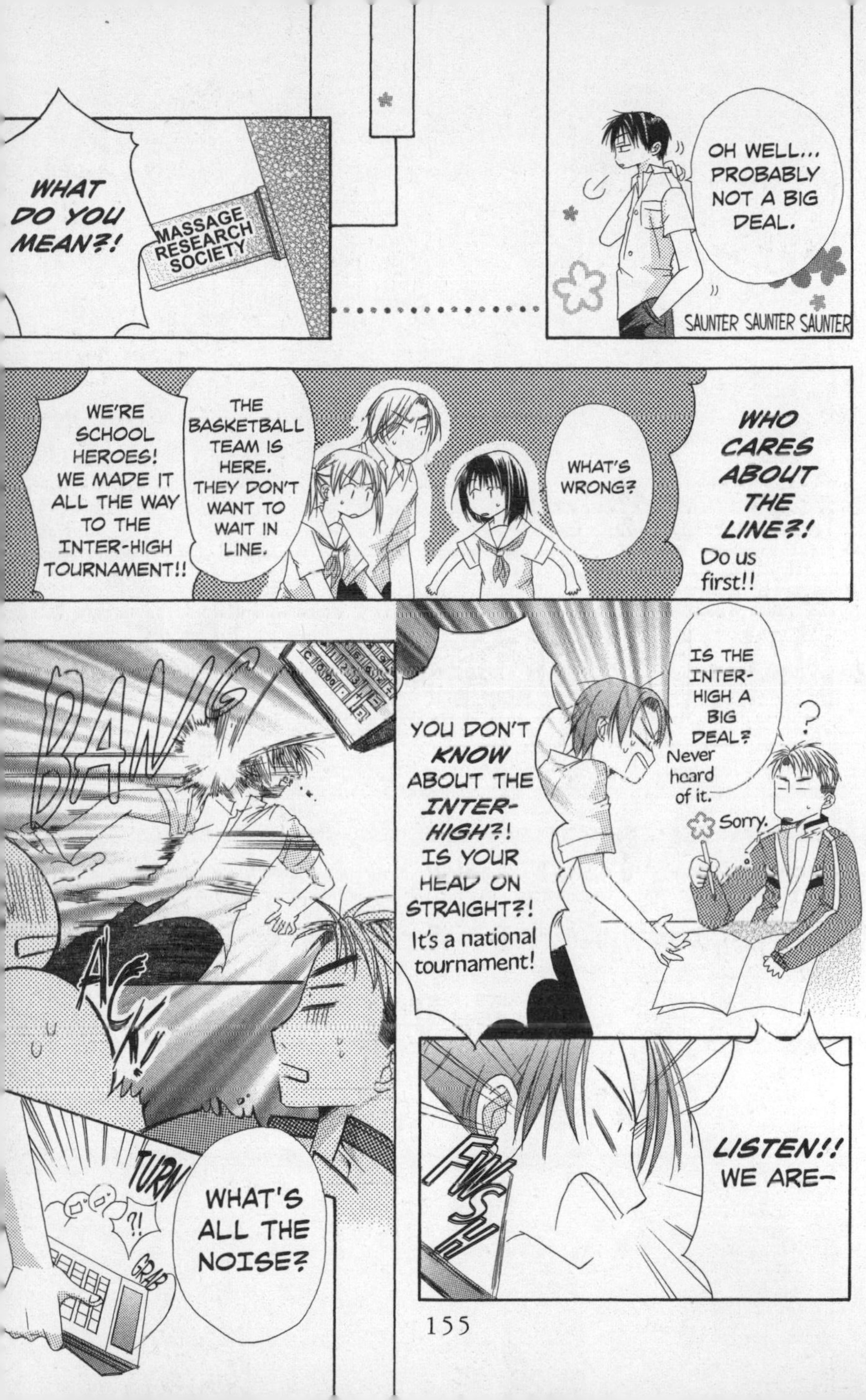
OH WELL... PROBABLY NOT A BIG DEAL.
SAUNTER SAUNTER SAUNTER
WHAT DO YOU MEAN?!
MASSAGE RESEARCH SOCIETY
WHO CARES ABOUT THE LINE?!
Do us first!!
WHAT'S WRONG?
THE BASKETBALL TEAM IS HERE. THEY DON'T WANT TO WAIT IN LINE.
WE'RE SCHOOL HEROES! WE MADE IT ALL THE WAY TO THE INTER-HIGH TOURNAMENT!!
IS THE INTER-HIGH A BIG DEAL?
Never heard of it.
Sorry.
YOU DON'T KNOW ABOUT THE INTER-HIGH?! IS YOUR HEAD ON STRAIGHT?!
It's a national tournament!
LISTEN!! WE ARE—
FWISH
BANG
ACK!
TURN
WHAT'S ALL THE NOISE?
?!
GRAB

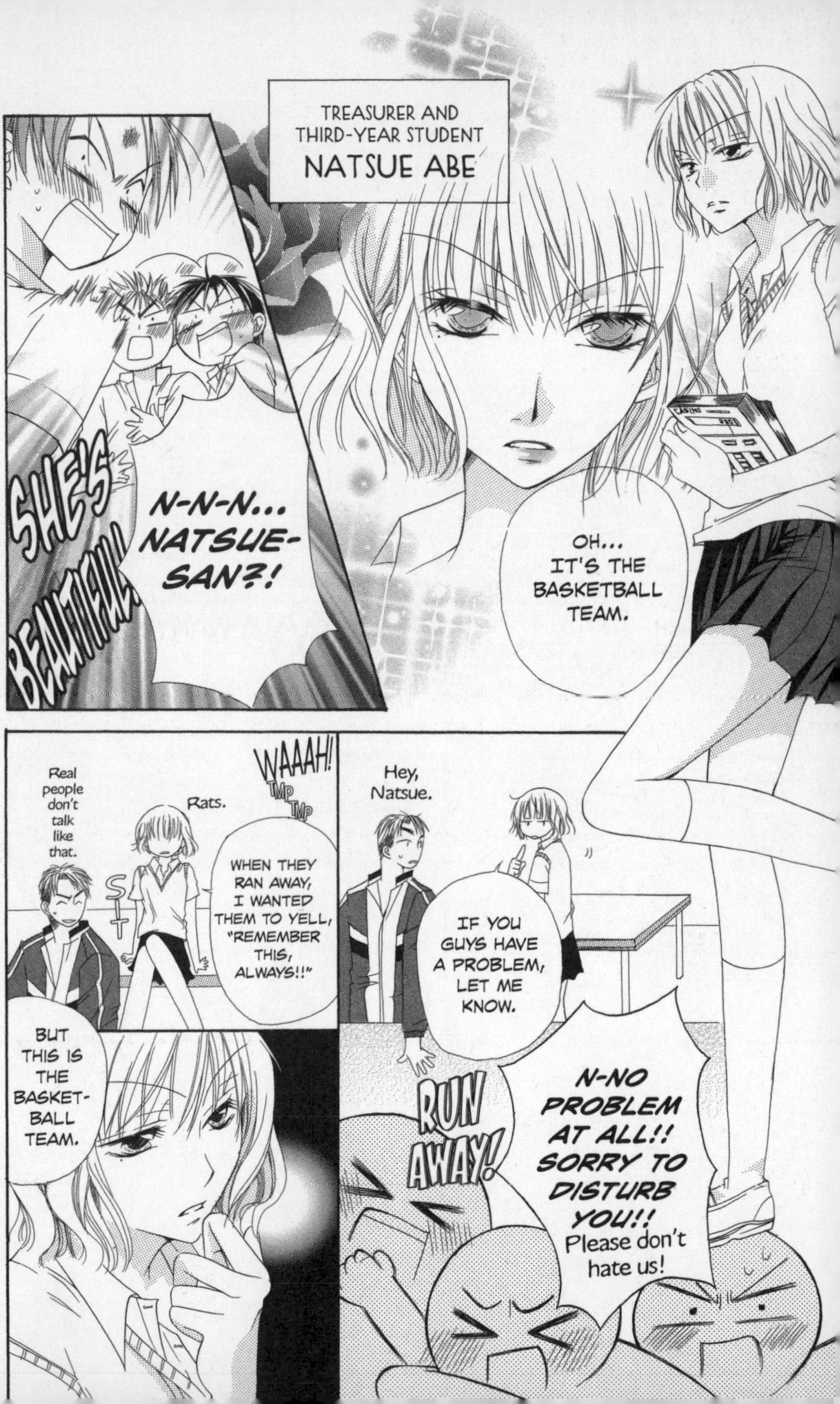
TREASURER AND THIRD-YEAR STUDENT
NATSUE ABE
OH... IT'S THE BASKETBALL TEAM.
N-N-N... NATSUE-SAN?!
SHE'S BEAUTIFUL!
Hey, Natsue.
IF YOU GUYS HAVE A PROBLEM, LET ME KNOW.
RUN AWAY!
N-NO PROBLEM AT ALL!! SORRY TO DISTURB YOU!!
Please don't hate us!
WAAAH!
TMP TMP
WHEN THEY RAN AWAY, I WANTED THEM TO YELL, "REMEMBER THIS, ALWAYS!!"
Rats.
Real people don't talk like that.
BUT THIS IS THE BASKET-BALL TEAM.

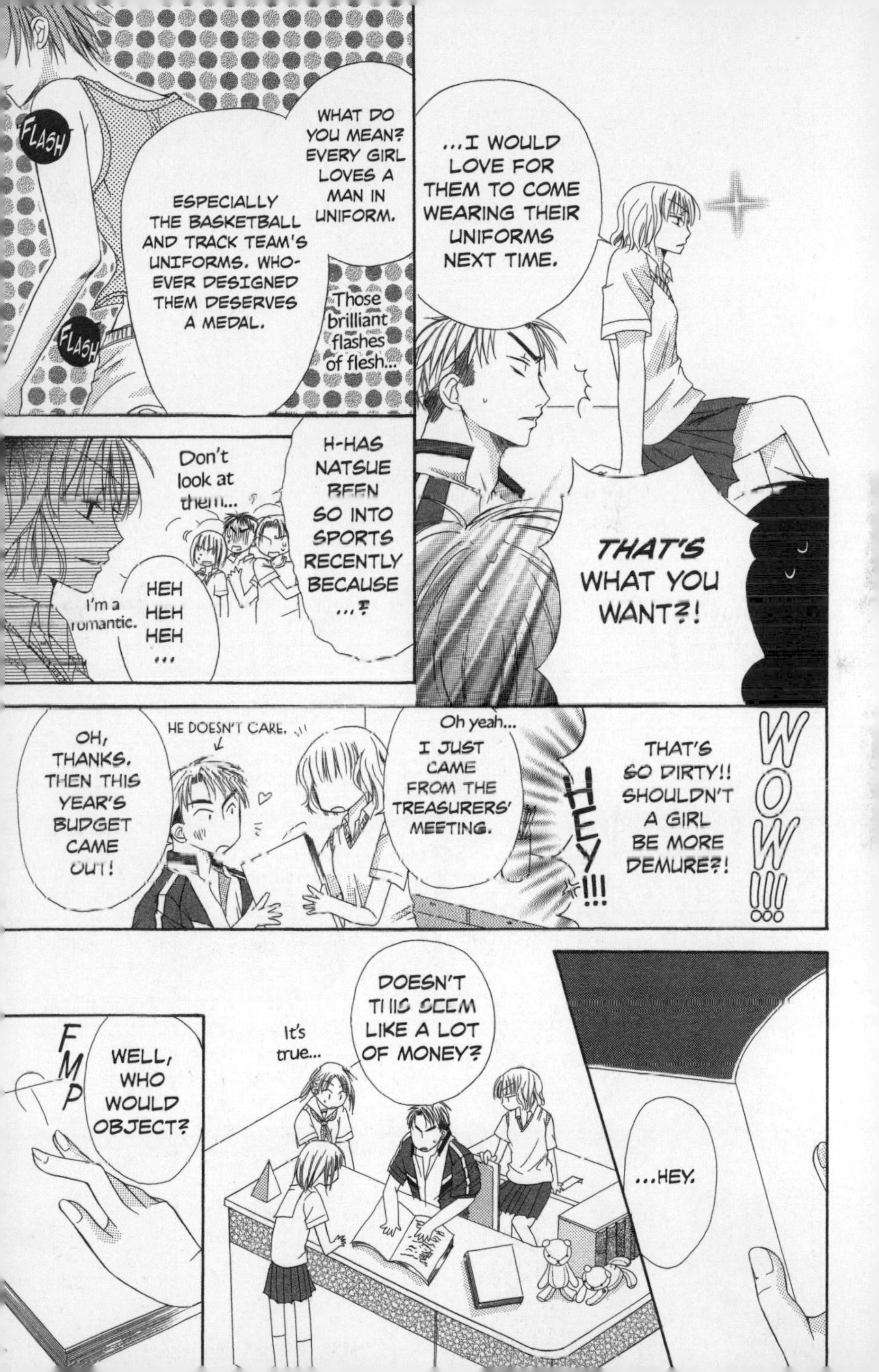
...I WOULD LOVE FOR THEM TO COME WEARING THEIR UNIFORMS NEXT TIME.
THAT'S WHAT YOU WANT?!
WHAT DO YOU MEAN? EVERY GIRL LOVES A MAN IN UNIFORM.
ESPECIALLY THE BASKETBALL AND TRACK TEAM'S UNIFORMS. WHO-EVER DESIGNED THEM DESERVES A MEDAL.
Those brilliant flashes of flesh...
FLASH
FLASH
H-HAS NATSUE BEEN SO INTO SPORTS RECENTLY BECAUSE ...?
Don't look at them...
HEH HEH HEH ...
I'm a romantic.
WOW!!!
THAT'S SO DIRTY!! SHOULDN'T A GIRL BE MORE DEMURE?!
HEY!!!
Oh yeah...
I JUST CAME FROM THE TREASURERS' MEETING.
HE DOESN'T CARE.
OH, THANKS. THEN THIS YEAR'S BUDGET CAME OUT!
...HEY.
DOESN'T THIS SEEM LIKE A LOT OF MONEY?
It's true...
WELL, WHO WOULD OBJECT?
FMP

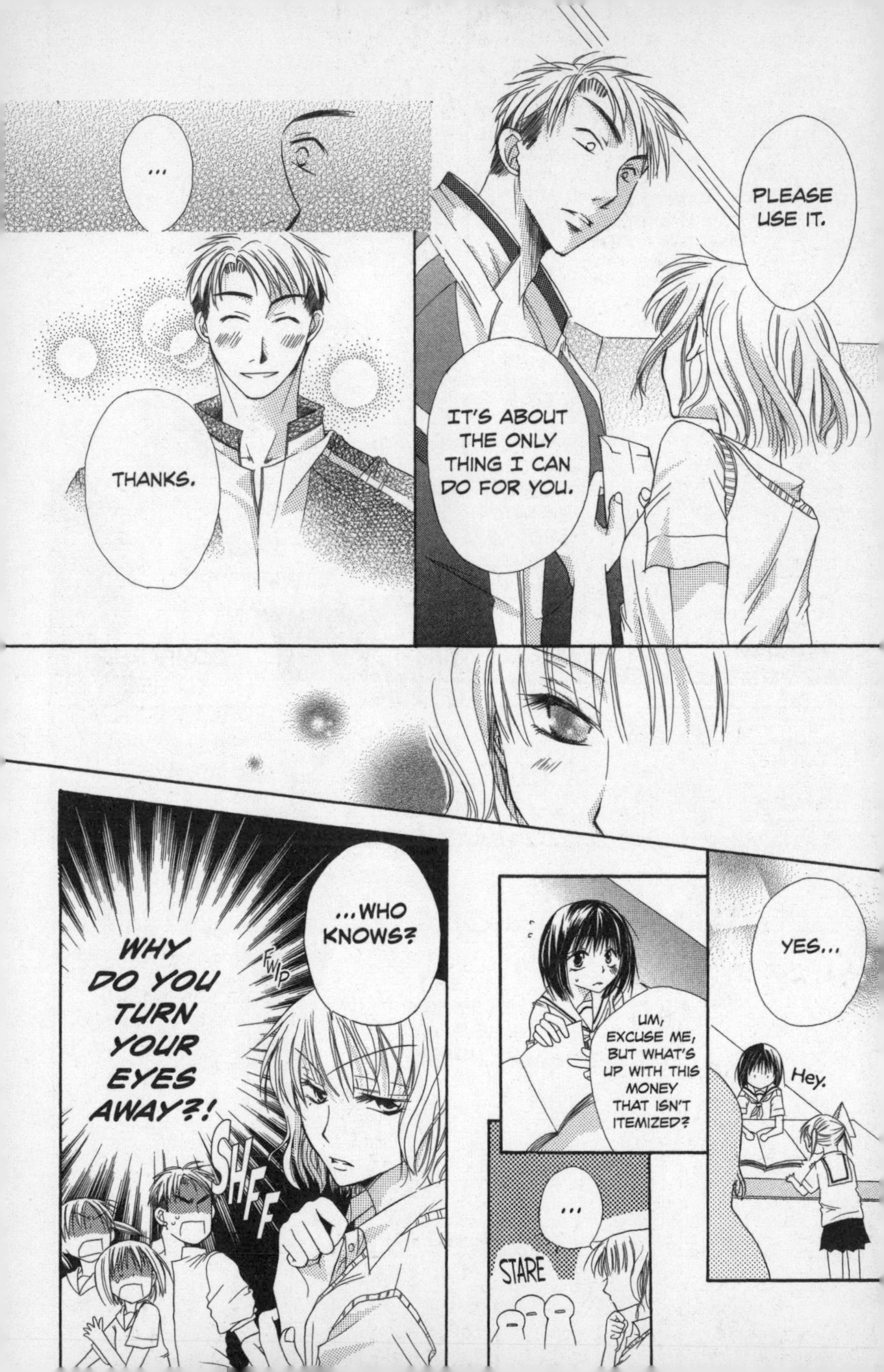
PLEASE USE IT.
IT'S ABOUT THE ONLY THING I CAN DO FOR YOU.
...
THANKS.
YES...
Hey.
UM, EXCUSE ME, BUT WHAT'S UP WITH THIS MONEY THAT ISN'T ITEMIZED?
...
STARE
...WHO KNOWS?
FWIP
WHY DO YOU TURN YOUR EYES AWAY?!
SHFF

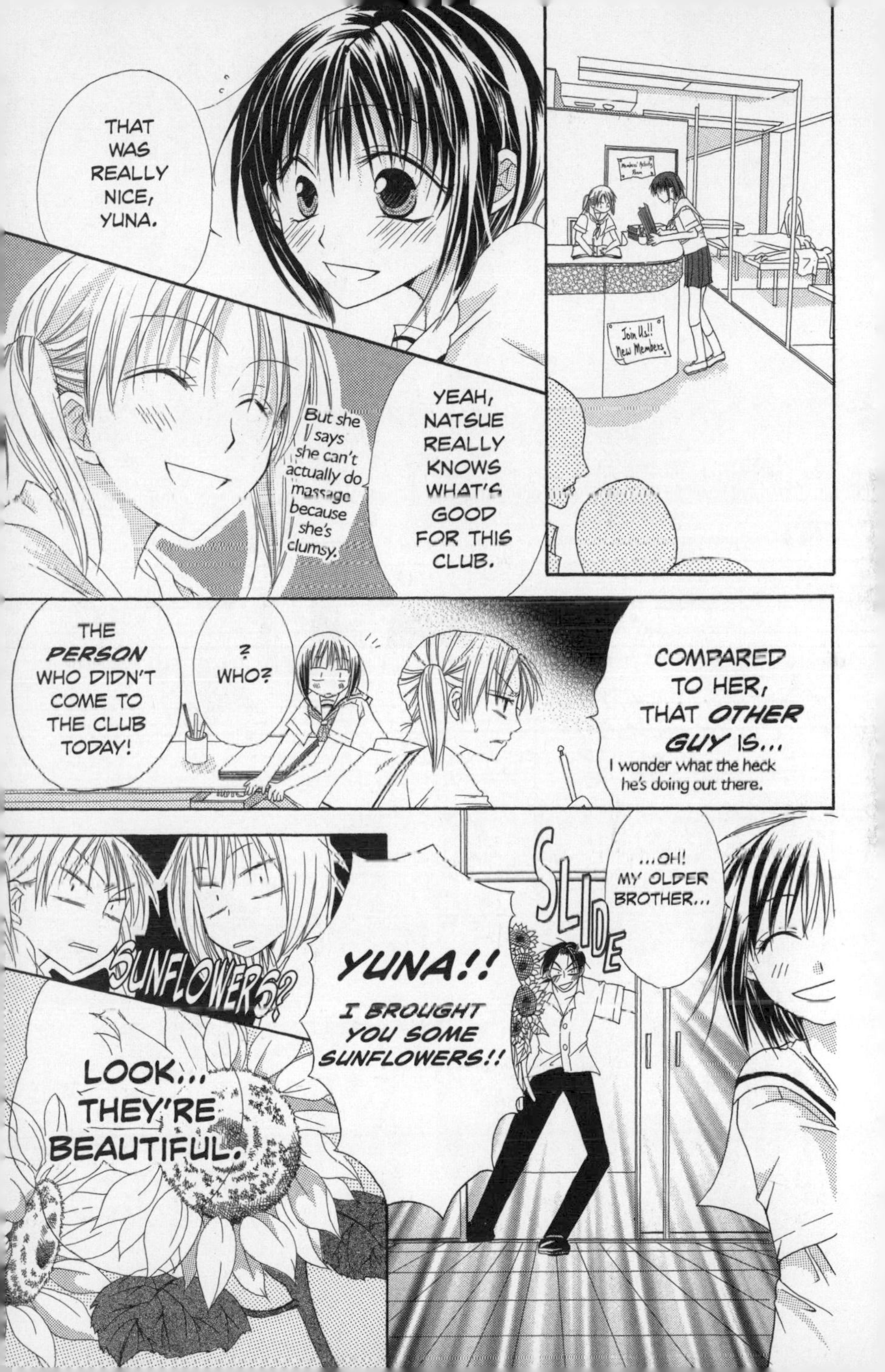
THAT WAS REALLY NICE, YUNA.
YEAH, NATSUE REALLY KNOWS WHAT'S GOOD FOR THIS CLUB.
But she says she can't actually do massage because she's clumsy.
COMPARED TO HER, THAT *OTHER GUY* IS...
I wonder what the heck he's doing out there.
? WHO?
THE *PERSON* WHO DIDN'T COME TO THE CLUB TODAY!
...OH! MY OLDER BROTHER...
SLIDE
YUNA!!
I BROUGHT YOU SOME SUNFLOWERS!!
SUNFLOWERS?!
LOOK... THEY'RE BEAUTIFUL.

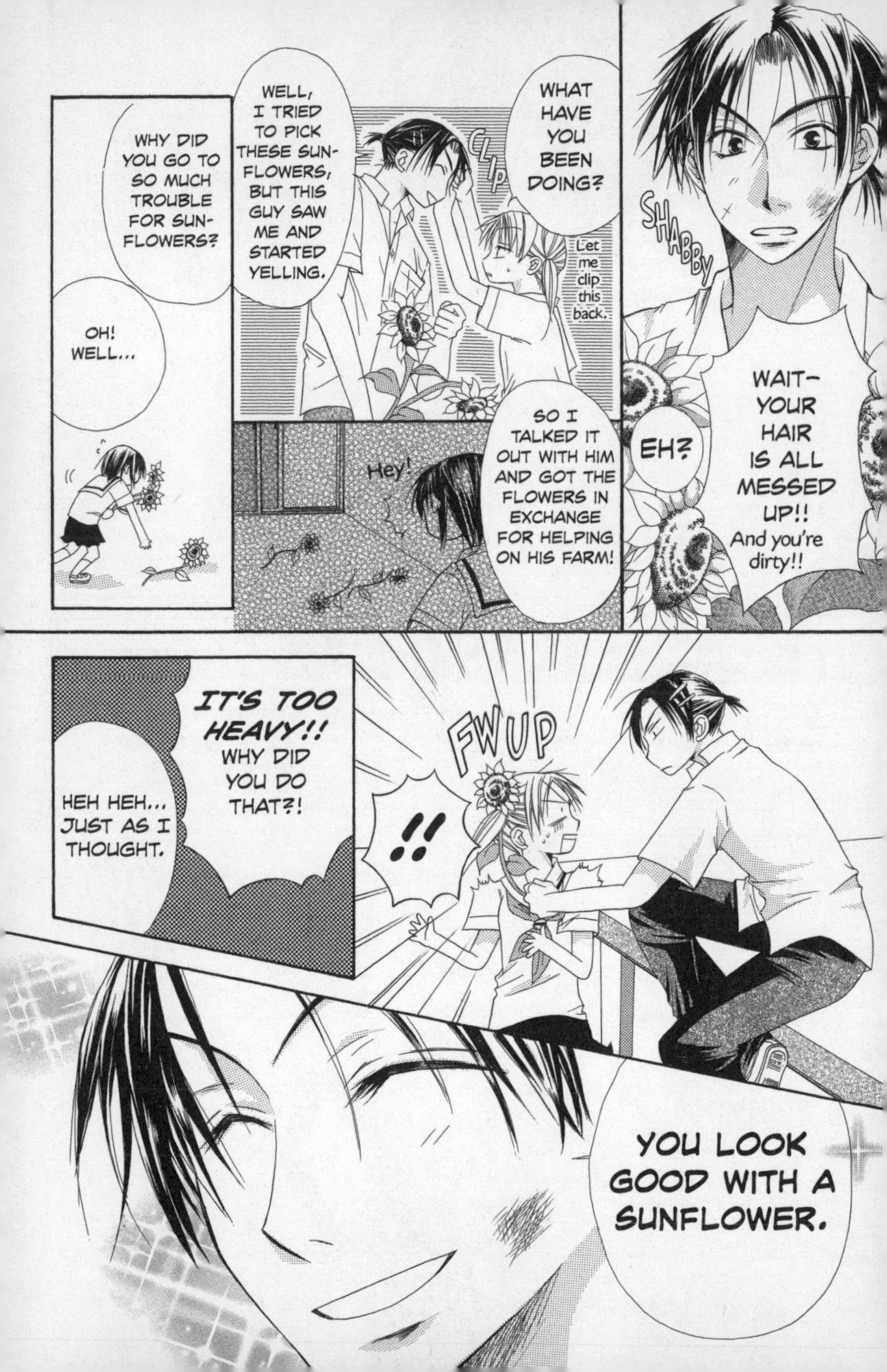
SHABBY
WAIT—YOUR HAIR IS ALL MESSED UP!! And you're dirty!!
EH?
WHAT HAVE YOU BEEN DOING?
CLIP
Let me clip this back.
WELL, I TRIED TO PICK THESE SUN-FLOWERS, BUT THIS GUY SAW ME AND STARTED YELLING.
SO I TALKED IT OUT WITH HIM AND GOT THE FLOWERS IN EXCHANGE FOR HELPING ON HIS FARM!
Hey!
WHY DID YOU GO TO SO MUCH TROUBLE FOR SUN-FLOWERS?
OH! WELL...
FWUP
!!
IT'S TOO HEAVY!! WHY DID YOU DO THAT?!
HEH HEH... JUST AS I THOUGHT.
YOU LOOK GOOD WITH A SUNFLOWER.

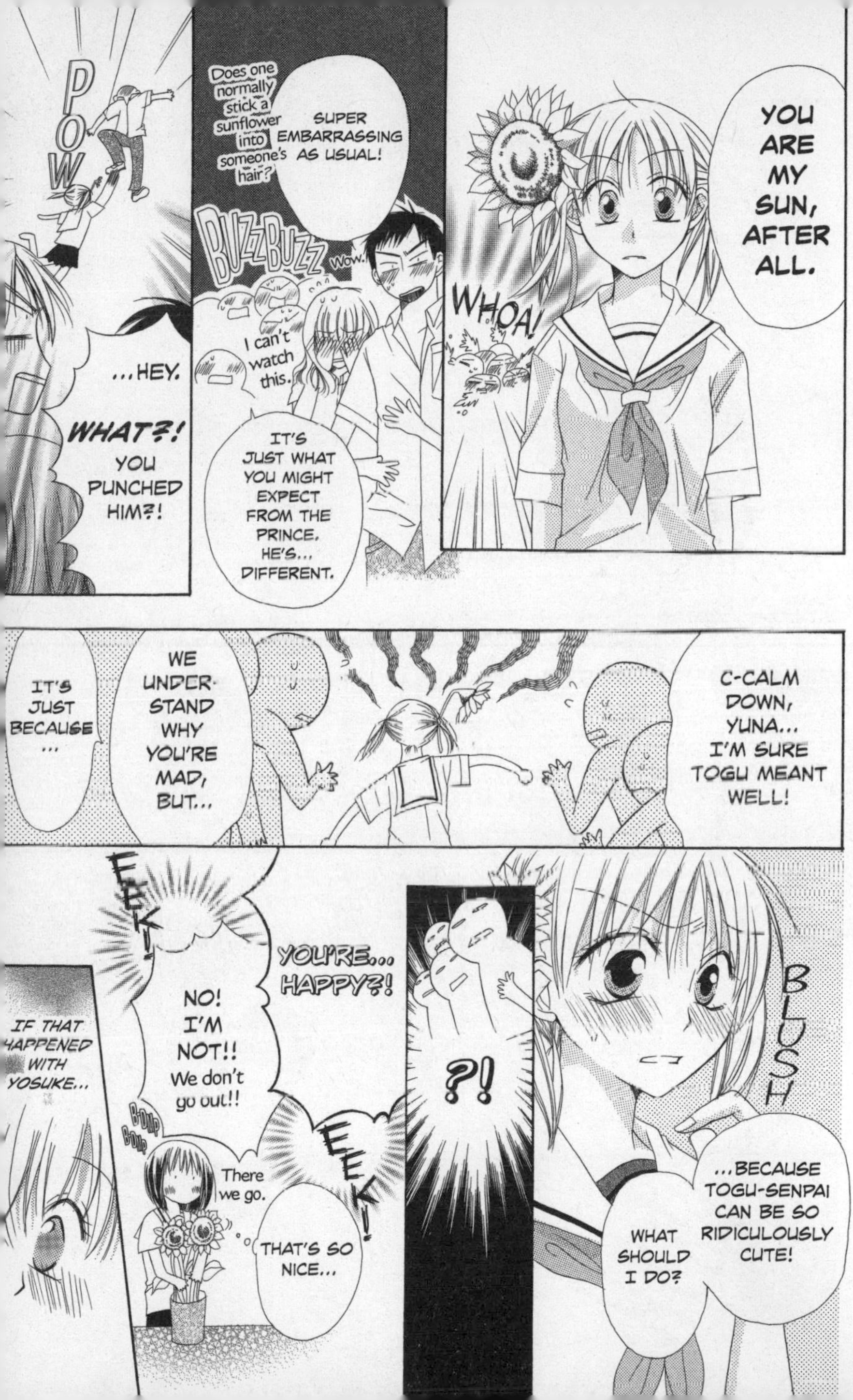
YOU ARE MY SUN, AFTER ALL.
WHOA!
BUZZBUZZ
Does one normally stick a sunflower into someone's hair?
SUPER EMBARRASSING AS USUAL!
wow.
I can't watch this.
IT'S JUST WHAT YOU MIGHT EXPECT FROM THE PRINCE. HE'S... DIFFERENT.
POW
...HEY.
WHAT?! YOU PUNCHED HIM?!
C-CALM DOWN, YUNA... I'M SURE TOGU MEANT WELL!
WE UNDERSTAND WHY YOU'RE MAD, BUT...
IT'S JUST BECAUSE...
BLUSH
...BECAUSE TOGU-SENPAI CAN BE SO RIDICULOUSLY CUTE!
WHAT SHOULD I DO?
?!
EEK!
YOU'RE... HAPPY?!
EEK!
NO! I'M NOT!! We don't go out!!
There we go.
THAT'S SO NICE...
IF THAT HAPPENED WITH YOSUKE...

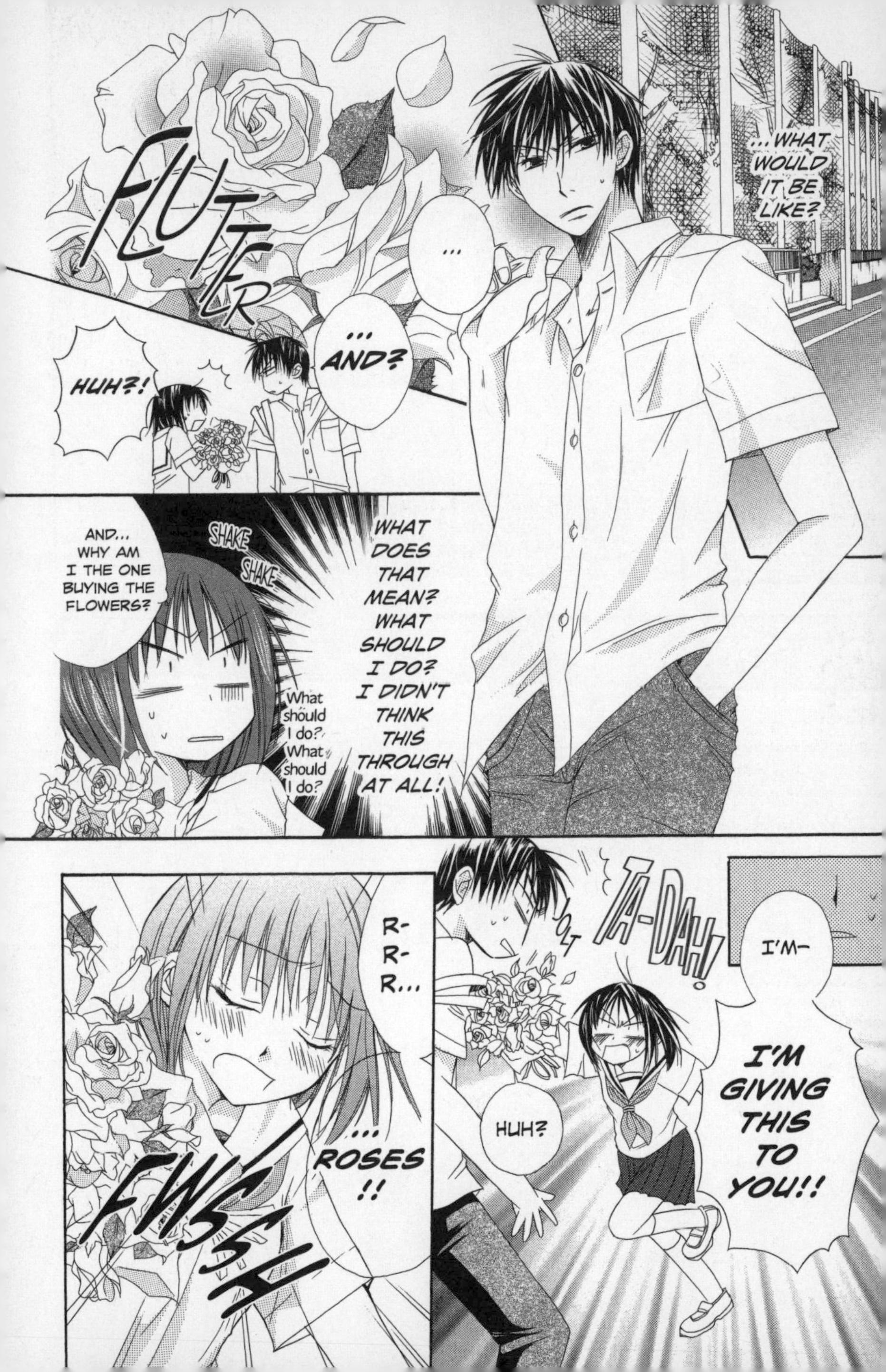

...WHAT WOULD IT BE LIKE?
...
FLUTTER
... AND?
HUH?!
WHAT DOES THAT MEAN? WHAT SHOULD I DO? I DIDN'T THINK THIS THROUGH AT ALL!
SHAKE
SHAKE
What should I do? What should I do?
AND... WHY AM I THE ONE BUYING THE FLOWERS?
I'M-
TA-DAH!
JOLT
I'M GIVING THIS TO YOU!!
HUH?
R-R-R...
... ROSES!!
FWSSH

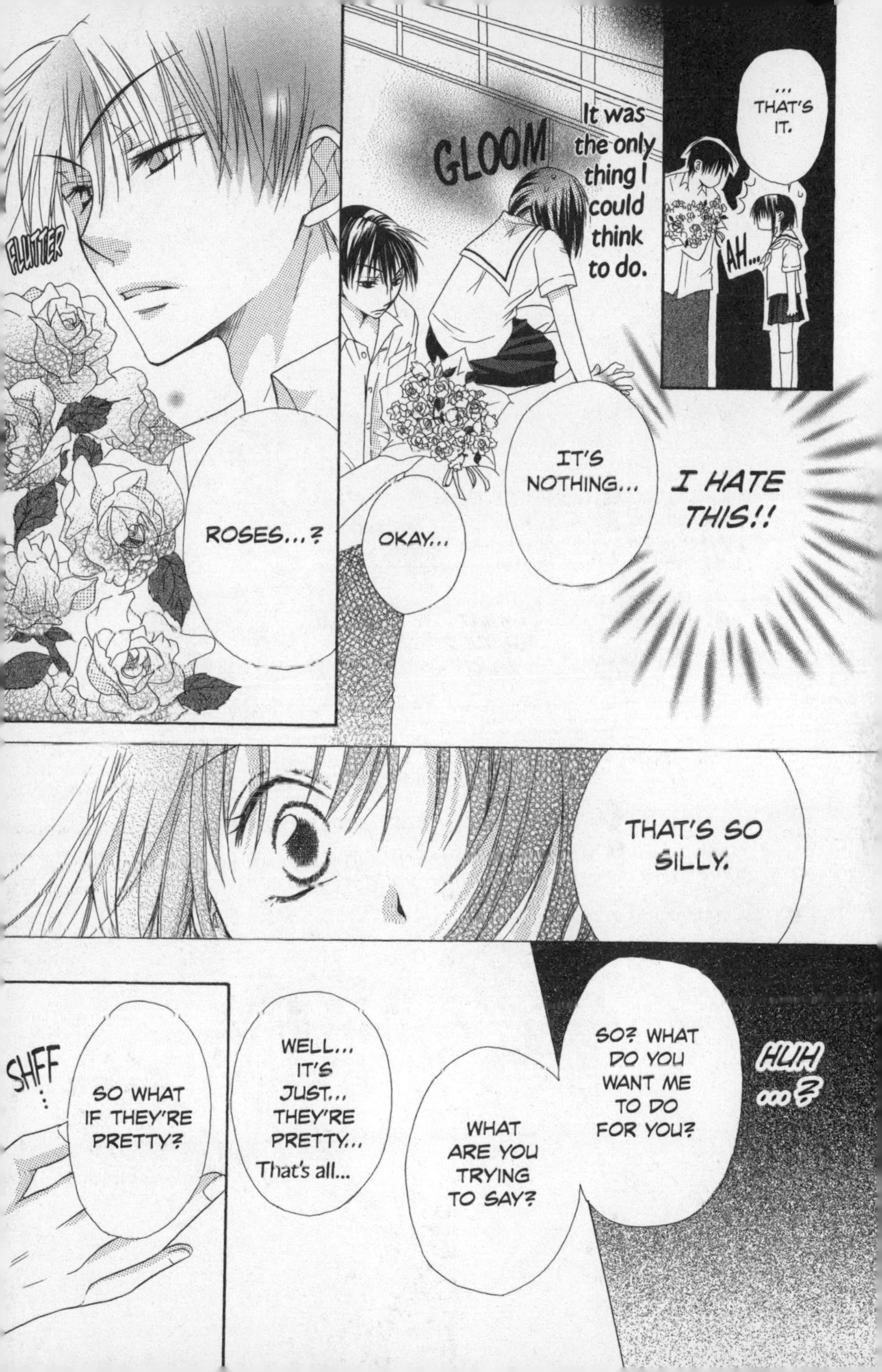
... THAT'S IT.
AH...
It was the only thing I could think to do.
GLOOM
I HATE THIS!!
IT'S NOTHING...
OKAY...
FLUTTER
ROSES...?
THAT'S SO SILLY.
HUH...?
SO? WHAT DO YOU WANT ME TO DO FOR YOU?
WHAT ARE YOU TRYING TO SAY?
WELL... IT'S JUST... THEY'RE PRETTY...
That's all...
SHFF...
SO WHAT IF THEY'RE PRETTY?

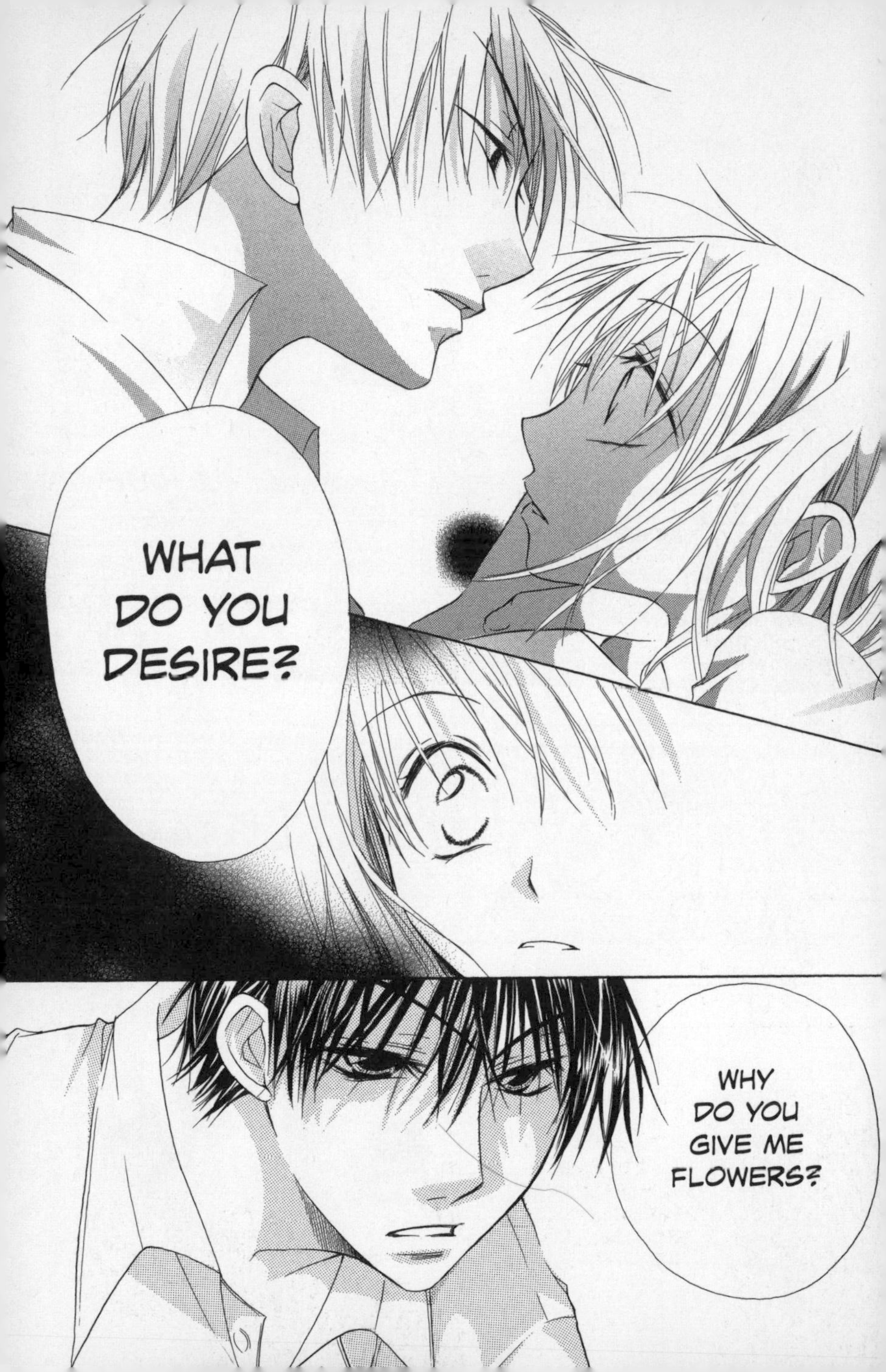
WHAT DO YOU DESIRE?
WHY DO YOU GIVE ME FLOWERS?

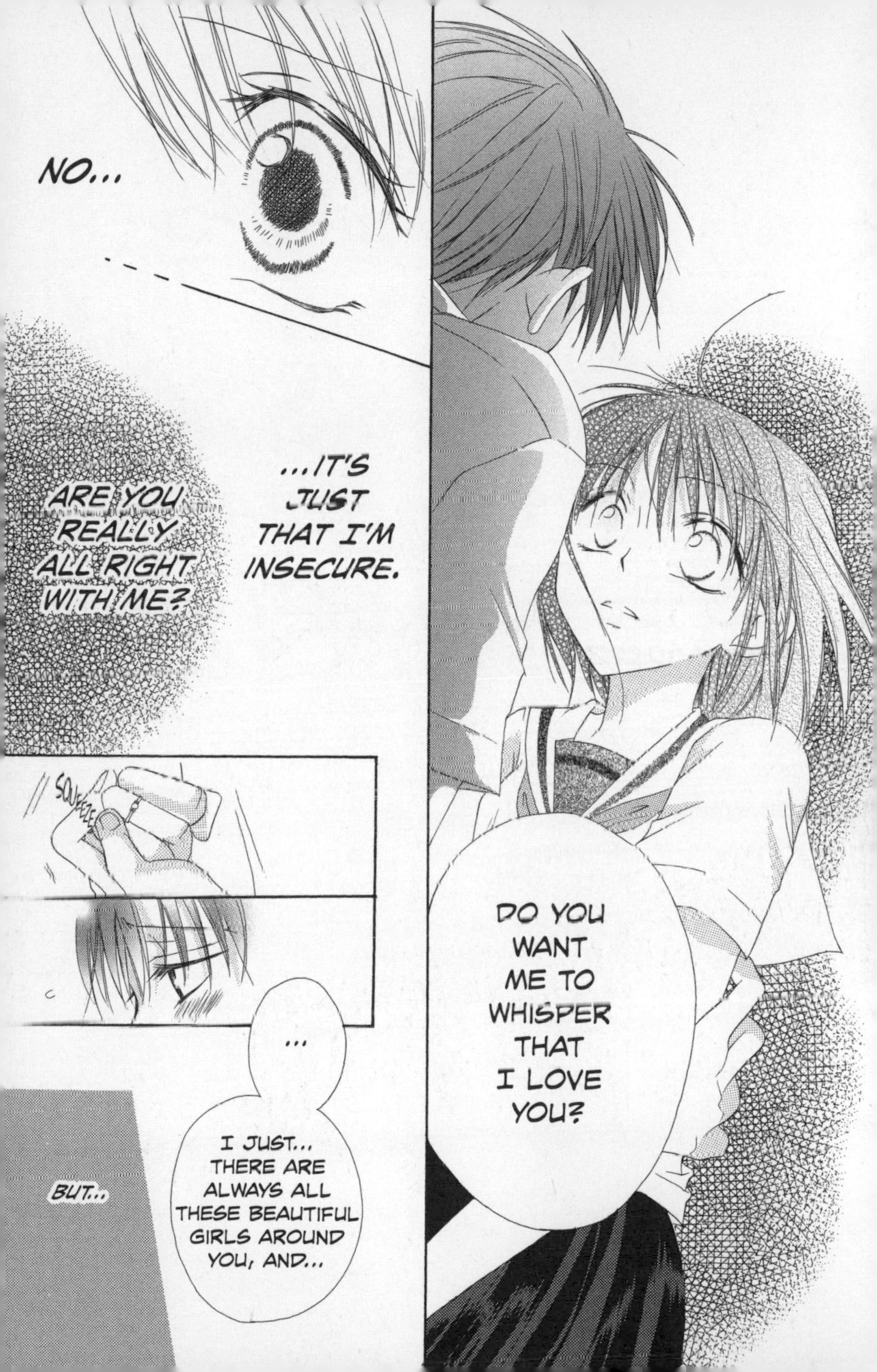
DO YOU WANT ME TO WHISPER THAT I LOVE YOU?
NO...
...IT'S JUST THAT I'M INSECURE.
ARE YOU REALLY ALL RIGHT WITH ME?
SQUEEZE
...
I JUST... THERE ARE ALWAYS ALL THESE BEAUTIFUL GIRLS AROUND YOU, AND...
BUT...

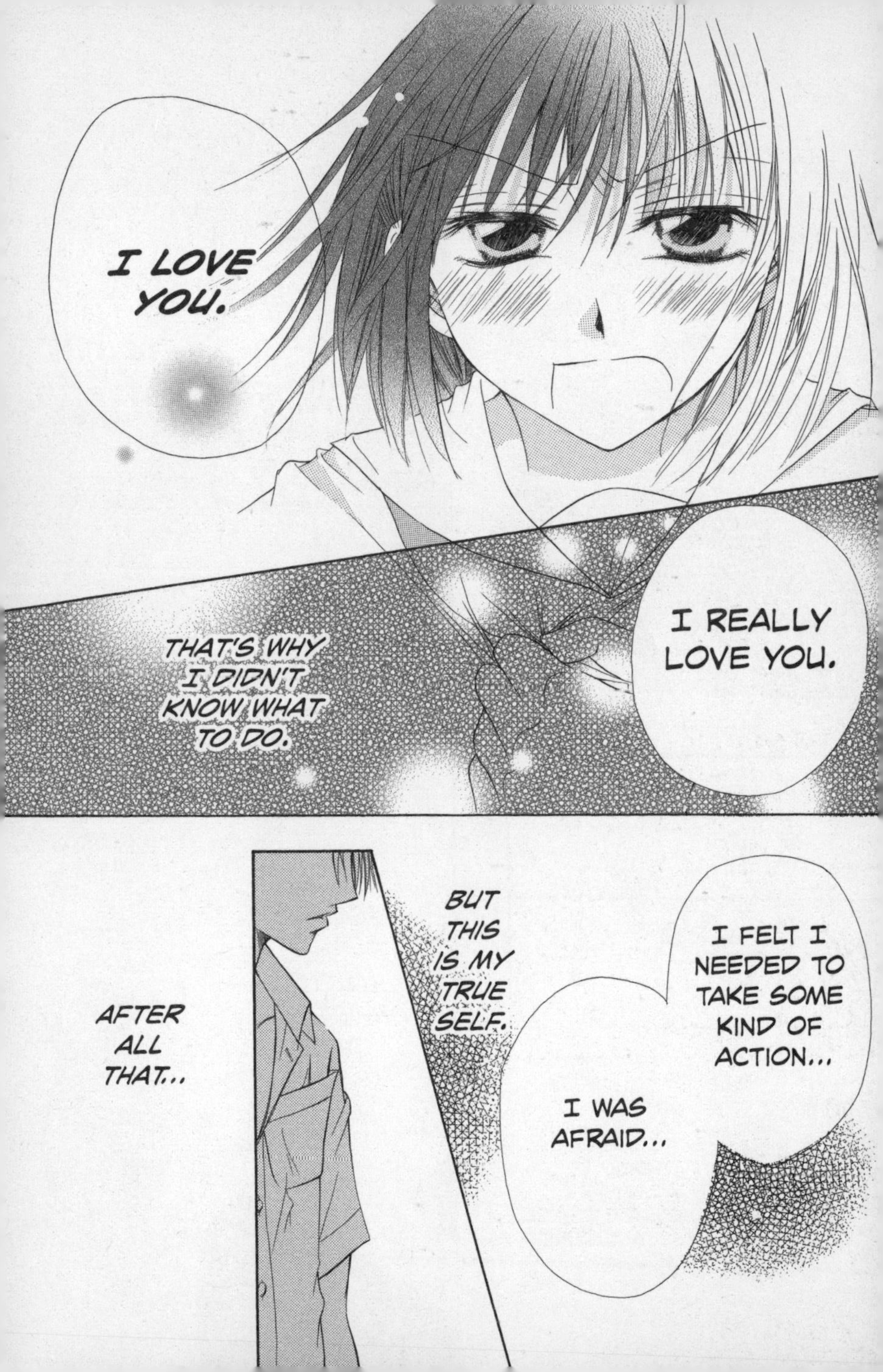
I LOVE YOU.
I REALLY LOVE YOU.
THAT'S WHY I DIDN'T KNOW WHAT TO DO.
I FELT I NEEDED TO TAKE SOME KIND OF ACTION...
I WAS AFRAID...
BUT THIS IS MY TRUE SELF.
AFTER ALL THAT...

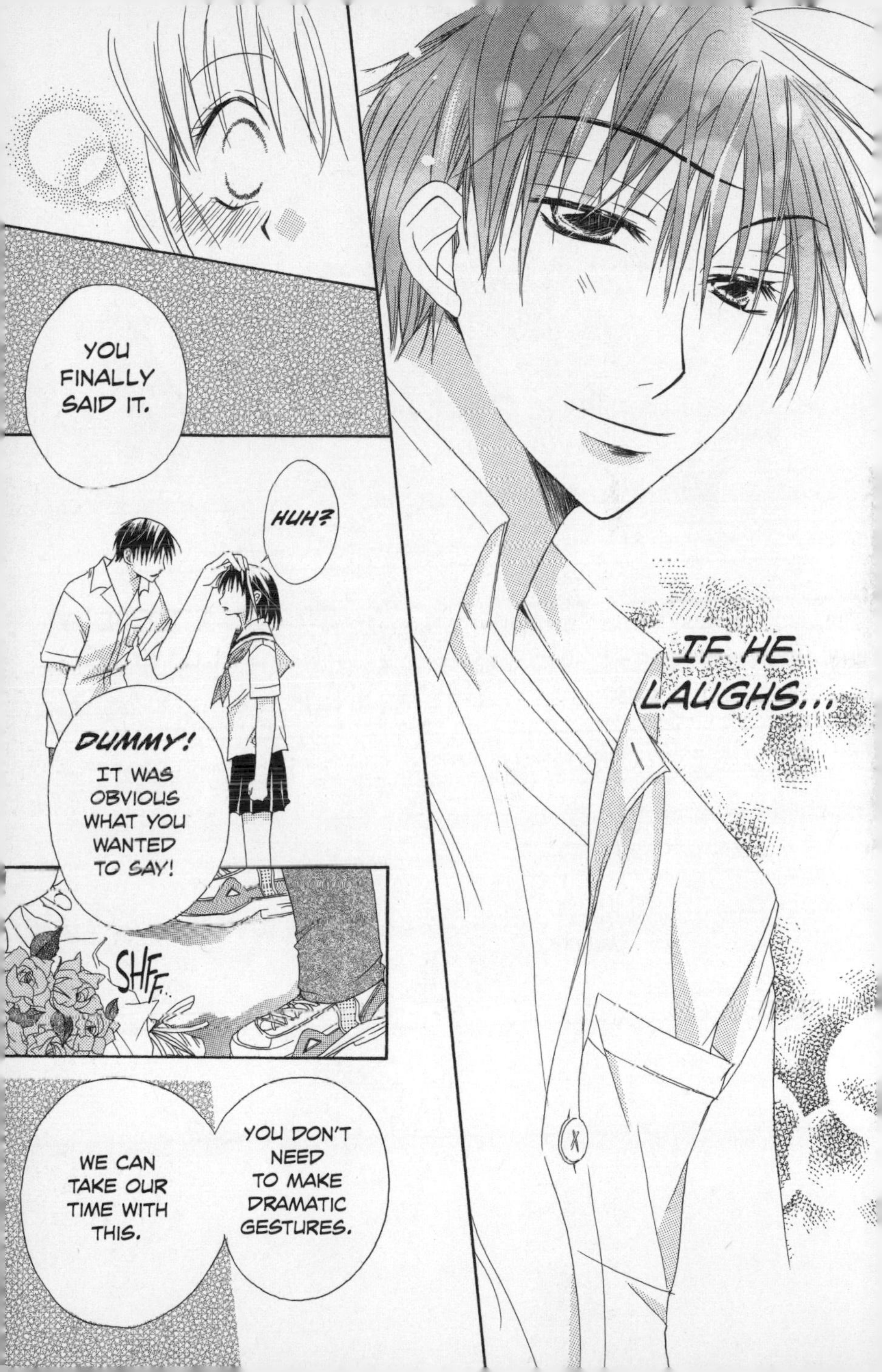
IF HE LAUGHS...
YOU FINALLY SAID IT.
HUH?
DUMMY! IT WAS OBVIOUS WHAT YOU WANTED TO SAY!
SHFF...
YOU DON'T NEED TO MAKE DRAMATIC GESTURES.
WE CAN TAKE OUR TIME WITH THIS.

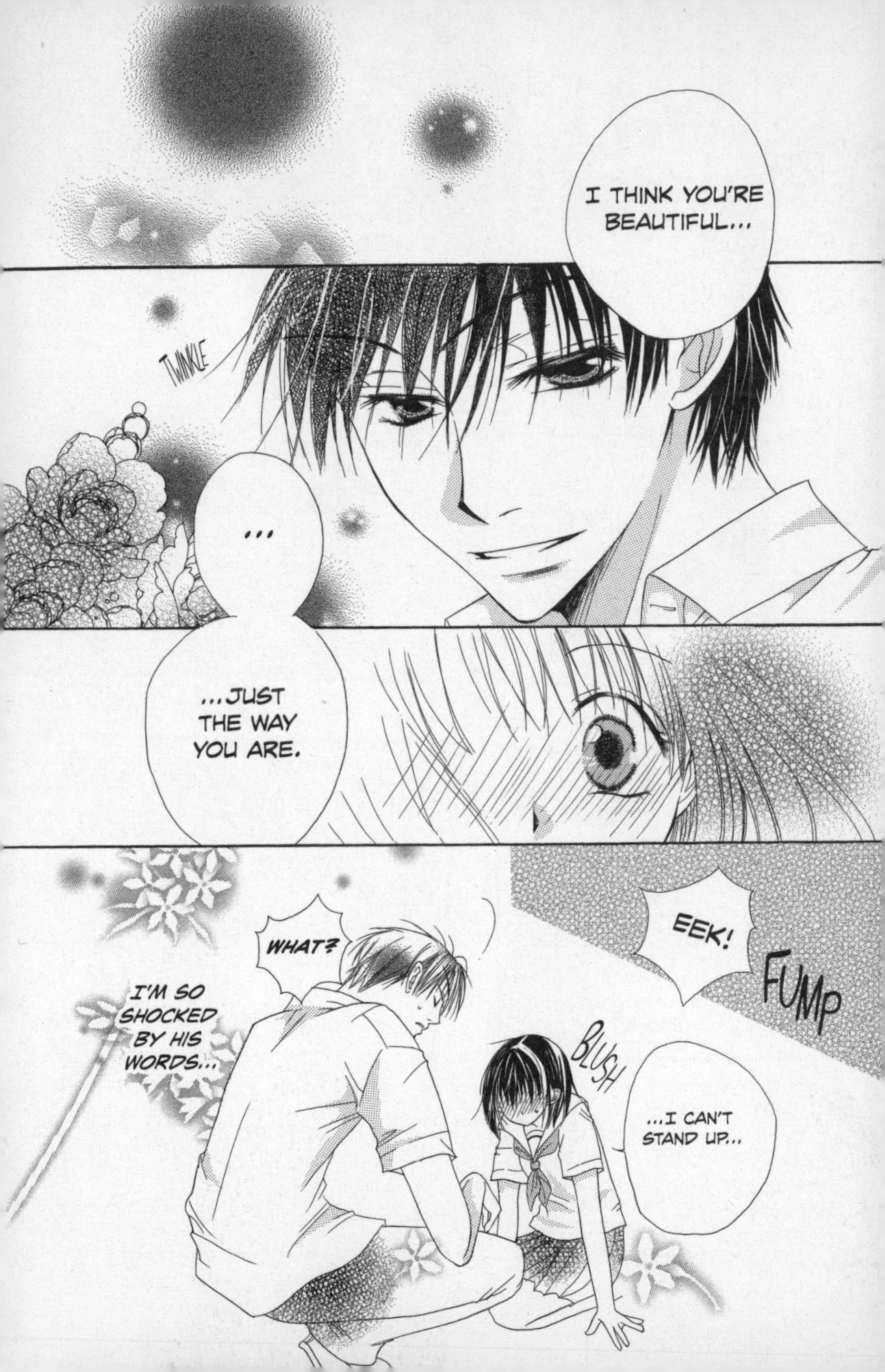
I THINK YOU'RE BEAUTIFUL...
TWINKLE
...
...JUST THE WAY YOU ARE.
EEK!
FUMP
BLUSH
...I CAN'T STAND UP...
WHAT?
I'M SO SHOCKED BY HIS WORDS...

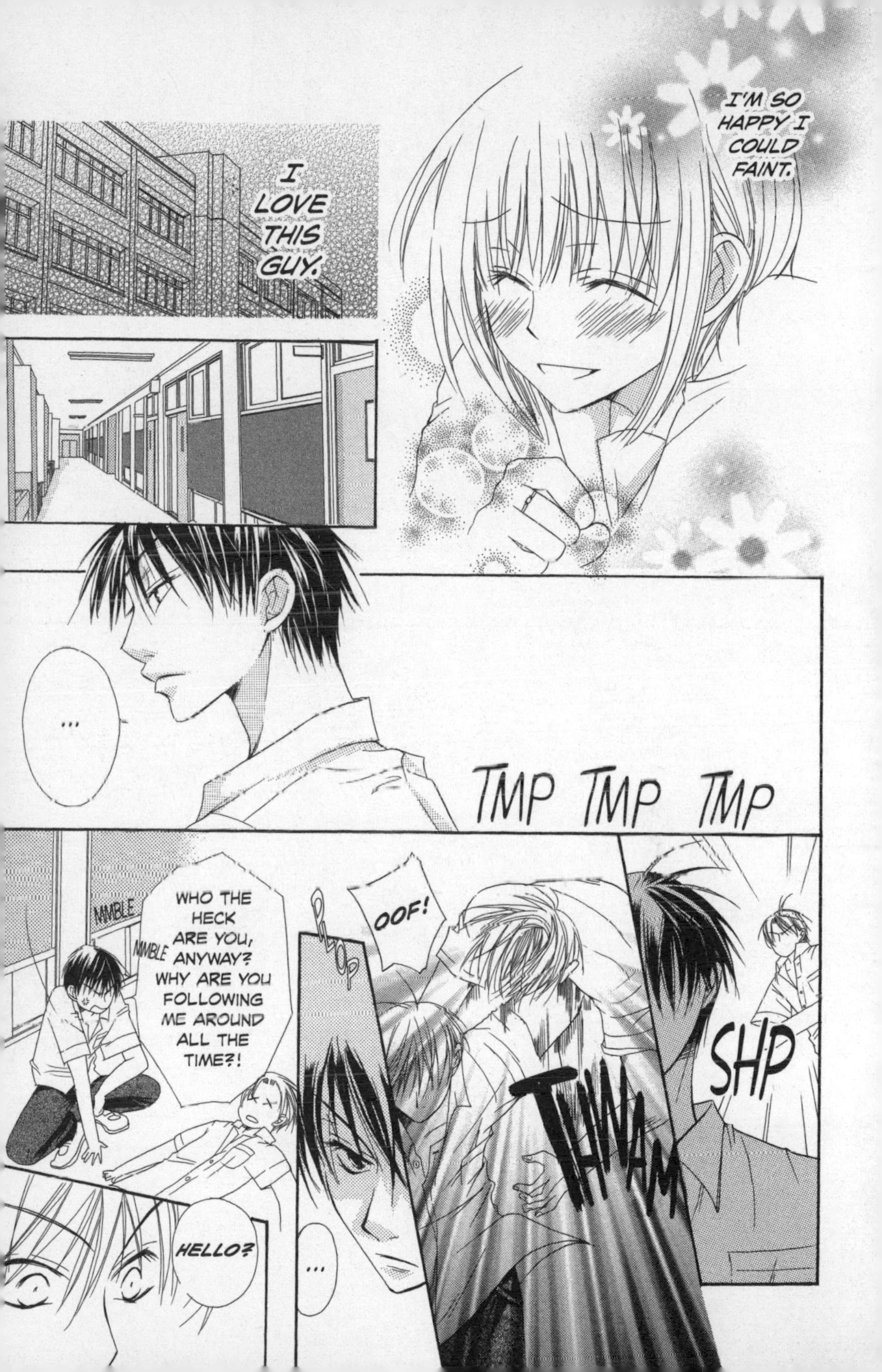
I'M SO HAPPY I COULD FAINT.
I LOVE THIS GUY.
...
TMP TMP TMP
SHP
THWAM
OOF!
PLOP
WHO THE HECK ARE YOU, ANYWAY? WHY ARE YOU FOLLOWING ME AROUND ALL THE TIME?!
MMBLE
MMBLE
...
HELLO?

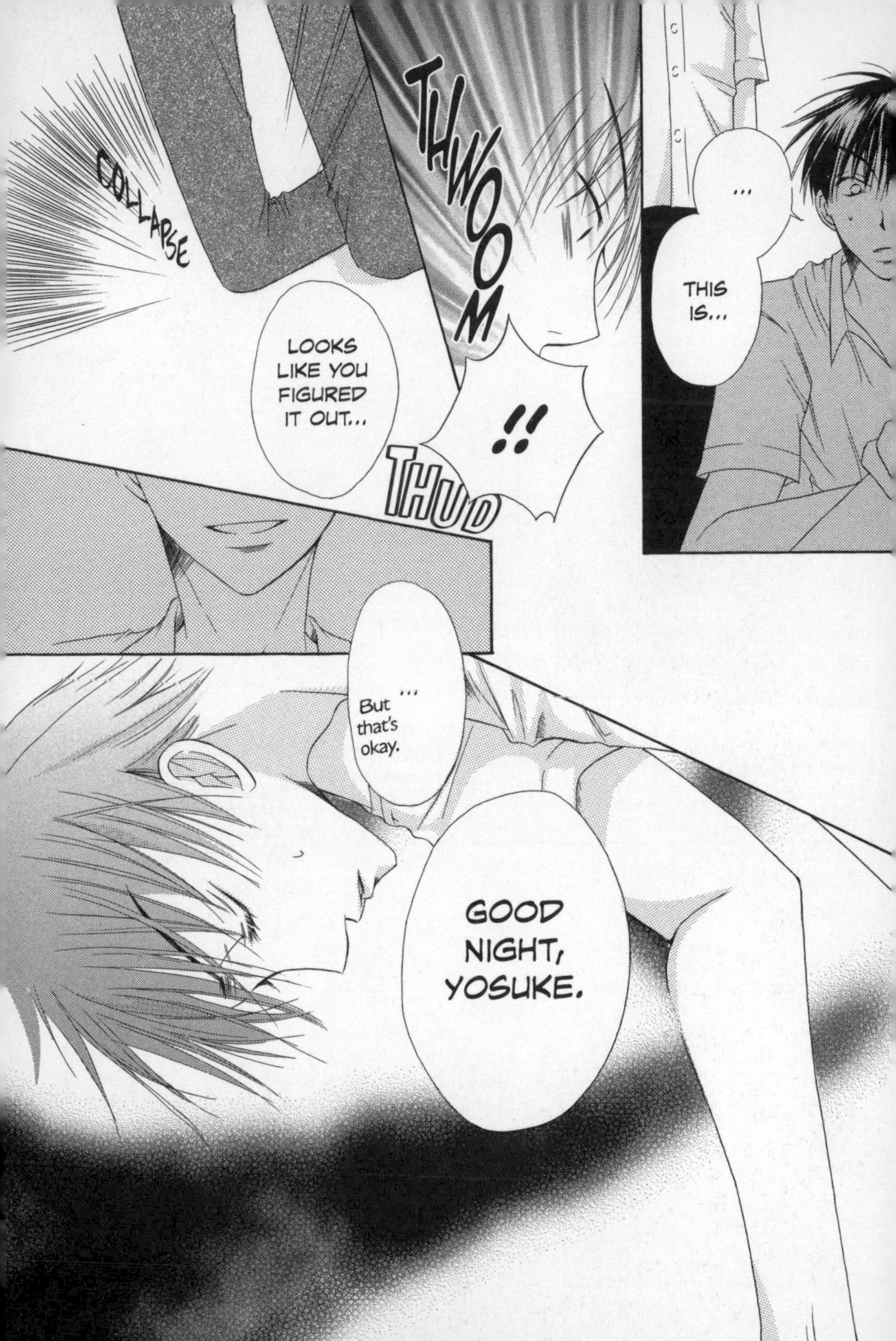
...
THIS IS...
THWOOM
COLLAPSE
LOOKS LIKE YOU FIGURED IT OUT...
!!
THUD
... But that's okay.
GOOD NIGHT, YOSUKE.

The Magic Touch, Part 4 / End

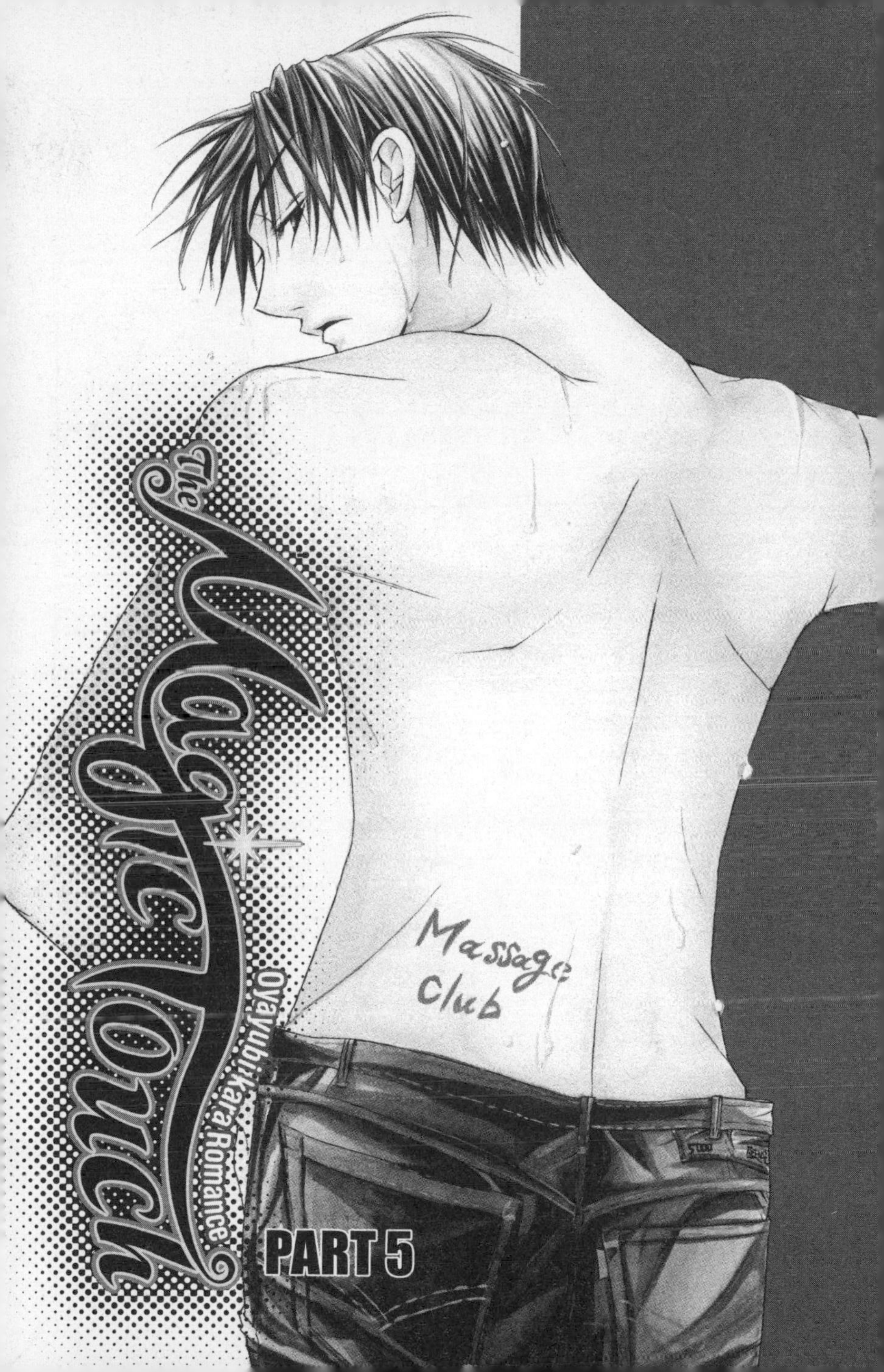
The Magic Touch
Oyayubi kara Romance
PART 5
Massage Club

INSIDE SCOOP: HOW THEY CHOSE THE TRAINING CAMP LOCATION

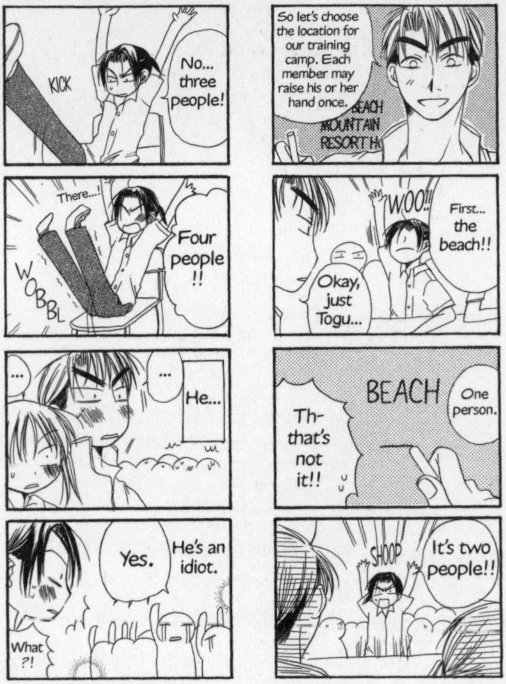
So let's choose the location for our training camp. Each member may raise his or her hand once.
MOUNTAIN
WOO!!
First... the beach!!
Okay, just Togu...
One person.
BEACH
Th- that's not it!!
It's two people!!
SHOOP
No... three people!
KICK
Four people!!
There...!
WOBBL
He...
...
...
He's an idiot.
Yes.
What?!

THEY ALL FELT SORRY FOR HIM.

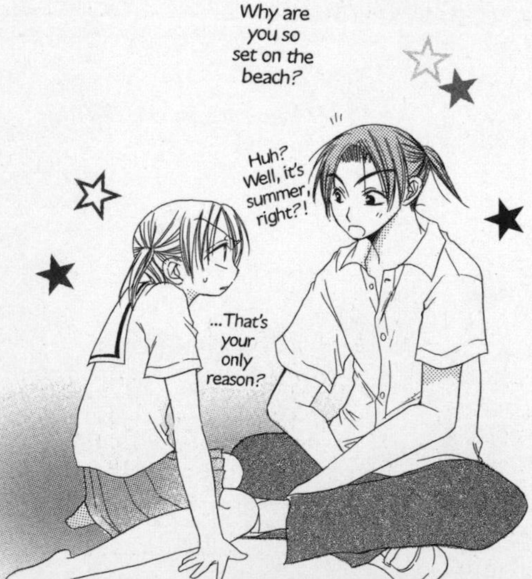
Why are you so set on the beach?
Huh? Well, it's summer, right?!
...That's your only reason?

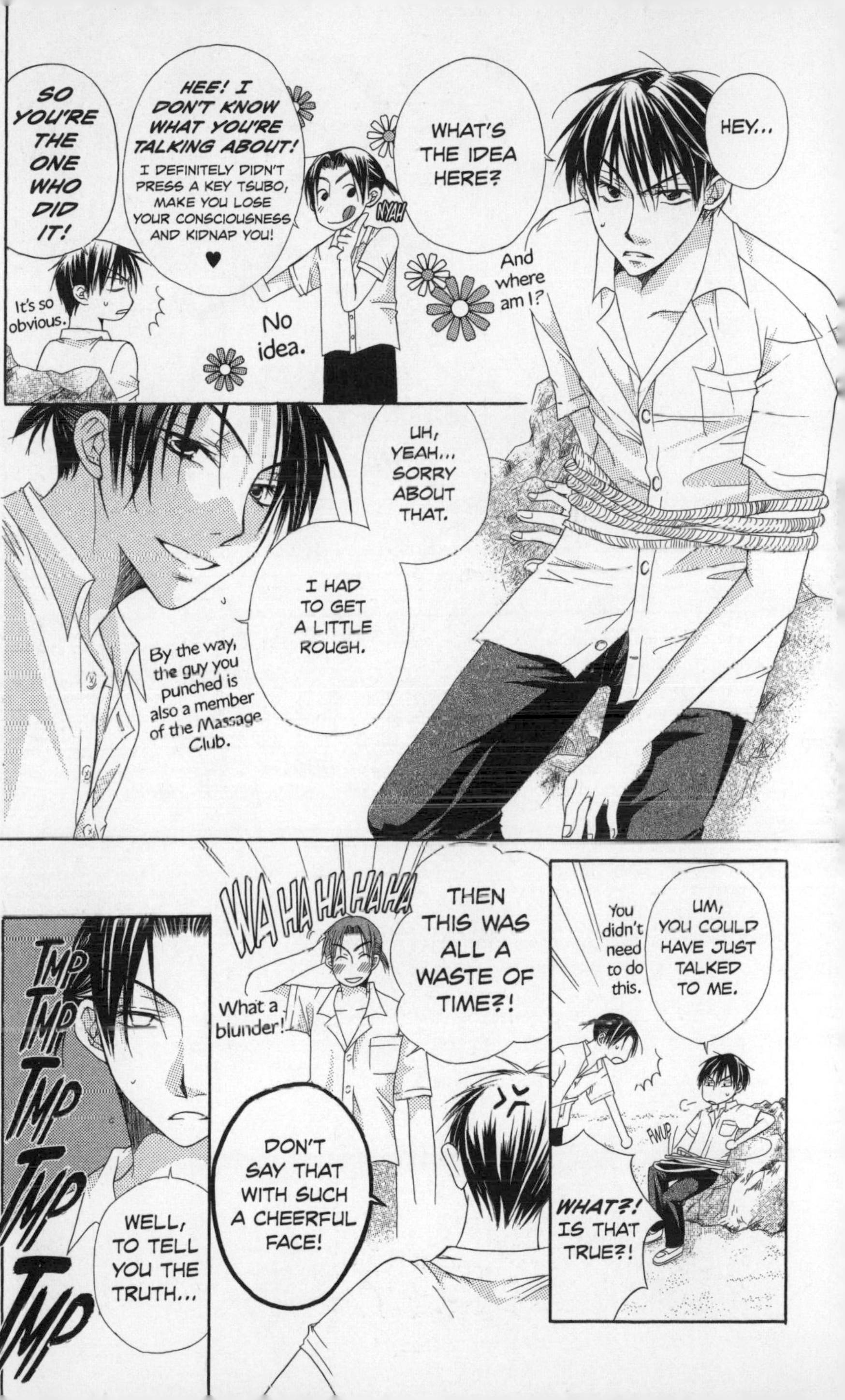
HEY...
WHAT'S THE IDEA HERE?
And where am I?
HEE! I DON'T KNOW WHAT YOU'RE TALKING ABOUT! I DEFINITELY DIDN'T PRESS A KEY TSUBO, MAKE YOU LOSE YOUR CONSCIOUSNESS AND KIDNAP YOU! ♥
NYAH
No idea.
SO YOU'RE THE ONE WHO DID IT!
It's so obvious.
UH, YEAH... SORRY ABOUT THAT.
I HAD TO GET A LITTLE ROUGH.
By the way, the guy you punched is also a member of the Massage Club.
UM, YOU COULD HAVE JUST TALKED TO ME.
You didn't need to do this.
FWUP
WHAT?! IS THAT TRUE?!
THEN THIS WAS ALL A WASTE OF TIME?!
WA HA HA HA HA
What a blunder!
DON'T SAY THAT WITH SUCH A CHEERFUL FACE!
TMP TMP TMP TMP TMP
WELL, TO TELL YOU THE TRUTH...

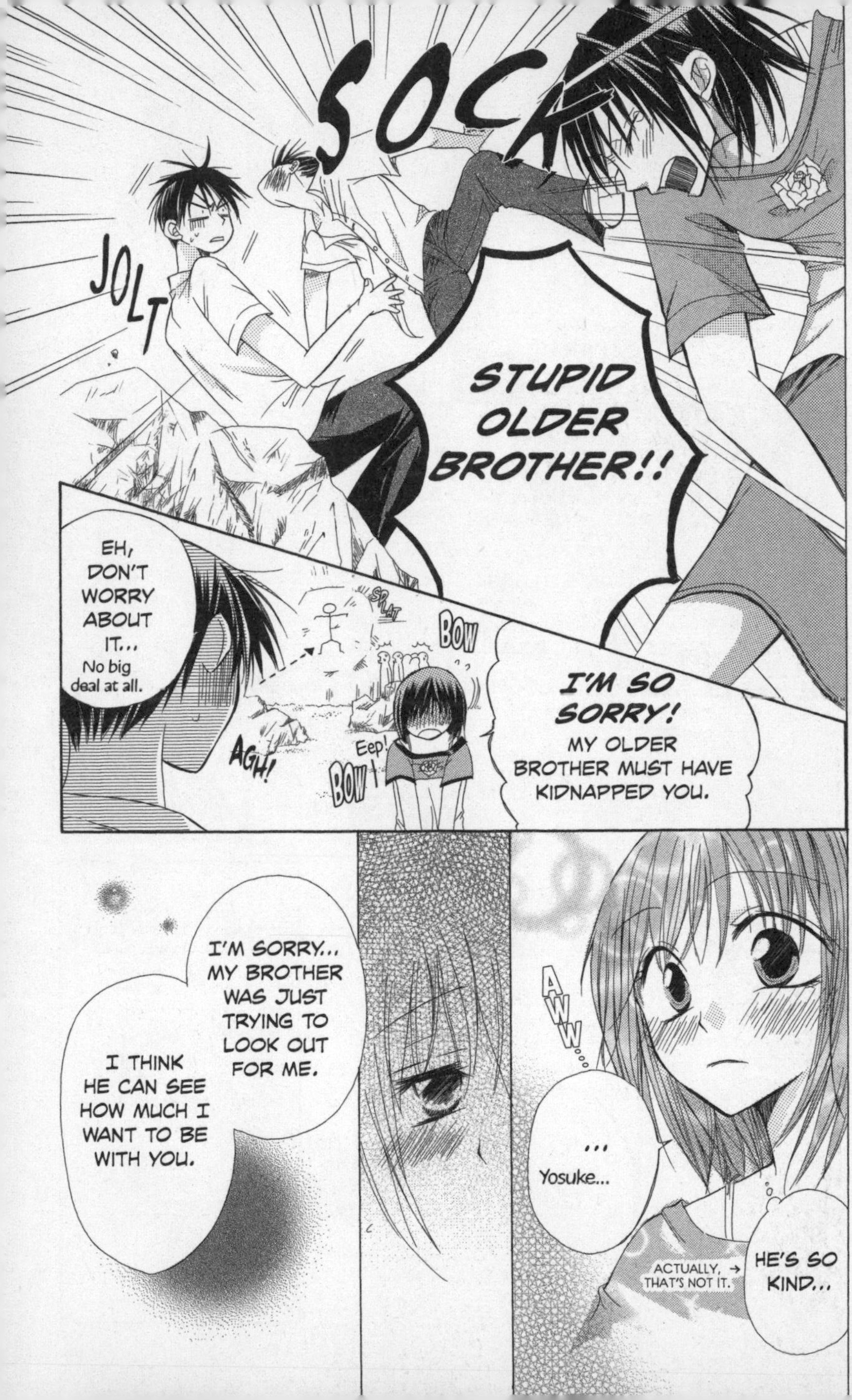
SOCK
STUPID OLDER BROTHER!!
JOLT
I'M SO SORRY! MY OLDER BROTHER MUST HAVE KIDNAPPED YOU.
BOW
SPLAT
Eep!
BOW
AGH!
EH, DON'T WORRY ABOUT IT... No big deal at all.
AWW...
... Yosuke...
HE'S SO KIND...
ACTUALLY, THAT'S NOT IT.
I'M SORRY... MY BROTHER WAS JUST TRYING TO LOOK OUT FOR ME.
I THINK HE CAN SEE HOW MUCH I WANT TO BE WITH YOU.

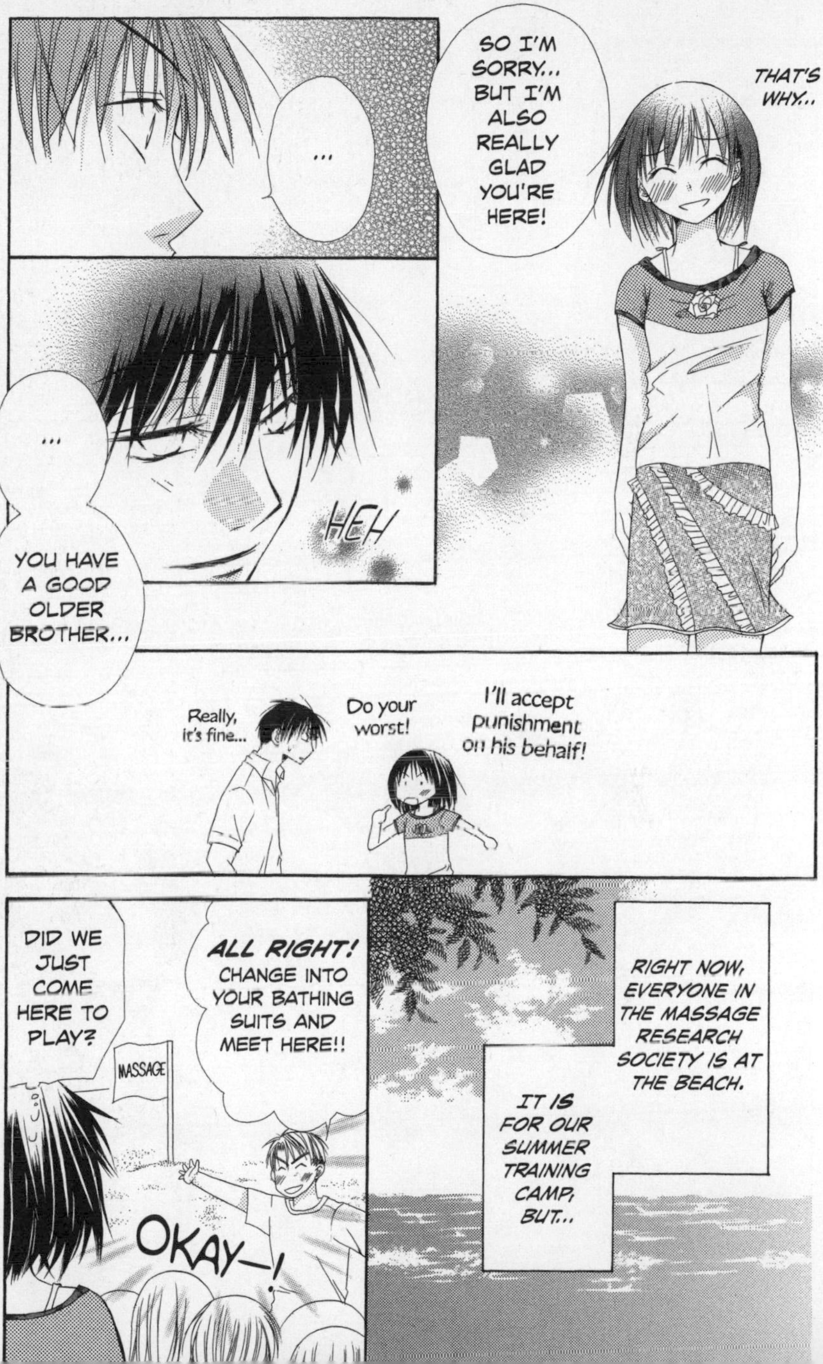
THAT'S WHY...
SO I'M SORRY... BUT I'M ALSO REALLY GLAD YOU'RE HERE!
...
...
HEH
YOU HAVE A GOOD OLDER BROTHER...
I'll accept punishment on his behalf!
Do your worst!
Really, it's fine...
RIGHT NOW, EVERYONE IN THE MASSAGE RESEARCH SOCIETY IS AT THE BEACH.
IT IS FOR OUR SUMMER TRAINING CAMP, BUT...
ALL RIGHT! CHANGE INTO YOUR BATHING SUITS AND MEET HERE!!
DID WE JUST COME HERE TO PLAY?
MASSAGE
OKAY—!

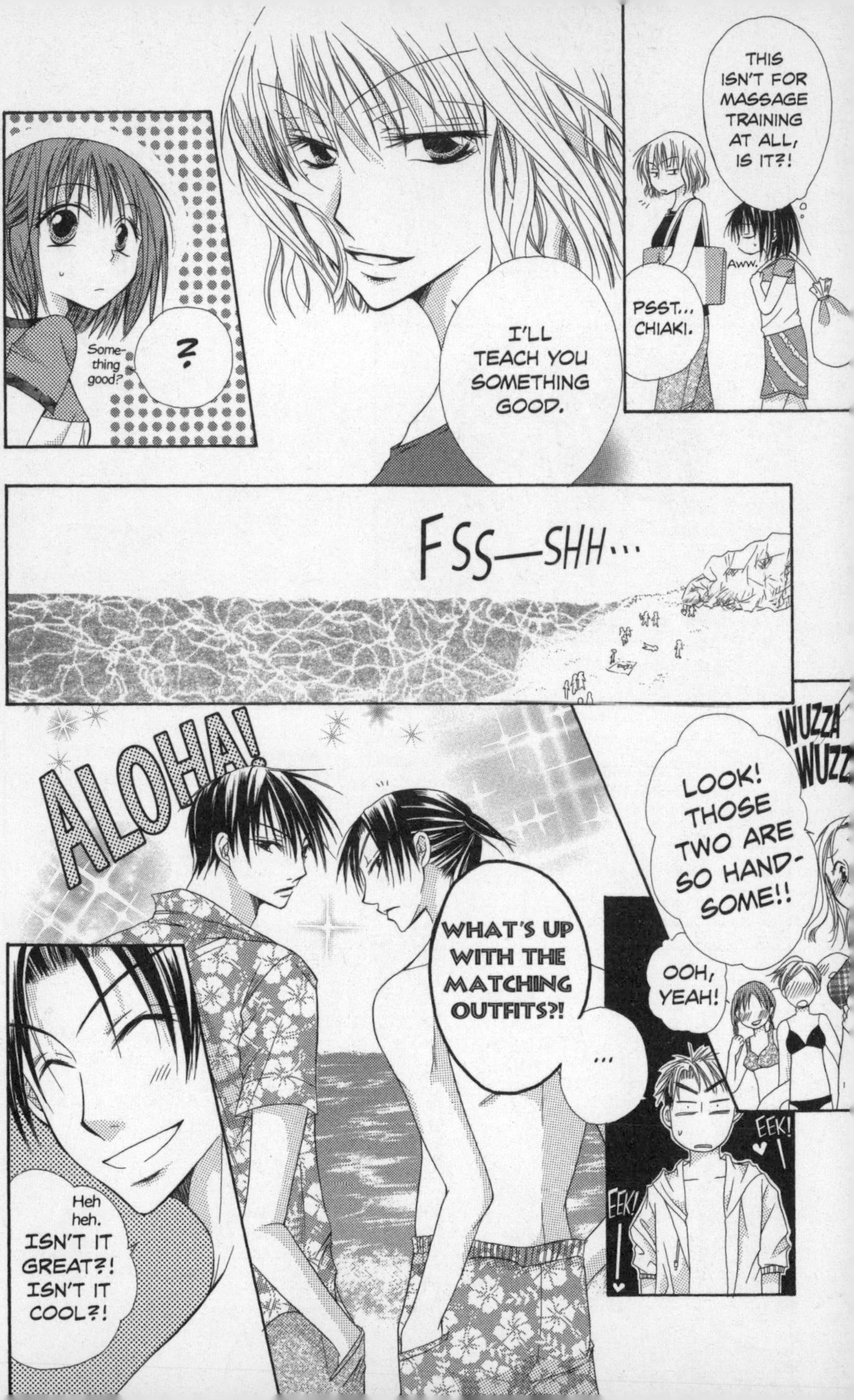
THIS ISN'T FOR MASSAGE TRAINING AT ALL, IS IT?!
Aww.
PSST... CHIAKI.
I'LL TEACH YOU SOMETHING GOOD.
?
Something good?
FSS—SHH...
WUZZA WUZZ
LOOK! THOSE TWO ARE SO HANDSOME!!
OOH, YEAH!
EEK!
EEK!
ALOHA!
WHAT'S UP WITH THE MATCHING OUTFITS?!
...
Heh heh. ISN'T IT GREAT?! ISN'T IT COOL?!

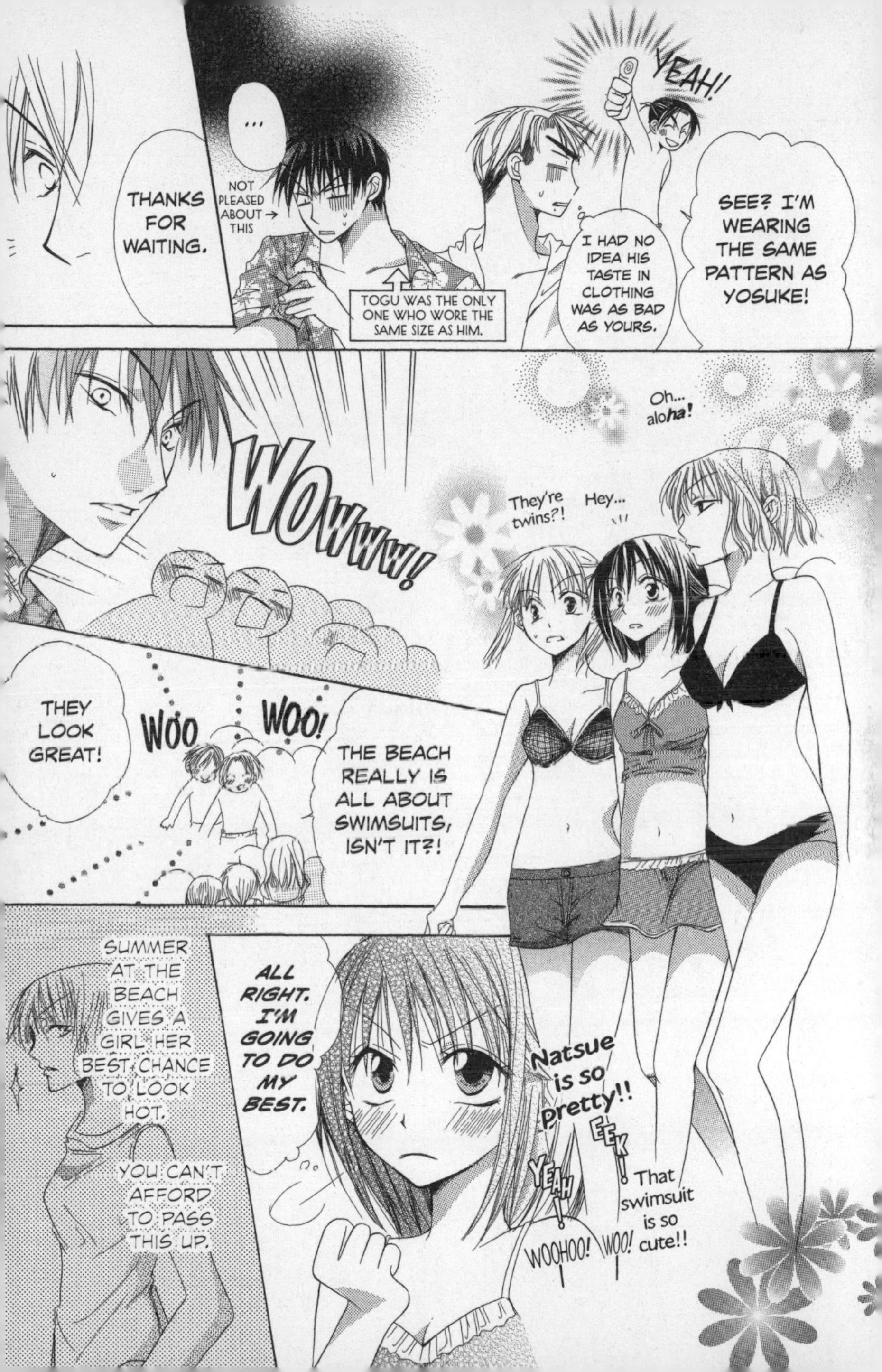

YEAH!
SEE? I'M WEARING THE SAME PATTERN AS YOSUKE!
I HAD NO IDEA HIS TASTE IN CLOTHING WAS AS BAD AS YOURS.
...
NOT PLEASED ABOUT THIS →
TOGU WAS THE ONLY ONE WHO WORE THE SAME SIZE AS HIM.
THANKS FOR WAITING.
Oh... aloha!
They're twins?!
Hey...
Natsue is so pretty!!
EEK!
YEAH!
That swimsuit is so cute!!
WOOHOO!
WOO!
WOWWWW!
THE BEACH REALLY IS ALL ABOUT SWIMSUITS, ISN'T IT?!
WOO
WOO!
THEY LOOK GREAT!
ALL RIGHT. I'M GOING TO DO MY BEST.
SUMMER AT THE BEACH GIVES A GIRL HER BEST CHANCE TO LOOK HOT.
YOU CAN'T AFFORD TO PASS THIS UP.

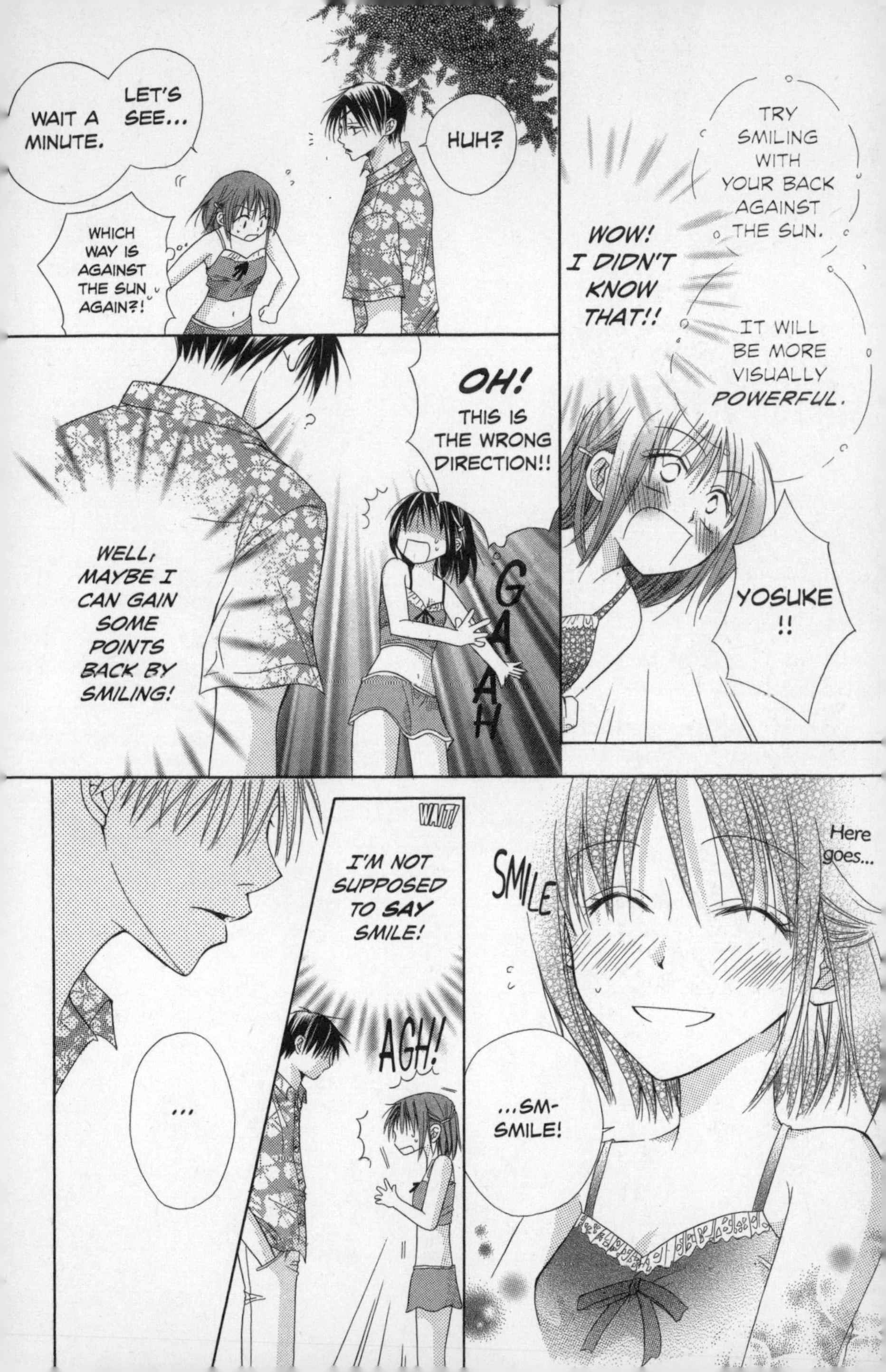
TRY SMILING WITH YOUR BACK AGAINST THE SUN.
IT WILL BE MORE VISUALLY POWERFUL.
WOW! I DIDN'T KNOW THAT!!
YOSUKE!!
HUH?
LET'S SEE... WAIT A MINUTE.
WHICH WAY IS AGAINST THE SUN AGAIN?!
OH! THIS IS THE WRONG DIRECTION!!
GAAH
WELL, MAYBE I CAN GAIN SOME POINTS BACK BY SMILING!
Here goes...
SMILE
...SM-SMILE!
WAIT!
I'M NOT SUPPOSED TO SAY SMILE!
AGH!
...

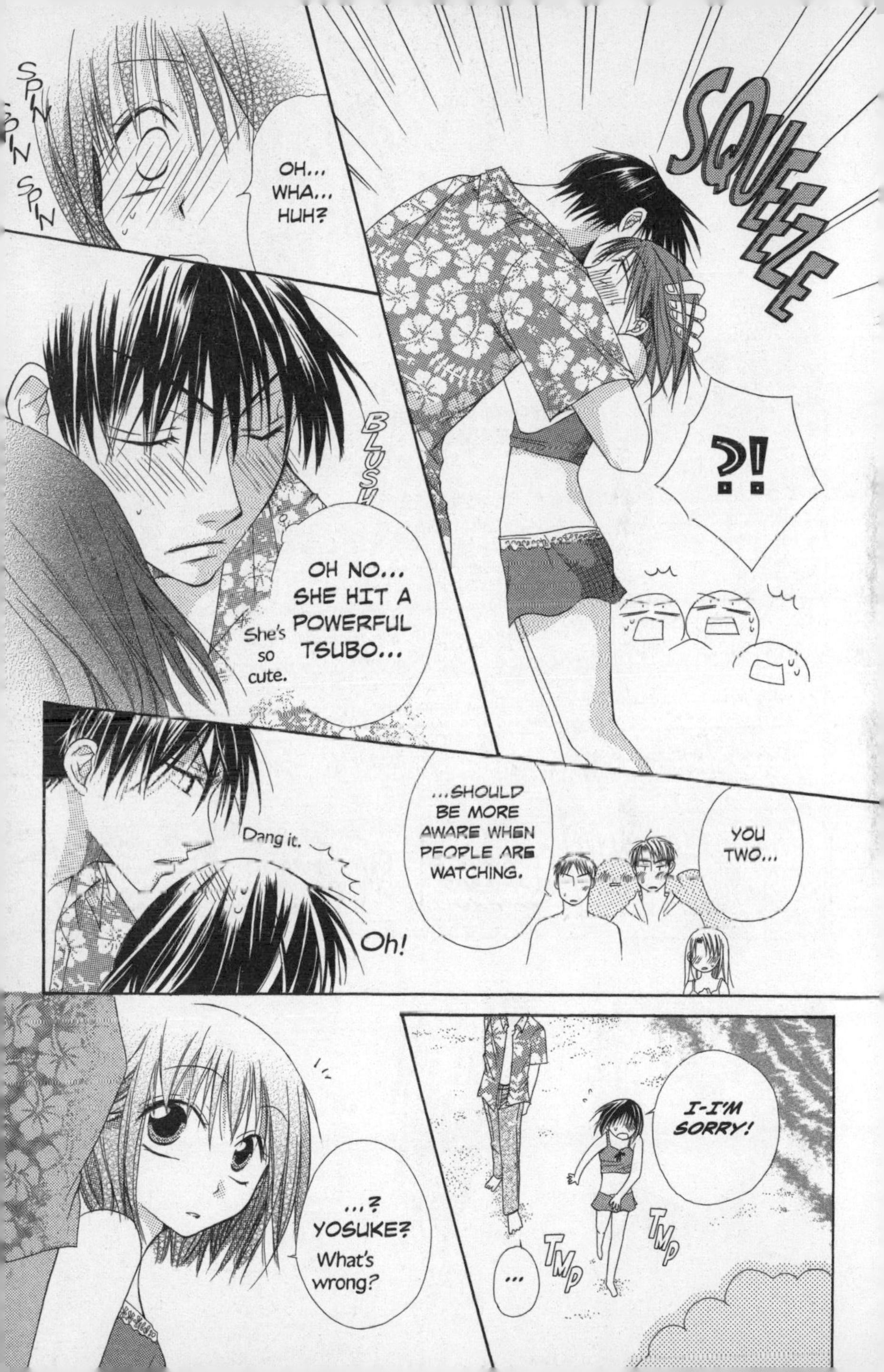
SQUEEZE
?!
SPIN SPIN SPIN
OH... WHA... HUH?
BLUSH
OH NO... SHE HIT A POWERFUL TSUBO...
She's so cute.
YOU TWO...
...SHOULD BE MORE AWARE WHEN PEOPLE ARE WATCHING.
Oh!
Dang it.
I-I'M SORRY!
TMP
TMP
...
...? YOSUKE?
What's wrong?

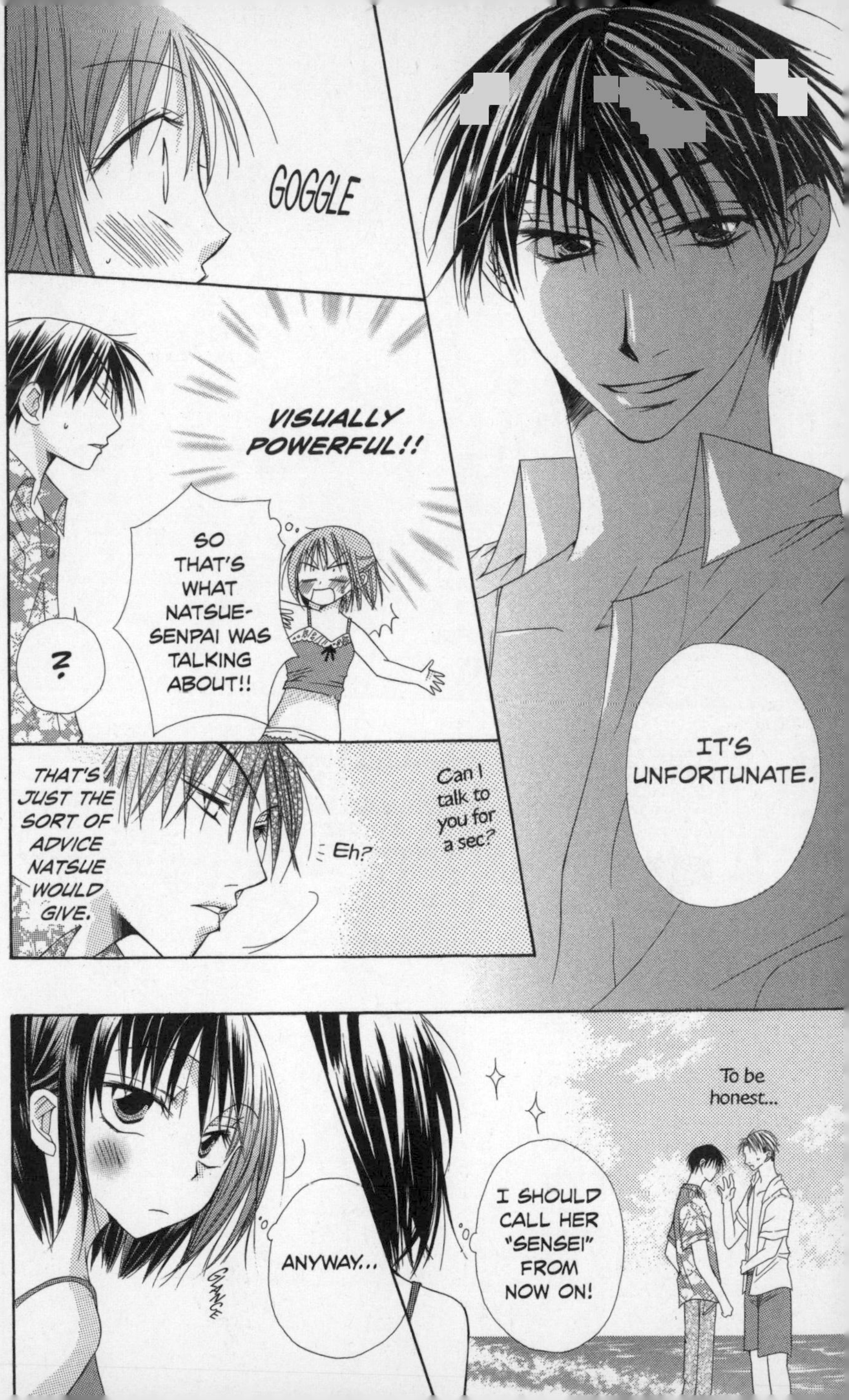
IT'S UNFORTUNATE.
GOGGLE
VISUALLY POWERFUL!!
SO THAT'S WHAT NATSUE-SENPAI WAS TALKING ABOUT!!
?
Can I talk to you for a sec?
Eh?
THAT'S JUST THE SORT OF ADVICE NATSUE WOULD GIVE.
To be honest...
I SHOULD CALL HER "SENSEI" FROM NOW ON!
ANYWAY...
GLANCE

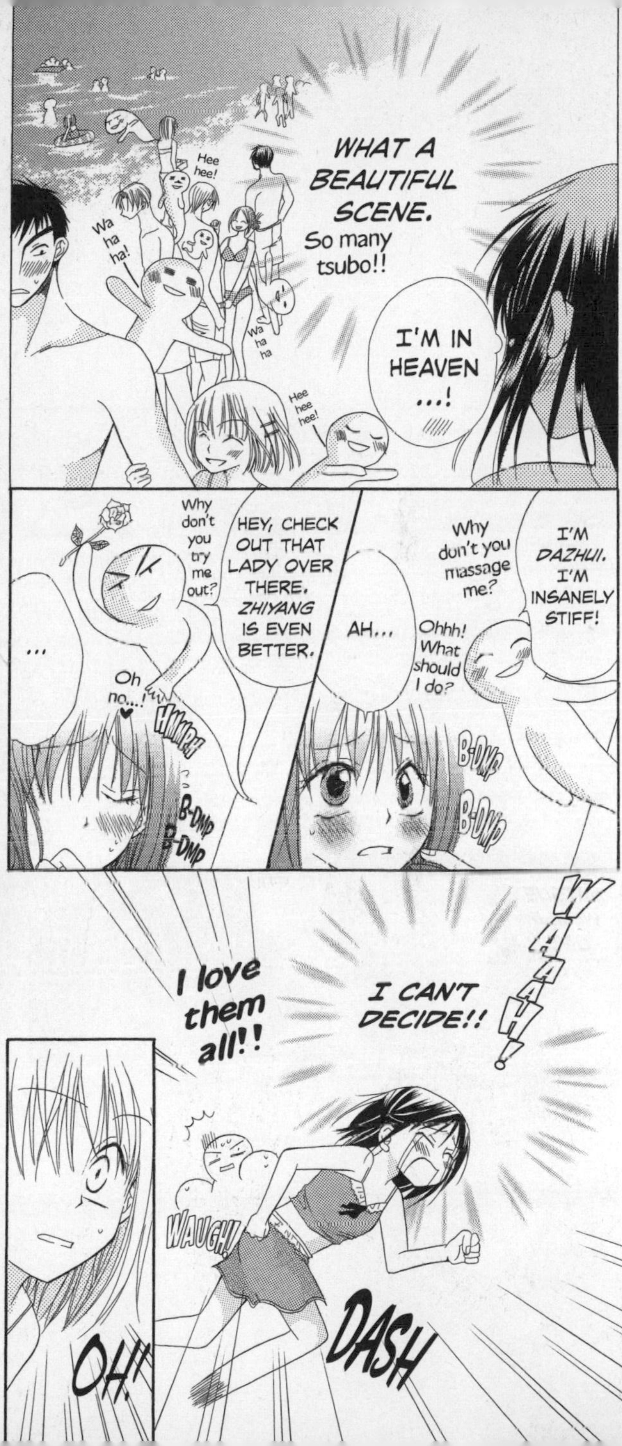
WHAT A BEAUTIFUL SCENE.
So many tsubo!!
I'M IN HEAVEN ...!
Hee hee!
Wa ha ha!
Wa ha ha
Hee hee hee!
I'M DAZHUI. I'M INSANELY STIFF!
Why don't you massage me?
AH...
Ohhh! What should I do?
B-DMP
B-DMP
HEY, CHECK OUT THAT LADY OVER THERE. ZHIYANG IS EVEN BETTER.
Why don't you try me out?
...
Oh no...!
HMMPH
B-DMP
B-DMP
WAAAAH!
I CAN'T DECIDE!!
I love them all!!
WAUGH!
DASH
OH!

School Uniform...?

Futouka Academy is a private school, so it has lots of different types of uniforms.* The students are allowed to arrange them—each individual gets to do whatever he or she likes.
For example, Natsue wears a sweater above her shirt.
⇩

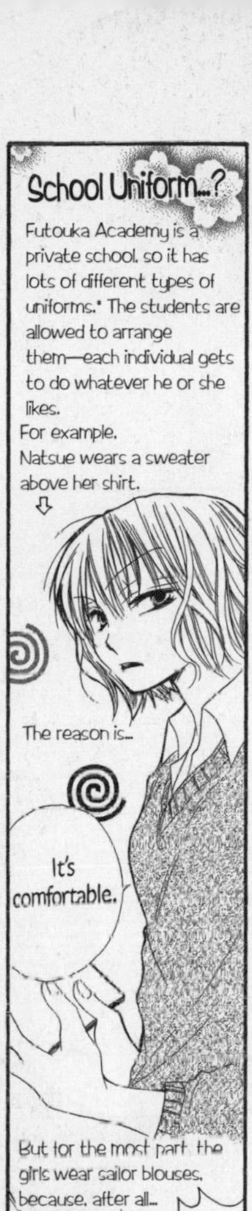
The reason is...
It's comfortable.

But for the most part the girls wear sailor blouses, because, after all...

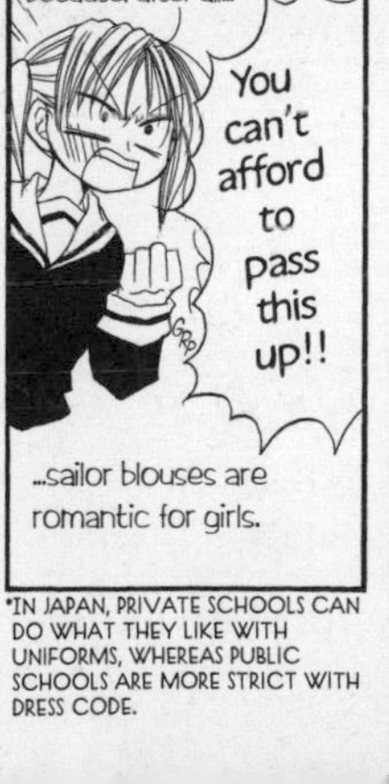
You can't afford to pass this up!!
GRR

...sailor blouses are romantic for girls.

*IN JAPAN, PRIVATE SCHOOLS CAN DO WHAT THEY LIKE WITH UNIFORMS, WHEREAS PUBLIC SCHOOLS ARE MORE STRICT WITH DRESS CODE.

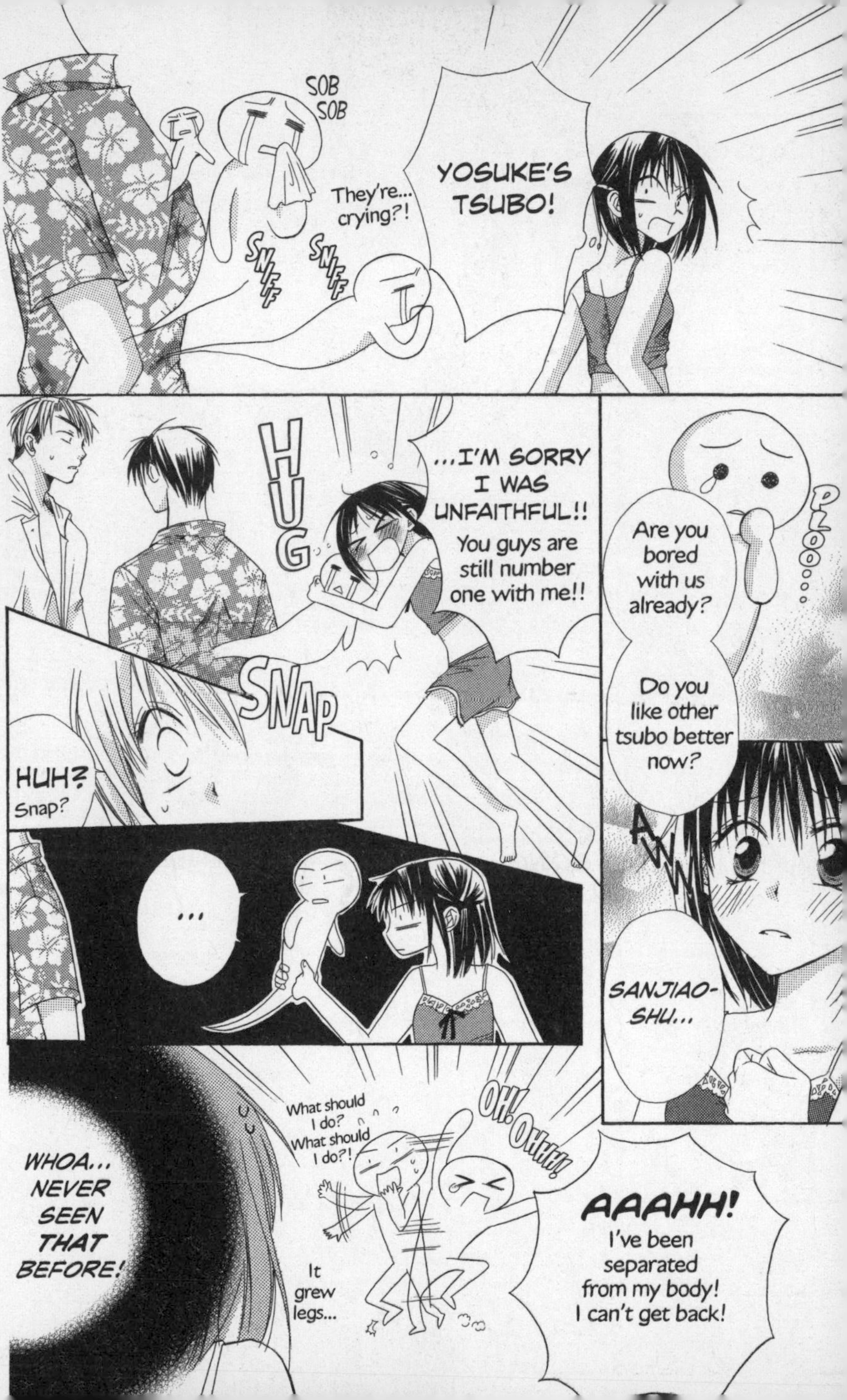
YOSUKE'S TSUBO!
They're... crying?!
SOB SOB
SNIFF SNIFF
Are you bored with us already?
PLOOO...
Do you like other tsubo better now?
AWW
SANJIAO-SHU...
...I'M SORRY I WAS UNFAITHFUL!! You guys are still number one with me!!
HUG
SNAP
HUH? Snap?
...
AAAHH! I've been separated from my body! I can't get back!
OH! OHHH!
What should I do? What should I do?!
It grew legs...
WHOA... NEVER SEEN THAT BEFORE!

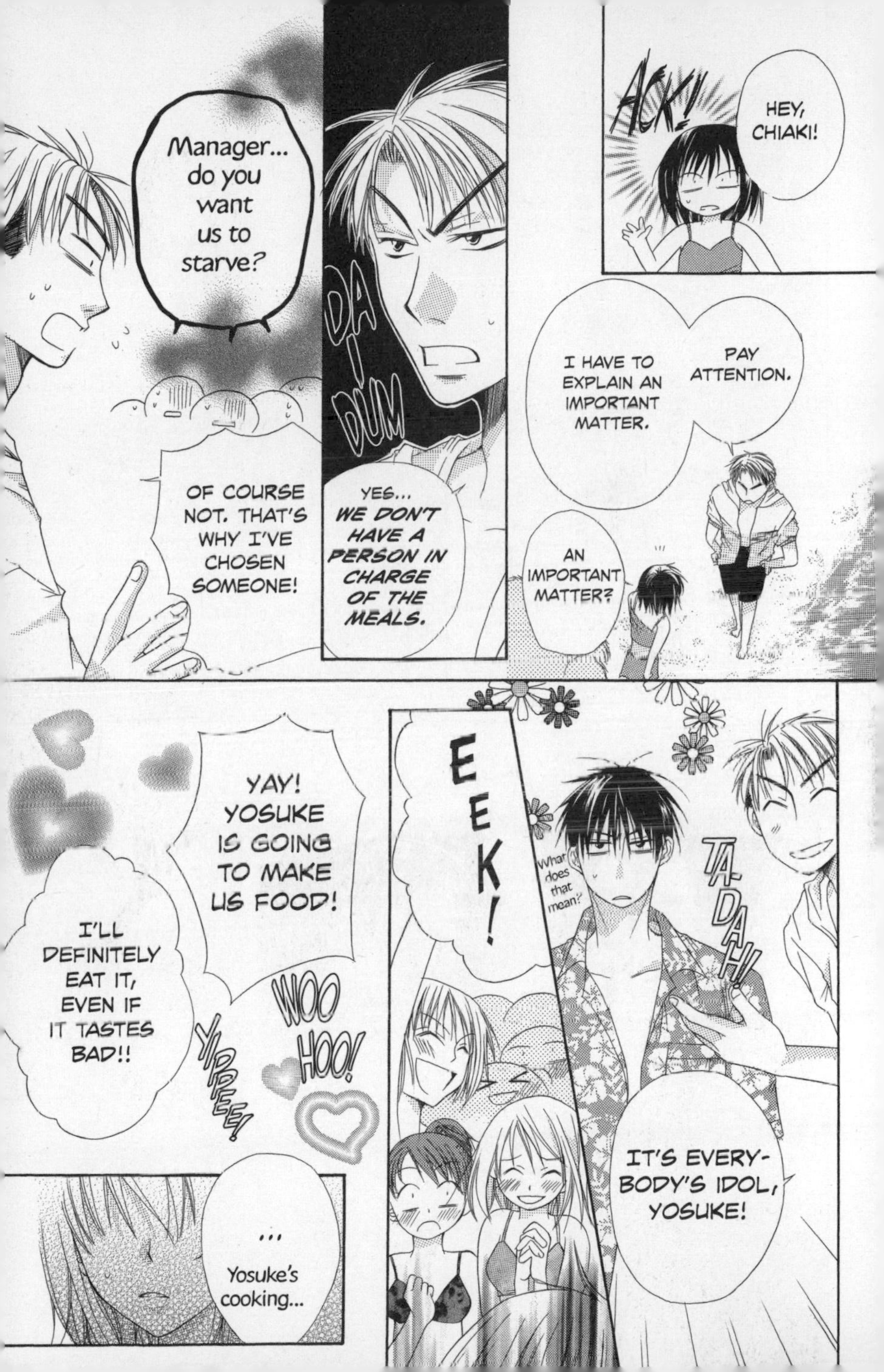
ACK!
HEY, CHIAKI!
PAY ATTENTION.
I HAVE TO EXPLAIN AN IMPORTANT MATTER.
AN IMPORTANT MATTER?
DA DUM
YES... WE DON'T HAVE A PERSON IN CHARGE OF THE MEALS.
Manager... do you want us to starve?
OF COURSE NOT. THAT'S WHY I'VE CHOSEN SOMEONE!
IT'S EVERY-BODY'S IDOL, YOSUKE!
TA-DAH!
What does that mean?
EEK!
YAY! YOSUKE IS GOING TO MAKE US FOOD!
I'LL DEFINITELY EAT IT, EVEN IF IT TASTES BAD!!
WOO HOO!
YIPPEE!
... Yosuke's cooking...

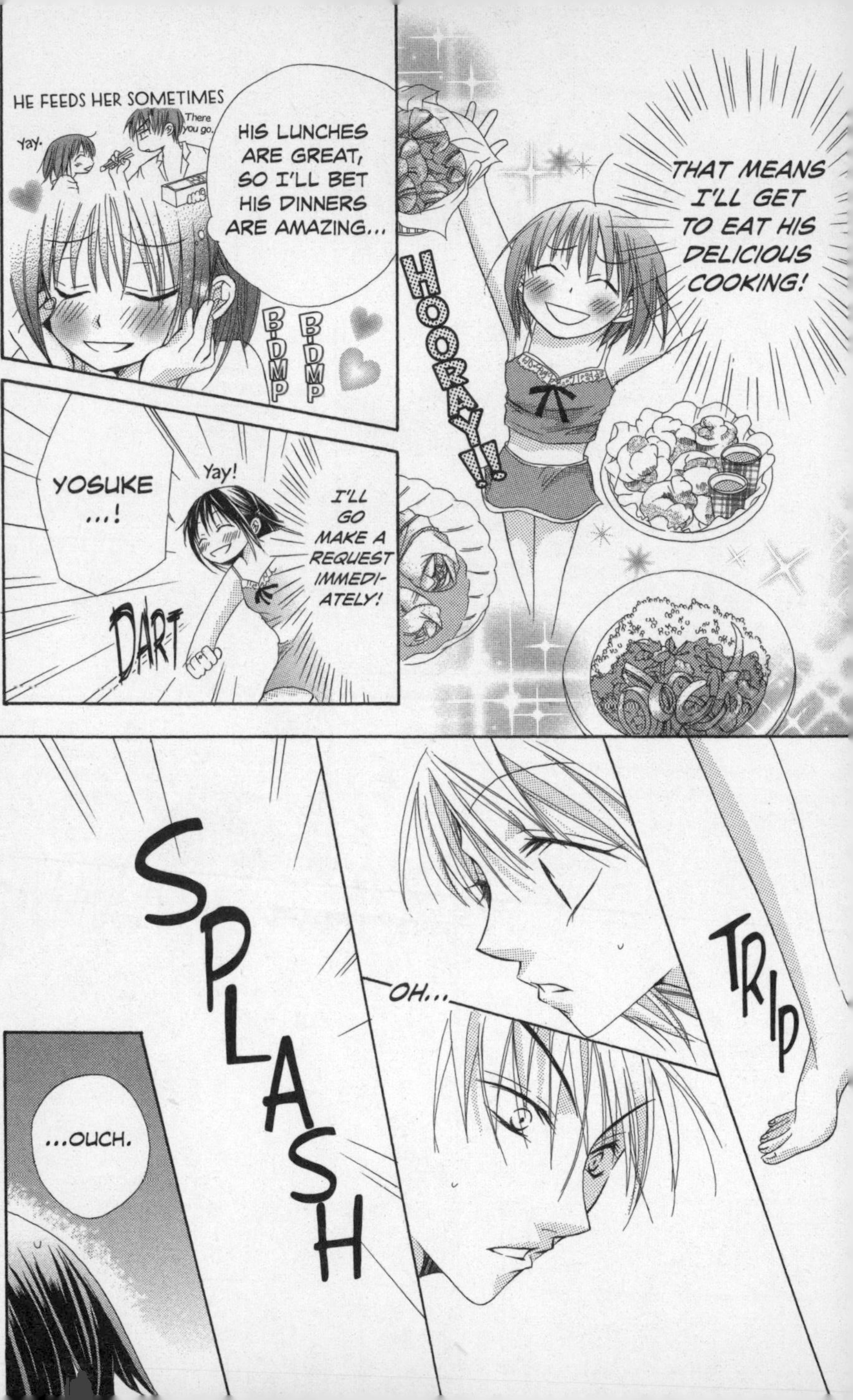
THAT MEANS I'LL GET TO EAT HIS DELICIOUS COOKING!
HOORAY!!
HE FEEDS HER SOMETIMES
There you go.
Yay.
HIS LUNCHES ARE GREAT, SO I'LL BET HIS DINNERS ARE AMAZING...
B-DMP
B-DMP
I'LL GO MAKE A REQUEST IMMEDIATELY!
Yay!
DART
YOSUKE ...!
TRIP
OH...
SPLASH
...OUCH.

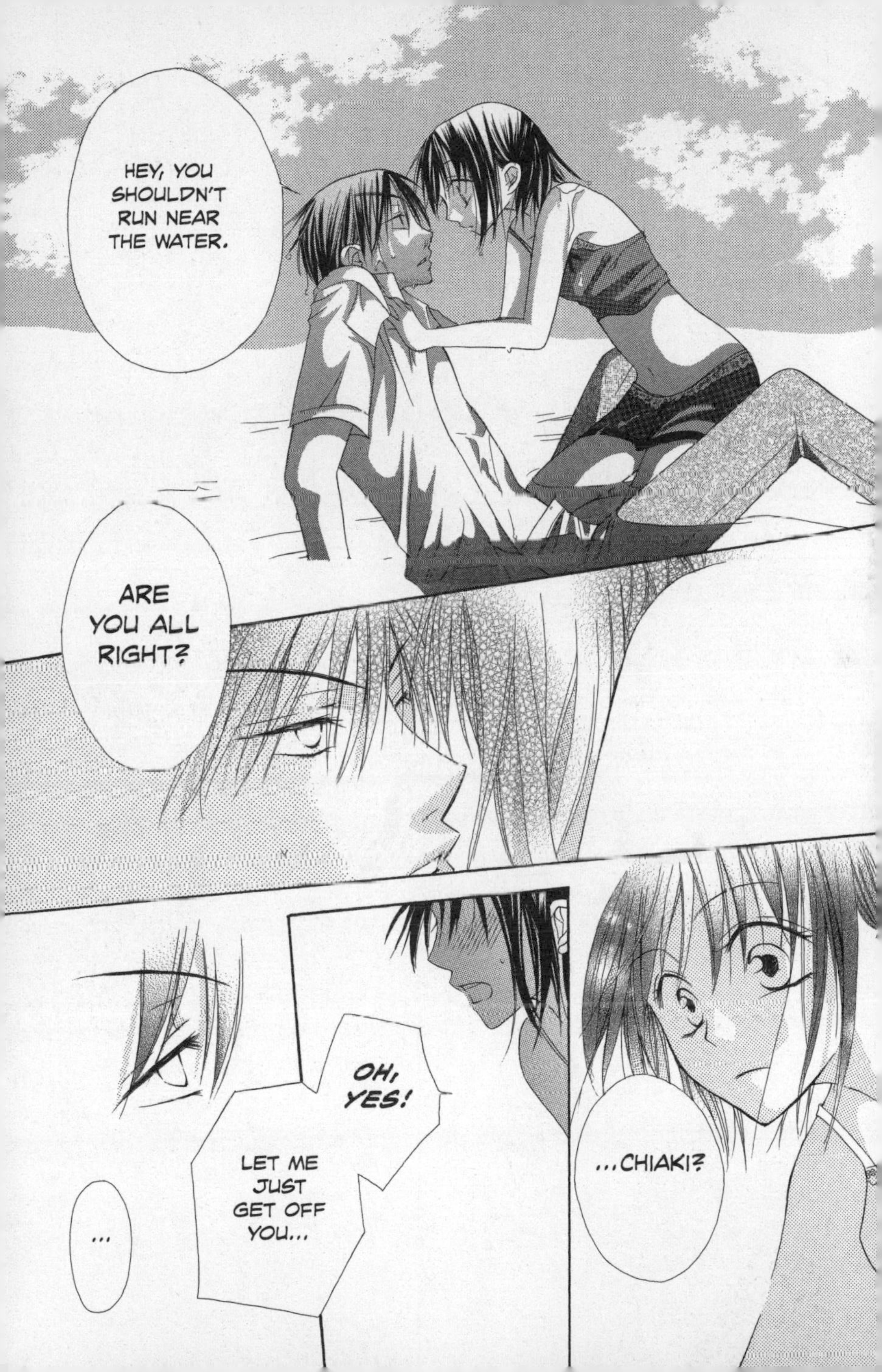
HEY, YOU SHOULDN'T RUN NEAR THE WATER.
ARE YOU ALL RIGHT?
...CHIAKI?
OH, YES!
LET ME JUST GET OFF YOU...
...

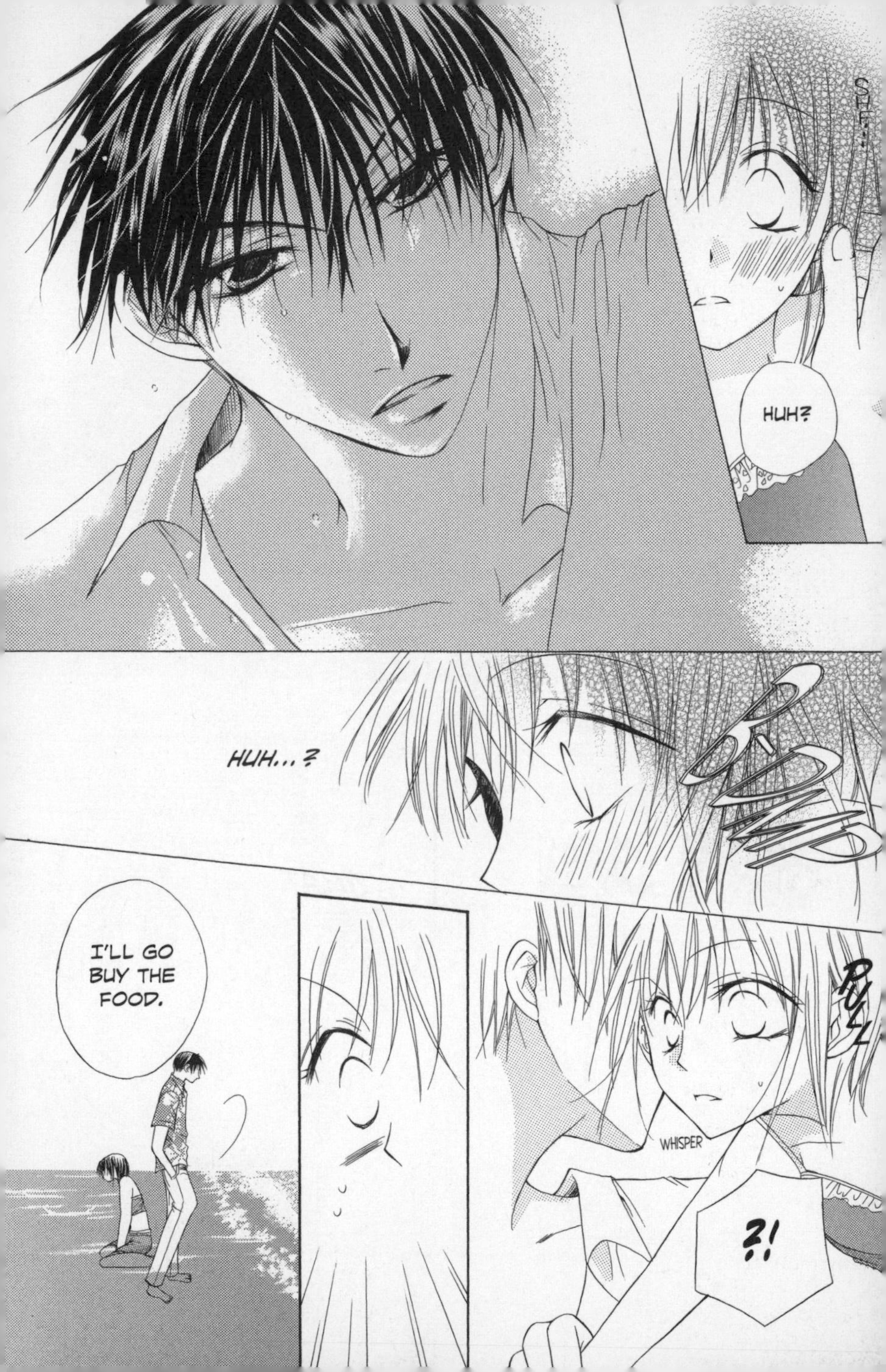
SHF...
HUH?
HUH...?
PULL
WHISPER
?!
I'LL GO BUY THE FOOD.

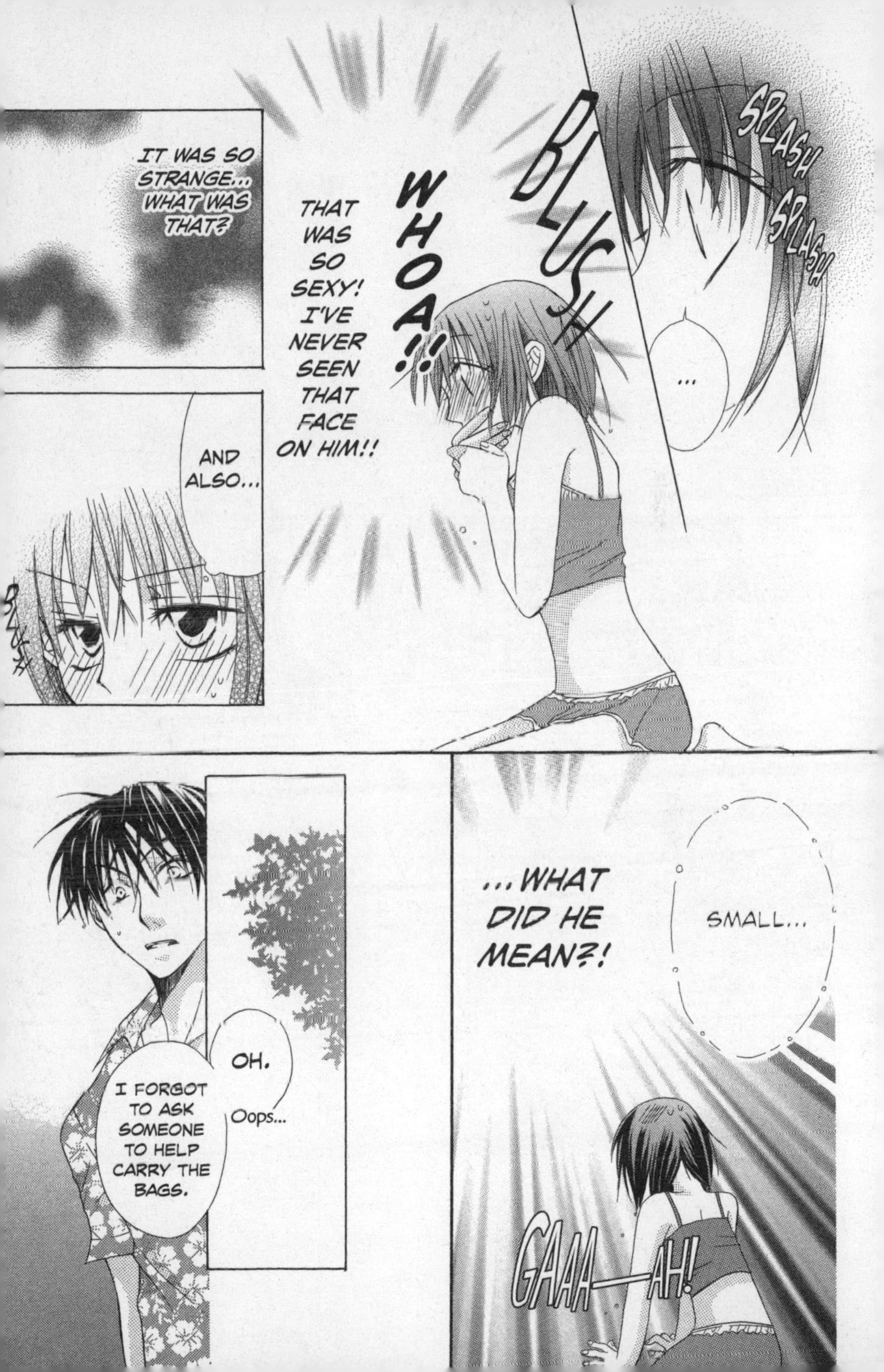
SPLASH SPLASH
...
BLUSH
WHOA!!
THAT WAS SO SEXY! I'VE NEVER SEEN THAT FACE ON HIM!!
IT WAS SO STRANGE... WHAT WAS THAT?
AND ALSO...
BLUSH
SMALL...
...WHAT DID HE MEAN?!
GAAA—AH!
OH.
Oops...
I FORGOT TO ASK SOMEONE TO HELP CARRY THE BAGS.

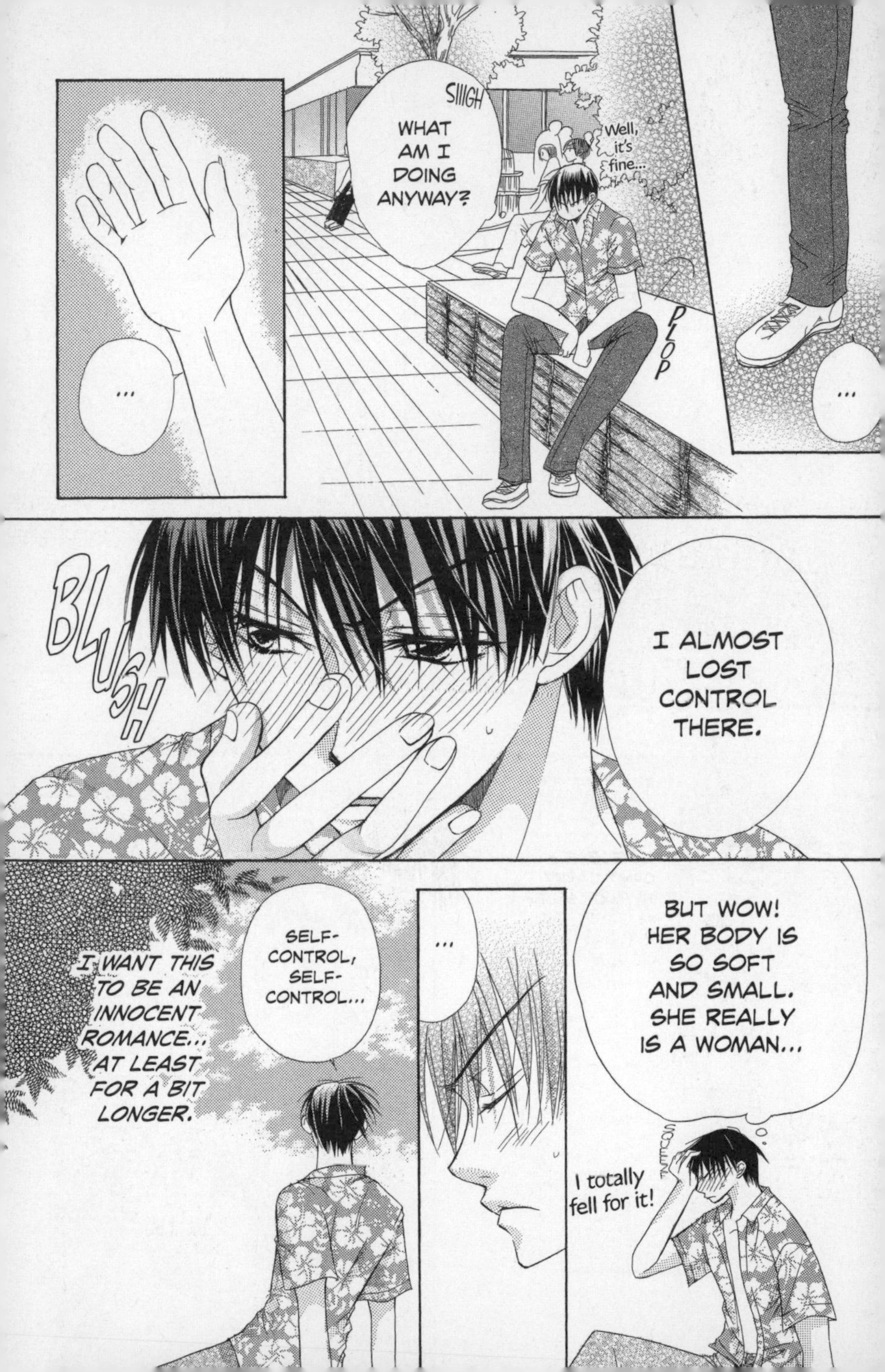
...
SIIIGH
WHAT AM I DOING ANYWAY?
Well, it's fine...
PLOP
...
I ALMOST LOST CONTROL THERE.
BLUSH
BUT WOW! HER BODY IS SO SOFT AND SMALL. SHE REALLY IS A WOMAN...
I totally fell for it!
...
SELF-CONTROL, SELF-CONTROL...
I WANT THIS TO BE AN INNOCENT ROMANCE... AT LEAST FOR A BIT LONGER.

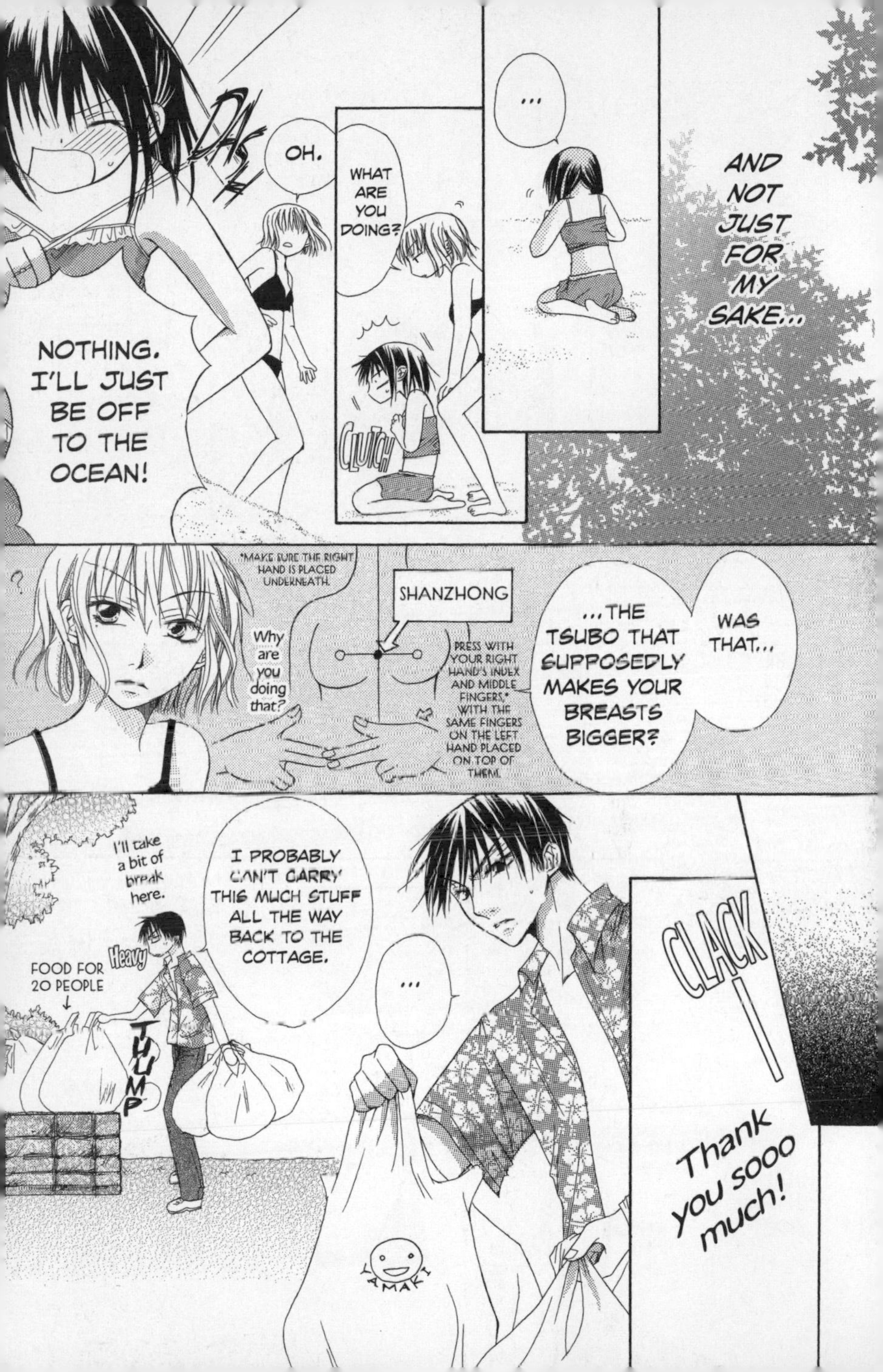

AND NOT JUST FOR MY SAKE...
...
WHAT ARE YOU DOING?
CLUTCH
OH.
DASH
NOTHING. I'LL JUST BE OFF TO THE OCEAN!
WAS THAT...
...THE TSUBO THAT SUPPOSEDLY MAKES YOUR BREASTS BIGGER?
SHANZHONG
PRESS WITH YOUR RIGHT HAND'S INDEX AND MIDDLE FINGERS,* WITH THE SAME FINGERS ON THE LEFT HAND PLACED ON TOP OF THEM.
*MAKE SURE THE RIGHT HAND IS PLACED UNDERNEATH.
Why are you doing that?
CLACK
Thank you sooo much!
...
YAMAKI
I PROBABLY CAN'T CARRY THIS MUCH STUFF ALL THE WAY BACK TO THE COTTAGE.
I'll take a bit of break here.
Heavy
THUMP
FOOD FOR 20 PEOPLE

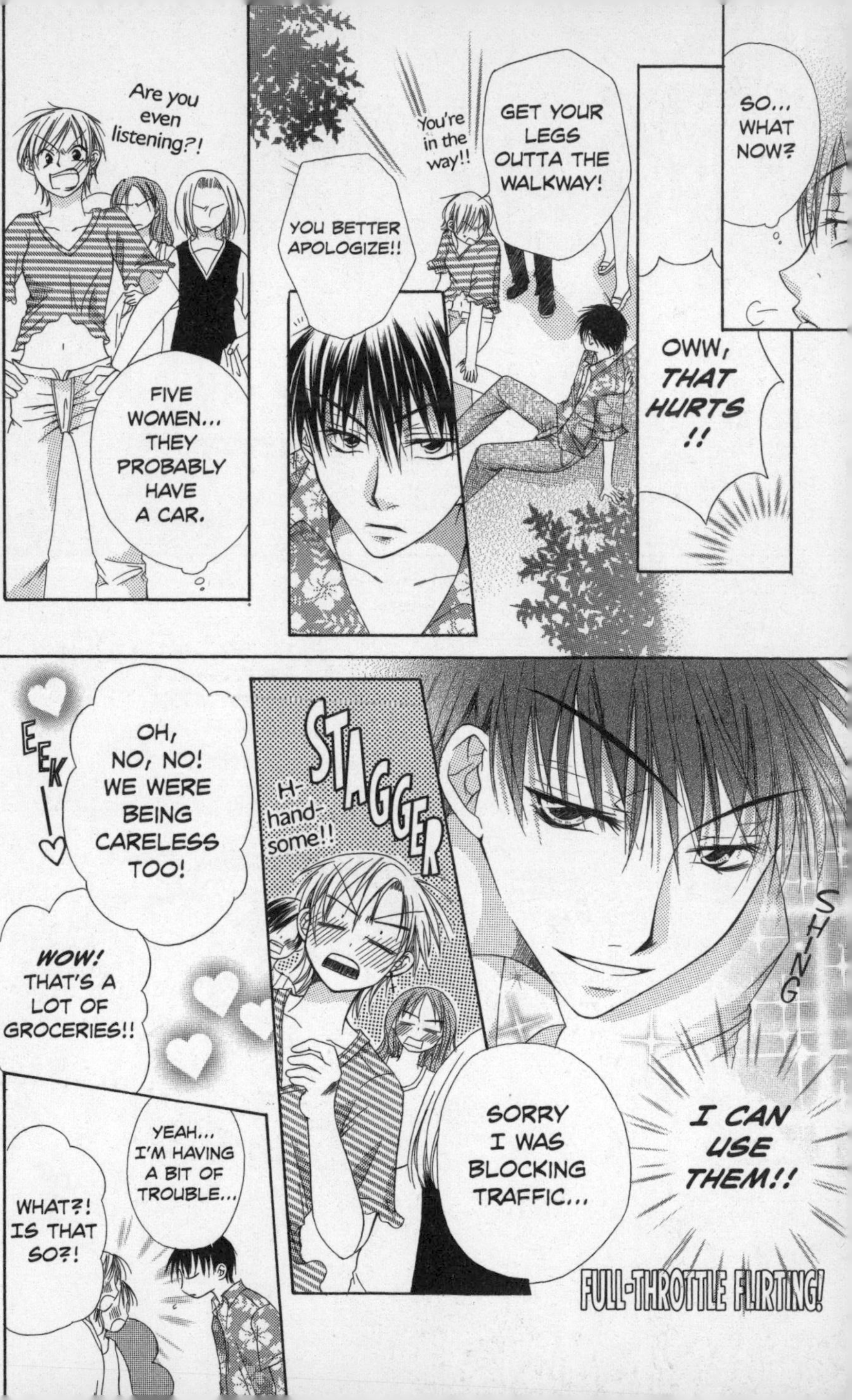
SO... WHAT NOW?
OWW, THAT HURTS!!
GET YOUR LEGS OUTTA THE WALKWAY!
You're in the way!!
YOU BETTER APOLOGIZE!!
Are you even listening?!
FIVE WOMEN... THEY PROBABLY HAVE A CAR.
SHING
SORRY I WAS BLOCKING TRAFFIC...
I CAN USE THEM!!
FULL-THROTTLE FLIRTING!
STAGGER
H-handsome!!
EEK
OH, NO, NO! WE WERE BEING CARELESS TOO!
WOW! THAT'S A LOT OF GROCERIES!!
YEAH... I'M HAVING A BIT OF TROUBLE...
WHAT?! IS THAT SO?!

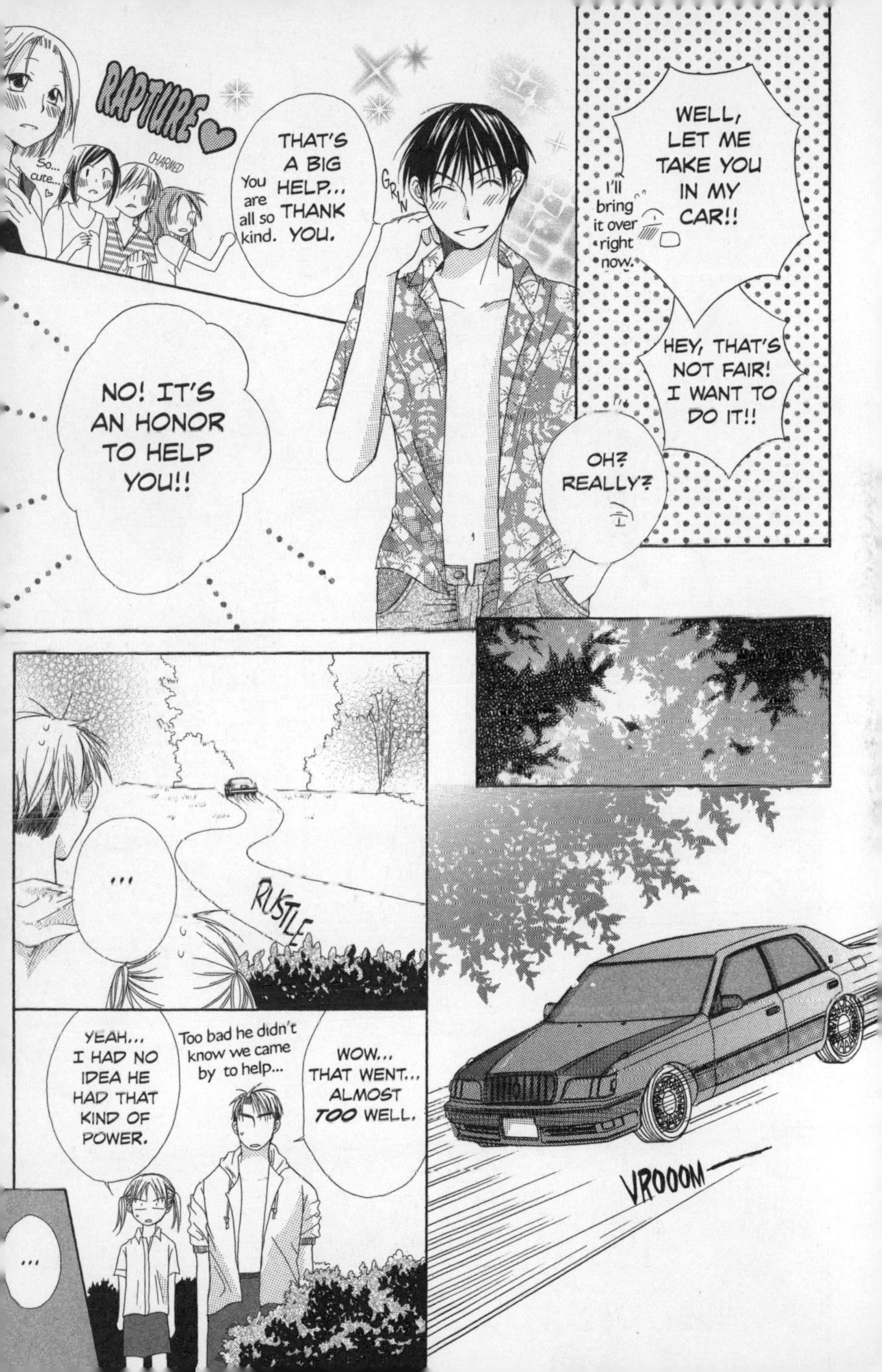
WELL, LET ME TAKE YOU IN MY CAR!!
I'll bring it over right now.
HEY, THAT'S NOT FAIR! I WANT TO DO IT!!
OH? REALLY?
THAT'S A BIG HELP... THANK YOU.
You are all so kind.
GRIN
RAPTURE
So... cute...
CHARMED
NO! IT'S AN HONOR TO HELP YOU!!
VROOOM
...
RUSTLE
WOW... THAT WENT... ALMOST TOO WELL.
Too bad he didn't know we came by to help...
YEAH... I HAD NO IDEA HE HAD THAT KIND OF POWER.
...

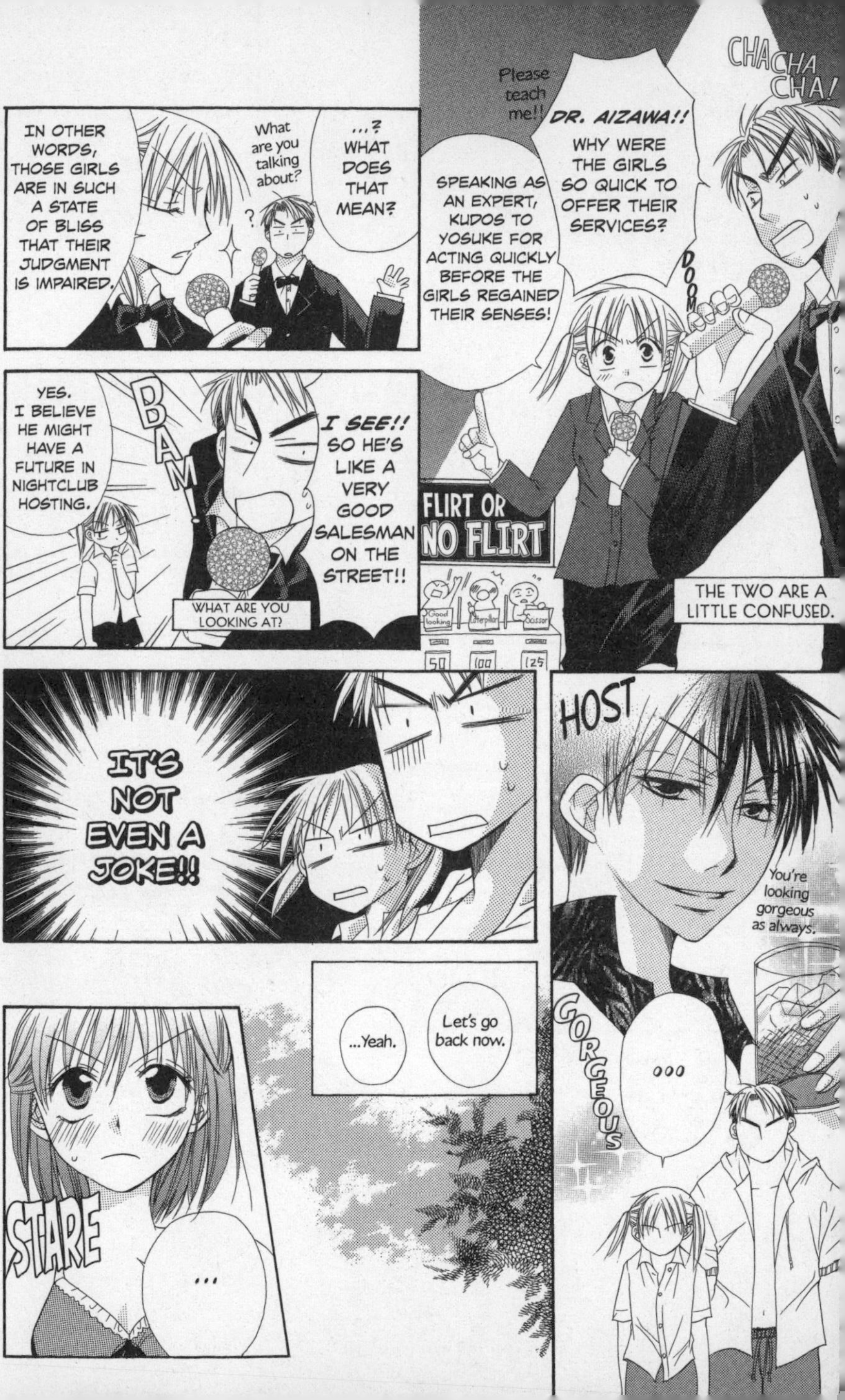
CHACHA CHA!
DR. AIZAWA!!
WHY WERE THE GIRLS SO QUICK TO OFFER THEIR SERVICES?
Please teach me!!
DOOM
SPEAKING AS AN EXPERT, KUDOS TO YOSUKE FOR ACTING QUICKLY BEFORE THE GIRLS REGAINED THEIR SENSES!
THE TWO ARE A LITTLE CONFUSED.
FLIRT OR NO FLIRT
Good looking
Caterpillar
Scissor
50
100
125
...? WHAT DOES THAT MEAN?
What are you talking about?
?
IN OTHER WORDS, THOSE GIRLS ARE IN SUCH A STATE OF BLISS THAT THEIR JUDGMENT IS IMPAIRED.
I SEE!! SO HE'S LIKE A VERY GOOD SALESMAN ON THE STREET!!
BAM!
YES. I BELIEVE HE MIGHT HAVE A FUTURE IN NIGHTCLUB HOSTING.
WHAT ARE YOU LOOKING AT?
HOST
You're looking gorgeous as always.
GORGEOUS
ooo
IT'S NOT EVEN A JOKE!!
Let's go back now.
...Yeah.
STARE
...

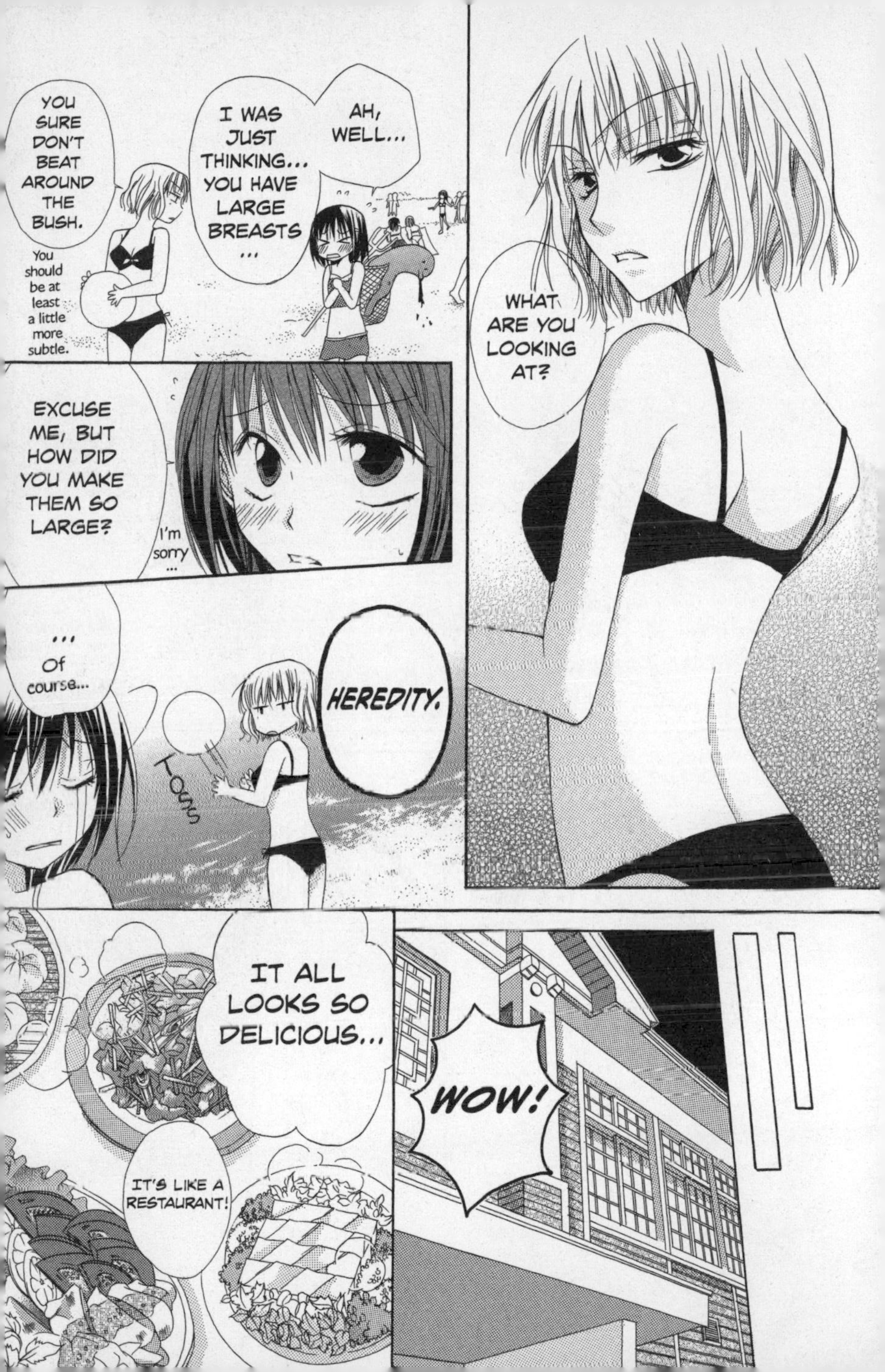
WHAT ARE YOU LOOKING AT?
AH, WELL...
I WAS JUST THINKING... YOU HAVE LARGE BREASTS ...
YOU SURE DON'T BEAT AROUND THE BUSH.
You should be at least a little more subtle.
EXCUSE ME, BUT HOW DID YOU MAKE THEM SO LARGE?
I'm sorry ...
HEREDITY.
TOSS
... Of course...
WOW!
IT ALL LOOKS SO DELICIOUS...
IT'S LIKE A RESTAURANT!

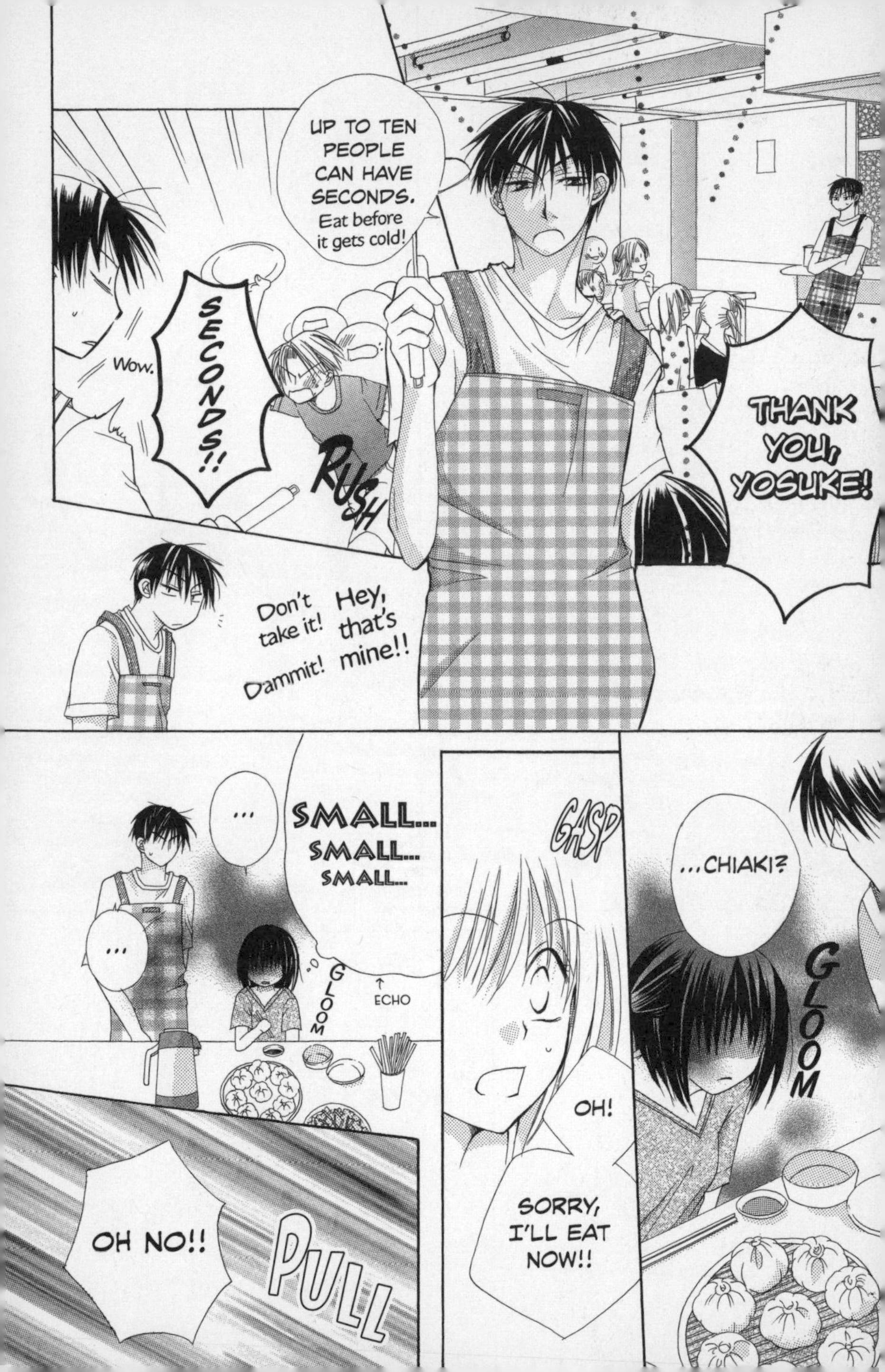
THANK YOU, YOSUKE!
UP TO TEN PEOPLE CAN HAVE SECONDS. Eat before it gets cold!
SECONDS!!
Wow.
RUSH
Hey, that's mine!!
Don't take it! Dammit!
...CHIAKI?
GLOOM
GASP
OH!
SORRY, I'LL EAT NOW!!
SMALL... SMALL... SMALL...
ECHO
GLOOM
...
...
OH NO!!
PULL

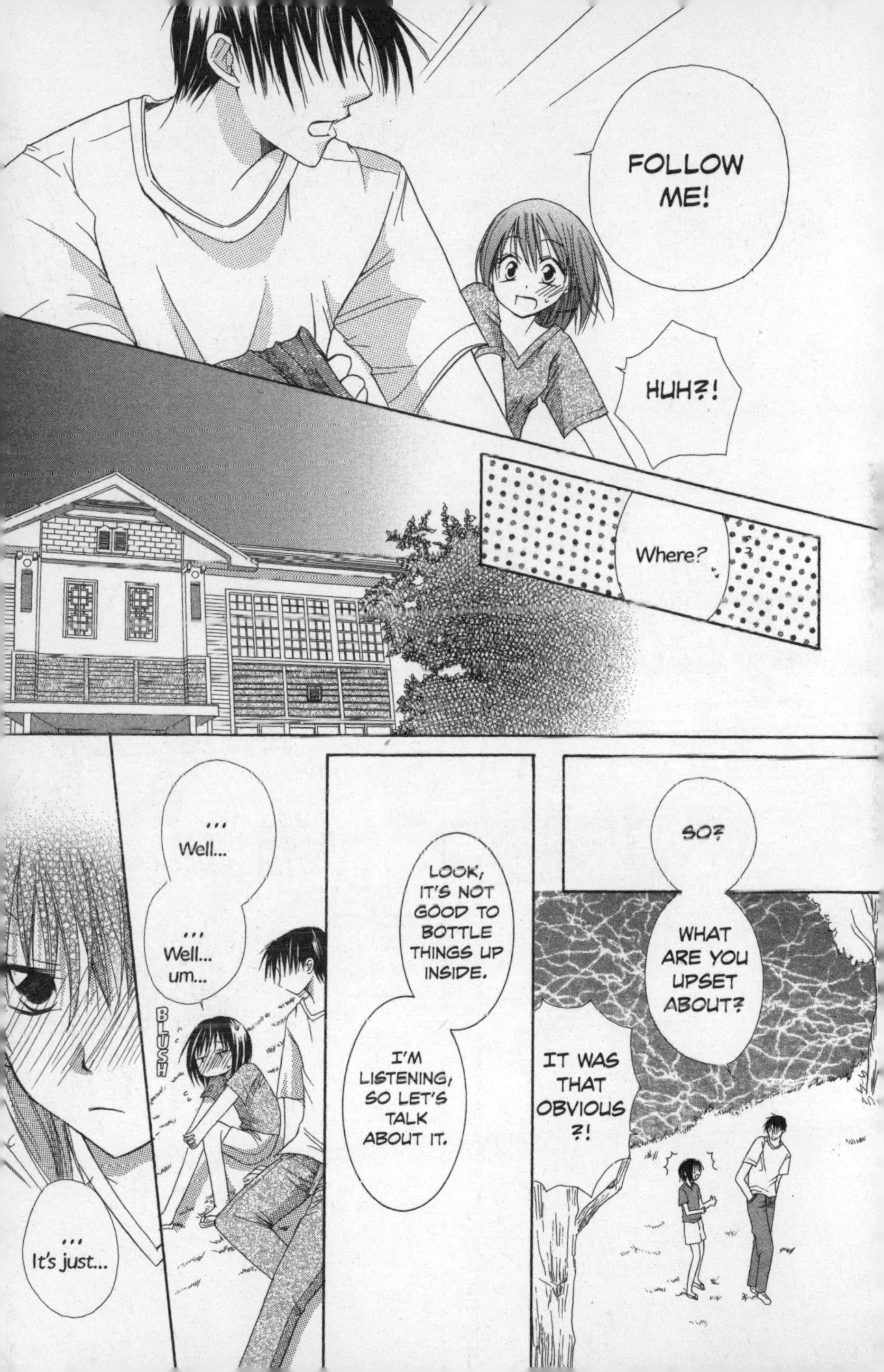
FOLLOW ME!
HUH?!
Where?
SO?
WHAT ARE YOU UPSET ABOUT?
IT WAS THAT OBVIOUS?!
LOOK, IT'S NOT GOOD TO BOTTLE THINGS UP INSIDE.
I'M LISTENING, SO LET'S TALK ABOUT IT.
... Well...
... Well... um...
BLUSH
... It's just...

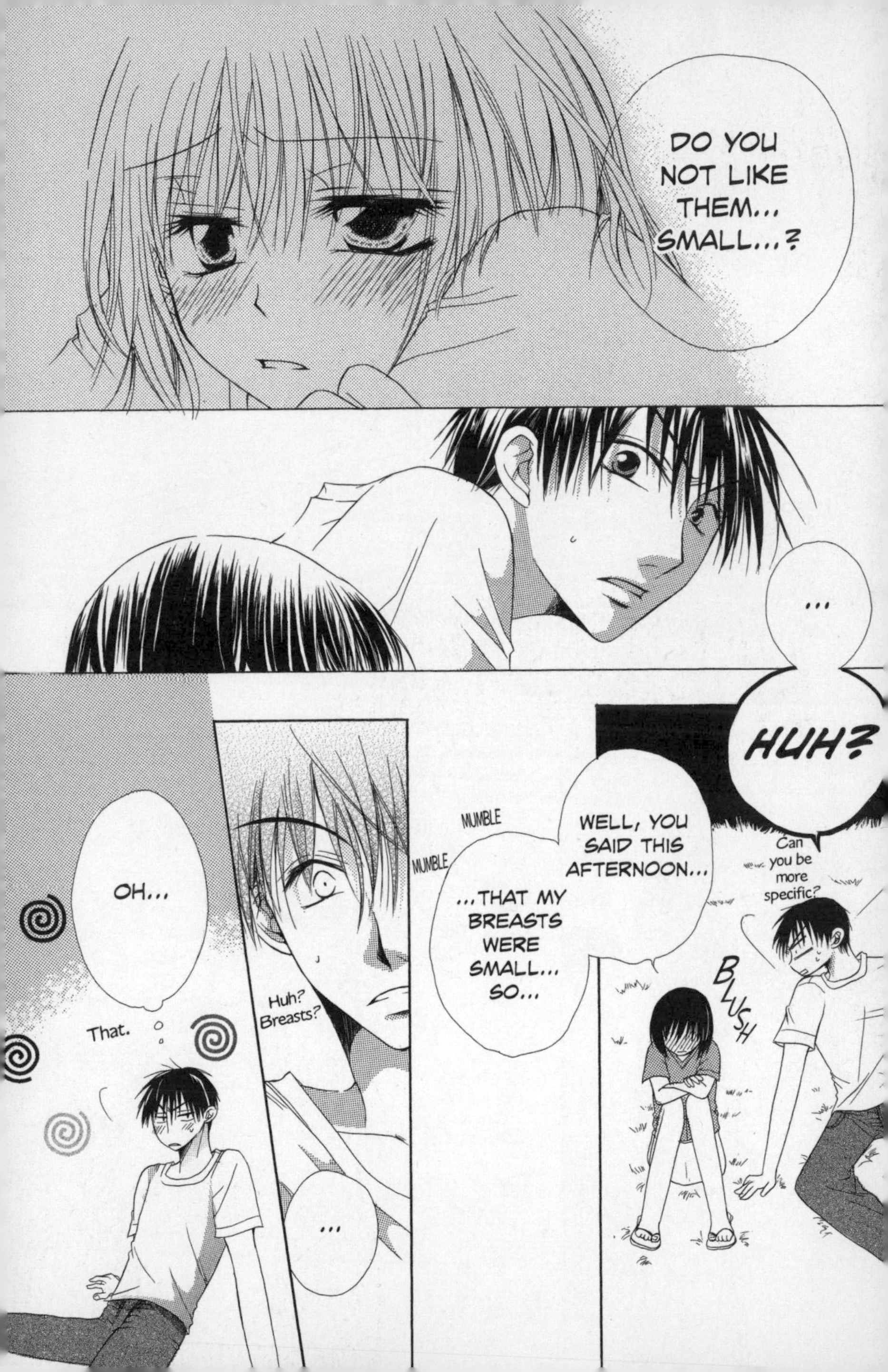
DO YOU NOT LIKE THEM... SMALL...?
...
HUH?
Can you be more specific?
BLUSH
WELL, YOU SAID THIS AFTERNOON...
...THAT MY BREASTS WERE SMALL... SO...
MUMBLE
MUMBLE
Huh? Breasts?
...
OH...
That.

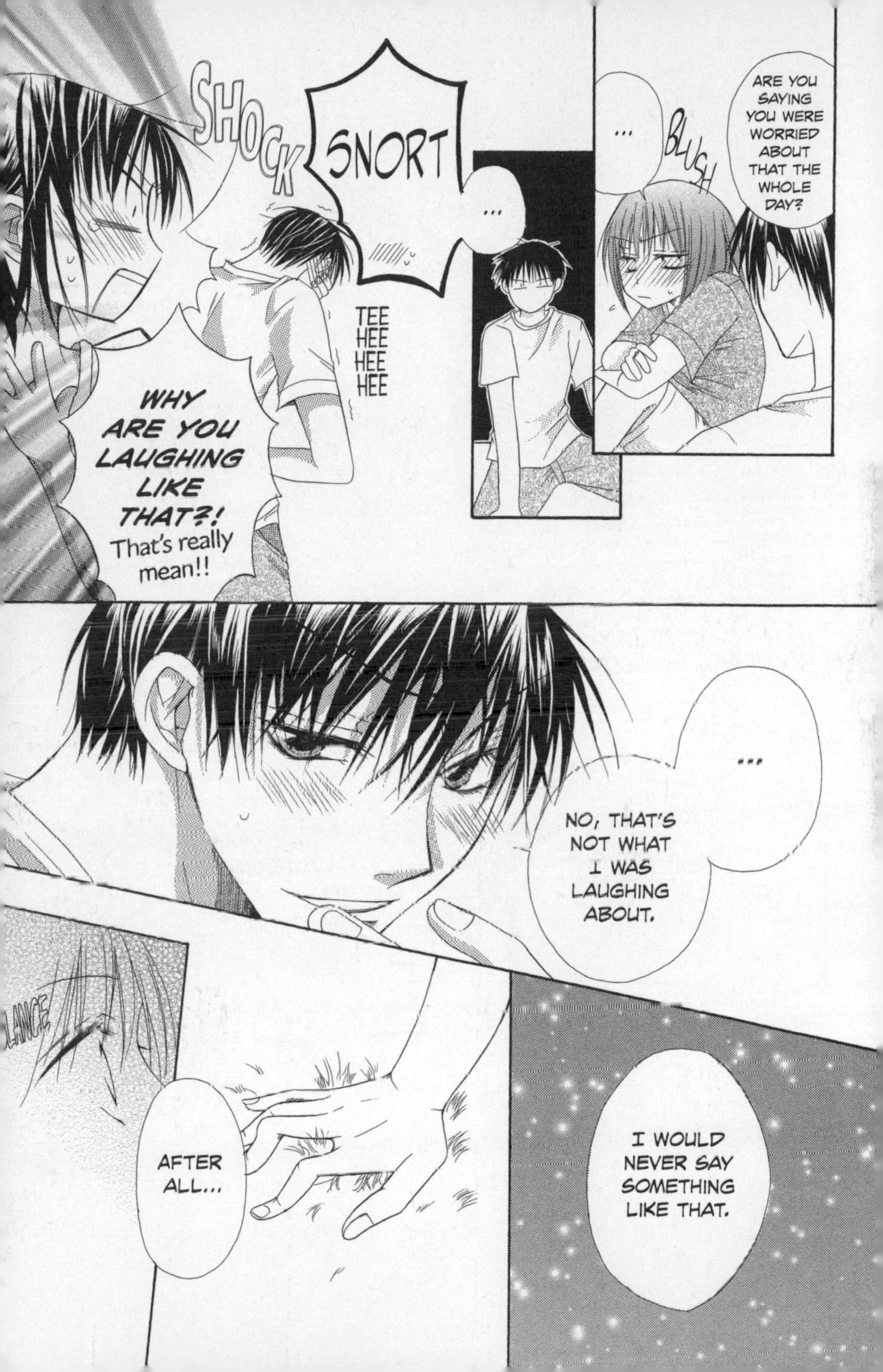
ARE YOU SAYING YOU WERE WORRIED ABOUT THAT THE WHOLE DAY?
...
BLUSH
...
SNORT
SHOCK
TEE HEE HEE HEE
WHY ARE YOU LAUGHING LIKE THAT?! That's really mean!!
...
NO, THAT'S NOT WHAT I WAS LAUGHING ABOUT.
I WOULD NEVER SAY SOMETHING LIKE THAT.
AFTER ALL...

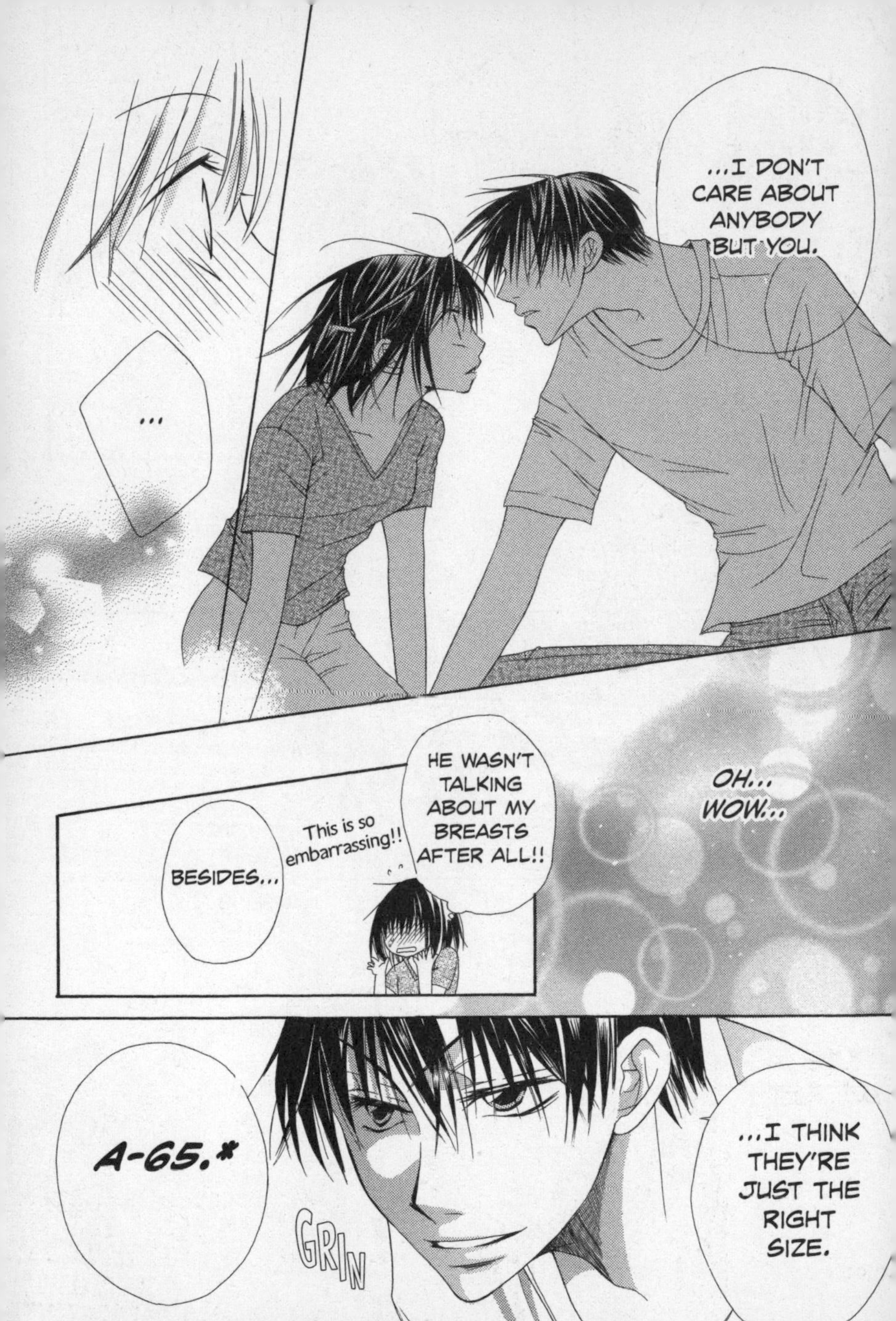
...I DON'T CARE ABOUT ANYBODY BUT YOU.
...
OH... WOW...
HE WASN'T TALKING ABOUT MY BREASTS AFTER ALL!!
This is so embarrassing!!
BESIDES...
...I THINK THEY'RE JUST THE RIGHT SIZE.
GRIN
A-65.*

*A BRA SIZE. SHE'D BE A 30AA IN THE STATES.

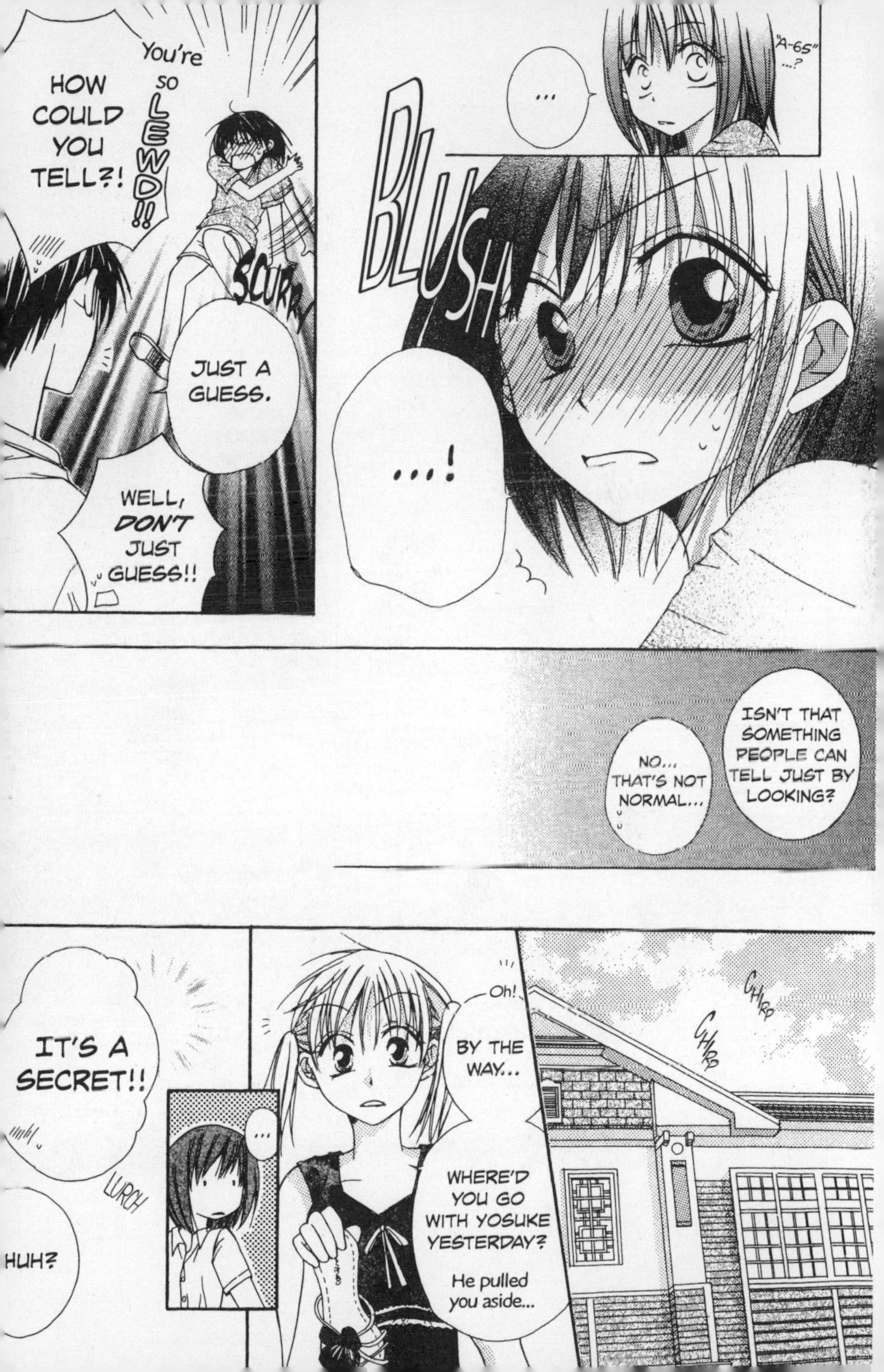
"A-65" ...?
...
BLUSH
...!
You're so LEWD!!
HOW COULD YOU TELL?!
SCURRY
JUST A GUESS.
WELL, DON'T JUST GUESS!!
ISN'T THAT SOMETHING PEOPLE CAN TELL JUST BY LOOKING?
NO... THAT'S NOT NORMAL...
CHIRP
CHIRP
Oh!
BY THE WAY...
WHERE'D YOU GO WITH YOSUKE YESTERDAY?
He pulled you aside...
IT'S A SECRET!!
...
LURCH
HUH?

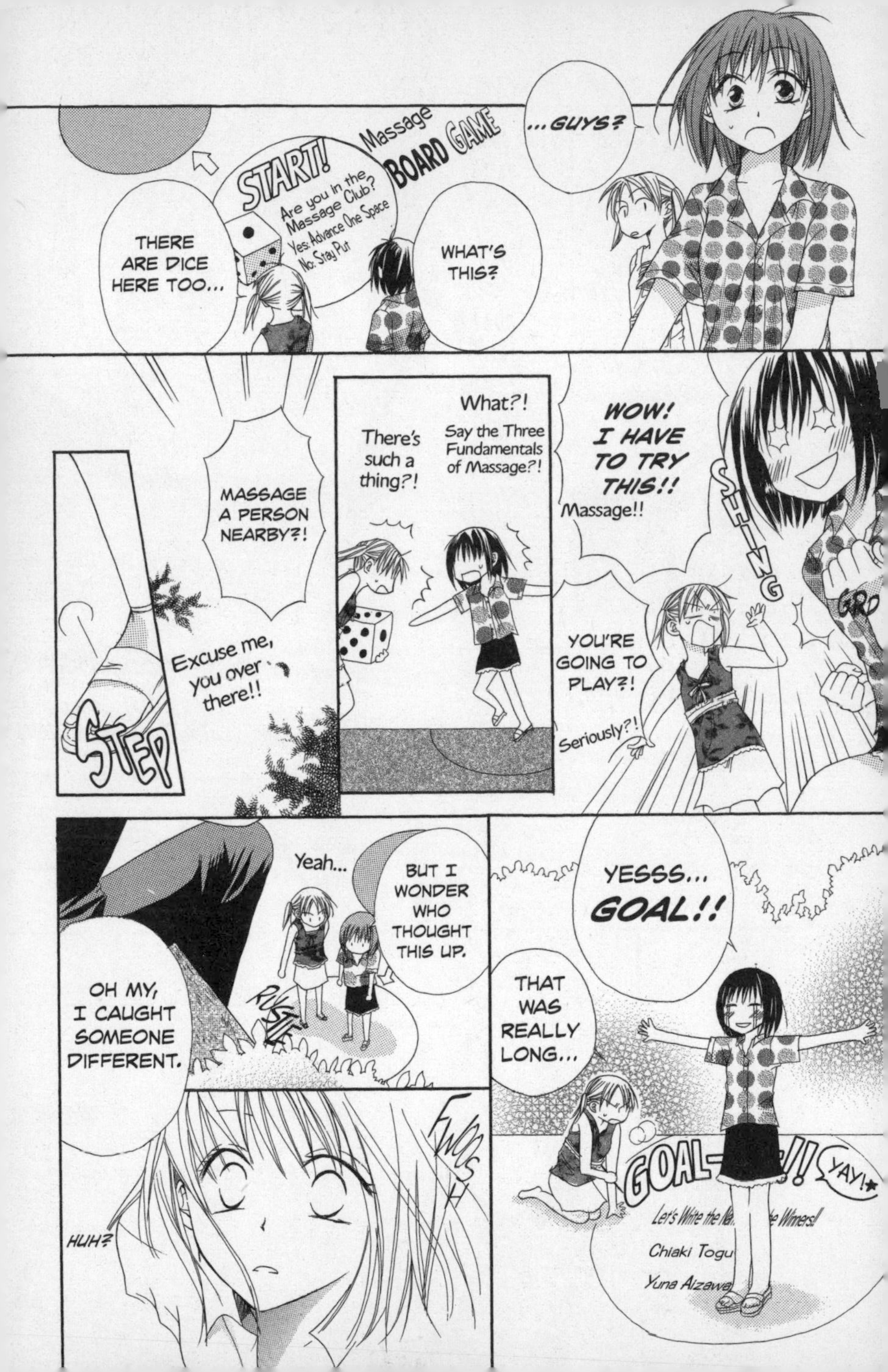
...GUYS?
WHAT'S THIS?
Massage BOARD GAME
START!
Are you in the Massage Club?
Yes: Advance One Space
No: Stay Put
THERE ARE DICE HERE TOO...
WOW! I HAVE TO TRY THIS!!
Massage!!
SHING
GRD
YOU'RE GOING TO PLAY?!
Seriously?!
What?!
Say the Three Fundamentals of Massage?!
There's such a thing?!
MASSAGE A PERSON NEARBY?!
Excuse me, you over there!!
STEP
YESSS... GOAL!!
THAT WAS REALLY LONG...
GOAL—!!
YAY!★
Chiaki Togu
Yuna Aizawa
Yeah...
BUT I WONDER WHO THOUGHT THIS UP.
RUSTLE
OH MY, I CAUGHT SOMEONE DIFFERENT.
FWOOSH
HUH?

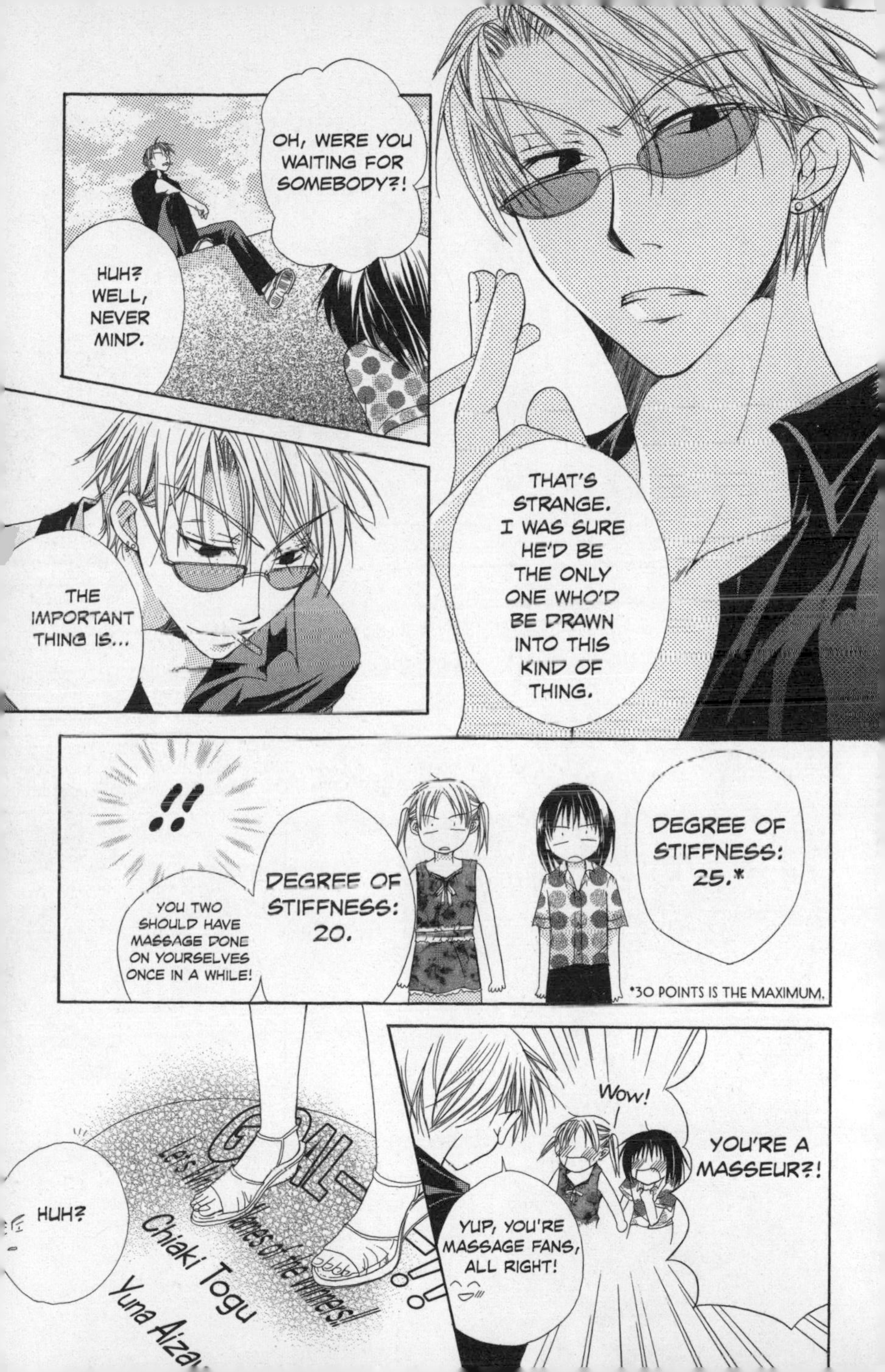
THAT'S STRANGE. I WAS SURE HE'D BE THE ONLY ONE WHO'D BE DRAWN INTO THIS KIND OF THING.
OH, WERE YOU WAITING FOR SOMEBODY?!
HUH? WELL, NEVER MIND.
THE IMPORTANT THING IS...
DEGREE OF STIFFNESS: 25.*
DEGREE OF STIFFNESS: 20.
YOU TWO SHOULD HAVE MASSAGE DONE ON YOURSELVES ONCE IN A WHILE!
!!
*30 POINTS IS THE MAXIMUM.
YOU'RE A MASSEUR?!
Wow!
YUP, YOU'RE MASSAGE FANS, ALL RIGHT!
Chiaki Togu
HUH?

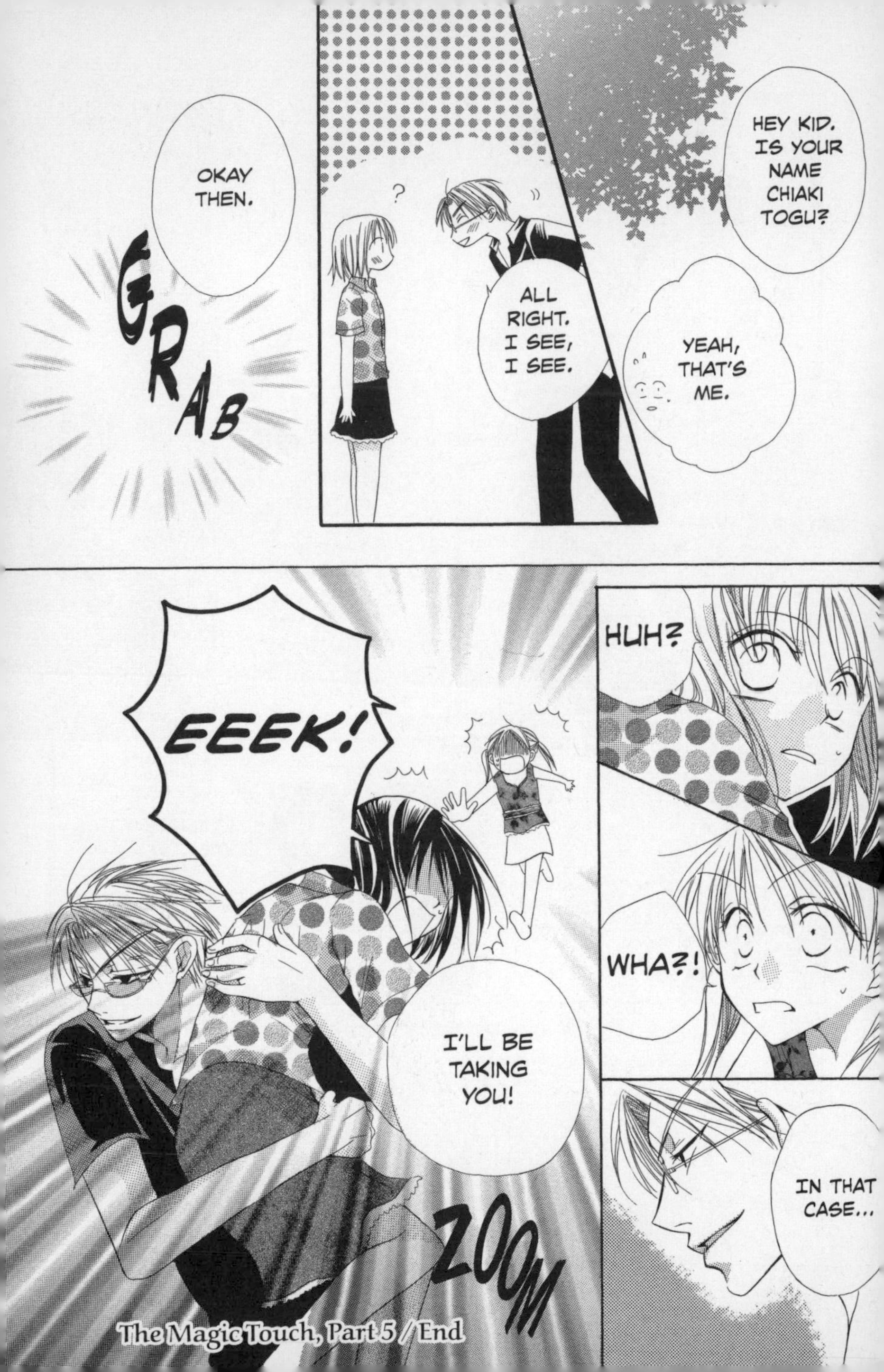
HEY KID. IS YOUR NAME CHIAKI TOGU?
YEAH, THAT'S ME.
ALL RIGHT. I SEE, I SEE.
OKAY THEN.
GRAB
HUH?
WHA?!
IN THAT CASE...
EEEK!
I'LL BE TAKING YOU!
ZOOM
The Magic Touch, Part 5 / End

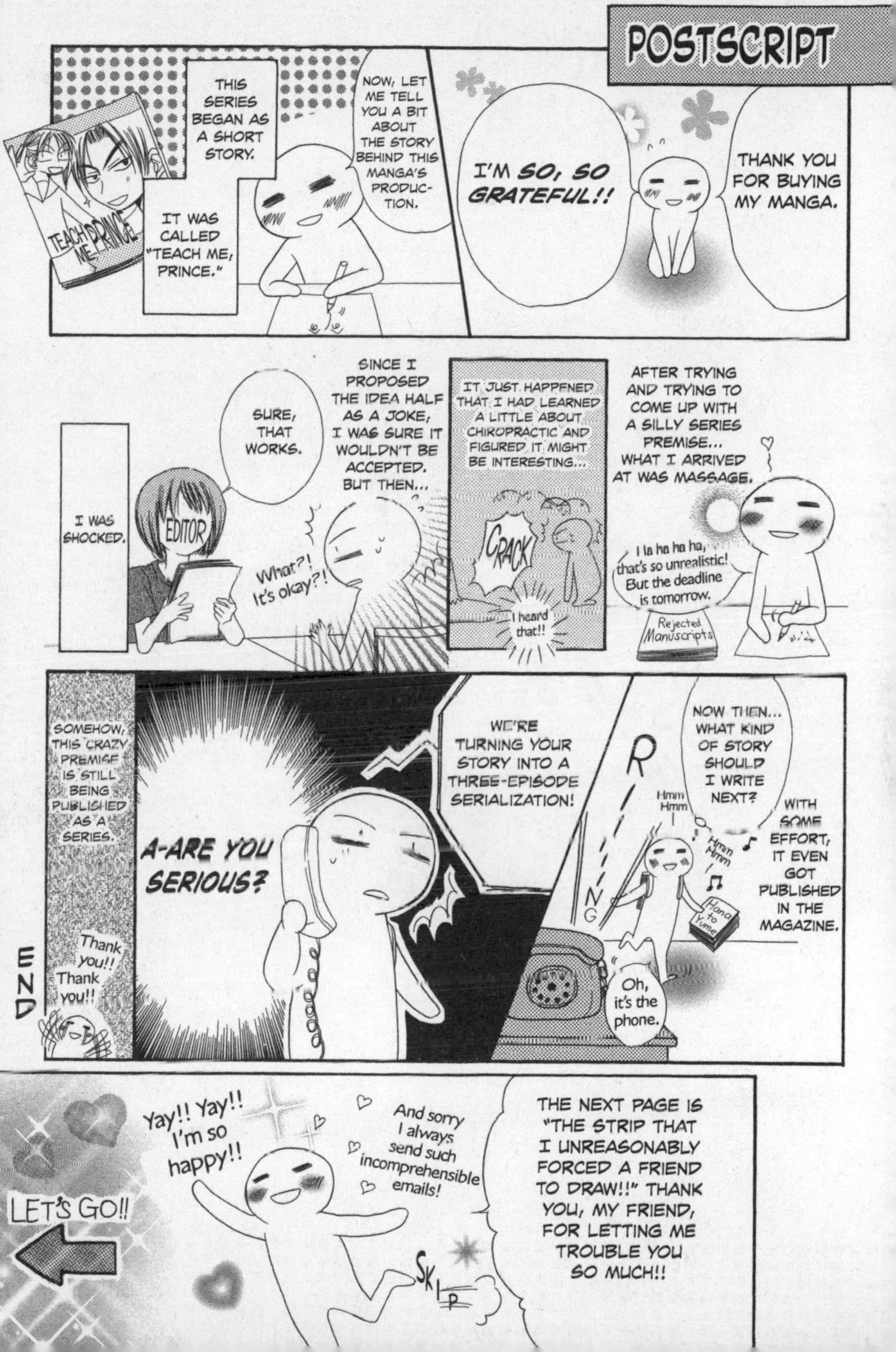
POSTSCRIPT
THANK YOU FOR BUYING MY MANGA.
I'M SO, SO GRATEFUL!!
NOW, LET ME TELL YOU A BIT ABOUT THE STORY BEHIND THIS MANGA'S PRODUCTION.
THIS SERIES BEGAN AS A SHORT STORY.
IT WAS CALLED "TEACH ME, PRINCE."
TEACH ME PRINCE
AFTER TRYING AND TRYING TO COME UP WITH A SILLY SERIES PREMISE... WHAT I ARRIVED AT WAS MASSAGE.
Ha ha ha ha, that's so unrealistic! But the deadline is tomorrow.
Rejected Manuscripts
IT JUST HAPPENED THAT I HAD LEARNED A LITTLE ABOUT CHIROPRACTIC AND FIGURED IT MIGHT BE INTERESTING...
CRACK
I heard that!!
SINCE I PROPOSED THE IDEA HALF AS A JOKE, I WAS SURE IT WOULDN'T BE ACCEPTED. BUT THEN...
What?! It's okay?!
SURE, THAT WORKS.
EDITOR
I WAS SHOCKED.
NOW THEN... WHAT KIND OF STORY SHOULD I WRITE NEXT?
WITH SOME EFFORT, IT EVEN GOT PUBLISHED IN THE MAGAZINE.
Hmm Hmm
Hmm Hmm
Hana to Yume
RING
Oh, it's the phone.
WE'RE TURNING YOUR STORY INTO A THREE-EPISODE SERIALIZATION!
A-ARE YOU SERIOUS?
SOMEHOW, THIS CRAZY PREMISE IS STILL BEING PUBLISHED AS A SERIES.
Thank you!! Thank you!!
END
THE NEXT PAGE IS "THE STRIP THAT I UNREASONABLY FORCED A FRIEND TO DRAW!!" THANK YOU, MY FRIEND, FOR LETTING ME TROUBLE YOU SO MUCH!!
And sorry I always send such incomprehensible emails!
Yay!! Yay!! I'm so happy!!
SKIP
LET'S GO!!

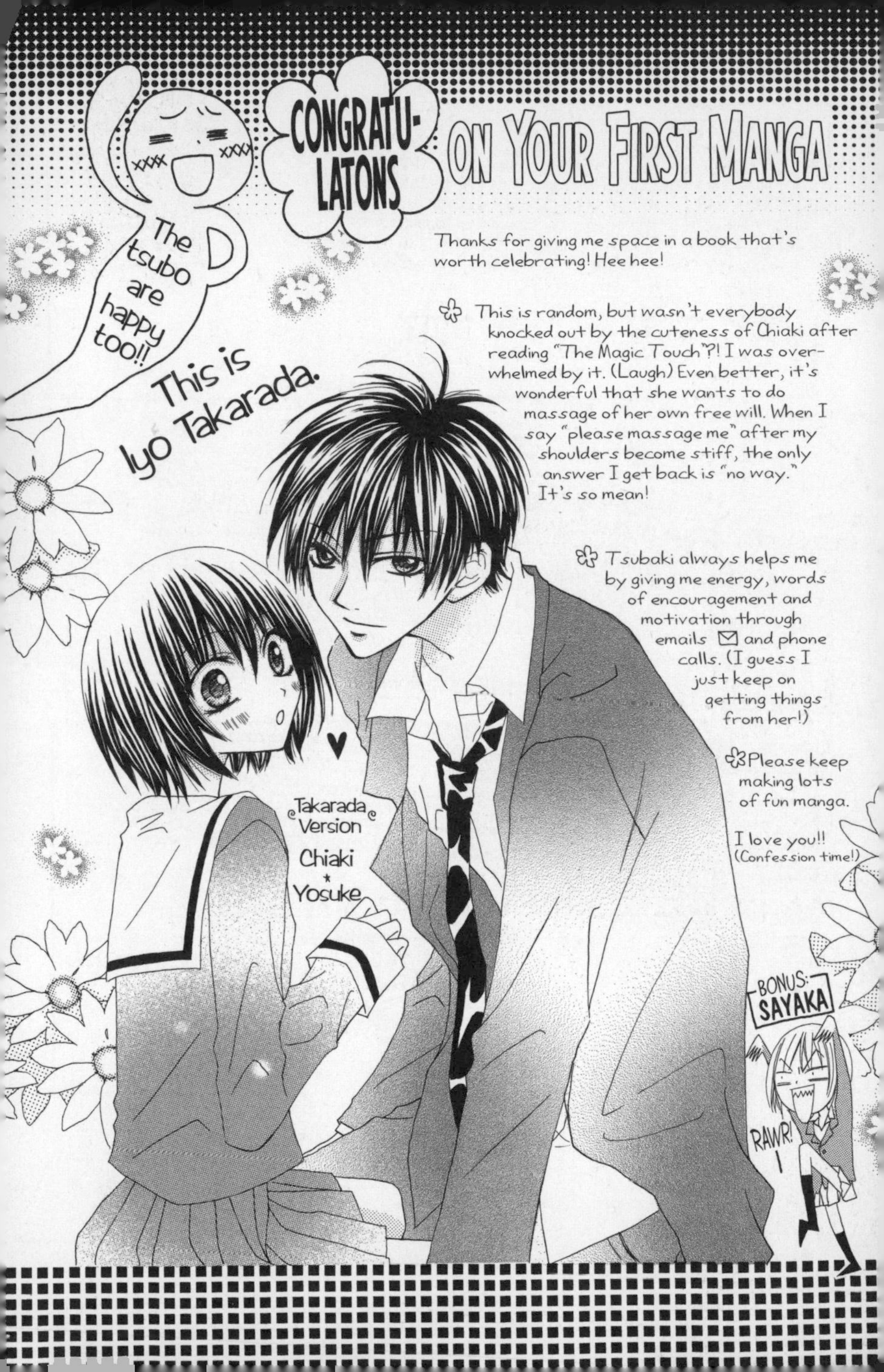
CONGRATU-LATONS
ON YOUR FIRST MANGA
Thanks for giving me space in a book that's worth celebrating! Hee hee!
✿ This is random, but wasn't everybody knocked out by the cuteness of Chiaki after reading "The Magic Touch"?! I was over-whelmed by it. (Laugh) Even better, it's wonderful that she wants to do massage of her own free will. When I say "please massage me" after my shoulders become stiff, the only answer I get back is "no way." It's so mean!
✿ Tsubaki always helps me by giving me energy, words of encouragement and motivation through emails ✉ and phone calls. (I guess I just keep on getting things from her!)
✿ Please keep making lots of fun manga.
I love you!! (Confession time!)
The tsubo are happy too!!
This is Iyo Takarada.
Takarada Version
Chiaki ⋆ Yosuke
BONUS: SAYAKA
RAWR!

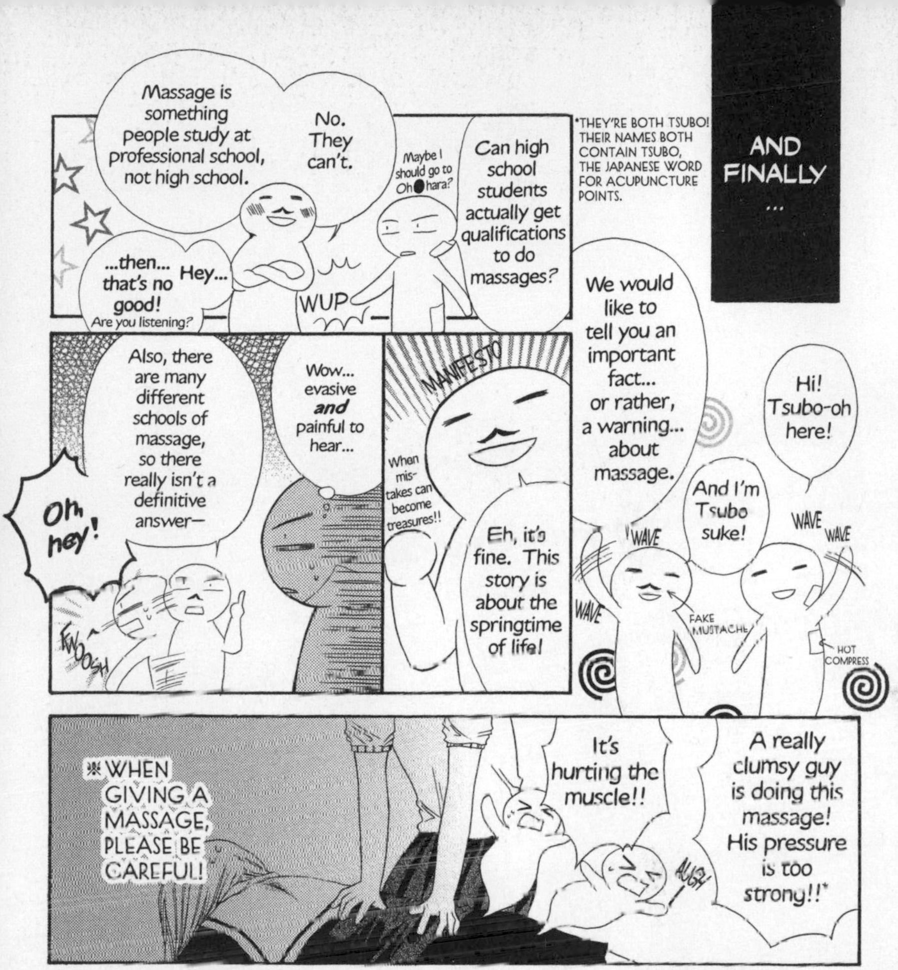
AND FINALLY...
Hi! Tsubo-oh here!
And I'm Tsubo suke!
WAVE
WAVE
WAVE
We would like to tell you an important fact... or rather, a warning... about massage.
FAKE MUSTACHE
HOT COMPRESS
Can high school students actually get qualifications to do massages?
Maybe I should go to Oh●hara?
No. They can't.
Massage is something people study at professional school, not high school.
Hey...
...then... that's no good!
Are you listening?
WUP
MANIFESTO
Eh, it's fine. This story is about the springtime of life!
When mis-takes can become treasures!!
Wow... evasive *and* painful to hear...
Also, there are many different schools of massage, so there really isn't a definitive answer—
Oh hey!
FWOOSH
A really clumsy guy is doing this massage! His pressure is too strong!!*
It's hurting the muscle!!
AUGH!
※WHEN GIVING A MASSAGE, PLEASE BE CAREFUL!
*THEY'RE BOTH TSUBO! THEIR NAMES BOTH CONTAIN TSUBO, THE JAPANESE WORD FOR ACUPUNCTURE POINTS.

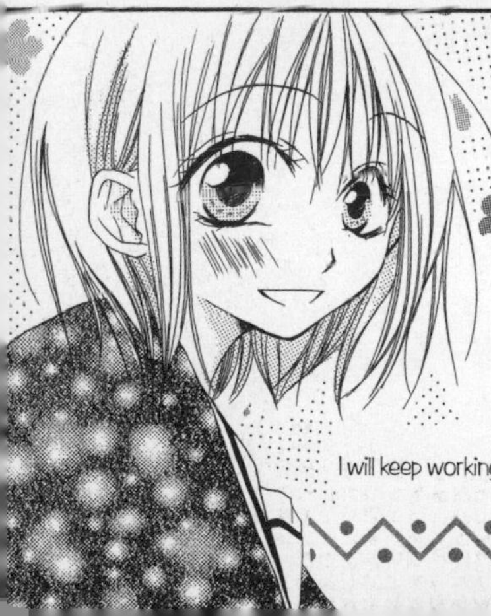

SPECIAL ♡ THANKS

Younger Sister (Thanks for the help!!)
My Family
The Editor

<<Thank You For Providing Names>>

(Yufuna. Chiaki. Chiaki. Tomoka. Non. Yoko. Nanae. Rumi. Tomitsuka. Abe. Katsuhisa. Baaba.)

And special thanks to you for reading this!
Thank you so much! ♡
I will keep working hard, so please keep reading this series.

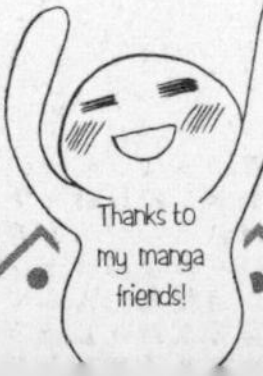
Thanks to my manga friends!

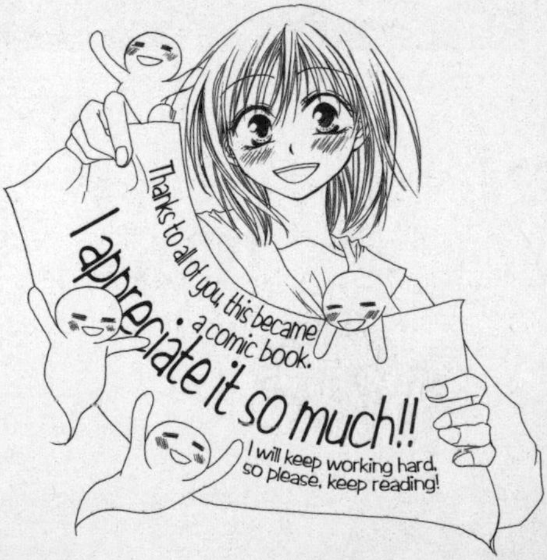
Thanks to all of you, this became a comic book.
I appreciate it so much!!
I will keep working hard, so please, keep reading!

Izumi Tsubaki began drawing manga in her first year of high school. She was soon selected to be in the top ten of *Hana to Yume*'s HMC (Hana to Yume Mangaka Course), and subsequently won *Hana to Yume*'s Big Challenge contest. Her debut title, *Chijimete Distance* (Shrink the Distance), ran in 2002 in *Hana to Yume* magazine, issue 17. In addition to *The Magic Touch* (originally published in Japan as *Oyayubi kara Romance*, or "Romance from the Thumbs"), she is also currently working on the manga series *Oresama Teacher* (I'm the Teacher).

Tsubaki-sensei hails from Saitama Prefecture, her birthday is December 11, and she confesses that she enjoys receiving massages more than she enjoys giving them.

THE MAGIC TOUCH
Vol. 1
Shojo Beat Edition

STORY AND ART BY
IZUMI TSUBAKI

English Adaptation/Lorelei Laird
Translation/Nori Minami
Touch-up Art & Lettering/James Gaubatz
Design/Sean Lee
Editor/Carol Fox

Oyayubi kara Romance by Izumi Tsubaki
© Izumi Tsubaki 2002
All rights reserved.
First published in Japan in 2004 by HAKUSENSHA, Inc., Tokyo.
English language translation rights arranged with HAKUSENSHA, Inc., Tokyo.

The stories, characters and incidents mentioned in this publication are entirely fictional.

Printed in Canada

Published by VIZ Media, LLC
P.O. Box 77010
San Francisco, CA 94107

10 9 8 7 6 5 4 3 2
First printing, February 2009
Second printing, May 2013

www.viz.com

www.shojobeat.com